THE COMPLETE IDIOT'S GUIDE® TO

Fishing Basics

Second Edition

by Mike Toth

ALPHA

A member of Penguin Group (USA) Inc.

ALPHA BOOKS

Published by the Penguin Group

Penguin Group (USA) Inc., 375 Hudson Street, New York, New York 10014, USA

Penguin Group (Canada), 90 Eglinton Avenue East, Suite 700, Toronto, Ontario M4P 2Y3, Canada (a division of Pearson Penguin Canada Inc.)

Penguin Books Ltd., 80 Strand, London WC2R 0RL, England

Penguin Ireland, 25 St. Stephen's Green, Dublin 2, Ireland (a division of Penguin Books Ltd.)

Penguin Group (Australia), 250 Camberwell Road, Camberwell, Victoria 3124, Australia (a division of Pearson Australia Group Pty. Ltd.)

Penguin Books India Pvt. Ltd., 11 Community Centre, Panchsheel Park, New Delhi—110 017, India

Penguin Group (NZ), 67 Apollo Drive, Rosedale, North Shore, Auckland 1311, New Zealand (a division of Pearson New Zealand Ltd.)

Penguin Books (South Africa) (Pty.) Ltd., 24 Sturdee Avenue, Rosebank, Johannesburg 2196, South Africa

Penguin Books Ltd., Registered Offices: 80 Strand, London WC2R 0RL, England

Copyright©2000 by Mike Toth

International Standard Book Number: 978-0-02-863884-3

Library of Congress Catalog Card Number: Available upon request.

10   09   08   14   13

Interpretation of the printing code: The rightmost number of the first series of numbers is the year of the book's printing; the rightmost number of the second series of numbers is the number of the book's printing. For example, a printing code of 00-1 shows that the first printing occurred in 2000.

Printed in the United States of America

Note: This publication contains the opinions and ideas of its author. It is intended to provide helpful and informative material on the subject matter covered. It is sold with the understanding that the author and publisher are not engaged in rendering professional services in the book. If the reader requires personal assistance or advice, a competent professional should be consulted.

The author and publisher specifically disclaim any responsibility for any liability, loss or risk, personal or otherwise, which is incurred as a consequence, directly or indirectly, of the use and application of any of the contents of this book.

Most Alpha books are available at special quantity discounts for bulk purchases for sales promotions, premiums, fund-raising, or educational use. Special books, or book excerpts, can also be created to fit specific needs.

For details, write: Special Markets, Alpha Books, 375 Hudson Street, New York, NY 10014.

Publisher
Marie Butler-Knight

Product Manager
Phil Kitchel

Managing Editor
Cari Luna

Senior Acquisitions Editor
Renee Wilmeth

Development/Copy Editor
Lynn Northrup

Production Editor
JoAnna Kremer

Content Reviewers
Will Ryan
Ken Schultz

Cartoonist
Brian Moyer

Cover Designers
Mike Freeland
Kevin Spear

Book Designers
Scott Cook and Amy Adams of DesignLab

Indexer
Angie Bess

Layout/Proofreading
Cyndi Davis-Hubler
Mary Hunt
Gloria Schurick

Contents at a Glance

Contents

Appendixes

Foreword

At 12 years of age, I had a paper route that probably brought in a whopping $2.00 per week. Not too bad, but the money was not the big deal for me. No, my motivation came from the fact that I also received "vouchers," maybe one a week, for a good delivery record. I could trade the 10 or 12 vouchers I accumulated for my choice of about 100 different items—baseballs, bats, tennis shoes, BB guns, and so on. My goal, and I attained it, was a Heddon River-Runt fishing plug, which I kept for several years.

I've thought a lot about that plug through the years, especially since fishing turned out to be my career. I wondered why I wanted that fish bait so badly. Did I think it would be this secret fish-catchin' lure that would fill my stringer? No, I don't think so. Did I think it was a new style and color that had never been seen before? No, not that either. In fact, I don't have the slightest idea why I wanted that River Runt. To be honest, I probably only wanted my own lure, to sharpen its hooks and clean it up before each fishing trip.

You see, I was consumed by fishing, and nothing you could do or say would have, nor could have, ever changed that. But that was the late 1940s and early 1950s, and there wasn't much TV, any computer games or little league sports, or much else that would occupy a kid (or grown-up for that matter).

With all the options open today, it may have taken you longer to become interested in fishing than it took me, but it's never too late to take up this fascinating sport that offers the opportunity to enjoy the outdoors. But you may need a little boost to get started. You could just walk into the sporting-goods store, perhaps with one of your kids, with angling on your mind. Now three things can happen here, and I have witnessed all three.

Situation #1 occurs when the salesperson doesn't have a clue about fishing and could no more help you than the man on the moon. You could walk out of the store completely discouraged. Fishing takes a reasonable amount of ability, about the same as the sport of golf. So would you go to a golf department and ask for advice from someone who has never participated in the sport? Of course not, and I rest my case on the #1 situation.

Situation #2 goes to the other extreme—you may be bombarded with a lot of high-tech equipment and fishing strategy by a salesperson who I know is scaring the heck out of you. You just want to find a simple—and that's a major word in this sport, *simple*—way to get started.

Situation #3 happens when you run into a tackle salesperson who has reasonable knowledge about fishing and lays a good, common-sense approach on you. The salesperson reinforces the idea that you can take fishing to any level you wish, and that this simple, down-to-earth game plan will work for almost any species of fish anywhere in the country.

Unfortunately, situations #1 and #2 occur far more often than #3. So be aware of that, try and find the right information from other sources, and digest it at your own pace. Then, by all means, pass it on.

"Other sources," you say. I think that *The Complete Idiot's Guide to Fishing Basics, Second Edition* can be a major asset in your growth in the sport of fishing.

This book offers a no-nonsense introduction to fishing. It helps you understand fishing theory and application, and the difference between the two. You'll learn how to find the species of fish you want to catch, select the right fishing equipment, and properly handle and clean your catch. And you'll learn the essentials for fishing in safety and comfort in various environments and weather conditions. If you want to try more challenging types of fishing, like flyfishing or fishing for big saltwater gamefish, you can read the later chapters for a look at how to get started.

When I was 12 years old and collecting vouchers from my paper route, I would have used those vouchers in a heartbeat for an informative fishing book like this, if it had been available.

—Jerry McKinnis, host of *Fishin' Hole*

Introduction

Why should anyone take up fishing? The reasons are as varied, and as individual, as fishermen themselves, and perhaps therein lies the answer: No other sport offers so many rewards to so many people.

On numerous occasions I've watched adolescents and senior citizens standing shoulder-to-hip on the bank of a pond in a pastoral park or in the shadow of a bridge on a warm summer afternoon, keenly eyeing their fishing lines. I've seen BMWs owned by young white-collar professionals in Buckhead—the trendiest section of Atlanta—go whizzing by with the tip of a fly rod poking out of the rear side window. While attending college in Pennsylvania, I skipped class one day to fish a recently stocked trout lake just outside of town, and found myself standing knee-deep in the cold water, chatting about the fishing with two middle-aged women with their hair up in curlers and spinning rods in their hands. I've fished for marlin on a charter boat in the Gulf Stream and had cocktails later that evening with fellow fishermen, some of them veritable millionaires, in the tony Florida Keys resort where I was staying—at the same time watching entire families with barely enough resources to own a rowboat fishing for snappers off the dock, just for fun.

Included in this tremendous cross-section of the population of the United States are people for whom fishing is an avocation: bass fishermen who think nothing of trailering their high-speed boats a couple hundred miles to a lake where the fishing is just so-so; trout fishermen who study tackle catalogs with the same enthusiasm as buyers studying models on the runway of a Paris fashion show, considering the merits of a $1,000 fly rod versus the half-a-dozen $500 rods they already own; middle-income earners who will scrupulously save up for five years to fish for pike and walleyes at a lodge accessible only by floatplane deep in the Ontario wilderness; and suburbanites who put every last discretionary dollar into the purchase of, maintenance on, and dock space for a sportfishing boat that allows them to spend as much spare time as possible probing the waters of a reservoir, river, bay, or ocean. For these people, fishing is their primary source of recreation, and they pursue it very seriously indeed.

One of these otherwise ordinary people might be your next-door neighbor, your co-worker, or your father-in-law—and after you finish this book, you'll become one of them, too. If you *don't* want to make new friends, spend more time outdoors, partake of a healthy and relaxing pastime, visit new regions of the country, possibly form new bonds with family members, discover a fascinating cuisine, and generally improve your overall life, stop reading now. Otherwise, turn off the TV and review this book to get off to a good start with the best hobby there is.

How to Use This Book

The Complete Idiot's Guide to Fishing Basics, Second Edition starts with the most fundamental facts about fish, fishing tackle, and fishing techniques, and builds upon them in later chapters. Therefore, if you're totally unacquainted with fishing, you can learn about the sport without any confusion or uncertainty. However, if you've fished before—and I'm sure many of you have—you may want to read some parts out of sequence. That's fine, but if you come across any term or methodology that you don't recognize, be sure to stop, check the table of contents for the chapter covering that subject, and read that chapter.

Here's how the book breaks down:

Part 1, **"Before You Get Your Feet Wet,"** covers the background of the sport, and provides a quick head-start on the basics of fishing. You'll get an idea of how popular fishing is, its demographics, and how much it will cost you to get started. You'll also learn how to find a place to fish, the species you'll find once you get there, and their habits and basic biological makeup.

In **Part 2, "Tackle and How to Use It,"** you'll take a look at fishing equipment. Like walking through a tackle shop, the chapters in this part identify and examine rods and reels (you'll also step outside and learn how to use them), line, hooks, lures, bait, and ancillary gear. And you'll learn to assemble a basic outfit for your needs.

Hit the water in **Part 3, "To Catch a Fish,"** and learn about the anatomy of lakes and streams to find out exactly where your quarry might be. Then cast to those spots with a variety of lures and baits. Learn to hook a fish, play it, bring it in, and keep it ... or put it back.

Part 4, **"Flyfishing,"** consists of a flyfishing primer, telling you all you need to know about this rapidly growing sport: the tackle, the casting techniques, the flies to use, and the proper form on the water.

Hit the beach and much more in **Part 5, "Saltwater Fishing,"** exploring the very different world of ocean fishing. Here you'll learn why saltwater fishing is so different from freshwater fishing—and so challenging. Equip yourself with the right tackle, the best bait and lures, and learn how to use them. Then review how to hire a guide, charter a boat, and catch a fish—maybe one that's bigger than you. Finally, delve into the ultimate fishing challenge: saltwater flyfishing.

Part 6, **"The Complete Angler,"** covers the rest of the story: rudimentary boat information and skills, the equipment you need to keep your stuff in, as well as the best boots, clothing, and safeguards to ensure your time on the water is happy and healthy. Then you'll come home with your catch and clean and prepare it, or bring it to the taxidermist, if you want a memory larger than a meal. Finally, look at how to stay within the law with a basic course on fishing licenses, seasons, limits, and special regulations.

Extras

On many pages throughout this book you'll find "bonus boxes." These contain information that deserves your special attention, as follows:

Loose Lines

These large boxes provide extra information related to the topic at hand: interesting facts and trivia, lessons, and stories.

Getting the Point

Look in these boxes for explanations and definitions of terms that you may not know.

School Notes

These boxes offer tips, tactics, techniques, or advice that will make you a better fisherman.

Cautious Casts

These boxes contain "red flags" that warn you of any specific dangers or practices you should avoid.

Acknowledgments

Many people have provided invaluable assistance on this book, including Anthony Acerrano, Dale Barnes, Frank Golad, Ted Kerasote, David Kiehm, Terry McDonell, Michael Mouland, Will Ryan, Ken Schultz, and Michelle Zaffino. I also thank my parents for their support, and my fishing buddies for their endless stories, many of which have found their way into this text. And finally, I thank my family: my wife, Reggie; son, Joey; and daughter, Caroline. This is for home.

Special Thanks to the Technical Reviewer

The Complete Idiot's Guide to Fishing Basics, Second Edition was reviewed by an expert who double-checked the technical accuracy of what you'll learn here, to help us ensure that this book gives you everything you need to know to begin fishing for fun and pleasure. Special thanks are extended to Rick Methot.

Mr. Methot is a former associate editor of *Outdoor Life* magazine and has been a newspaper desk editor for more than 30 years. He is also an award-winning writer on the outdoors whose work has appeared in numerous newspapers and national magazines. Mr. Methot has fished for salmon in Northern Ireland, tarpon in the Florida Keys, bonefish in Bermuda, and trout in New Zealand, as well as for scores of other species. He has fished with the author on several occasions. Mr. Methot lives near the Delaware River in Titusville, New Jersey.

Trademarks

All terms mentioned in this book that are known to be or are suspected of being trademarks or service marks have been appropriately capitalized. Alpha Books and Penguin Group (USA) Inc. cannot attest to the accuracy of this information. Use of a term in this book should not be regarded as affecting the validity of any trademark or service mark. The following trademarks and service marks have been mentioned in this book:

Ande®	Kevlar®
Bomber®	Maxima™
Dacron®	Red Lobster®
DarDevle®	Spiderwire®
Dramamine®	Stren®
Gore-Tex®	Top-Sider®
Ironthread®	Trilene®

Part 1

Before You Get Your Feet Wet

If you've never fished before, or have only attempted to fish a couple of times, learning the sport can seem daunting if not outright intimidating: all that gear, all those fish, all that water. But it's not hard to get started—especially if you take the time to learn some background information before you jump in. This part of the book presents that background information.

Millions of people from all walks of life fish today, and if they can do it, you can, too. It doesn't have to cost you a lot of money, and there are plenty of excellent places to go wet a line. And fish really aren't as smart as some people make them out to be. You just have to understand why they do what they do.

Chapter 1

So, You Want to Fish?

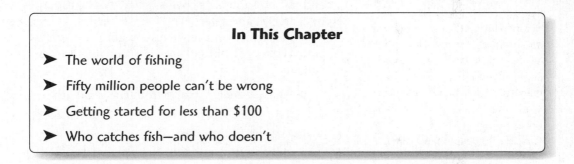

In This Chapter

➤ The world of fishing

➤ Fifty million people can't be wrong

➤ Getting started for less than $100

➤ Who catches fish—and who doesn't

The spring I graduated from college, three friends and I spent the better part of a month camping and fishing the trout streams in and around Yellowstone National Park. One day we decided to fish an extremely remote section of the Snake River in Idaho. We drove on a dirt road until the van could go no farther, then hiked down a steep cliff to reach the water. We were fishing for no more than an hour when two anglers in a drift boat came by. They stopped and we all started quizzing each other about the fishing—until two of my friends and one of the other fishermen realized they knew each other, as they all had grown up in the same small town in New Jersey, 2,000 miles away.

Coincidence? Yes, but not for the reasons you might expect. After all, millions of people fish because it's fun, not too expensive, and not difficult to learn. And fishermen encompass an amazing cross-section of the U.S. population, from all ages and income groups. However, as you'll also learn in this chapter, only a minority of the millions of fishermen are very good at it.

Welcome to the Party

Imagine walking into a huge party and being introduced to all kinds of people whom you have never met—people with different personalities, interests, and backgrounds. Although you may like many of them, eventually you will gravitate toward one group of people with whom you are most comfortable, who you find most entertaining, or who challenge you with their ideas.

So it is with the world of fishing. There are so many areas and categories and specialties that the beginner may not know where to start. And I can't tell you that either; you'll have to find out for yourself what you like best. But I can tell you what's out there.

The first major classification of fishing is that of the water type: fresh water, which includes all ponds, lakes, reservoirs, brooks, creeks, streams, and rivers; and salt water, which covers oceans, bays, estuaries, tidal creeks, and rivers. The type of fishing you choose depends largely on the water you are fishing. The basic types of fishing (some of which are obvious) include

➤ *Bank fishing*. Casting from the shore (or a dock or pier) of a still body of water or a large river.

➤ *Stream fishing*. Casting from the shore or while wading in the water of a brook, river, or creek.

➤ *Boat fishing*. Casting from a boat anchored in the water.

➤ *Drift fishing*. Fishing from a boat that is being moved by wind, tide, or current.

➤ *Trolling*. Fishing from a boat motoring slowly through the water.

➤ *Surf fishing*. Casting from a beach into salt water.

➤ *Jetty fishing*. Casting from a man-made structure that extends into salt water from shore.

➤ *Inshore fishing*. Fishing from a boat in a bay, tidal river, or on the ocean within a mile or two of land.

➤ *Offshore fishing*. Fishing from a boat on the ocean that's well off the coast.

Cautious Casts

If you're planning to fish in fresh water (and, in some states, in salt water) anywhere in the U.S. or Canada, you will need a fishing license. You should also be acquainted with the open seasons, minimum sizes (how big a fish has to be in order to be kept by the angler), and creel limits (how many of those fish you can keep in one day's fishing). For details on licensing and laws, see Chapter 30, "Hello, Warden."

Getting the Point

A **fishing reel** holding **fishing line** attaches to a **fishing rod**— a long, slender, flexible, and light-weight tube made of fiber-glass, graphite, or a composite. Fishermen use rod, reel, or line to cast, hook, and retrieve fish.

Within these general types are three basic styles of fishing, which are determined by the species you are after and/or the tackle you pursue them with:

1. *Baitfishing.* Fishing with a live or dead organism on a hook, such as a worm or a minnow.

2. *Lure fishing.* Fishing with a wood, plastic, or metal device that imitates or simulates something that fish eat.

3. *Flyfishing.* Fishing with a fly rod using artificial flies, which resemble insects or other fish.

Later chapters will detail these styles of fishing, the tackle you need to do it with, and the type of fish you will catch.

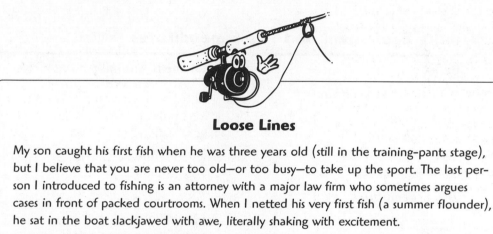

Loose Lines

My son caught his first fish when he was three years old (still in the training-pants stage), but I believe that you are never too old—or too busy—to take up the sport. The last person I introduced to fishing is an attorney with a major law firm who sometimes argues cases in front of packed courtrooms. When I netted his very first fish (a summer flounder), he sat in the boat slackjawed with awe, literally shaking with excitement.

Fishing U.S.A.: Who We Are

Fishing is the second most popular form of recreation in the United States. The first is swimming (and the fact that people pursuing the second sometimes accidentally become involved in the first isn't reflected in surveys).

So how many anglers are out there, anyway? The exact number is impossible to determine, but recent studies indicate a large group indeed. Every five years, the U.S. Department of the Interior publishes a "National Survey of Fishing, Hunting, and Wildlife Associated Recreation." Undertaken by the U.S. Fish and Wildlife Service, and done in conjunction with other government organizations such as the Bureau of the Census, the National Survey for 1996 (the most recent Survey available) states that 35.2 *million* U.S. residents went fishing that year. And that figure counts only those 16 years old and older.

The Survey reveals other interesting (and sometimes startling) statistics about fishing and fishermen. For example

➤ People fished for an estimated total of 625.9 million days in 1996.

➤ Fishermen took an estimated 507 million fishing trips in 1996.

➤ Fishermen spent approximately $37.8 billion on direct fishing-related expenditures in 1996, and had a combined direct and indirect impact on the U.S. economy that year of more than $71.9 billion.

All these fishermen contribute to the economy in many ways, from buying a $1 can of worms at the local tackle shop to mortgaging a half-million-dollar sportfishing boat. The following table provides examples of the items anglers buy and how much they spend on them.

Fishing Equipment and Trip Expenditures

Item	Total Spent Annually
Equipment Expenditures	
Rods and reels	$2.3 billion
Lures and bait	$880.9 million
Line	$490.9 million
Hooks and sinkers	$376.7 million
Trip Expenditures	
Food	$4.2 billion
Private transportation	$3.2 billion
Boating costs	$2.9 billion
Lodging	$1.7 billion

(Figures are rounded. Source: "1996 National Survey of Fishing, Hunting, and Wildlife Associated Recreation," U.S. Fish and Wildlife Service.)

In 1995, fishermen spent close to $320 million on ice alone. But you don't need to break into your 401(k) retirement plan to get started. Actually, you might have enough in your wallet right now.

Loose Lines

Wallop-Breaux is an excise tax collected each year by the U.S. Treasury Department on fishing equipment and recreational motorboat fuel. Funds are allocated to each state for sportfishing enhancement and restoration. In 1997, Wallop-Breaux generated almost $178 million in revenue.

Basic Equipment, Basic Costs

You can put together the basic elements of freshwater fishing tackle—all decent stuff, too—for less than $50. By basic elements, I mean

➤ A *fishing rod*, which allows you to cast to the fish via ...

➤ A *fishing reel*, which is attached to the fishing rod and holds the ...

➤ *Fishing line*, to which is tied ...

➤ A *hook*, onto which is threaded ...

➤ *Bait*, something that fish eat. You can use imitation bait instead, which is called ...

➤ A *lure*.

You'll learn more about tackle, the various kinds, and what it does in Part 2 of this book. For now, though, to get an idea of the prices involved, note the cost of assembling a basic freshwater rod-and-reel outfit and some lures (which were priced at a sporting-goods store), detailed in the following table.

Costs of Basic Freshwater Tackle

Item	Cost
Spinning rod-and-reel combination, rated for 6- to 12-pound-test line, medium action	$34.99
Three spinners @ $1.99 each	5.97
250 yards of 8-pound-test monofilament line	4.99
Subtotal	$45.95
Sales tax @ 6 percent	2.76
TOTAL	$48.71

One major manufacturer offered a "ready to fish" spinning rod-and-reel combination that came with a free tackle starter kit—either three spinners or a small assortment of plastic worms and hooks—for $35. Conversely, for about $100 you can buy an excellent warranty-backed rod-and-reel outfit, one that will last for more than a decade, and still have money left over for your license. For now, though, I recommend going with a mid-priced outfit, because your desires may change in the future. There's no point investing heavily in, say, a lightweight trout-fishing outfit now when you may wind up doing most of your fishing in big reservoirs for heavyweight largemouth bass.

The cost of putting together a basic saltwater-fishing outfit with rudimentary tackle is slightly higher, as detailed in the following table.

Costs of Basic Saltwater Tackle

Item	Cost
Conventional rod-and-reel combination, rated for 12- to 20-pound-test line, medium action	$60.00
Eight hooks, assorted sizes	1.99
300 yards of 15-pound-test monofilament line	6.99
Six bank sinkers, assorted sizes	1.80
Bait (clams, squid, worms, etc., available at bait shop)	5.00
Subtotal	$75.78
Sales tax @ 6 percent	4.55
TOTAL	$80.33

It's possible to spend even less on tackle; the same store offered starter rod-and-reel outfits for less than $15. These were spincasting (also known as "pushbutton") outfits with line already on the reel, and in some cases blister-packaged with a hook or a lure. This is where the "you get what you pay for" philosophy applies, because, cheap tackle is just that. Poor-quality rods don't cast well, lack proper balance, and are usually either as stiff as broomsticks or as whippy as rope. Inexpensive reels are typically clumsy to operate, malfunction often, and break easily. Learning to cast and eventually fish with such cheap tackle is difficult, frustrating, and possibly detrimental to your learning the sport. In the end, a cheap rod and reel will send you back to the tackle shop for what you should have bought in the first place.

Manufacturers of quality rods and reels include (but are not limited to) Abu Garcia, All Star, Berkley, Daiwa, Eagle Claw, Fenwick, G. Loomis, Lamiglas, Lew's, Mitchell, Penn, Quantum, Shakespeare, Shimano, St. Croix, and Zebco.

A number of mail-order houses specialize in fishing tackle, and their prices are competitive, usually beating those at local tackle shops. But be aware of two caveats if you're considering buying an outfit over the phone:

➤ Looking at a photograph of and reading the catalog copy about a particular rod or reel doesn't provide that all-important "feel" of it. One rod labeled "light action" may be similar to a "medium action" rod by another manufacturer, and you can't compare rod actions by looking at a glossy catalog page.

➤ The cost of shipping (not to mention the risk) may negate any potential savings.

Loose Lines

Many deep-discount department stores sell fishing tackle (some even specialize in it). They offer decent selections and their prices are good. However, the sales clerk may not be well acquainted with the merchandise, and may not be able to offer much assistance. If you need sales help, you're much better off patronizing a small tackle shop staffed with knowledgeable employees. You'll pay a bit more for your tackle, but with it will come expertise.

Why Only 10 Percent of Fishermen Catch 90 Percent of the Fish

The primary objective of fishing is to catch fish, but the actual enjoyment of the sport stems from many of its aspects. Just standing in front of a cold, gurgling brook, rowing across a glass-still pond at dawn, or riding the ocean swells on a sportfishing boat on the way to the fishing area provides enough enjoyment for many people; actually catching a fish while they're enjoying the scenery is nice but not necessary. For others, "getting away from it all" (whatever "it" may be) is enough reason to grab a rod and find some water. Camaraderie (or solitude), getting some sun, and an excuse for having a picnic are all reason enough for plenty of people to go fishing.

Well, that's not good enough for me—and, we can assume since you've read this far, not for you either. Granted, I love the outdoors, and one of my favorite moments on a fishing trip is arriving at a lake, stream, or dock in the half-light of dawn, witnessing the creation of a new day. But I'm there to catch fish—or at least attempt to. That's my primary goal. Many fishermen hit the water with hopes that they'll catch fish, but either they don't consider it a serious pursuit or they don't know enough about the sport itself. The vast majority of these types of fishermen go home empty-handed.

Getting the Point

My wife, Regina, is a **fisherman**—the term "fisherwoman" doesn't exactly roll off the tongue (it also invites comparison to the term "fishwife," which Reggie doesn't appreciate), and a "fisher" is a small fur-bearing animal. **Angler** (derived from the Sanskrit word "anka," meaning bend, referring to a curved fishhook) is proper. But "fisherman" is a widely accepted reference. (And I have yet to answer the phone one night and have a friend say, "Hey Mike! Let's go angling tomorrow!")

That's why only 10 percent of all fishermen catch 90 percent of all fish caught. This is not an original statement—I've heard it repeated ever since I was old enough to understand it—and I know of no survey proving the numbers. But I've witnessed its truth many times, and so can you. Drive to a popular fishing area right now and you'll see an assortment of anglers. I guarantee that at least one of the fishermen would not be fishing right at the moment. He or she would be gazing around, talking to another fisherman or half-heartedly fumbling with tackle. At least a couple more anglers would be actively fishing but casting to the wrong place, fishing with the wrong bait or lure, or even using the wrong rod-and-reel outfit for the conditions. At least one of them might have it all correct—focusing on the water, using the right equipment—but the line on his or her reel is weakened because it hasn't been replaced in three years, and the knot he or she tied is more granny than good, and what is that grinding sound coming from the reel, anyway? What's more, all the people you would see there could very well be fishing at the wrong time of day, during the wrong tide, or even during the wrong time of year.

Like many pursuits, fishing is easy to initiate but not so easy to do well. Just realizing how much goes into successful fishing will make you a better fisherman even before you make your very first cast.

The Least You Need to Know

➤ There are numerous types and styles of fishing, all with varying venues to pursue different types of fish.

➤ Billions of dollars are spent annually on fishing, by approximately 35.2 million people.

➤ It costs less than $100 to assemble rudimentary fishing tackle.

➤ The "you get what you pay for" philosophy applies to fishing tackle. Avoid low-end prices.

➤ Fishing is an easy sport to take up, but it's not so easy to become proficient at it. The sport offers numerous rewards, but the primary one—catching fish—requires focus, experience, and knowledge.

Chapter 2

First Step: Finding a Place to Fish

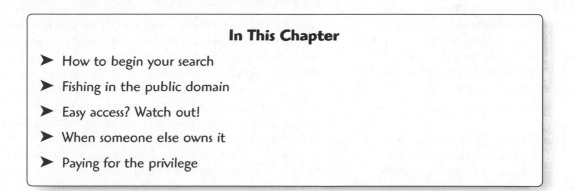

In This Chapter

➤ How to begin your search

➤ Fishing in the public domain

➤ Easy access? Watch out!

➤ When someone else owns it

➤ Paying for the privilege

You have to know where you will be fishing before you first set foot inside a tackle shop, because even the best rod, reel, line, bait, and lures won't help you catch a fish if you're using it in areas that don't hold many fish. Judging fishing waters accurately on looks alone takes time and experience, but this chapter will at least get you started finding waters, both public and private, that you can fish, as well as help you recognize waters that you should avoid.

According to *The Water Encyclopedia* (Frits van der Leeden et al., 1990) there are 3,249,000 miles of streams—that is, moving water—and 64,480 square miles of lakes and reservoirs in the United States. When considering the additional millions of square miles of fishable salt water, first-time fishermen may feel intimidated when it comes to finding a good place to cast a line.

So Much Water, So Few Fish

To begin your search, first narrow down your possibilities. Don't focus so much on finding a great place to fish (that will come later) as finding one that isn't far from home—within walking distance or a short car ride away.

This is important because many basic fishing skills—reading the stream or lake, setting the hook, playing the fish—can only be practiced on the water. Also, as an extremely general rule, fish are more active early in the morning and late in the day, when the sun is not shining directly on the water. For now, the less time spent getting there and the more time there, the better.

When you're just beginning to learn to fish, pick a small body of water rather than a large one. A one-acre pond, for instance, is basically a 1,000-acre lake in miniature. Various types of shoreline, submerged drop-offs and humps, vegetation, and varying temperature zones are all there, only in scaled-down form and thus much easier to identify. The same is true with fishing a creek instead of a river, or a back bay instead of the ocean: There's less water to fish, which makes navigation easier and simplifies the process of narrowing down likely areas to focus on.

Cautious Casts

Make sure the water you're fishing isn't so polluted that the fish you catch will be unfit for consumption—or even devoid of fish. Large amounts of foam in quiet waters of a stream or near a lake's shoreline, an unpleasant odor, or a constant brownish or milky hue generally indicate pollution.

However, don't pick too small a body of water. If you decide to fish a brook that's narrow enough to jump across, or a pond so small that you can easily cast across it to the opposite bank, you stand a very good chance of scaring or "spooking" the fish before you even begin fishing. Most fish are extremely sensitive to abrupt changes in their environment, such as vibrations from heavy footfalls on the shoreline, or shadows suddenly appearing or moving across the bottom. Even an ill-placed cast can send fish scurrying into hiding, where they'll remain for an hour or longer without feeding or moving. Fishing small waters requires extra patience, a good degree of stealth, and an ability to accurately cast a bait or lure when standing well back from the bank or shoreline. (Even many otherwise experienced anglers don't know how to fish small waters effectively.) The first-timer needs a wide and forgiving margin of error.

Public Waters

If you don't know of or can't find a place to fish, one telephone call can put you in (cool) water. Each state has a government department that manages that state's fisheries. These "state fish and game departments," as they are generally known, are charged with setting the dates for fishing seasons, implementing and enforcing the rules regarding the size and the number of fish taken, enforcing those rules, and generally caring for those waters harboring fish. They work and operate both actively (such as constructing boat-launch sites and fishing platforms, surveying fish stocks, and monitoring their health) and in a watchdog sense (such as reporting polluters to the proper authorities).

Each state fish and game department can provide a free listing of the public fishing waters in an area. Sometimes these waters are listed in a compendium, or abstract, that summarizes the current (annual) fishing rules and regulations. These compendiums are available free from fishing license agents. If the compendium doesn't list all public waters, call your state's fish and game department and ask. See Appendix A for a list of all fish and game department phone numbers.

There are also many miles of waters that are under federal jurisdiction, presided over by the Department of Agriculture and the Department of the Interior (the latter consisting of the Bureau of Land Management, the U.S. Park Service, the U.S. Fish and Wildlife Service, the Bureau of Reclamation, the Department of Defense/U.S. Army Corps of Engineers, and the Tennessee Valley Authority). Your state's fish and game department will include these federal waters in their lists of fishable waters; details about them are available by contacting the individual department.

State fish and game departments have jurisdiction in salt water as well. Most bays, tidal rivers, and beaches have numerous public accesses. Again, your state fish and game department can provide details.

Stocked Waters

Many state fish and game departments run intensive "stocking" programs, in which hatchery-raised fish are released into suitable waters.

Many programs are "put-and-take" in nature, meaning that the department is not stocking the fish in hopes of developing a naturally reproducing population or augmenting an existing one (although this does happen on occasion). The fish are released simply to provide fishing opportunity. Most trout stockings, for example, occur before the opening of trout season and throughout the spring. Many states list trout-stocked waters in their compendium of fishing rules and regulations, and the outdoor columns of many newspapers provide details on the number of trout being released into particular waters on certain days.

If It's Convenient and Accessible, It's (Probably) Not That Good

Even if you've never fished before, you've probably seen people fishing: from the side of a bridge spanning a picturesque creek, in a man-made pond in the middle of an office park, or on a beach a short distance from swimmers and sunbathers. Now think: How often have you seen any of these people actually catch anything of substance?

School Notes

If the only place you have to fish receives a lot of pressure from other anglers, try to get there as early in the morning as possible, before anyone else gets there. Then walk around a bit, away from those well-worn spots and trails created by fishermen. The combination of fishing at first light, in areas that are rarely cast to, may result in a strike from a fish bigger than you thought existed there.

Probably not very often, because one problem with convenient and accessible waters is that so many anglers know about them. Finding a good place to fish is not necessarily akin to finding a good diner, where a lot of 18-wheelers parked outside is an indication of decent fare (although some exceptions exist, especially with some species of saltwater fish that "school up" in specific areas at certain times of the year). Besides the fact that fish are sensitive to changes in their environment, any body of water that receives a lot of fishing pressure—people constantly walking the banks, lures and baits constantly plopping into the water, boats drifting or motoring back and forth—can actually alter the habits of the fish. Intense fishing pressure often causes fish to become exclusive nocturnal feeders; that is, instead of feeding throughout the day (especially at and near dawn and dusk), the fish will seek seclusion during the day and not feed at all, saving all their energy for nighttime activity.

Another reason that the beginning fisherman should avoid such high-popularity, low-result fishing areas: You probably aren't going to learn much about fish habits and habitat. Other anglers there could have beat the water to a froth with their casts and spooked every fish in the vicinity for the rest of the day. This means that you could be doing everything right and still not be catching anything. On less-frequented waters, you could at least guess at the reasons for your lack of success—wrong bait or lure, wrong time of day, too windy. (The mark of an experienced fisherman is having a host of excuses, available at any time, for not catching anything.)

Knocking on Doors

One spring weekend some years ago my father, a friend, and I made a trip to upstate New York's Adirondack mountains to fish for trout in the beautiful, cold, crystal-clear lakes and streams that drain those majestic peaks. The scenery was beautiful, as always, but a late winter had left the rivers high and roily, and many of the large lakes still had crusts of ice on some shorelines. We fished three lakes and two streams and had absolutely nothing to show for our efforts—none of us even had a bite.

We had just begun our drive home Sunday afternoon when we passed a gravel road that led through a small woods, through which we saw a house and the faint glimmer of water. This was at a lower elevation than were those lakes and streams we had just fished, and the air felt a little warmer here. So, on a hunch, we turned around, drove down the gravel drive, parked in front of the house, and politely asked the landowner if we could fish his pond. Be my guest, the man said.

Well, the black flies were thick there—so thick that we had to wear headnets and apply insect repellent to every inch of exposed skin—but we caught so many brook trout in two hours of fishing (we only kept enough to eat) that we hardly noticed the flies. That totally spontaneous attempt to gain permission to private water salvaged the entire three-day trip.

That's an example of one aspect of the advantages of fishing private water. The fishing isn't always that good on non-public lakes, streams, and ponds, of course, and many "private" waters are actually open to fishing for anyone. But the point is that a little bit of effort can pay off when seeking a place to fish. And there are countless farm ponds, meadow creeks, resort lakes, even privately held sections of shoreline on bays and oceans that the fisherman may gain access to.

There's no standard method or trick to finding good private fishing waters (if there was, the places would be mobbed with anglers). You have to spend some time searching for them: driving around, taking roads that you aren't familiar with, getting out of the car and walking around, asking questions at gas stations and convenience stores. A map of the area will help you from getting totally lost, and it may show some waters, but it's surprising how many ponds, brooks, and small lakes aren't included on state and county maps.

If you discover a promising-looking body of water that you know—or even suspect—is in private hands (the lack of "No Trespassing" signs is not an indication that the water is open to the public), you should follow certain procedures to increase your chances of gaining permission to fish it:

School Notes

When approaching a landowner for the first time, make sure you're dressed in clean clothes that are in good condition. You don't have to change into a suit or a dress—after all, you're there to fish—but don't wear clothes that are ready for the rag bin or that make some type of social or political statement (like a T-shirt that reads "Nuke the gay whales").

➤ *Don't drive your vehicle right up to the landowner's house.* Park far enough away so that the owner can see you approaching. You don't want to intimidate the owner, or have him or her believe you're a door-to-door salesman (yes, they still exist, especially in rural areas) before you even greet him or her.

➤ *Be polite when you greet the landowner, but don't stand there talking about the weather.* Get to the point—after all, you are already on his or her property without permission.

➤ *Explain what you want to do ("I'd like to fish your pond from the bank"), when you want to do it ("for a few hours late this afternoon"), and with whom ("I'll have one friend with me").* Make sure the landowner knows you aren't asking for permission to fish there the rest of the year, and that you are a responsible sort—you won't leave gates open (or close gates that are already open, so you don't disrupt

any livestock or farming activity on the land), you won't litter, build fires, consume alcohol, or otherwise do something that might disturb or anger him.

➤ *If you are planning to keep some fish, offer part of your catch to the landowner.* Many property owners—farmers and ranchers especially—like to fish but they don't have the time.

➤ *Offer the landowner a card or paper listing your name, address, phone number (as well as that of anyone else who will be fishing with you), and your license plate number.* You know where the landowner lives; he has a right to know where you live as well.

➤ *If the landowner refuses to grant permission, politely ask why.* It's very possible that he or she has had a bad experience with previous fishermen, and you may be able to convince him that you won't behave in that manner.

➤ *If the landowner still refuses (and the reason may have nothing to do with you personally, such as liability concerns), thank him for his time and leave immediately.* Time to go look for another spot—and it's always possible that the landowner will change his mind if you ask him again the following year. One friend requested trespass rights for four years—by both personal visits and letters—before the landowner let him on!

Those Pay-to-Fish Places

Across the U.S. are a number of private enterprises that sell access to waters that are heavily stocked with fish. These places vary from a half-acre man-made pond (situated on one acre of land) to thousand-acre-plus "resorts" or "preserves" complete with overnight accommodations, restaurants, tennis courts, jogging paths, and many other amenities. The basic business premise is the same, though: Guests pay for the privilege to cast a line in waters that are heavily and frequently stocked with fish, usually trout. Typically there is an admission charge as well as a per-pound charge for fish kept, and at many of the pay-to-fish places that I know about, anglers can't throw back any fish they catch.

There are both advantages and disadvantages to these enterprises. On the plus side: If you want the makings for a fresh-fish dinner, you'll come home with something to fry (even if you don't catch anything, which is highly unlikely, you can usually buy fresh trout on site). Beginning anglers (and children) who haven't had much luck on non-pay waters can at least find out what it's like to have a fish on the end of the line, and practice skills such as setting the hook on, playing, landing, and unhooking a fish. And most are clean, well-run, and efficient. After all, they want your return business.

The disadvantages: The waters are like nothing found in nature. These businesses make their money by people killing fish—remember, no throwbacks—and for that reason want to make sure that customers don't have to work hard to catch some. If the fish are in the mood to eat—and they usually are, since a minimum of natural forage exists in these waters and the abnormally high numbers of trout in them creates fierce competition for what is there—it's possible to catch fish almost as quickly as you can cast a bait or lure to them (as an adolescent I once caught a trout at a pay-to-fish operation on a bare hook). This means that you can catch $30 or $40 worth of trout in less time than it would take you to buy them in a store. Finally, because catching fish is so easy, the beginning angler learns nothing about real-life fishing: reading and approaching the water, casting accurately, making a proper presentation, discovering natural forage of the fish, finding out what the fish will hit through experimentation with various lures and baits, and so on.

If you really must kill a fish one day, you should definitely visit one of these enterprises. Actually, I recommend at least one trip for every fisherman at some stage of his or her life, simply for comparison purposes. But I'll bet you'll come home with misgivings along with your dinner.

School Notes

A number of the larger pay-to-fish operations have at least one body of water dedicated to fly-fishing only. You'll definitely learn a lot about casting, setting the hook, and playing a fish, which is much more difficult at first on fly tackle than it is with a spinning or spincasting outfit. Some places also allow you to catch fish and then release them.

The Least You Need to Know

➤ Try to find water that's not too far from home, so you can start building your fishing skills as soon and as often as possible.

➤ Select a small body of water so you can learn its makeup quickly—but not too small, where the fish tend to be flighty.

➤ Contact your state's fish and game department for names and locations of public waters near you.

➤ Waters that offer easy access to a lot of people usually suffer from overfishing.

➤ Many waters on private land offer good fishing, but you must be willing to spend some time both finding them and gaining permission to fish them.

➤ Visiting a commercial operation that charges admission to a heavily stocked body of water and levies a fee on fish that you catch offers good fishing, but their artificial nature means you'll learn few skills that carry over into "real world" waters.

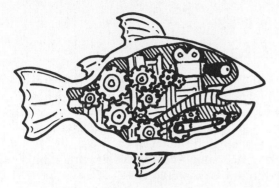

Chapter 3

How Fish Work

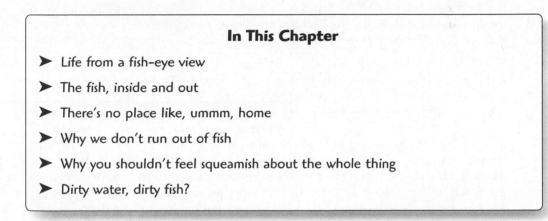

In This Chapter

➤ Life from a fish–eye view

➤ The fish, inside and out

➤ There's no place like, ummm, home

➤ Why we don't run out of fish

➤ Why you shouldn't feel squeamish about the whole thing

➤ Dirty water, dirty fish?

Considering the fact that civilized humans—humans at least bright enough to seek shelter in caves—have been on Earth for 50,000 to 100,000 years, you might think we'd have this business of fishing down pat. Fish do have the advantage of time, though, because they've been around for an estimated 400 million years. On the other hand, they still have a brain about the size of a pea. And it's not much of one, being pretty much an enlargement of the spinal cord.

Ironically, that itself is a clue as to why catching a fish isn't a simple and straight-forward process. Fish are slaves of their senses; they don't ponder abstracts and permutations like humans do, they *react* to various stimuli. If you've ever been around a four-year-old when he or she hears the jingle of a nearby ice-cream truck, you've already grasped this concept. Also, the stimuli that fish react to are very different from those that you and I react to (and I refuse to write a simile or metaphor about *that*, because fishing is a wholesome activity). But the point is that it can be difficult to catch fish consistently if you don't understand, say, how the heck they can live in water in the first place. This chapter introduces concepts that can help you become better at catching fish.

Hal's Story: A Day in the Life of a Fish

Hal (not his real name; he doesn't have a name) is a foot-long largemouth bass who lives in a 100-acre lake in a state with a moderate climate. Hal was born in the lake three years ago, one of about one thousand fertilized eggs that hatched in late spring. When he was an inch long—by which time more than half of his nestmates had been eaten by other fish—he was on his own, seeking shelter in the weeds of the cove where he was born. Hal has spent most of his life in that cove, leaving it only when the water there became too warm, too low, or too cold.

At sunrise this summer morning, Hal is hovering just inside the edge of the bed of lily pads that extends 10 feet from the shoreline. His belly is full of various minnows, insects, and one unlucky frog that Hal ate during the course of the previous night. Hal roamed the entire cove finding this forage, but now he is staying under the cover of the lily pads, avoiding the direct sunlight.

A school of 3-inch long shiners, a dozen in all, swims past the edge of the lily pads, looking for insects and any tiny aquatic creatures that will fit into their minuscule mouths. Hal sees the school and remains motionless. He will not go after the school and expend energy chasing them. However, the last shiner in the school is a bit smaller than its mates and must swim harder to keep up. This effort sends vibrations through the water that do not synchronize with the vibrations made by the rest of the school. Hal waits until the shiners are almost past him, then darts out and opens his mouth behind the last shiner. By this time the entire school has sensed the presence of the predator and has begun swimming quickly toward the deeper water of the cove, but already the last shiner is in Hal's mouth. Hal turns the shiner around in his mouth and swallows it headfirst while swimming back to his station in the weeds.

Hal remains there for a couple more hours, eating one more shiner in a similar manner. By now the sun is higher in the sky and Hal moves to a deeper, and thus cooler and darker, section of the cove, where he is more comfortable and less likely to be seen by predators. Hal stays in the depths for most of the day, moving around close to the bottom, finding and eating two small crayfish.

Hal's Evening

Toward dusk, when the sun is off the water, Hal moves back to the lily pads. A not-quite-grown green frog jumps off one lily pad and begins swimming toward another. The sight of the frog and its vibrations trigger Hal into movement. He rises to near the surface, studies the frog for a few seconds, and with one powerful burst shoots up and out of the water, grabbing the frog in his mouth in the process. He swims back down and swallows the frog, again headfirst.

Minutes later something splashes down on the water in almost the same place where Hal captured the frog. Again, Hal is triggered into movement, but as he rises near the object, it moves in a most unfroglike manner, moving way too fast through the pads, at one point sticking to a pad stem and making it quiver and shake. Hal moves quickly away from the object disturbing the environment and leaves the lily pads altogether, dropping down to the bottom of the cove.

The fisherman standing on shore yanks on his fishing rod, eventually disentangling his lure from the weeds, reels up, and casts again elsewhere.

The sun sets. That night Hal moves around the cove again, searching for shiners and other small fish. A cricket falls into the water just inches from the shoreline and Hal, being only a few feet away, blasts into the shallows to eat it. Later, a field mouse swims across the water and Hal rises up, studying the rodent. But suddenly a bass nearly twice as big as Hal appears from the other side of the cove and engulfs the mouse in a shower of spray. Hal moves off, and as the light from the early morning sun hits the water, goes back to the refuge of the lily pads.

Cautious Casts

Some fishing lures are good at catching fish, others are good at catching fishermen. When you're buying lures, don't fall for fancy packaging or ornate designs. A good lure either imitates the natural forage of the water you intend to fish—long, slim, silver minnows, perhaps; or small crayfish—or will provoke a strike because of its action in the water. (More on lures in Chapter 11, "Lures: Virtual Reality to Fish.")

Loose Lines

Many people, even experienced anglers, assume that a fish will hit a bait or lure because it's hungry. This is true most of the time, but certainly not always. For example, fish that are protecting their nests of eggs or young will often attack a lure retrieved past them, only to defend their progeny. And certain species of fish, like shad and some salmons, that migrate up a river or stream to spawn (mate) sometimes aggressively hit an angler's offering. But if you open a migrating shad's belly, you'll find it empty. When spawning, these fish hit lures only out of reflex.

Just Another Survivor ...

Hal's life may not seem to be a particularly pleasant one because everything he (and every other fish) does revolves around survival: eating; competing with other fish for the same food supply; locating to various parts of the water to avoid extreme cold, heat, or light; and staying away from predators (reproduction, another survival instinct, will be covered later in this chapter). Hal's life is not a Disney movie; anthropomorphizing may be fun but it won't help you catch fish. Hal isn't cagey or crafty or plotting; he is simply a survivalist.

He is also quite tasty when filleted, dipped in milk, rolled in flour, and fried to a crispy golden brown.

Fish Physiology 101

Fish are cold-blooded (meaning their body temperature is not internally regulated) vertebrates (meaning they possess a spinal column) that live in waters the world over. About 17,000 species of fish are now known.

There are two basic biological groups of fish: bony fish, which have skeletons made of bone and are the quarry of most fishermen; and cartilaginous fish, which have skeletons made of cartilage. The latter group consists mainly of sharks, rays, and skates, found primarily in salt water. The females of most bony fish discharge their eggs into the water, where males fertilize them with their *milt* (semen). The eggs of cartilaginous fish are fertilized in the female's body.

Bony fish share many characteristics, as indicated in the following illustration.

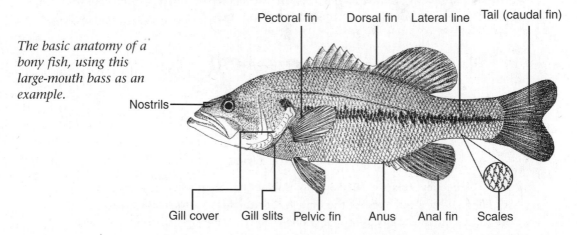

The basic anatomy of a bony fish, using this large-mouth bass as an example.

Pectoral fin   Dorsal fin   Lateral line   Tail (caudal fin)

Nostrils

Gill cover   Gill slits   Pelvic fin   Anus   Anal fin   Scales

Most bony fish have two sets of paired fins: the pectoral fins, which are typically located just behind the gills; and the pelvic fins, found on the fish's belly below the pectoral fins. There are also three vertical fins: the dorsal fin, which is on the fish's back (some fish have front and rear dorsal fins); the anal fin, which is at the rear of the belly, and the caudal fin, which is the tail. Fins provide mobility and balance.

Fish must take in oxygen from the water and eliminate carbon dioxide from their circulatory systems. This is performed via the gills, which bring the fish's blood supply in close contact with the water. Bony fish have four pairs of gills, which are located on either side of the fish just behind the head. A fish "breathes" by closing the gill slits and opening its mouth, taking in water. The water is then forced through the gill chambers, over feather-like gill filaments that absorb oxygen from the water and remove carbon dioxide from the blood. The water is then passed out through the opened gill slits.

The skin of a fish is covered with a thin layer of slime, which performs a number of vital functions. First, the slime serves to protect the fish from parasites and disease. Second, it allows the fish to move easily through the water (which is why some long-distance swimmers coat their bodies with grease before a competition). Third, the slime prevents water from entering the fish's body.

Beneath the slime on most bony fishes are scales, which serve as another form of protection. Scales are layered in rows on the fish's body, much like shingles on a roof. One edge of each scale is attached to the skin of the fish. Scales are not living tissue, somewhat resembling fingernails. Some fish species have no scales; some have tiny, practically invisible scales; and some have large ones. People who eat large-scaled fish like perch with the skin on, such as when baking, should remove the scales before cooking. This can be done with a scaler, which resembles a dull-edged, large-saw-toothed knife. (See Chapter 29, "In the Pan or On the Wall?" for more information on fish cleaning and preparation.)

The lateral line on a fish is a long, thin canal that runs horizontally on each side of the fish's body, from just behind the gills to the base of the tail. On some fish it is also continued on the head and may have numerous branches off the main line. The lateral line is filled with sensory organs with which the fish is able to detect low-frequency sounds and changes in temperature,

Getting the Point

An **anadromous** fish is one that migrates from the ocean to a freshwater river to spawn, such as shad and striped bass. Salmon that have been transplanted to the Great Lakes still exhibit this behavior, moving from the lake to a tributary to spawn. Fish that migrate from freshwater rivers to oceans in order to spawn are called **catadromous** fish.

pressure, and water current. Fish also possess an inner ear, and numerous pits on the skin containing nerve endings detect touch. All this makes for a very vibration-sensitive creature.

Fish taste things via specialized taste organs located in and around the mouth. Fish may also be able to detect taste via additional organs on their body. A number of species, such as catfish, have *barbels* (commonly referred to as "whiskers"), or thin protrusions emanating from the mouth area. These are very sensitive to taste.

Fish smell (that is, they are able to) via nostrils on either side of the head. Nerves connect the nostrils to the brain and allow the fish to search for food. Some fish, most notably sharks, have highly refined senses of smell and rely on it more than they do eyesight to find food. Some fish use their sense of smell to find particular waters. Anadromous fish such as salmon live in oceans but always migrate to the stream in which they were born. Their senses of smell allow them to detect the odor of their home stream.

What Fish See and Don't See

Fish see things very much like humans see things, although there are some important differences.

First, with the exception of some sharks, fish don't have eyelids and tear glands. Because the fish is in constant contact with water, there is no need to rewet the eye and clean it.

Second, most fish can't regulate the size of their iris, which is the colored ring on the eye. The human iris can widen or shrink to adjust to the amount of light, leaving just a dot in the center when the light is bright, or exposing the whole lens in dim conditions. Fish, therefore, must move to different areas of their environment to adjust to the amount of light in the water. (Of course, light under water never reaches the same brilliance as does light above it.) This is why fish rarely expose themselves to bright sunlight.

Third, the lens of a fish is round (when looking from the side), not disk-like as in humans. Fish focus on objects by altering the position of the lens, instead of changing its shape, as we do.

Fourth, because fish have eyes on either side of their head, they can see objects to either side of them simultaneously (although most fish can't focus on the same object with both eyes). This also means, however, that fish have a "blind spot" directly in front of their heads, because the line of vision from each eye intersects at a certain distance in front of them—from a few inches to a few feet, depending on the fish.

Fifth, some fish species are farsighted, some are nearsighted; others have no problem focusing on both distant and close objects. This last group can focus their eyes independently on different objects at different ranges as well. Authorities agree that the various vision capabilities of fish depend on the environment and habits of the particular species. For instance, a bottom-hugging catfish has no need to see objects at a long distance; the fish is suited to living and feeding in dark and often silty waters. This makes perfect sense when considering that catfish have those taste organs on their barbels, which allow them to identify food without having to get a clear picture of it. Conversely, brown trout—which often feed on insects floating on the surface of the water—need good long-range vision to search for and identify forage.

Fish see color very well, at least as well if not better than humans can, and can distinguish contrasts, brightness, and shade. This holds true mostly for comparatively shallow-water species. Because light does not penetrate water very well, fish that live in the depths have no need to distinguish colors, as most aren't visible there anyway.

School Notes

Because fish don't like bright light, casting to large areas of shallow, sunlit waters is usually wasted time. This is one reason why dawn and dusk are usually good times to fish. Also, if you can easily see a fish, that means it can also see you, and any sudden movement will scare it into hiding. Back off slowly and cast from a distance.

Where Fish Live

Different species of fish prefer various types of habitat, depending on their biological needs. Often, that habitat is determined by the temperature of the water. Because fish cannot internally regulate their body temperature, they must seek water in which they are comfortable.

Brook trout, for example, require very clean, cool (never reaching higher than 65°F), well-oxygenated water to survive. Picture a gushing cold mountain stream, and you've defined ideal brook-trout habitat. The brown trout, though, prefers water in the 60°–65° range, but it can tolerate much warmer water than can the brookie—up to 75°F, or, in some cases, 80°F. Brown trout can live practically anywhere that brook trout live, but brookies can't survive in many waters where brownies thrive. The two species, though, share many of the same food sources—mainly aquatic and terrestrial insects, crustaceans, and smaller fish—so if you're fishing a stream that harbors both fish, you're liable to catch either type if you are using, say, an earthworm for bait.

Compare that with the temperature preferences of the largemouth and smallmouth bass. Largemouths prefer water temperatures from 68° to 78°, but can survive in lakes and rivers that reach higher and lower temperatures. This means that the largemouth

Getting the Point

A **terrestrial** is a life form that lives on or in the ground (*terra firma*) instead of in the water. Terrestrials play a significant role in the diets of many fish. Ants, grasshoppers, crickets, mosquitoes and their larvae, grubs, mealworms, mice, and, of course, earthworms are all eaten by numerous species.

School Notes

Good fishermen check the temperature of the water they intend to fish. Although fish can detect minute differences in temperature—as little as one degree, according to some studies—most of us can't accurately gauge the temperature of water by sticking our hand in it. Water thermometers, which are sold in tackle shops, come with a long cord so temperatures can be checked at various levels.

can survive, even thrive, in a large variety of waters, and it does: Largemouths are found in almost every state in the U.S., in waters ranging from huge reservoirs to slow-moving rivers to spit-across-size ponds. The smallmouth bass—a close relative of the largemouth—requires water near the 70° mark, and therefore is limited in range to cool rivers and large lakes and reservoirs. The range of the smallmouth is limited to the northern half of the U.S. (and some deep and therefore cool man-made waters throughout the South, where the smallmouth was stocked). There are a number of waters that hold both largemouth and smallmouth bass, but because largemouths prefer warmer water than the smallmouth, you usually won't find them inhabiting the same area.

For example, one day a friend and I went fishing at a large reservoir in the Northeast for largemouth bass. We were planning to hit the coves first thing in the morning, casting to weedbeds and to the numerous felled trees that littered the shoreline. We launched the boat and started motoring to one long, narrow cove not too far away. At the entrance to the cove, a rock bluff entered the water at a steep angle, and the depth obviously dropped off quickly. There were no weeds. It wasn't an ideal place to fish for largemouths, considering that this was mid-spring and the water was still quite cool. But in our anxiousness to begin fishing, we cut the motor and cast to the bluff. Bang! A fish grabbed my lure (a jig with a white plastic trailer; see Chapter 11 for more information about lures), and a few minutes later, I brought a 2-pound smallmouth to the net. I was pleased but also surprised because I had no idea that the reservoir even contained smallmouths.

We cast a few more times to the bluff with no results. So we fired up the motor, turned into the cove, cut power, and dropped anchor. On my second or third cast to the downed trees, a 1-pound largemouth nailed my lure—the same jig that fooled the smallmouth.

The following table lists the preferred habitats and water temperatures of popular freshwater species.

Fish Habitats and Temperature Zones

Species	Preferred Habitat	Preferred Temperature Zone (°F)
Brook Trout	Streams, lakes, ponds	52–56
Brown Trout	Reservoirs, streams, lakes	60–65
Lake Trout	Reservoirs, lakes	48–52
Rainbow Trout	Reservoirs, streams, lakes	55–60
Largemouth Bass	Rivers, reservoirs, lakes, ponds	68–78
Smallmouth Bass	Reservoirs, lakes, rivers, streams	67–71
Spotted Bass	Streams, reservoirs	73–77
Bluegill	Streams, lakes, ponds	75–80
Pumpkinseed	Streams, lakes, ponds	70–75
Black Crappie	Rivers, reservoirs, lakes	70–75
White Crappie	Rivers, reservoirs, lakes	70–75
Chain Pickerel	Streams, lakes	75–80
Muskellunge	Rivers, lakes	67–72
Northern Pike	Reservoirs, lakes, rivers, streams	50–70
Walleye	Reservoirs, lakes, rivers, streams	65–75
Yellow Perch	Reservoirs, lakes, rivers, ponds	65–72
Striped Bass	Rivers, reservoirs	65–75
White Bass	Reservoirs, lakes, rivers	65–75
White Perch	Reservoirs, lakes, rivers, ponds	75–80
Blue Catfish	Reservoirs, rivers, ponds	77–82
Channel Catfish	Reservoirs, lakes, rivers, ponds	75–80
Black Bullhead	Streams, lakes	75–85
Brown Bullhead	Streams, lakes, ponds	78–82

Loose Lines

A good reason to know temperature preferences of various species, and to check the temperature of the water you're fishing, is the thermocline. The *thermocline* is a horizontal band of water in a lake or pond that marks a rapid temperature change. If you've ever gone swimming in a lake and, upon entering a deep section, noticed that the water at your feet was much colder than the water at your belly, you felt the top layer of the thermocline. Fish will often seek out and remain in the thermocline because the water temperature they seek is within the thermocline's zone.

How Big Fish Make Little Fish

Bony fish reproduce by the female discharging eggs through her vent into the water, where a male releases milt, or semen, from his vent to fertilize them. (If you turned to this page first in hopes of finding some NC-17 material, sorry, that's it, the show's over.) *Spawning*, as fish reproduction is called, is an instinctive rite for fish and not much is known about the actual triggers for it, although experts in the field agree that water temperature and light have something to do with it. Some fish species will change hues and color patterns during the spawn—some turn bright, others go dark.

Various species go about spawning in slightly different ways. The brown trout and the largemouth bass, two very popular species in the United States, provide two good examples of the differences.

The brown trout spawns in the fall or the early winter, depending on the region. Brown trout in streams will deposit eggs in *redds*, or a shallow depression on the gravel bottom dug by the female trout with her tail. The male and female will lay side by side over the redd, depositing eggs and milt. After fertilization, the female covers the eggs in the redd with more gravel. The current holds the eggs, which number from 500 to a few thousand, depending on the size of the fish, in place in the redd. The male and female browns then leave. The eggs hatch the following spring.

Largemouth bass, however, spawn in the spring. The male (not the female, as with trout) prepares a nest—again a shallow depression—in a sandy or gravelly bottom of a lake in only two or three feet of water. The male then tries to attract a female to spawn. If successful, the male and female lay eggs and release milt over the nest. This may happen several times in one nest, with the same or a different female. The eggs hatch in a week or two, during which time the male guards the nest, defending it from all real and imagined predators, including lures cast by fishermen.

Although the reproductive habits of the brown trout and the largemouth bass differ, both species—as well as hundreds of other species—are very successful spawners in the U.S., enough so that natural propagation keeps thousands of waters filled with fish.

Do Fish Feel Pain?

This is a question commonly asked by those new to fishing. And it's a good question, too; many otherwise experienced anglers don't know the answer. Actually, it's difficult to prove scientifically whether a fish feels the sting of a hook in its mouth the same way that I would feel that same hook in my mouth (that has never happened to me, although a friend of mine once hooked himself in the nose while flyfishing on a very windy day, and he said it hurt quite a bit).

We do know that fish *respond* to being hooked: They fight and leap and pull toward the bottom, always putting pressure against the angler's fishing line (never in my life have I hooked a fish that came directly to my hand or net). But that still does not signify pain as we know it. As a matter of fact, fish exhibit some traits from which we can construe that they don't feel pain at all.

School Notes

Fish eggs are popular forage for many fish, notably rainbow trout and steelhead (which are ocean or Great Lakes rainbows that spawn in rivers). A popular bait for both fish are salmon eggs, which are sold in jars. One pea-sized egg is usually impaled on a similar-sized gold-colored hook. Often the pale yellow salmon eggs are dyed in bright colors (usually orange) and/or scented for extra fish appeal.

Loose Lines

Because bass are very vulnerable to fishermen when they are spawning, some states don't open the bass fishing season until after the spawn is complete. On very heavily fished lakes, it would be possible to decimate the bass population if fishermen caught and kept all those males guarding the nest.

For instance, many times I have had a fish on my line—including bass, pickerel, bluegills, and numerous saltwater species—that I lost moments after I hooked it. These fish had the point of the hook embedded far enough into their mouths to respond to it by fighting. For whatever reason—I didn't set the hook hard enough, the hook point itself was dull, I didn't keep a tight enough line—the fish was able to dislodge the hook from its mouth ("throwing" or "spitting" the hook, as it is commonly referred to). Yet on one of my next few casts, I would hook *the very same fish*.

When I was young, sometimes I would lie down on a small boat dock and fish for the little bluegills and pumpkinseeds that took refuge in the shade of the structure. I would dangle a worm-baited hook just a foot or so under the surface and watch the panfish come out from the shade, observing the worm. Eventually one of them would dart over and try to grab the worm—try, because often the mouths on those diminutive bluegills would be too small to engulf the whole worm. So it would become a matter of striking exactly when just the point of the hook was positioned at, or just inside of, the fish's mouth. So many times I would have a bluegill on the hook for a matter of seconds, watching while it tugged against the line and tried to swim back to the safety of the dock's shadow, and then it would throw the hook. I'd reel in, rebait with a fresh worm, drop it back in the same place, and witness that same bluegill come out, study the worm, and try to eat it again.

Similarly, I have fished lakes for bass with a topwater lure (which imitates a frog or a mouse or a wounded baitfish) and had a bass jump up, grab the lure, and start swimming away. Now, many surface lures are made of hard plastic and feel very much unlike a frog, not to mention the shiny and sharply honed hooks dangling from them. The bass would shake its head, losing the hook, and then come back to hit it again.

Also, many people have witnessed sharks in a "feeding frenzy" that are so keyed into eating that one shark will occasionally take a bite out of another. That wounded shark would then—as gruesome as it may sound—turn and actually begin feeding on itself.

Some people may argue that fish *do* feel pain; the reason that they don't react to it is that their sense of hunger—the predatory instinct—is much stronger than their sense of pain. But I've also fished enough times when, for whatever reason, the fish just won't eat anything, to disallow that reasoning. My personal, unscientific theory is that fish do feel *something* when they're hooked, but it is not at all the same sensation that humans would experience. In other words, it doesn't *hurt* them.

School Notes

If I catch a fish that I intend to keep, and don't have the means to keep it alive until I clean it or fillet it, I kill it. Besides putting the fish out of its misery, it ensures good-quality meat. Fish that jump around until they expire may acquire an off-taste.

Loose Lines

Sometimes a fish gets away from the angler by breaking the line, with the hook still embedded in its jaw. Surprisingly, many fish survive such an event, because the hook will rust and fall away. I have even caught fish with an old fishhook still attached to them, and they didn't show any outward signs of being affected by it (obviously they were still well enough to eat). Fish that swallow the hook are a different case, and there have been numerous—and conflicting—studies on whether or not the majority of such fish survive. The type and size of the hook, where in the fish it is located, the species of the fish, and the water it is in are all factors.

Pollution and How Fish Deal with It

I used to live near a picture-perfect trout stream in rural Pennsylvania that had signs posted on trees along its banks notifying anglers that the water was polluted. Chemicals had leached from some old barrels that had been buried near the stream some time ago, and tests had shown that the fish carried the chemicals in their bodies. The state fish commission no longer stocked the stream. That was OK, because it was brimming with brown trout that had "held over" from previous stockings years ago. My friends and I caught and released hundreds of trout from that stream over the course of a couple of years, and they were beautiful, sparkling fish. One day there I caught a brown trout that was no more than five inches long—proof that the trout were successfully reproducing.

At one time I also lived close to a river that had one color year-round: brown. Street sewers drained into it and various manufacturing companies released who-knows-what from discharge pipes along its length. Occasionally the river would emit a distinct and very unpleasant odor. Its shores were lined with garbage and waste. Yet the river held fish—a healthy population of carp and a few species of panfish.

Many fish species are hardy and can withstand pollution to an amazing extent. The problem with fishing in polluted waters—besides the obvious loss of aesthetic value—is that the fish might be dangerous to eat, because of the build-up of chemicals inside their bodies.

Loose Lines

The carp is an extremely hardy and prolific species of fish that is native to Europe, where it is highly regarded as a gamefish. In the U.S., however, where the species was introduced into a number of waters in the late 1800s, carp are disdained by many fishermen. This is because carp are considered ugly by those who pursue trout, bass, and other "glamour" species; they muddy waters because of their widely wandering bottom-feeding habits; and possibly because they can survive where no other fish species can, such as highly polluted lakes and rivers. Yet carp grow to tremendous sizes, exceeding 40 pounds in many waters. They are also edible (when skinned and the dark meat removed), and are an ingredient in gefilte fish. Smoked carp is also considered delicious.

Cautious Casts

Many of the harmful chemicals found in fish that live in polluted waters collect mainly in the organs, which are not normally consumed, and the skin. If you know or suspect that the water is polluted, remove skin before cooking.

Fortunately, U.S. waters are less polluted now than they were just two decades ago, thanks to rigid enforcement of environmental regulations. Also, state fish and game departments keep close track of the degree of pollution in fishable waters, and institute dietary guidelines for people who intend to keep and eat their catch. There are many different types of pollutants present in our waters, but basically there are two types of guidelines issued if necessary: Either no fish should be consumed, or no fish should be consumed by children under a certain age or by pregnant women. Contact your state fish and game department for details about specific waters, species affected, and guidelines.

The Least You Need to Know

➤ A fish's instinct is keyed to eating, survival, and reproduction.

➤ Some fish senses are highly developed, especially touch and smell.

➤ Fish don't see things like humans do, but they are very sensitive to light, and they can see color very well.

➤ Water temperature is the most important factor in determining where fish will be, and different fish have different preferences.

➤ Fish reproduce, or spawn, at different times of year depending on the species, and one of the parents usually defends the nest.

➤ Fish probably do not feel pain as humans know it.

➤ Some species can tolerate water pollution remarkably well, but fish from polluted waters may not be safe to eat. Contact your state fish and game department for details about specific waters, species affected, and guidelines.

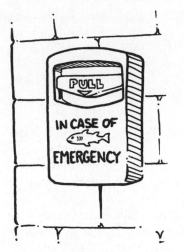

Chapter 4

Emergency Fishing Guide

In This Chapter

➤ Scenario 1: fishing a pond from shore

➤ Scenario 2: fishing a lake from a boat

➤ Scenario 3: fishing a river or stream

It's 9 P.M. on a Friday night. Tomorrow, you're going fishing—with friends, co-workers, a son or daughter, or on your own—and you don't know a thing about it.

Relax. You don't have to read this entire book between now and sunrise to get by. Although the rest of this book is written and organized in a manner that takes the beginning fisherman through every single step of the process, with every term clearly explained before it is used in context, this chapter is an exception. It serves as an emergency summary of what you have to do to have fun, or at least not feel like a fool, tomorrow on the water. The rest of the book provides all the details on the techniques and the equipment, plus the specialty areas such as flyfishing or saltwater fishing, which you can read at your leisure.

If you need specific info about one particular topic, simply look it up in the contents page at the beginning of this book or in the index.

This chapter contains three common freshwater fishing scenarios. Read all three, as basic information is presented chronologically, then pick the one that's closest to your situation tomorrow and follow that. You many not catch a fish, but you'll probably come away pleased with yourself—and eager to try it again!

Shore Fishing

The first thing you'll probably need is a fishing license. If you don't have one, get it tomorrow. Most bait and tackle shops sell them. For details on who needs one and the cost, ask at a tackle shop or contact the fish and game department of your state (phone numbers and Web sites are listed in Appendix A, State Fish and Game Departments).

Cautious Casts

Some states require that you display your fishing license while fishing. Most all tackle shops sell inexpensive little plastic holders that pin onto your clothing.

School Notes

It pays to invest in a tackle box in which you can carry your gear. Tackle bags, or satchels, are made of cloth and hold smaller, individual boxes. You can buy additional boxes as your tackle collection grows.

Wear rubber boots, or sneakers that you won't mind getting wet and muddy. You may not intend to step in the water, but the banks of lakes and ponds are wet places. Also bring one extra layer of clothing (you can leave it in the car) no matter what the season because the weather is always cooler near water. Wear a brimmed hat to keep the sun off your face. Sunscreen and insect repellent are also good to have. (See Chapter 28, "Sense and Safety on the Water," for more information on what to wear and bring.)

We'll assume that you already have a fishing rod and reel, and that there's line on the reel. You also should have some hooks, bait, split-shot sinkers (also called weights), and some clippers to cut the excess line after you tie a knot. You can buy all this stuff at the bait shop (ask the clerk to help you), and carry it all in a tackle box or even a backpack. Optional items are a couple of bobbers (floats), lures (imitation bait), needlenose pliers, and a rag or small towel.

If you're not going with someone who has fished before and who would show you where to start fishing, you'll have to find a spot on your own. It's not difficult. First, walk down to the water and look around. If you see "No Trespassing" signs or any other indication that the water is on private property, ask the landowner for permission to fish there or find another place to fish. Search for any kind of structure—a boat dock, a weedbed, a tree that fell into the water—and head there. What you want to avoid when fishing is featureless water. If you see no structure, look at the lay of the land on shore. If you see a point of land that sticks into the water, walk out to the end of it. If you see a cove, walk to that. If you can't find or recognize any of these things, walk the shore until you come to water that seems deeper than the rest.

Take your rod and thread the line through the guides on the rod, which are the wire circles along its length. First you have to allow line to come freely off the reel. If your reel has a *button*, it's a *spincasting* reel. Push the button down to release the line. If your reel has a *C-shaped wire*, called a *bail*, it's a *spinning* reel. Pull it back until it stops. Run the line through the guides and let about 5 or 6 feet of line dangle from the end of the rod. Then turn the reel handle—the arm coming off the reel—to stop any more line from coming out.

Take a hook and thread the line through the hole on the end. Then use an improved clinch knot to tie the hook to the line. (The tear-out card inside the front cover of this book shows you how to tie this knot. See Chapter 8, "It's All on the Line," for more about knots in general.) Moistening the line with water or saliva will help the knot close tight.

Then take a split-shot sinker out of the container. If you have a variety, use the middle size; you can always adjust later. Pinch the split shot onto the line about a foot above the hook. Use your fingers or pliers to clamp it on tightly.

If you have worms for bait, pick one up and push the hook through it, about in the middle of the worm. Now reel up the line until the split shot is dangling about 6 inches below the rod top.

If you have a spincasting reel, hold the rod so the button is on top. Push the button down with your thumb and hold it there. If it's a spinning reel, hold the rod so the reel is on the bottom. Clamp the line in the first crook of your index finger and flip the bail open with your other hand.

Face the water and swing the rod tip back until it's just behind and to the side of you. Then bring the rod forward with a quick sweeping motion. As you're bringing the rod forward, either let go of the button or straighten out your finger to release the line. The weight of the sinker and worm will carry the line over and into the water.

Cast first near any structure. Try to drop your bait just to the side or front of the boat dock, at the edge of a weedbed, beside the fallen tree. Lacking that, cast to the deep water, aiming for where the shallow water drops off into deep.

School Notes

Boat docks are convenient and comfortable places to fish from, and you'll often catch fish from one simply because the dock juts into deeper water. But don't stay on one if you're not catching anything. Move around on shore and cast to different areas until you find fish.

School Notes

Worms are often sold in cups or shallow foam containers with lids. These are convenient places to keep the worms when you're fishing, but if you intend to save any leftovers, you'll need a bigger container—a coffee can will do, or you can buy a special worm box at a tackle store. You'll also need to add soil, leaf mulch, and some moisture to keep the worms alive.

Once you have the bait in the right place, turn the reel handle to close the reel. Continue turning the reel until there's no slack in the line, but not so tight that you move the worm from its place on the bottom. Then, wait—five minutes is not too long—and keep a sharp eye on your line. Reel in any slack that forms in your line. If your line doesn't move or you don't feel a tug, reel up and cast to a different area— say, 5 or 10 feet away from where you first cast. If you don't get a touch there, cast 5 or 10 feet away from that spot. In this way you can methodically cover all the water that's in front of you.

Occasionally it's worthwhile to use a bobber, which is a float that attaches to your line above the bait. A bobber serves to both indicate a fish hitting your bait—the bobber wiggles, moves around, and disappears beneath the surface—and to keep the bait off the bottom, if that's your desire. It pays to use a bobber if your line is constantly getting snagged on the bottom. Generally, you want to place your bobber so that your bait is somewhere between the bottom and halfway to the surface.

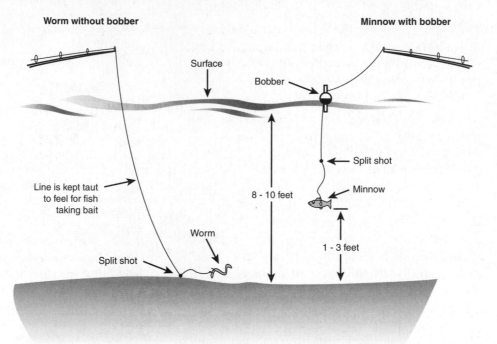

How to fish a worm without a bobber, and a minnow with a bobber. A worm can be fished with a bobber in the same manner.

If you do feel a tug—sometimes it's so negligible that you almost sense it rather than feel it—wait for a second tug. Then, making sure your line is tight, lift the rod up sharply to set the hook. Keep a tight line as you reel in the fish. Don't rush it, but don't dawdle, either. When the fish appears to tire out, reel up until there's a few feet of line between the rod tip and the fish, then swing it out of the water and onto the bank in one motion.

Hold the line just above the fish and grasp the fish with your free hand. Watch out for sharp fins that may poke you; holding the fish with a rag gives you a more secure grip. Carefully pull the hook out of the fish's mouth by twisting it back and forth. (Because bait hooks have barbs, twisting is usually the only way to remove the hook.) Pliers make this job easier. If the fish swallowed the hook, cut the line as close as possible to the fish's mouth and tie on a fresh hook later. If you're going to keep the fish (be sure you checked the regulations that came with your license—the fish may be too small or out of season), impale it on a stringer and put it into the water, tying the stringer to a secure shoreline object, such as a rock or tree root. If you want to return the fish to the water, perform all the above steps as gently as possible.

School Notes

If you intend to keep fish, you can keep them on a stringer—either a rope with a large needle on one end and a metal ring on the other, or a chain with large locking snaps—or in a cooler with ice. Keep the stringer in the water, and keep ice in the cooler. A forked branch works in a pinch.

Fishing from a Boat

Once you're at the spot you want to fish—a weedbed, cove, point, fallen tree, or an area of shoreline where the bottom drops off quickly from the shore—drop anchor. Make sure the boat is within casting range of the water you intend to fish. If it isn't, pick up the anchor, get closer, and drop anchor again. If there's any wind, the boat will probably slowly swing around in a shallow arc. That's fine, as long as it doesn't swing over your target water.

If you're fishing with minnows, drain some water from the minnow bucket and grab one. Hold it gently but firmly between your thumb and first two fingers, so the tail is pointing out. Insert the hook just behind the dorsal fin (the long top fin on the minnow's back). Don't place the hook right in the center of the minnow or you will sever its spine and paralyze the minnow. Add a split shot to the line a foot or so above the minnow, to keep it from swimming to the surface. Unless you're fishing very deep water, also put a bobber on the line, so that the minnow will be suspended about halfway between the bottom and the surface.

Cast gently to the edge of any structure (weeds, fallen tree, etc.) and turn the reel handle to close the reel. Reel in any excess line and watch the bobber closely. Unlike when using a worm for bait, the bobber will probably jiggle a bit and slowly move back and forth. That's caused by the minnow swimming around. Leave a minnow bait in one area for a good five minutes before casting again.

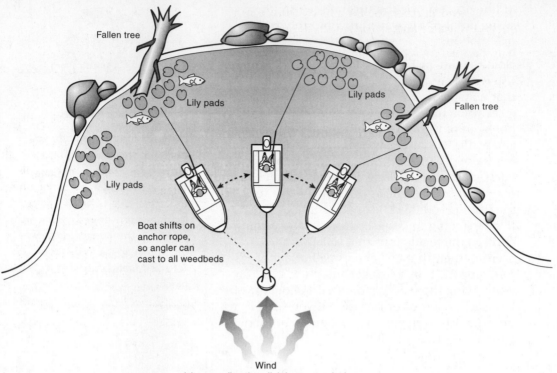

Fallen tree

Lily pads

Lily pads

Fallen tree

Lily pads

Boat shifts on
anchor rope,
so angler can
cast to all weedbeds

Wind
(changes direction slightly on occasion)

Anchor a boat so that it is within casting distance of the structure you want to fish. Make sure the wind doesn't push the boat into weeds or rocks.

If the bobber begins moving erratically—dancing about or moving quickly in one direction—get ready. That means a fish either is chasing the minnow or already has it in its mouth. At this point you may have to open the bail (or, on a spincasting reel, push the button) to allow line out, because if a fish feels resistance, it will drop the bait. Wait until the bobber goes completely under the water, count to five, tighten your line, and swing the rod back sharply over your shoulder to set the hook.

As the fish runs (and possibly jumps) about, keep a tight line. Reel in line when you get the opportunity, but don't be overly aggressive about it, or you may pull the hook out of the fish's mouth. Also, you have to allow the fish to tire out a bit before you attempt to bring it into the boat.

Once you get the fish close to the side of the boat, have your partner net it. Don't reel the fish so close that you're pointing the rod down at the water. Instead, reel in just enough so that you can hold the rod comfortably and control the fish's movement. Your partner should put the net into the water, with the opening facing the fish. Then, as you swing the rod and the fish toward the net, your partner should be simultaneously swing the net toward the fish. As soon as the fish is in the mesh of the net, your partner should quickly lift the net out of the water and swing it into the boat.

If you're fishing alone, hold the rod in one hand while you net the fish with the other. Leave about a rod's length of line between the rod tip and the fish, and lift the rod up while you scoop up the fish with the net. Remember to net the fish head-first.

If you want to fish with a minnow-imitating lure, knot it on—with most lures you don't need to add a split shot to the line—and cast to your target area. Lures do one of four things:

➤ Float at rest and when you reel it in

➤ Float at rest but dive under the surface when retrieved

➤ Sink continually at rest and stay under when retrieved

➤ Sink to a certain level and stay close to that level when retrieved

Cautious Casts

The temptation to stand up in the boat may be very strong. If the boat is large and stable, and the water is calm, you'll probably be okay. But to maintain a steady boat, and to make sure that you don't rock your partner overboard, you're better off remaining seated or, if you feel more comfortable, kneeling on the seat.

If you don't know what your lure does, watch it closely as soon as it hits the water, and when retrieving.

After you cast, close the reel immediately. If the lure floats and remains floating when retrieved, reel it in *slowly*, stopping and starting intermittently. If it floats at rest but dives when retrieved, reel it in steadily. If it sinks at rest, wait a few seconds for the lure to sink down before you begin reeling it in. When fishing sinking lures, it pays to fish different levels, so let the lure sink deeper each time you cast (you can do this methodically by counting seconds as soon as the lure hits the water, then adding to the count on successive casts). If you catch a fish, be sure to let the lure sink down to that same level on all casts in that area.

If a fish hits the lure, you'll feel it—your line will stop, or move to the side, or begin pulling back. As soon as you feel pressure, lift the rod sharply to set the hook. Then play the fish back to the boat.

The plastic worm is another very popular lure, especially for largemouth bass. To fish one, add a split shot or a sliding sinker to the line above it. Cast it out and, as soon as it hits the water, close the reel. Then allow it to sink all the way to the bottom. However, keep a tight line when it is sinking, as a fish will often hit a sinking plastic worm. When it reaches bottom, begin retrieving very slowly. Lift your rod up occasionally and let the worm sink back down to the bottom. Keep it on the bottom until it's back to the boat.

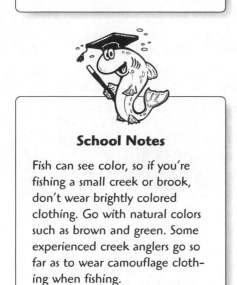

Fish often take a plastic worm gently. You may feel a jerk on the line, or simply a little bit of pressure, or a sense that the worm is no longer on the bottom. If this happens, wait one or two seconds—sometimes fish will mouth the worm, as if they're testing it, before engulfing it—and then set the hook. If a fish is on, you'll feel it immediately.

Fishing Moving Water

Whether it's a tiny meadow brook or a big roaring river you're facing, certain techniques for fishing moving water apply.

Before you make a cast, remember two things: There is always a current in moving water, and fish always face into the current. So you have to make sure your bait or lure gets in front of the fish, not behind it.

If the water you are fishing is fast-moving and studded with rocks, look for a pool—an area where the water runs deeper and quieter than the rest of the river. Often the area directly downstream of a rocky stretch of water contains a pool. If the water is slow-moving and has no obvious rocks, look for structure such as a tree lying in the water, or an area where the water is deep directly out from the bank. Lacking those, find an area where the river bends; typically the water is deeper right at a curve. Obviously, what you are looking for is deep water.

Walk to the edge of the water. You may even enter the water if you are wearing hip boots or waders, but do so quietly and slowly. Remember that fish can sense vibrations from your footsteps, even if you remain on land. And if the water you are fishing is small or narrow, keep a low profile. Skylining yourself will spook fish.

If you are fishing bait, such as worms or minnows, add a split shot to the line a foot or so above the hook to keep the bait from rising to the surface as it swings downstream. And be sure to have different-sized split shot on hand, because the current flows at varying speeds throughout a creek or river, and you'll have to adjust the size of your split shot to keep the bait close to the bottom, where fish will find it.

Put your worm on the hook as described earlier. If you're using a minnow, don't hook it through the back. Instead, put the hook through *both* lips of the minnow, from the bottom up. (This allows the minnow to "swim" naturally when you're retrieving it back through the current. If it was hooked in the back, the minnow would twirl at the end of your line in a most unfishlike fashion.)

Reel up until the split shot is just below your rod tip. Pick out an area where you want the bait to go, and cast above—upstream—of that area. If your target area is directly in front of you, you will have to cast at about a 45° angle upstream, because as soon as the bait hits the water, it will start moving downstream. The idea here is to present the bait to the fish as if it was a natural piece of forage flowing down the stream.

As soon as the bait hits the water, turn the reel handle to close the bail. Reel in just enough line so that you can feel the split shot bouncing along the bottom. If your bait plummets straight down and remains in one spot, you have too much weight on your line. If the current carries your bait quickly downstream and close to the surface, you need more weight on your line. Add and remove split shot as necessary. This sounds tedious, but you will soon get a feel for what size split shot you'll need in a given stretch of water, and you won't have to change very often.

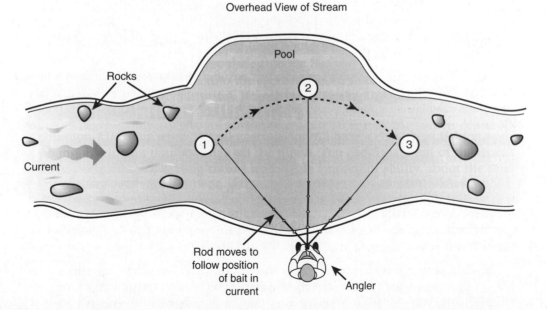

To cast in moving water, the angler first casts to a spot about 45° upstream of his position (1). As the current drags the bait along the bottom, the angler lifts his rod and reels in a bit to keep a tight line (2). As the bait moves downstream, the angler lowers his rod to keep the bait swinging in an arc until it's directly below him (3).

School Notes

When fishing a rock-filled stream, be sure to let your bait or lure drift into the water just behind the downstream side of large rocks. Those areas—some only a foot or two in diameter—are protected from the current, and fish often gather in those miniature pools.

So let's say that you do everything right: You cast to the right place, you can feel the split shot bouncing along the bottom, at about the same speed of the current. Soon—in maybe just a couple of seconds—your bait will be directly across from you. Now you'll have to raise your rod to keep in contact with the bait. Then, as the bait moves past you, slowly lower your rod to allow the bait to proceed downstream. Moving the rod like this keeps the bait moving naturally through as much water as possible while you keep your line tight enough to feel if a fish hits the bait.

Eventually, your line will straighten out at about a 45° angle downstream from you. When this happens, just let the bait swing in a short arc until it is directly downstream from you. Then reel in slowly and cast again, a bit farther out this time, or maybe a few steps upstream or downstream.

When you fish a current in this manner, one of two things will happen: Your line will snag on a rock or branch, or a fish will take your bait. And sometimes it's difficult to distinguish between the two, though snags are more common. (Getting snagged occasionally is actually a good sign, because it means that you are fishing properly: keeping the bait moving naturally along the bottom, where fish can see it.)

If your line stops moving, raise your rod tip until the line is taut. If you feel a *tap-tap*, or if you see or feel the line moving against or crossways to the current, a fish has your bait. Immediately lower your rod tip so the fish doesn't feel any resistance. Count to three, then raise your rod tip sharply to set the hook. When playing the fish, you may have to move upstream or downstream a bit, because the fish will use the current to its advantage. It may also wrap your line around an obstruction. Let the fish run, but don't let it take too much line out.

If your line stops moving and you don't feel a fish, you're probably (but not definitely) snagged. Usually, the sinker gets caught under a rock or between two of them. Simply pulling on the line usually just worsens the problem. The best course is to move upstream of the snag and reel in.

When fishing moving water, remember to keep moving. Fish each area thoroughly, but don't concentrate on one stretch of water if you aren't catching anything. Occasionally, you just need to move a few feet to put your bait in the fish zone.

Conversely, and especially on slow-moving and/or cold waters, you'll get better results if you cast the bait out and let it sit. Sometimes fish are sluggish and won't chase after a bait; other times (and especially with species such as catfish), they need to examine the bait before they'll eat it. This is called still-fishing, and it's best done in a deep pool or a slow-moving stretch of the river or stream. Put on enough split shot so that the current won't move the bait after it sinks to the bottom. Cast out, let it sink, then reel up until the line is taut. You can even put the rod down on shore: Just cut a dead branch into a Y shape, and stick the bottom of the Y into the bank. Lay the rod in the fork of the Y, with the bottom of the rod touching the ground. But keep a close watch on the rod—if a fish finds the bait, the rod tip will start jiggling, and you'll have to grab it quickly and set the hook. More than once I've been distracted by something or someone on shore and had to go chasing after the rod after a fish took the bait and began dragging the rod into the water.

Methods for fishing lures in moving water are somewhat similar to fishing bait. Spinners work well in moving water because the current automatically makes the blade on the spinner turn, flashing and vibrating and attracting fish. To fish a lure, cast at about a 45° angle upstream of your position. Turn your reel handle to close the bail as soon as the lure hits the water, and keep turning the handle. You don't have to reel fast, you just want to keep the lure moving. (If you reel too fast, the lure will rise to the surface.) Occasionally, in fast currents, all you have to do is keep your rod tip up and let the current work the lure for you. But always keep a tight line, because a fish may hit the lure at any moment.

Be especially attentive when the line tightens downstream of you and the lure begins swinging in an arc toward the bank. Fish often hit a lure at this point, because the lure enters the "seam" between fast water and slow water, and fish often congregate in this area. When the lure reaches the end of the arc, reel it back in slowly, pausing the lure occasionally, which may tempt a fish into hitting it.

Loose Lines

Fish long enough and sooner or later you're going to fall in. You can avoid this mishap by taking obvious precautions, such as not standing up in a boat, not wading into rivers with extremely fast currents, and not walking in places with insecure footing, such as moss-covered rocks or steep muddy banks. Sometimes, though, you're going to fall in no matter what you do. When my son, Joey, was three, I took him fishing at a local pond. I had just set my tackle down on the bank and was talking to Joey, who was facing me, with his back to the water. He took one step to see me put a worm on a hook and put his foot right into a fresh little pile of goose droppings. His feet went right out from under him and he fell backwards into the pond. I quickly reached down, grabbed him by the shirt and yanked him out of the water, coughing and crying. So what did we do? We drove home, changed clothes, and went right back to the pond. And we steered clear of goose poop after that.

The Least You Need to Know

➤ Before going fishing, make sure you have a fishing license, rod and reel with line, hooks, bait, and sinkers. Consider bringing bobbers, lures, extra clothes, sunscreen, insect repellent, rag, needlenose pliers, and something to carry it all in.

➤ When casting from shore, search for weeds, docks, fallen trees, rocks, points of land, or just deeper water.

➤ Always allow a few seconds for the fish to take the bait securely in its mouth. Then, don't just start reeling in—make the line taut by reeling in slack and then raise the rod sharply to set the hook.

➤ When fishing from a boat, locate the craft within reasonable casting distance of the area you want to cast to. Drop the anchor and make sure the wind doesn't swing the boat over your target area.

➤ In moving water, fish always face the current, so you must put your bait or lure in front of the fish. Always cast upstream and let your bait or lure move downstream with the current.

➤ In rivers and streams, concentrate on pools—deeper, slower sections of water—bends, deep areas near banks, and the "seam" between fast and slow currents.

Part 2

Tackle and How to Use It

Rods, reels, line, hooks, lures, bait: These make up the heart of fishing tackle, and to someone who is not familiar with all the various sizes, qualities, and applications of each, the task of assembling a proper combination for a particular style of fishing can be frustrating indeed. Walk into a tackle shop and you'll see an army of fishing rods, reels of all sizes stacked in counter displays, racks of line, boxes of hooks, and enough lures and bait to catch seemingly every fish in the ocean. And what about those sinkers and floats, wires and pliers, buckets, boxes, and nets? Where to begin? Where does it end? Hmmm…wasn't fillet of sole on sale at the grocery store?

Don't worry about the huge selection. If you know where you'll be fishing, and what species you are likely to encounter there, you'll be able to eliminate about 80 percent of the merchandise in front of you. And knowing the basics of each type of equipment will help you narrow down your selection even further. After that, it's a matter of individual needs and cost. This part of the book will walk you through the entire process. (Besides, the sole is probably spoiled anyway.)

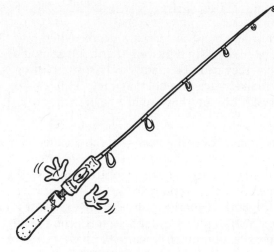

Chapter 5

Don't Spare the Rod

In This Chapter

➤ Today's fishing rods

➤ Get in on the action

➤ Weighty stuff

➤ Fishing-rod anatomy

You need a fishing rod for two basic reasons: first, to be able to put your lure or bait into water farther away than where you are standing; and second, so that a fish doesn't break your fishing line. Rods must be able to bend when casting and when reeling in a fish, so that the spring-like action of the rod allows the fisherman to impart more velocity to the lure (it's the same principle as someone bouncing on a trampoline). Also, the bend of the rod allows a fish to surge, dive, and run when hooked without breaking the line, like a car's springs absorbing shock when driving on a rutted road. Rods also provide many other advantages—among them the abilities to fish with extremely lightweight lures and baits, attach a fishing reel to hold line, keep the line taut to feel a fish take the bait or lure, set the hook firmly, and prevent the fish from throwing the hook. Given a rod's benefits, fishing with a line alone, while possible, puts the fisherman at a tremendous disadvantage.

Understanding the fishing-rod basics covered in this chapter will go a long way toward both finding the best rod for your purposes as well as using it efficiently.

What Rods Are Made Of

Because fishing rods must be straight at rest and bend to a certain degree when pressure is applied at the tip—and also must be reasonably lightweight enough so that an angler can cast one without tiring quickly—they can't be made out of just anything. The earliest prehistoric fishing "rods" were likely tree branches, as they exhibit these qualities. Kids throughout time have noticed this, and have used tree branches to fish with as well.

Fishing rods have been made of many substances over the years—notably cane, bamboo, and even steel—but most all of today's models are constructed of either fiberglass, which has been used to make rods for scores of years; or graphite, which was first developed for rod manufacture by the Fenwick company in the 1970s. Some rods are made of a combination of the two. Both of these substances are excellent for fishing-rod use, because after various construction methods (and secrets), the finished rods are lightweight and stiff. They will bend easily under pressure yet have excellent "memory," meaning they will go back to their original form when pressure is removed. The rods will accept necessary hardware, such as grips, reel seats, and guides. Finally, the materials are not expensive, which makes the rods affordable. Graphite is lighter and stiffer than fiberglass, and is the more popular choice of rod material.

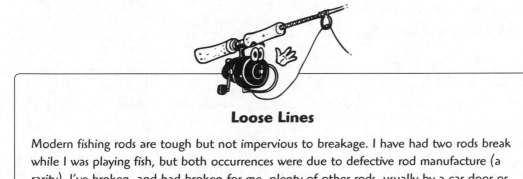

Loose Lines

Modern fishing rods are tough but not impervious to breakage. I have had two rods break while I was playing fish, but both occurrences were due to defective rod manufacture (a rarity). I've broken, and had broken for me, plenty of other rods, usually by a car door or trunk slamming shut on the rod or by someone's foot stepping down where it shouldn't have.

Rod Actions: The Wiggle Factor

The action of a rod, which is noted on the rod itself, identifies when the rod begins to "load," or resist bending when under pressure, given the same amount of pull. Rods stop bending—that is, the rod displays a curve at a certain place under a certain amount of pressure—at a certain point along the rod shaft, depending on the type of action. Although exact determinations vary from manufacturer to manufacturer, there are four general, recognized action types in fishing rods, which hold true for all rods used in all fishing. These are described in the following table and illustrated in the figure that follows.

Fishing Rod Actions

Action Type	Location of Most Curvature
Extra fast	Upper ¼ of rod
Fast	Upper ⅓ of rod
Moderate	Upper ½ of rod
Slow	Progressive curve from tip to butt

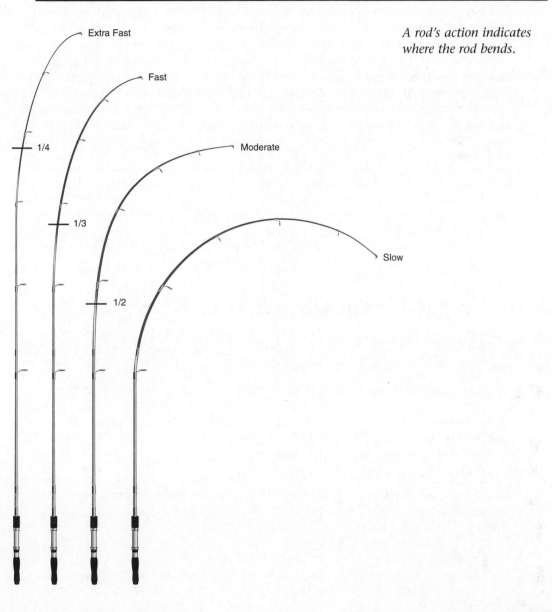

A rod's action indicates where the rod bends.

Different actions have advantages for different applications. Generally, a fast-action rod has more sensitivity than a slow-action rod. This is advantageous because it lets the angler feel a fish taking a lure or bait, which sometimes is so delicate that the line hardly moves at all. A fast-action rod also clearly transmits vibrations of the lure, so the angler can easily tell when his lure is hitting bottom. Fast-action rods also allow quick hook-setting, because less of the rod has to bend before the line becomes taut. Some anglers believe that fast-action rods are best because of all these important reasons.

However, slow-action rods have their place as well. For instance, many baits, such as worms, minnows, and salmon eggs, are soft and need to be cast gently, or the bait might tear off from the hook. A slow-action rod allows a soft cast, while a fast-action rod might snap the bait right off. Also, a slow-action rod is preferable when casting a substantial bait or lure with very light, narrow-diameter fishing line—again, a fast-action rod with its unforgiving give, as it were, might snap the line. Finally, because some fish sometimes mouth a lure or bait before deciding to eat it, a slow-action rod prevents the angler from jerking the offering out of the fish's mouth.

So, which action for you? Personally, I don't go for either extreme, because I might change a bait or lure dozens of times on one fishing trip, and often the "optimal" action will change from extra fast to slow and back to extra fast again. For the beginner, I suggest going with a moderate-action rod, no matter what the species or conditions. Such a rod is still sensitive enough to feel what's going on at the end of the line, but is forgiving enough when you're learning how to cast lures and baits of different weights. It's also rewarding to see your rod bend mightily, even when you've only hooked a 6-inch bluegill.

Rod Weights: From Ultralight to Heavy

The weight of a rod, which also is listed on the rod itself, is different from the action of a rod in that it defines the rod's strength rather than its flexibility. Some manufacturers use the term "power" when referring to rod weight.

There are seven basic rod-weight classifications: ultralight, light, medium light, medium, medium heavy, heavy, and extra heavy. Basically, the bigger the fish you are going after, and/or the heavier bait or lure you will be using, the heavier the rod you need within a particular style. (These styles—spinning, spincasting, baitcasting, and flyfishing—will be detailed in later chapters.)

The following chart details the information that is listed on fishing rods, including the size of the rod, its weight, and the recommended weight of lures and strength of line to use with it.

Rod Model	Rod Length	Rod Weight
↓	↓	↓
LX60	6'6"	MED. LT.
LURE ⅛–⅜	LINE 6–10 LB. TEST	
↑	↑	
Lure Weight Range in Ounces	Line Strength Range	

So, how do you decide which rod weight is right for you? It's difficult to pinpoint one exact weight for each species and fishing style, but there are some guidelines you can follow. First, though, it's important to note that many manufacturers make it easy to pick the right size of rod, because they classify their rods according to the species they are sized for. Many manufacturer and mail-order catalogs have charts that help you narrow down the field. If you're at a tackle shop, the sales help should have catalogs available for this purpose (it's a simple matter of checking the rod model number against a master list). One rod manufacturer, G. Loomis, has cross-reference classifications for 20 different freshwater and saltwater species. Fenwick, another manufacturer, organizes many of their rods via a species "class," making selection even simpler. This is important to the beginning angler because a medium-weight panfish rod is nowhere near as powerful as, say, a medium-weight bass rod. (You eventually will develop a "feel" for rods and you won't have to rely on catalogs and sales help. Just seeing and holding the rod will tell you plenty.)

Again, to choose the right weight, you have to know the general size of the fish you're going after, and, just as important, the size of the bait or lures you'll be using. Because the largemouth bass is the most popular freshwater species in the United States, the following table gives some theoretical spinning-rod weights for that fish using particular lures (by weight) as an example.

Example Spinning-Rod Weights for Bass

Rod Weight	Lure Weight (Oz.)	Bass Size (Lbs.)
Medium light	⅛–⅜	1–2
Medium	¼–⅝	2–4
Medium heavy	⅜–1	4–8
Heavy	½–1½	8 and higher

So, if you will be fishing small lakes, where the average bass weighs only a pound or two, and you'll be using small lures, go with the medium light-weight rod. But if you'll be fishing in large lakes or reservoirs, where the bass can run to double-digit weights—and therefore, where you'll be using large lures and heavy baits—the heavy-weight rod will be justified.

Cautious Casts

Although you can use lures and baits that are a bit lighter or heavier than recommended for a particular rod, don't stray from the recommended line strength range. Line that is lighter than recommended won't cast well and will break more easily. Using line that is much heavier than recommended may harm the rod itself, and may even break it if your hook is snagged and you pull the rod too hard.

Lure weight ranges for each rod weight (which also are printed on the rods themselves) are recommended, but not mandatory. In other words, you won't break the rod if you cast a lure that's a half-ounce larger or smaller than the recommendation (although it will make it harder to cast).

Also notice that the lure weights overlap from rod to rod. Manufacturers know that most anglers don't fish just one type of water for just one size range of just one species their entire lives. So, if you were going to fish a number of waters for bass—from farm ponds to huge reservoirs—the medium-heavy rod from our example would be the best "all-around" rod.

The weight of the rod you use also will determine the strength of fishing line you will need. Manufacturers also print the recommended strength of line, measured in breaking strength (pound test, which is covered in Chapter 8, "It's All on the Line") on the rod.

Balancing all of these factors together—size of fish, lure weight, and line strength—to pick the one best rod weight isn't always a simple matter. Beginning fishermen are usually better off going for the middle ground—that is, medium weight—within each rod family. Or you can do what I do when I can't decide between two rods: Buy them both.

From Butt to Tip and in Between

It's important to know the parts of a fishing rod, because they are not put there by the manufacturers just for decoration. Each part performs a specific function. While spinning, spincasting, baitcasting, and flyfishing rods differ in form and function, they all share the same basic anatomy, as shown in the illustration that follows.

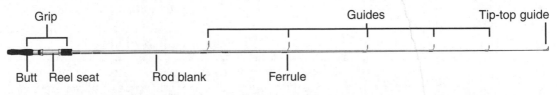

The basic parts of a fishing rod.

The bottom of the rod, below where the reel fits, is called the rod *butt*. Often a plastic *butt cap* is fitted on the very end, to protect the rod when it is set down.

Above and below where the reel fits is the rod *handle*, also called the *grip*. Most rods today have either cork handles, which are made from rings of cork glued together and sanded smoothly, or closed-cell foam handles. Both allow the angler to keep a good grip on the rod, even when it's wet from precipitation or perspiration.

The *reel seat*, located above the butt, is a short, flattened section that allows the fishing reel to be attached to the rod. This is accomplished via slots that the reel foot (a narrow horizontal projection) fits into, and one or two locking rings, depending upon the rod. It sounds more complicated than it is: The angler simply fits one end of the reel foot into the fixed slot, slides the movable slot down or up onto the other end of the reel foot, and turns the threaded locking ring (which, on some rods, is actually that part of the handle above the reel seat) until tight. This holds the reel securely to the rod. Some rods have two movable slots and two locking rings, which allows a little bit of adjustment in the exact placement of the reel.

Many ultralight rods used for small fish sport a pair of simple, non-tightening rings that hold the reel in place, to eliminate unnecessary weight. Conversely, some extra heavy-weight rods (those designed for battling big gamefish such as sharks and marlin) feature double locking rings and a metal bracket that holds the rod and reel together via bolts and wing nuts, for additional support.

The *guides* on a rod are rings along the length of the rod through which the fishing line passes. Guides are attached to rods by closely wrapped thread around the guide foot. Because guides are subject to a lot of friction by line passing and slapping through them at high speeds (and because the line itself could become damaged if subject to a rough surface at high speeds), they must be made of a hard, smooth material. Ceramic and carbide guides are considered best. The very last guide at the tip of the rod is called the *tip-top*. Some rod manufacturers put an extra-high-quality tip-top on their rods, as that guide suffers from the most friction.

Cautious Casts

You can carry and store rods and reels either assembled or taken apart, whichever is more convenient. But don't store the rod so it's bent or under pressure, as doing so will damage the rod or create a permanent curve in it.

School Notes

Rod handles come in various diameters, so it's important to be sure the rod(s) you want fits your hands. You should be able to cast the rod repeatedly and hold it in various positions without experiencing fatigue or cramping. Cork handles can be sanded down if they feel too large.

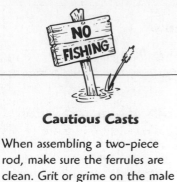

Some fishing rods are one piece, meaning that they don't come apart. Two-piece rods do, which allows for easier storing and portability. Two-piece rods usually come apart at about the middle of the shaft. The two pieces fit together via *ferrules*. The male ferrule tapers to a narrow end and fits into the hollow female ferrule. Many rods today have integral ferrules, meaning that the rod pieces naturally taper and open at the ends. All two-piece rods made decades ago, and some rods still made today, have metal ferrules, which are attached to the rod-piece ends. Generally, integral ferrules are preferable because metal ferrules can and usually do impede the action of the rod.

Long Rods Versus Short Rods

Many rods can be of the same action and weight, and take the same line strength and lure weights, yet be of different lengths—say, a 6-footer and a 7-footer. Which one is better? It depends on your fishing situation, your angling aptitude, your hand-eye coordination, and your taste.

Here's why. All else being equal, a long rod casts farther and with less effort than a short rod. Generally, and within reasonable length limits, it's easier to make accurate casts with a long rod.

On the other hand, short rods are easier to handle all-around. They are less prone to snagging or tangling on shoreline brush, and are easier to cast when you don't have much elbow room, such as when fishing beneath overhanging trees. Shorter casts are easier with a short rod. Finally, because of its comparatively narrow angle between rod and line, a short rod requires less muscle when fighting a large fish.

Often, the best way to determine whether a long rod or a short rod is better for you is to hold it, preferably with a reel attached to it. You should feel comfortable with its balance and heft, and such personal "fit" varies from individual to individual.

One feature of modern rods is what is termed *blank-through* handles, which means that the fishing rod blank, or shaft, extends all the way down through the handle. This provides for more sensitivity when holding the rod, because vibrations caused by a fish hitting a bait are more easily felt by the angler.

The Least You Need to Know

➤ Modern rods are highly technological products, making them lightweight, sturdy, sensitive, affordable, and much better than rods made a few decades ago.

➤ A rod's action is determined by the point where it bends when under a certain amount of pressure. Fast-action rods are very sensitive; slow-action rods are very forgiving.

➤ A rod's weight is determined by the overall strength of the rod in that rod's class. Ultralight is for small fish; extra heavy is for the monsters.

➤ All rods share the same important characteristics and features, although some rods exhibit higher-quality parts than others.

Chapter 6

The Reel Thing

In This Chapter

➤ Reel operating principles

➤ The all-important click

➤ When a drag can save you from losing a fish

➤ How does your reel rate?

A fishing rod without a reel is pretty much an expensive stick, because without a reel—and except when flyfishing—it would be very difficult to cast a lure or bait any reasonable distance. This is not a new concept, as reels have been in use for centuries, with the first written reference of a fishing reel appearing in the 17th century, and depicted in drawings as far back as the 13th century. Some sources indicate use of a fishing reel as far back as the 3rd century.

Reels back then were simply devices to hold excess fishing line. That is still true today, although reels serve many other important purposes as well—some so important that they have permanently altered, and tremendously improved, the practicality of the sport itself. This chapter explains why.

Reels and How They Function

All fishing reels consist of a spool, around which is wrapped fishing line, mounted in a housing that fits onto a fishing rod. The reel allows the angler to control the fishing line, and thus the bait or lure in the water. A handle or crank on the reel lets the fisherman reel in line and adjust the amount of line in the water. All reels feature a release device that lets line come off the spool freely, which allows the angler to cast. The momentum of the lure or the bait as it moves through the air when cast pulls line off the spool.

All reels fall into two basic categories: those with spools that revolve, and those with spools that are stationary. Revolving-spool reels that fit on the top of the rod with the spool perpendicular to the axis of the rod are known broadly as *conventional* reels. They are based on the same principle as a bobbin used for sewing. When the handle is turned, the spool revolves and line wraps itself around the spool.

Conventional reels are popular for use in saltwater fishing. Large conventional reels, which can hold many hundreds of yards of strong fishing line, are used for offshore trolling for large species such as marlin and tuna. These are sometimes called big-game reels or saltwater trolling reels, and are not used to cast to fish.

A conventional reel that is small enough for an angler to hold comfortably when mounted on a fishing rod, and is designed so that the angler can cast with it, is known as a *baitcasting* reel (see the following figure). Most baitcasters are used for larger freshwater fish (such as bass and pike) and light saltwater species. Both conventional and baitcasting reels have a switch or a lever on the reel housing that, when depressed or moved, puts the reel in freespool, allowing line to come freely off the spool. The angler casts a baitcaster by putting the reel in freespool, placing his or her thumb on the spool to keep it from moving, and then releasing his thumb when casting so the weight of the lure or bait pulls line from the spool. Turning the handle automatically engages the reel—that is, takes it out of freespool mode so the angler can retrieve line. Learning to cast a baitcasting reel isn't as easy as it is with fixed-spool reels (casting instructions are detailed in the next chapter).

A typical baitcasting reel, used for large freshwater species.

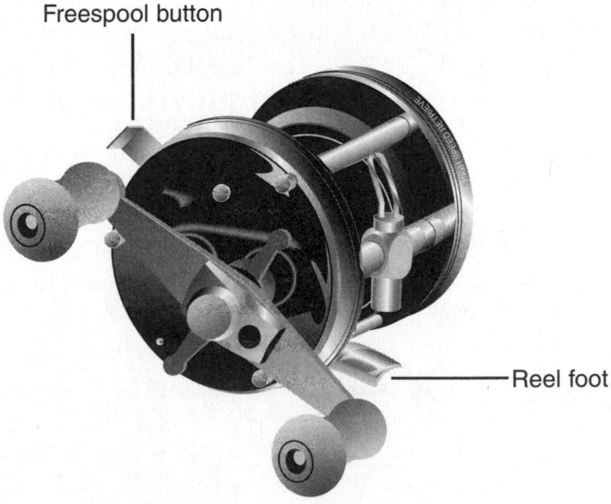

Freespool button

Reel foot

Most baitcasting reels today incorporate a *brake*, or an anti-backlash device to prevent the spool from turning faster than the lure is moving through the air. Such devices are adjustable and make learning how to baitcast much less problematic, with fewer time-consuming tangles. However, they are not foolproof. While they reduce the risk of backlashes, they don't prevent them altogether.

Fixed-spool reels come in different forms. The *spinning* reel (see the following figure) is so named because a housing that fits around the fixed spool, which is parallel to the axis of the rod, spins around it when the handle is turned. A device on this outer housing, called a pickup bail, distributes line around the spool as the handle is turned. At the same time, gears within the reel move the spool in and out of the spool housing, so the line fills the spool in neat layers. An angler casts a spinning reel, which is attached to the bottom of a fishing rod, by first lifting the pickup bail, which puts the reel into freespool. Then he holds the line with one finger, releasing it when casting. Turning the handle automatically drops the bail back into place. Learning to cast a spinning reel is easier than learning to baitcast.

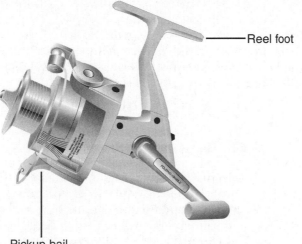

Reel foot

Pickup bail

A spinning reel—the most common reel type in use today.

The *spincasting* reel (see the following figure) is a sort of hybrid between a conventional reel and a spinning reel. Although spincasters feature a fixed spool, they usually go on the top of rods. Spincasters are also called *pushbutton* reels because they are operated via a button or a lever: When the angler presses and then releases the button with his thumb, line flows freely from the spool. The spool itself is housed inside of a cone-like hood, at the tip of which is a small hole through which the line comes out. After a cast, the angler turns the handle, which automatically engages an internal pin, guiding line onto the spool as the angler reels in. Spincasters are very easy to operate, and are a good choice for kids and beginning anglers.

A spincasting reel is easy to operate.

Freespool button

Reel foot

Some relatively new spincasting reels fit on the bottom of the rod, and instead of a pushbutton, feature a long lever that puts the reel in freespool. Some anglers feel that these trigger-type spincasters are easier to operate, and are better balanced than typical spincasters because the reel and its weight are on the bottom.

There are pros and cons to each type of reel, as detailed in the following sections.

School Notes

Fishing rods are matched to the style of reels they take. Spinning rods have a very large first guide, so the coils of line coming off the reel can pass through easily. Casting rods (both bait- and spin-types) do not, and some casting rods feature a protuberance opposite the reel side, called a *trigger*, which eases handling.

Baitcasting

Advantages: Sensitive to movement at the end of the line; an inherently strong design that can be built in large sizes and used in conjunction with large lures and bait; accurate when casting because the angler can control the lure's flight by "feathering" the spool with his thumb.

Disadvantages: Not available in ultralight-line sizes; comparatively difficult to learn how to cast; are prone to "backlash" tangles when casting, caused by line coming off the spool faster than the lure is traveling through the air.

Spinning

Advantages: Fairly easy to learn to cast; available in sizes from ultralight to medium heavy; no possibility of backlash because the spool is fixed.

Disadvantages: Cumbersome to use in larger sizes and/or with heavy lures and baits; not as sensitive as baitcasters; prone to line twist because the line turns 90 degrees when being wrapped onto the spool.

Spincasting

Advantages: Simple to learn to use; inherently stronger than spinning reels and less cumbersome in large sizes; very quick to cast with.

Disadvantages: Even less sensitive than spinning reels to movement at the end of the line; poor casting accuracy and lure/fish control; prone to line twist.

Cautious Casts

Rods used in fresh water are basically maintenance-free. Reels should be lubricated according to manufacturer's directions. Be sure to rinse and lubricate the reel if you drop it in sand, mud, or dirt.

That Clicking Sound

Baitcasting, spinning, and some spincasting reels all share a necessary feature called an *anti-reverse* mechanism, typically a small lever or switch on the reel housing. When the anti-reverse is engaged, the reel's handle can be turned, placing line onto the spool. Many reels emit a soft ticking or clicking sound when the anti-reverse is on and the handle is turned. But the handle cannot turn in the opposite direction, allowing line to come off the reel, unless the anti-reverse is disengaged.

There are several reasons why an anti-reverse is necessary, and why the ability to turn it on and off is important. The first is practicality. If no anti-reverse existed, and the handle was free to turn backwards at all times, the angler would have to maintain a very tight grip on the reel handle at all times when fishing. With the anti-reverse on, you can hold onto the rod with just one hand when fishing and still maintain a tight line. This may not sound so necessary when sitting in a comfortable chair in a climate-controlled room, but when you are fishing, there are plenty of reasons to do so. You want to put a piece of gum in your mouth or hand a friend a worm (and you certainly don't want to confuse the two). Or you want to adjust your hat or throw your hand out for balance.

The second reason: When you're playing a fish, there are times when you do not want to reel in and simply let the fish run and jump. This is when you want the reel's drag (covered in the

Cautious Casts

Some reels don't click when the anti-reverse is engaged and the handle is turned. If yours doesn't, be sure to familiarize yourself with the position of the switch so you don't fish with the anti-reverse off.

Getting the Point

Certain bait-casting reels feature a device called a **levelwind** which distributes the line evenly along the length of the spool when the handle is turned (sometimes the entire reel is referred to as a levelwind).

following section) to take over. With no anti-reverse mechanism, the drag wouldn't function and the reel's handle would spin backwards as line would peel off the spool. Stop it too forcefully and the line might break. And how would you be able to grab a fish or net it if you needed both hands on the rod at all times?

Reels are not made in permanent anti-reverse mode because there are times when you want to let line out by turning the handle backwards—to adjust the amount of line hanging from the rod tip before a cast, say, or to increase the amount of line in the water when fishing with live bait. As a rule, though, the anti-reverse mechanism should be engaged when you are actively fishing, as long as the reel's drag is set properly.

It's a Drag, and You Need It

The *drag* of a reel is an adjustable mechanism that controls the amount of line coming off the spool when the anti-reverse is engaged, or when it is not engaged and the angler is holding the reel handle still. Drags allow a hooked fish to take line out under pressure without the line breaking. This allows the angler to play a fish without having to worry about when to give the fish line, because the drag does it automatically.

Drag systems differ from reel to reel. Generally, they consist of washer-like disks stacked under spring pressure. That amount of pressure should be adjusted by the angler to a point under the breaking strength of the line. The drag adjustment device on most baitcasting reels and on some spincasting reels is often a flat, star-shaped

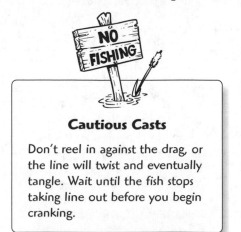

Cautious Casts

Don't reel in against the drag, or the line will twist and eventually tangle. Wait until the fish stops taking line out before you begin cranking.

piece of metal or plastic (called a star drag) at the base of the reel's handle. Some baitcasters feature a lever that adjusts drag. On spinning reels, the drag adjustment is either a turning cap on the top of the spool or a knob at the back of the spinning reel housing. Turning the star, lever, cap, or knob in one direction increases the amount of drag—that is, it applies more pressure and makes it increasingly difficult for line to come off the reel. Tightened all the way, drag is eliminated—resulting in a line with no give that could be snapped by a fish. Turning the drag device in the other way decreases the amount of drag.

Drag works because, when you are playing a fish, it often runs and lunges and dives erratically. If the fish is especially large for the rod and reel—and thus the line strength—you are using, the fish could very well break the line. Usually you can't move the rod or run after the fish to adjust for such movement. Putting the reel in freespool and letting the fish take line unhindered would allow the fish to throw the hook or wrap the line around an underwater obstruction (which happens often enough even with a tight line). So the drag takes over, letting the fish take line when it has to, all the time allowing you to maintain control of the fish.

Drag works only if it is adjusted properly for the line on the reel. For instance, if you are fishing with 6-pound-test line, which means the line won't break unless there is a minimum of 6 pounds of pressure on it (details are in Chapter 8, "It's All on the Line"), your drag should be set for 3 or 4 pounds. There is no standard rule for the amount of drag necessary, but the common belief is that it should be set strong enough to set the

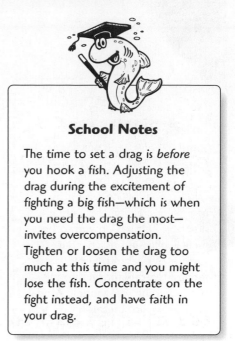

School Notes

The time to set a drag is *before* you hook a fish. Adjusting the drag during the excitement of fighting a big fish—which is when you need the drag the most—invites overcompensation. Tighten or loosen the drag too much at this time and you might lose the fish. Concentrate on the fight instead, and have faith in your drag.

hook on a fish without giving up line, but not so tight that line comes off the reel grudgingly when you pull it by hand. Also, because knots actually reduce the strength of fishing line, you should adjust your drag to compensate.

Read the brochure that comes with your reel to find how to adjust the drag properly. Experiment with and adjust the drag setting *before* you fish. It's a good idea to tie the end of your line to a tree or some other solid object, back off a couple dozen feet, and pull to see how and when the drag gives up line at certain settings. Eventually you'll become familiar with your drag and be able to quickly adjust it to the proper setting.

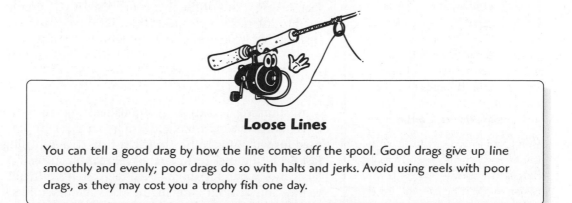

Loose Lines

You can tell a good drag by how the line comes off the spool. Good drags give up line smoothly and evenly; poor drags do so with halts and jerks. Avoid using reels with poor drags, as they may cost you a trophy fish one day.

The Ratio You Need to Know

All fishing reels operate at certain speeds, meaning that they retrieve varying amount of line when the reel handle is turned. This *retrieve ratio* is based on the number of times one "wrap" of line is placed on the reel's spool for each complete revolution of the reel handle. A reel with a ratio of 4.5:1, for instance, puts 4½ turns of line around the spool for each complete turn of the reel handle.

Reels used for casting (as compared to those big conventional reels used for trolling big fish) must have some stepped-up gearing, otherwise fishermen would spend most of their time reeling in after a cast. And it would seem that the faster the retrieve rate, the better, because fewer turns of the handle are necessary to bring in line, which makes reeling a less tiring activity. To a point, this is true, and modern reels have higher ratios than before. High-speed reels allow anglers to bring in lures very quickly with minimal effort. And in some fishing situations, the lure or bait is in the fish "zone" for only a small amount of time. High-speed reels therefore allow the angler to reel in quickly and recast once the lure or bait is out of a fish's reach.

However, there is a law of diminishing returns. A reel that has an extremely fast retrieve can make lure or bait control difficult for beginning anglers, as it allows little margin for retrieval error. Turn the reel handle just a quarter-turn, and the lure can move a couple of feet, taking it out of the fish zone. Also, if you aren't used to the reel's high speed, you could be cranking in line too fast—a chronic problem with beginning fishermen, and even with experienced anglers when fishing in dark or murky waters where the lure or bait can't be seen.

Most spinning, spincasting, and baitcasting reels today have ratios varying from a low of about 2.5:1 (those used for winching in heavyweight fish) to a lightning-fast 6:1 and more. Fortunately, reel manufacturers label and hype super-high-speed reels, so it's difficult to buy one without knowing it. Also, manufacturers design reels with optimal ratios for their size and probable intended use, so chances are you won't get a reel with a too-high or too-low ratio.

The Least You Need to Know

➤ Different styles of reels have different applications. Baitcasters are strong but can be difficult to use, spinning reels are easier to operate but cumbersome in large sizes, and spincasting reels are simple to use but lack accuracy and sensitivity.

➤ The anti-reverse mechanism keeps the reel handle from turning in the opposite direction, allowing unencumbered fishing and drag operation.

➤ The drag lets a fish take line at the point before the line would break.

➤ The retrieve ratio refers to the speed of the reel, or how fast it takes in line when the handle is turned. Generally, high-speed retrieve ratios are preferable.

Chapter 7

How to Cast with the Perfect Pair

In This Chapter

➤ Push a button, catch a fish

➤ Spinning around

➤ Conventional (reel) wisdom

One day earlier this year, my son Joey and I went to fish a tiny pond in a nearby park late in the afternoon. We were figuring on catching some catfish, so we baited up with worms and cast out. We had just missed one hit about half an hour later when a young boy showed up with his mother in tow. He was carrying a brand-new spincasting outfit that had a huge shiny lure tied to the end of the line. He walked over to us on the bank, asked if we had caught anything, and proceeded to cast. His first attempt put the lure back on the bushes behind him. His second cast left the rod tip sideways, so his lure flew right over both of our lines. On his third cast—at this point, after I had untangled the three lines, I was keeping a wary eye on him—the lure zoomed a safe 10 inches or so past my face and hit the ground at Joey's feet. I glanced at the boy's mother, who was looking at a book, oblivious to her son's actions.

"Hey, Joey, the fish aren't biting," I said. "Want to go get some ice cream?"

"Okay," he agreed. Even his four-year-old mind was able to register the futility of it all.

Maybe I should have stayed and taught the kid some casting basics. (Then again, maybe I should find the kid's mother and give her a copy of this book.) The point, though, is that if you can't use your rod-and-reel outfit correctly, you aren't going to catch fish. And learning to cast, while it might seem challenging at first, is actually fun and quite rewarding, once you get the feel for it. Here's how.

Spincasting: The Easiest of Them All

Fishing with a spincasting rod-and-reel outfit is literally as simple as pushing a button because that's how you control the outflow of line. Although spincasting does have its detractions, as pointed out in Chapter 6, "The Reel Thing," it's ideal for the first-timer, especially someone who has never even held a fishing rod before.

School Notes

With any rod, you'll know if you're casting correctly if you watch the rod tip. The rod must "load," that is, gain energy by bending at the tip to impart speed to the lure. As you bring the rod forward to cast, the rod tip should be bent back a bit behind (away from) you. If it's not bending, you're not being forceful enough with the forward motion.

To make a cast, follow these steps:

1. Hold the rod with the reel facing up. The rod trigger (that little curved extension on the other side of the rod, below the reel) should fit comfortably between your index finger and your third finger. If it doesn't feel right, place the trigger between your third and fourth fingers. In either case, your thumb should be able to rest on the button of the reel.

2. Push the button with your thumb and hold it there. If you accidentally release it, putting the reel into freespool and letting line out, simply turn the reel handle to re-engage the reel. Reel up so that there is about 6 inches of line between the rod tip and the lure or bait, and push the button again, keeping it depressed.

3. Look at your target and swing the rod up and back in a smooth motion. Your arm should be bent about 90° at the elbow. Don't pivot your shoulder so that your arm is behind you. Instead, cock your wrist to bring the rod back.

4. Without pausing, bring the rod forward sharply. When the rod tip is pointing above the target at about a 45° angle, release the button. The lure should then shoot out toward it.

5. When the lure hits the target, turn the handle clockwise to engage the reel.

If you put too much energy into the cast and you realize the lure will probably shoot past the target, you can check the line outflow simply by pressing the button. Unfortunately, the effect is sudden, and because the lure or bait will jerk to a stop in midair, it will plop down into water in a most ungentle manner, possibly spooking any fish in the vicinity. On the other hand, better to waste one cast than wind up casting your lure into the top of a tree. Once you become familiar with the basic spin-casting motion, you'll find that it's possible to slow the line outflow somewhat with the fingers and palm of your rod-holding hand, allowing you to at least get the lure close to your target instead of missing it completely.

When using a spincaster, you must always reel in when the line is under tension, or else the line won't wrap properly around the spool under the cone, and you'll wind up with a bird's nest of line underneath it. If you have a lot of slack line after a cast, use the fingers of your rod-holding hand to gently squeeze the line as you reel. And never reel in against the drag, as doing so will twist the line, creating more tangles later.

The Basics of Spinning

Casting with a spinning rod and reel is a bit more challenging than with a spincasting rig, but you can learn the rudimentary aspects of the skill in one afternoon. The basic spinning cast is as follows:

1. Hold the rod with the reel on the bottom. Place the reel foot between your second and third fingers. If this is not comfortable, place it between your index finger and second finger, or between your third and fourth fingers.

2. Turn the reel handle clockwise until there's about 6 inches of line between the rod tip and the lure. Reel in a bit less or a bit more so that the line pick-up mechanism on the bail—where the line bends beneath a little roller—is at the top of the reel.

3. Extend your index finger and hold the line coming off the reel in or just above the crook of that finger's first joint.

4. With your other hand, flip the bail back into the open position until it locks into place.

5. Point the rod tip at the target and swing the rod up and back behind you, to a point just past vertical. Cock your wrist to create the angle; your arm should not be behind your shoulder. Without pausing, swing the rod swiftly to the front. You should see or feel the rod bend a bit at this point (see the following figure).

School Notes

It's a good idea to practice casting in a yard, field, or park. Avoid casting on pavement or hardtop as your line may abrade with repeated casts.

When casting, the rod should flex so it imparts power to the cast. It's not necessary to swing your casting arm behind your shoulder.

6. When the rod is at about a 45° angle above the target, straighten your index finger to release the line.

7. When the lure hits the target, turn the handle to close the bail and engage the reel.

The typical problem that beginners have when casting with spinning tackle is learning exactly when to straighten the index finger to release line and send the lure on its way. Most first-timers either release the line too early, sending the lure up like a bottle rocket; or release it too late, splashing it down at their feet.

If you put too much power into the cast and it appears that the lure will overshoot the target, you can slow it down by extending your index finger. The coils of line coming off the reel will slap against your finger, thus reducing speed. With some practice, you can "finger" a too-fast lure right to your intended target.

As when spincasting, never reel in against the drag; doing so will result in twisted line and future tangles.

One major advantage of spinning is that you can carry spare spools of line with you. Spools on most spinning reels are removed in moments by either depressing a plunger-type button on the spool or by unscrewing a

Getting the Point

A **practice plug** is a lure-sized, hookless, soft-plastic or rubber object designed to be used for practice casting. These are obviously safer to use than the real thing and won't hook interested bystanders or inquisitive pets. Tackle shops carry them.

cap on top of the spool. This enables you to go to a stronger or lighter line on the spot, or use the same reel for light-line fishing one day and heavy-line fishing the next (as long as the lines are within the range of the rod and reel itself).

Conventional Wisdom: Baitcasting

The biggest advantage of baitcasting is its inherent accuracy. Although it is the most difficult of all rod-and-reel disciplines (barring flyfishing) to learn, baitcasting's accuracy advantage makes it the overwhelming favorite for expert fishermen where the situations and the species allow it. The basic baitcasting method is as follows:

1. Read the instructions that come with the reel so you can locate and adjust the reel's spool brake, or anti-backlash mechanism. The brake controls the freedom of movement of the spool when the reel is in freespool mode, and is usually a knob or a dial situated on the reel housing (although its location differs from reel to reel). If you don't have the instructions, adjust the brake so that a lure tied to the end of the line drops slowly to the ground when the reel is in freespool mode, and the spool stops turning when the lure stops moving.

2. Hold the rod with the reel on top, with about 6 inches of line hanging from the rod tip. Place your thumb firmly on the coils of line on the reel spool (see the following figure) and press the button (or bar, on some reels) that puts the reel into freespool mode.

To begin a cast, place your thumb firmly on the baitcaster's spool, and keep it there.

3. Turn your rod hand 90° so that your knuckles are facing up, and point the rod tip at your target.

4. Keeping your elbow at the side of your body, bend your wrist to bring the rod tip up and back over your shoulder to a point at or just past vertical.

5. Without pausing, bring the rod forward again in a snapping motion, again bending your wrist. If you're doing it right, the upper part of the rod should bend at this point.

6. As the rod springs forward, lift your thumb from the spool. You need to do this exactly when the lure will fly toward the target, and at its highest momentum. The lure should sail out on a fairly low and slightly curved trajectory.

7. As the lure nears the target, place extremely light thumb pressure on the spool ("feather" it). Apply gradually increasing pressure as the lure gets closer and closer. Then thumb the spool to a stop when the lure lands.

8. Turn the handle clockwise to engage the reel.

Remember that all the steps in making a cast are done in one smooth, easy motion, as shown in the following figure.

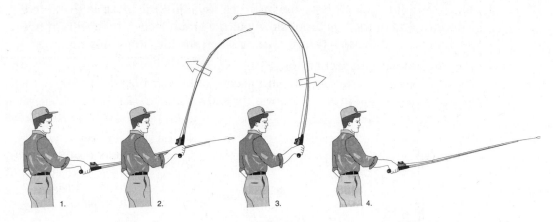

To baitcast: 1. Face the target and point your rod tip at it. 2. Lift the rod to a vertical position. 3. Snap the rod forward, simultaneously releasing your thumb from the spool. 4. Feather the line with your thumb to slow and eventually stop the lure's flight.

You won't become an accomplished baitcaster until you learn exactly when to apply thumb pressure to the spool, and how much you need to apply. The amount of anti-backlash adjustment you make, the weight of the lure, and the distance of the cast (and thus the power you put into it) are all factors that affect the cast. Practice until you get a "feel" for the right combination.

However, the ability to use that "feel" is what gives baitcasters such an advantage. When all goes right, you'll be able to drop a lure or bait exactly where you want it. Some accomplished baitcasters can feather in a cast so softly that the lure barely makes a splash as it enters the water.

While you're practicing your baitcasting, you will create some backlashes (not might create, *will* create), or tangles of line at the reel. Even the most experienced fishermen will experience the occasional "professional over-run," as the euphemism goes. Remember that backlashes are caused by the spool spinning at a speed faster than the speed of the lure as it is cast, and are often caused by conditions that the angler can remedy:

➤ The most common reason for a backlash is an improperly adjusted spool brake. Remember to adjust the brake every time you change to a lure of a different weight.

➤ If you don't apply enough pressure with your thumb, the spool will continue to spin. Try overcompensating.

➤ Using too light a lure for the line (or too heavy a line for the lure) will create a backlash, as the lure will lose momentum quickly. Switch to a heavier lure.

➤ Casting into a strong wind will retard the lure's flight. Cast in a different direction or wait for a lull in the wind.

School Notes

When practicing your casts with any type of rod and reel, it's wise to aim at a specific target to hone your skills. Start off with a hula hoop or a bicycle tire laying flat on the ground. When you hit that consistently, switch to a bucket. When you start getting cocky, put a coffee cup out there.

If you get a backlash, put the reel in freespool, then pull the loops of line out slowly, one at time, until all are clear. Then reel in the slack line under tension and try again.

Loose Lines

Sometimes a fish can cause a backlash on a baitcasting reel. It occurs when the angler has the drag set too loose and a fish grabs the bait or lure and sets off on a powerful run. Even though the reel isn't in freespool, the loose drag allows the spool to spin madly as the fish surges, but when the fish stops, the spool continues to spin. So there you are, with a big fish at the end of your line and your reel out of commission. And I can tell you that it's quite difficult to pick knots out of a baitcasting reel while simultaneously attempting to subdue a particularly large and feisty fish. For some reason, my companions that day thought the whole thing very amusing.

The Least You Need to Know

➤ Spincasting is the easiest of the disciplines to learn, although it lacks potential for accurate casts.

➤ Spinning is more difficult to master than spincasting, but it enables you to cast more accurately. Spinning also offers the option of changing line spools on the water.

➤ Baitcasting is the most challenging of the three methods, and offers pinpoint accuracy and delicate presentations.

Diameter and Pound Test

All fishing line, except for fly line, is classified according to its diameter and its strength. The diameter is measured in hundredths, thousandths, or even ten-thousandths of an inch. The strength is classified by the number of pounds the line can hold before breaking, called *pound test*. Thus, 8-pound-test line can hold 8 pounds of weight before breaking, and, theoretically, an 8-pound fish. The higher the pound test, or the stronger the line, the thicker its diameter.

Most lines sold today—Ande, Maxima, Ironthread, Spiderwire, Stren, and Trilene are all good brands, and there are many others—actually have a breaking strength that's a bit higher than the pound test listed on the box. (Many knots actually reduce the breaking strength of the line, as can abrasion.) The rule of thumb when picking the proper pound-test line—other than to be sure your rod and reel is compatible with its strength—is to go with the lightest possible for the species, the lures and bait, and the conditions. All else being equal, lighter line casts farther and easier than heavier line. It won't impede a lure's action in the water, and can't be seen by fish as easily.

For example, let's say you plan on fishing for bass in a medium-sized natural lake. The bass average 2 pounds or so, with some going to 5 pounds and a few reaching 8. One angler caught a 10-pounder last year (or so you've heard). Your medium-weight spinning rod and reel are rated for 8- to 12-pound-test line, and you'll be casting jigs and crank-baits that weigh ¼ or ⅜ ounce to the shallows in the morning. What line do you use?

I'd suggest the 8-pound-test, as it fits the rod, reel, lures, conditions, and fish. Even if you were lucky enough to hook into a bass that weighed more than 8 pounds, it wouldn't necessarily break the line from its weight alone. Remember that the fishing rod absorbs a lot of energy by flexing, and that your reel's drag should be set below the breaking strength of the line. (Some anglers even specialize in fishing with very light tackle and line, considering it more challenging and thus more sporting. They routinely catch fish that weigh much more than the pound-test strength of the line.)

Here's a different scenario: same rod, reel, and lures, except now you'll be fishing a large, deep reservoir. The fish are the same size, too, but here, limbs and branches from flooded trees protrude from the water off the steep shorelines, and that's where you'll be fishing. In this case, I'd suggest 10-pound-test line (and advise packing a spool of 12-pound-test) because if you hook a bass in that thick stuff, you'll need to get it out to open water quickly, before it can wrap your line around a submerged limb. The stronger line makes that easier and is less likely to break if you have to "turn" a fish around an obstruction.

Another reason to go with heavier line is if the fish you are after have sizable teeth. Freshwater species such as pickerel, pike, and muskies; and many light-tackle salt-water species such as bluefish, weakfish, sea trout, and summer flounder, can bite

Chapter 8

It's All on the Line

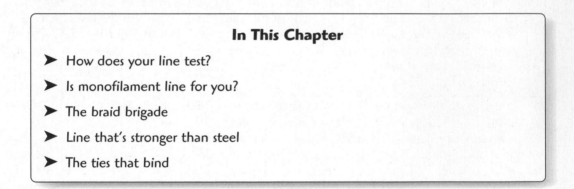

In This Chapter

➤ How does your line test?

➤ Is monofilament line for you?

➤ The braid brigade

➤ Line that's stronger than steel

➤ The ties that bind

Fishing line is changing and advancing so rapidly that some types didn't even exist a few years ago. New components and manufacturing processes have made the fishing line industry a highly technological, and extremely competitive, enterprise. While anglers have never had a better selection of line, it can create a lot of confusion, because with so many types to choose from, and all those manufacturer's claims to sort through, it can be difficult to make an informed decision.

While the history of fishing line development is interesting, with everything from braided horsetail hair to silks and linens used in the past, it really has no bearing on choosing and using line today. Most all fishing lines sold today are inexpensive, sturdy, thin, and reliable. If there's a common mistake made by anglers when selecting line, it's choosing the wrong line for their rod and reel and the fish they are after, rather than choosing the wrong brand. This chapter will guide you through the line selection process, and show you what to do with that line.

right through a line if the fish is hooked deeply enough. (Many anglers use a wire or heavy-line leader, which is a short length of line tied between the bait or lure and the end of the reel line, when fishing for these species. More on leaders in Chapter 12, "Yes, You Should Sweat the Small Stuff.")

Although there are numerous variables and exceptions to the proper pound-test line to use for each species, the following table gives you a *general* guide for freshwater fishing.

Remember that your choice of tackle—rod, reel, lures, and bait—also has a bearing on your line choice. The kind of line you use is a factor as well.

General Pound-Test for Various Fish

Species	Pound-Test Range
Largemouth bass, northern U.S.	6–12
Largemouth bass, southern/western U.S.	10–20
Trout, streams and small rivers	2–6
Trout, large rivers and lakes	6–14
Trout and salmon, Great Lakes	17–20
Perch and panfish	2–6
Catfish less than 5 pounds	6–10
Catfish more than 5 pounds	10–20
Pickerel	6–12
Pike and muskies	10–20

Loose Lines

Fishing line is sold on spools in various lengths. The minimum length sold for filling a reel (for the lowest pound-test lines) is 100 yards. Some lines come in 200- to 400-yard lengths, which is enough to fill most reels that accommodate that particular strength. Some spools contain 1,000 to 3,000 yards of line. Remember to check the line capacity of your reel spool and buy a spool that contains more than enough to fill it.

Monofilament: One with Nylon

The most common and popular fishing line on the market is nylon monofilament. This line has been around for more than 50 years, and the "mono" of today is better than ever. The angler has a lot of choices, too: mono in clear, whites, greens, blues, and fluorescents; extra-tough, extra-supple, or extra-thin; in all pound-test classifications and lengths.

Loose Lines

What's the best color of monofilament to use? I like to use clear or white-translucent line, but some fishermen prefer blue or green translucents, whichever better matches the color of the water they'll be fishing. Manufacturers do run underwater visibility tests, so it's doubtful that you'll end up using a line that fish will readily see. One advantage of tinted line is that you can easily see it above the water, so you know where your lure or bait is, and can watch the line for a light take from a fish.

School Notes

Always cut a few feet off the end of your line before each fishing trip, and occasionally when fishing in obstruction-filled waters. That tag end is subject to the most wear, and cutting it back reduces your chances of losing a fish.

Monofilament is easy to handle. It casts well and is easy to tie knots in, because it is somewhat stiff (compared to, say, sewing thread). Mono can be used on spinning, spincasting, baitcasting, and conventional reels. It's translucent and becomes nearly invisible underwater. Because mono stretches, it excels at absorbing energy. This can be an advantage, such as when setting the hook on a very large fish; if the line didn't stretch, it would be possible to break the line, or even the fishing rod. Mono is also relatively inexpensive.

Monofilament's detractions include, ironically, its stretch when wet, which translates into decreased sensitivity, especially if you have a lot of line out. This means that mono is not a good choice when fishing at great depths for deep-water species. It also has memory, which means that it tends to spiral or coil when not under tension, displaying its placement on the reel spool (it looks a bit like a Slinky). It can also absorb some water, which may cause knots to loosen. Heat and sunlight can also weaken monofilament.

You should replace monofilament lines on fishing reels at least every season, more often if you fish a lot. Those memory coils can turn into kinks over time, and abrasions from rubbing against rocks, docks, boat gunwales, and other objects can cause them to break, always at the most inopportune time, such as when fighting the biggest fish of your life. (Yes, it happened to me.) These abraded areas are difficult to spot, so you're better off playing it safe and buying new line. It's a relatively inexpensive investment.

Dacron: The Old Braid

Braided Dacron line has been used by anglers for decades, mostly for long-line fishing such as deep trolling. Dacron braid has a few specific advantages over monofilament, such as very little stretch and great sensitivity, which is important when you have 100 feet or so of line out. Monofilament's stretch would make it difficult to feel a fish take a lure or bait at that distance. Dacron also absorbs very little water, so it retains its sensitivity when wet, and resists deterioration from sunlight. It is almost as strong as nylon monofilament, so the diameters of Dacron and monofilament in the same pound-test ranges are close.

Dacron, however, is opaque. In very clear water you must tie a leader—a length of monofilament line—to the end, and tie your hook or bait to that, otherwise fish may spot the line and shy away from your offering. And because Dacron is so limp, it doesn't take well to use on spinning and spincasting reels, as it promotes tangles. Conventional and baitcasting reels handle Dacron best.

A recent development in fishing lines has supplanted both nylon monofilament and braided Dacron in many fishing applications. It just may be the line of the future.

Multifilaments: The Super Lines

These are the newest lines on the market, and every year brings a new improvement. Basically, multifilament lines are braided lines made of a type of polyethylene. Their make-up isn't as important as their primary advantage: They are as sensitive as Dacron, but with a diameter about one-third that of monofilament. These polyethylene strands are five to ten times stronger than steel by weight. (One manufacturer's multifilament is made of Kevlar, a DuPont fiber that is used to make bulletproof vests.) This translates into an extremely thin line for its strength.

Some multifilament manufacturers designate their line according to the equivalent diameters of monofilament line. For instance, a spool of 10-pound-test multifilament line has the same diameter as 2-pound-test monofilament line (about .003 inch). This means that anglers can use much stronger line for the same purposes, or stay with the same strength yet be able to use a much smaller-diameter line. This advantage, combined with superb sensitivity, no memory, and extremely little stretch, makes multifilament sound perfect indeed.

But all is not perfect, of course. Multifilament works best on conventional and baitcasting reels. On spinning and spincasting reels, the line's limpness can make for awkward manipulation, as it doesn't "spring" off the reel like monofilament. Also, going up in line strength while maintaining the same diameter requires careful use of the rod. If you're using an outfit rated for 6- to 10-pound-test line, and you spool up with a multifilament that has an 8-pound-test monofilament diameter but is rated at, say, 30-pound-test, it's possible to break the rod or crack the reel spool if you apply too much pressure. This can happen if your hook is irretrievably snagged on the bottom and your only option is to break the line. Pull hard enough with a screwed-down drag and the rod could shatter. (The solution would be to cut the line as close to the snag as possible, or use a monofilament leader that will break first.)

Also, knot-tying is more difficult with the multifilaments. The knots themselves don't cinch down as easily as they do on mono, and they are prone to slipping. Some manufacturers offer a type of super glue to apply to multifilament knots.

Finally, multifilaments are expensive, sometimes quadruple the cost of equivalent monofilament. This can run into a bit of an expense, especially considering that the line is so thin that you need more of it to fill a reel spool.

All things considered, however, multifilament's advantages outweigh its disadvantages for many situations, especially when fishing for larger species such as largemouth bass, pike, pickerel, and many saltwater fish, with a conventional or baitcasting reel. That's my preference, and I use monofilament on my spinning outfits.

Knots for the Fumble-Fingered

While many pamphlets describe how to tie scores of different knots in line, the beginner can fish effectively by mastering just four of them. Not that others aren't worth knowing; the point is that you don't have to become familiar with them all to catch a fish.

Practice these knots at home so you won't waste valuable fishing time messing around with them.

The Slip Knot

This knot is used to attach fishing line to a reel spool. Don't use this knot to attach your line to terminal tackle, as it is not an essentially strong one. Be sure to run the end of the new line backward through the rod guides first, so you can reel the line onto the reel later. On spinning reels, it's usually easier to remove the spool, tie the line on, and replace the spool before reeling (open the bail before replacing the spool).

1. Pass the line around the spool. If putting line on a levelwinding baitcasting reel, pass the tag end through the levelwind, around the spool, and back out through the levelwind. Tie a simple overhand knot in the tag end. Pull tight and clip the excess.

2. Pass the tag end around the other strand of line, and tie an overhand knot around it.

3. Hold the standing line (the line going to the spool of new line) and pull tight. The first knot will slide up tight to the second and cinch tight.

Cautious Casts

When putting line on a spinning or spincasting reel, have someone hold the new-line spool facing you (so you see the label) when reeling. On a baitcasting reel, the spool should be sideways to you. With both, make sure the line is coming off the spool the same way it is going onto the reel, or the line will twist.

Tying a slip knot to a spinning-reel spool.

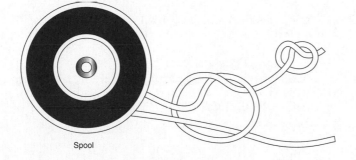

Spool

The Improved Clinch Knot

This is one of the best, and easiest, knots for attaching terminal tackle (hooks, lures, swivels, or snaps) to your line. The "improved" part is the last turn of the line.

1. Pass the line through the eye of the hook (or lure, swivel, or snap). Make five turns around the standing part of the line, using the fingers of your other hand to hold the loop formed by the first turn.

2. Pass the tag end through the first loop above the eye.

3. Pass the tag end through the wide loop just formed.

4. Pull the standing line while holding the tag end, so it doesn't slip back through the loop. The coils should form a neat spiral and not overlap.

5. Clip the tag end close to the knot.

83

Tying an improved clinch knot to a hook eye.

The Surgeon's Knot

This knot is used to tie together lines of greatly different diameter, such as a heavy leader to a standing line.

1. Place the two lines parallel, overlapping about 6 inches, with the ends pointing in opposite directions.

2. Hold the two lines together and, treating them as one line, tie an overhand knot. Pull the entire leader through the loop. Don't pull the knot tight.

3. Pass the line through the loop a second time, so it looks like the middle portion of the following figure.

4. Hold the lines on either end of the knot and pull tight. Clip the tag ends.

Tying two lines together with a surgeon's knot.

School Notes

Knots are usually easier to pull tight if the line is wet. You can use saliva or dip the knot in the water.

The Loop Knot

A loop at the end of your line is useful for attaching swivels or large sinkers. It's also handy for keeping line on the rod when you put your tackle away temporarily. Simply make the loop, pull the line out of the tip-top guide, place the loop over the rod tip, and reel tight.

1. Double the end of the line to form a loop.

2. Tie an overhand knot with the doubled section. Don't pull tight.

3. Pass the loop through the knot a second time.

4. Hold the standing line and the tag end in one hand and pull the loop with the other. Clip the tag end close to the knot.

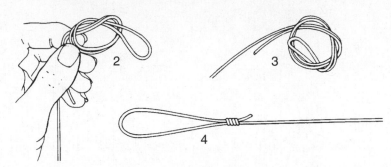

Making a loop with a loop knot.

The Least You Need to Know

➤ All fishing line is measured by its diameter and its breaking strength. A 6-pound-test line will hold 6 pounds of weight before breaking. The lighter the line, the smaller the line's diameter.

➤ Always fish with the lightest line acceptable for the conditions, the species, and the tackle.

➤ Nylon monofilament is popular and inexpensive. Although it stretches quite a bit and is subject to abrasion, its translucency, castability, and easy knot-tying qualities make monofilament a good all-around line.

➤ Braided Dacron line is more sensitive than monofilament and is a better choice when you have a lot of line out, such as when trolling or fishing in deep water.

➤ The new multifilament lines are replacing both monofilament and Dacron for many situations. Its greater strength for the same diameter as mono or Dacron makes multifilament superior, especially for larger fish on baitcasting or conventional reels.

➤ As long as you know how to tie line onto a reel and how to tie a hook or a lure onto line, you're ready to fish.

Chapter 9

Hooks: The Point of It All

In This Chapter

➤ Penetrating facts

➤ Hook nomenclature

➤ The best hook for the situation

What fishing all comes down to is the ability to put a hook into a fish's mouth. For that reason, fishhooks are one of the most important pieces of tackle that an angler owns (if not the most important), as you'll learn in this chapter. They are also inexpensive, compared to other necessary gear, yet it's surprising how many fishermen don't give hooks the attention they deserve, both when purchasing and using them.

Once, when fishing for trout in Montana's Madison River, I couldn't seem to hook any of the rising trout I was casting to. Every ten seconds or so a trout would lift up from the bottom to snatch an insect floating on the surface, and my dry fly matched the real bugs in size and color. On about every third cast, one of the trout would snatch my fly. I'd go to set the hook but couldn't sink it into any of the fish. I repeatedly cast to these trout, thinking I was striking either too early or too late. Then, one large brown trout took the fly, I set the hook, and I had the fish on—for about three seconds. That's when I checked my fly and ruefully noted that the entire hook point had broken off, probably from ticking a rock on one of my backcasts. I changed flies and caught a trout on my very next cast.

I inspect my hooks all the time now.

How Hooks Hook Fish

It's difficult to pinpoint exactly when humans began using hooks to catch fish, as rudimentary prehistoric hooks made of bone, antler, and other natural materials have been unearthed in archeological digs. The very first fishhook was actually a "gorge," a short, straight shaft with pointed ends that, when buried in a bait and swallowed by a fish, would turn and lodge in the fish's gullet as the angler tugged on the line. Other prehistoric hooks that have been unearthed closely resemble modern versions— a curved object with a point on one end and a notch to tie line on the other end— except, of course, for the fact that they might have been made from the angler's dead neighbor.

Getting the Point

A fish that is **foul-hooked** is one that is hooked anywhere besides the mouth; such as the body, gill, or tail. Sometimes fish hit a lure or bait so explosively that they don't get it in their mouth, but manage to hook themselves anyway.

A hook works by its point becoming embedded in a fish's mouth or gullet. However, it's up to the fisherman to cause this to happen and to keep it that way until the fish is at hand. There are three things a fisherman must do to accomplish this:

1. *Keep hooks sharp.* The sharper the hook point, the easier it enters the fish. Most all fishhooks have a barb, which is a sharp, angled protuberance below the hook point. The hook must sink into the fish past the barb to ensure a solid hookset. If it doesn't, the fish stands a good chance of getting off. A hook sharpener (see Chapter 12, "Yes, You Should Sweat the Small Stuff") costs about as much as a package of a dozen small hooks, and you can hone the point of a hook with one in five or ten seconds.

2. *Set the hook solidly.* This is the most common fault of beginning fishermen I've known: They feel a fish hit the bait, then start reeling in. The fish feels the pressure, opens its mouth, and bait and hook pop out. Rarely does a fish hook itself solidly (unless it swallows the bait, which often doesn't occur until five or ten seconds after it mouths the bait, during which time the fish might feel the hook and spit it out anyway). Whether you are using a bait or a lure, you must lift the rod sharply, with no slack in the line, to drive the hook point deep enough into the fish's mouth for the barb to penetrate.

3. Keep *a tight line.* Even if you have set the hook solidly, a fish can break the hookset as it pulls and turns in different directions. Many fish have bony mouths, and it takes a lot of pressure to sink a hook solidly. Also, considering how much monofilament line can stretch, what you thought was a deep hookset could be a very shallow one, with the point of the hook barely penetrating the fish's mouth.

It's also important to use the right size and style of hook, covered next.

Hook Types and What They're For

Most all fishhooks are made of steel. All hooks have basic parts and measurements (shown the following figure) and they all share three basic identifying characteristics: their size, their weight, and their style.

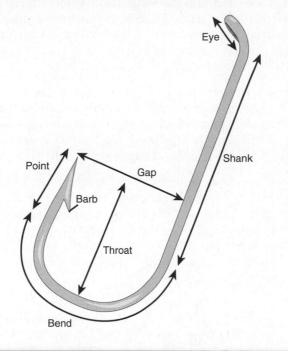

Parts and measurements of a fishhook.

Hook size is designated by a number. The higher the number, the smaller the hook. A No. 4 hook is bigger than a No. 6 hook within the same style. Hooks bigger than No. 1 take a zero, and the number progression is reversed, so that a No. 2/0 hook is smaller than a No. 3/0 hook. However, this numerical system is not standardized, and the actual lengths of the hooks differ among manufacturers and styles. The hook's *gap*, which is the distance from the point of the hook across to the *shank*, which is the straight part of the hook, determines hook size, along with the length of the shaft itself. A hook with a ¼-inch gap is usually a No. 6. And a standard No. 6 hook with a standard-length shank measures anywhere from ⅝- to ⅞-inch long, again depending on the hook style.

Hooks can also be *long-shanked* or *short-shanked*. This is also designated by a number, which is followed by an "X." The number indicates how many sizes longer or shorter the shank is for its size. For instance, a 2X Long hook has the same shank length as a hook two sizes larger, and a 2X Short hook has a shank length of a hook two sizes smaller. So a No. 6 2X Long hook would have a shank the same length as that of a standard No. 4.

The correct size of hook to use depends on the bait you're using and the type of fish you're after. The larger the fish, the larger the hook required to ensure a good hold.

The hook must be small enough, however, so that it doesn't scare the fish and/or is too large for the bait. For instance, a whole garden worm fits well on a No. 8 hook. A long-shanked hook is preferable when fishing for large-toothed species, so that when hooked, the fish bites on the shank instead of the fishing line. (Long-shanked hooks also figure in flyfishing, when using flies called streamers, which imitate baitfish. A long, narrow hook most closely resembles the shape of a small fish.) Long shanks also make hook removal easy, which is a consideration with species that are difficult to unhook, such as flounder.

Hook weight, other than standard, is also designated by a number accompanied by an "X," meaning it is *fine wire* or *heavy wire*. A 1X Fine hook has the same diameter as a hook one size smaller, and a 1X Stout hook has the same diameter as a hook one size larger. Generally, a fine-wire hook penetrates a fish's mouth more easily than a heavy-wire hook, and does not impede the action of live bait—a minnow impaled with a heavy hook won't swim normally. However, heavy hooks don't bend (or break) as easily as fine ones. Heavy hooks also hold better in fish.

A hook's style is determined by a number of features. The eye of the hook, which is where the line is tied, can be *ringed*, in which it is parallel to the shank; *turned up*, in which it is angled away from the point; or *turned down*, meaning it's angled toward the point. The theory is that turned-up eyes allow more clearance between the shank and the point, which is a consideration when using very small hooks. Turned-down eyes are said to penetrate easier because of the better angle of the point to the fishing line. Ringed eyes are the compromise.

Getting the Point

Some hooks don't have barbs (and are called, logically enough, **barbless hooks**). Although barbless hooks don't hold as well as barbed versions, some fishermen, such as those who intend to release all the fish they catch, prefer them because they are easier to remove from a fish. To make a barbed hook barbless, just press down the barb with pliers.

Hooks that are designed to hold bait such as worms have *slices* (protrusions) along the shank, which are extra barbs that keep the bait secured to the hook. Other bait-style hooks are *curved-shanked*. A hump or bend in the shank also helps hold the bait on the hook.

A *weedless hook* is one that features one or more thin wires that extend from the hook eye to the point. The idea is that the wires will keep weeds from snagging on the hook, but will bend inward when a fish strikes. They work—to a degree. (A more appropriate term would be weed-*resistant*.)

A *double hook* has one eye and shank with two points. They are most often used when fishing in salt water with very large baits. A *treble hook* has one eye and shank with three points. These are most common on lures (artificial baits), and many lures have two or three sets of treble hooks on them. While doubles and trebles do offer more hooking potential than single hooks, they may be too large for a fish's mouth (especially smaller fish), they foul with weeds much more readily, and they make unhooking a fish that much more difficult.

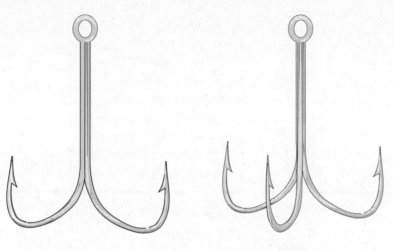

Double Hook   Treble Hook

A double hook has one eye and shank with two points; a treble hook has one eye and shank and three points.

How to Pick the Right Hook

There is no one perfect size or style of hook to use in one particular situation or for one particular species. Rather, the size range is more important.

Fortunately, hook manufacturers have made it easy for us to pick the right hook in many cases. Many hooks come packaged as "bass hooks" or "trout hooks," and if the angler buys a small assortment of sizes, he's ready to go. Hooks that are designed to be used with a particular bait also are sometimes labeled as such. A "salmon-egg hook," for example, is about the size of your pinkie nail and has an extremely short shank, which enables the angler to insert the entire hook (up to the eye) inside the egg. Also, some hooks are sold "snelled," meaning they have a monofilament leader already tied onto them. Some snelled hooks have a loop at the end of the line, meaning an angler can attach a snelled hook to his fishing line simply by fashioning a loop on the end of the main line, inserting the hook through the loop, then passing the hook through the loop on the end of the leader and pulling it tight.

Again, because the proper hook size depends on the bait (covered in Chapter 10, "Bait: Getting Your Bona Fides in Order") and on the species sought, there is no one "best" hook size. However, the following table can serve as a rough guide to hook sizes for freshwater fish.

Hook Size Ranges and Styles for Freshwater Species

Species	Hook Size Range and Style
Small panfish	No. 6 to 12 long-shanked
Large panfish	No. 1 to 6 long-shanked
Small trout	No. 6 to 14 fine wire
Large trout	No. 1/0 to 6 baitholding
Largemouth bass	No. 4/0 to 2 baitholding
Smallmouth bass	No. 2/0 to 4 baitholding
Walleyes	No. 3/0 to 2 baitholding
Small catfish	No. 1/0 to 4 baitholding
Large catfish	No. 5/0 to 1/0 baitholding
Pickerel/Northern pike	No. 4/0 to 1/0 baitholding

It pays to carry an assortment of hook sizes at all times, even if you know you're going to be fishing for just one species of one particular size range that day, because you may discover that you need a larger or smaller size to hook fish, or to fish with a different bait. I often change to a larger hook size if I discover that many of the fish I'm catching are swallowing the hook.

Here's an extreme example of the advantage of bringing a variety of hooks. I was in the Florida Keys with some business associates to fish for tarpon early one spring, and we woke up that first morning to discover that no mullet (a preferred forage fish for tarpon) was available at area tackle shops. So there we were, geared up with heavy-duty tarpon rods and reels to do battle with these 100-pound-and-up fish, stuck at the dock. Luckily, one of us had brought an "emergency" tackle box with him, including a selection of (comparatively) small baithooks. We fashioned some handlines and drifted in the shallows, using tiny pieces of shrimp, to fish for pinfish—a type of saltwater panfish, also preferred tarpon forage—that we could use as bait. We did this every morning for the three days we were there. If it wasn't for my companion's foresight in bringing a supply of extra hooks in various sizes, we wouldn't have been able to fish at all effectively for tarpon.

Interestingly enough, the tarpon weren't in a very cooperative mood on that trip (although I did have a big one on for a short time), but everyone had a blast trying to catch, without a rod or a reel, a day's supply of those 6-inch pinfish every morning. Those small hooks saved the trip in more ways than one.

Loose Lines

Some hooks, especially those designed for use in salt water, are made of stainless steel, and resist corrosion much better than standard (non-stainless) steel hooks. There are two differing views on stainless hooks. One is that because they are strong, they are less apt to break as they age, as is true with standard hooks. And although stainless hooks cost a bit more, they don't need to be replaced as often. The opposing viewpoint is that because stainless hooks take a very long time to decompose, any fish that breaks the line with a stainless hook in its throat may have difficulty surviving.

Because many species of fish must be of a certain size to be kept, many undersized fish must be released. If a fish has swallowed the hook, the fish stands a much better chance of surviving if the angler simply cuts the line close to the fish's mouth and drops the fish back in the water as soon as possible, instead of holding it and digging into its throat, trying to remove a deeply embedded hook. If the hook is stainless, however, the fish's chance of survival are diminished.

The Least You Need to Know

➤ Hooks must be kept sharp, and the angler must set the hook properly and keep a tight line to bring in the fish.

➤ The higher the number, the smaller the hook, except when a zero follows the number, in which case the opposite is true. Some hooks have features, such as its length or extra barbs, for specific applications.

➤ There is no one "best" size of hook for certain fish and situations. But there are preferred size ranges, and fishermen should carry a good assortment of hooks.

Chapter 10

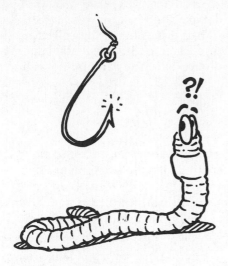

Bait: Getting Your Bona Fides in Order

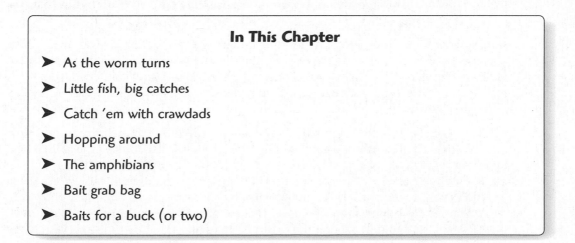

In This Chapter

➤ As the worm turns

➤ Little fish, big catches

➤ Catch 'em with crawdads

➤ Hopping around

➤ The amphibians

➤ Bait grab bag

➤ Baits for a buck (or two)

Using the right bait—whether it's fresh or frozen, alive or dead, pickled or freeze-dried—is the most effective way to catch fish, if it is chosen correctly and used properly. There are many different types of baits—earthworms alone vary in size and color, for example—but in this chapter I'll be covering basic bait types.

Some people are squeamish about putting bait, such as a minnow, on a hook. If you feel this way and want to flip directly to the chapter on lures, go ahead. (But if you feel funny about touching a worm, you'll be a riot when it's time to take a fish off the hook.)

In many cases, acquiring the bait on your own is an adventure in itself. On a trip to a nearby lake last year, my son and I scared up a bunch of grasshoppers while walking through a small grassy field on the way to the water. We dropped our tackle and tried to grab a few of them, because I knew that they'd make good bait for the panfish and small bass we were after. It turns out that Joey had just as much fun collecting them—chasing after one of the flying, jumping bugs, catching it, and gently cupping (or at least attempting to gently cup) his little four-year-old hands around it—as he did fishing with them afterwards. In truth, so did I.

The Not-So-Lowly Worm

There are few freshwater fish that will turn up their noses (or at least their scent glands) at a well-presented worm. Such soft, undulating, defenseless, protein-filled creatures are usually snatched up by fish, even though they don't seem to appear in water with any regularity. (I'm sure that plenty of worms wash into lakes and streams after a storm or during a high-water period, but of the hundreds of trout that I've cleaned over the years, I found a worm in the stomachs of only a couple of them.)

Worms come in different sizes. *Red worms* average 1 to 3 inches long and have a pinkish hue. They are good for catching panfish and trout, especially in low and clear water. They are also called manure worms because they tend to be found in that organic matter. (Yes, that.)

Garden worms run from 3 to 5 inches long and are good baits for sunfish, trout, bass, walleyes, and catfish at any time of year. You can dig your own garden worms in, obviously, a garden, lawn, field, or anywhere you find soft, loamy soil. Use a shovel or fork and dig about a foot down, gently breaking up the clods of soil with the tool as you search for worms.

Night crawlers (also called *night walkers*) are large earthworms, measuring from 4 to 6 inches when relaxed, and are good bait for the species noted above, especially when targeting bigger fish. Night crawlers seem to work best in high, murky water. They are named for their tendency to come out of the ground at night, especially when the ground is wet. You can collect night crawlers by checking lawns after dark with a weak-beamed flashlight, or by covering the lens of one with a thin cloth or colored-plastic wrap, so you don't spook the crawlers. Take one step at a time and search the ground carefully. Most night crawlers don't come out of the ground completely, so if you see one, try to pinch it close to its hole. Gently pull on the worm, giving it time to contract so it will come out of its hole.

You can also buy garden worms and night crawlers at any bait shop. They're usually inexpensive; a few dollars will buy you enough worms to fish for a morning.

Keep worms in a ventilated can (a standard coffee can with some holes punched in the plastic lid is fine) or a box filled with damp (not wet) soil and leaf detritus, and keep the container in a cool, dark place. Occasionally throw some bits of eggshell in the soil for nourishment. Tackle shops sell special boxes to store worms: large ones with handles for keeping a supply at home and/or taking with you on a boat, and small ones with loops that you can strap onto your belt—allowing you to reach for a worm easily while fishing.

Worm Rigging and Fishing

There are many ways to fish with worms as bait. The simplest and most common method is to hook the worm through the collar, which is a short, tough band on the worm's body (see the following figure). Impale the worm once or twice on the hook, so it hangs naturally; don't skewer it like a corn dog. If you're fishing for bait-nibbling panfish, use a very small hook and cover the entire hook with a short piece of worm. You should use a baitholder hook (the kind with slices along the shank) to keep the worm in place. The right size hook depends on the size of the worm. As a rule of thumb, use Nos. 4–6 hooks for night crawlers, Nos. 8–10 for garden worms, and Nos. 10–12 for red worms.

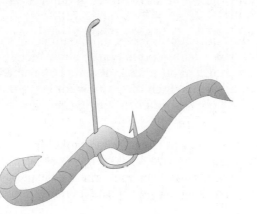

Hook a worm through its collar on a baitholder hook. Impale the worm again if it's a long one. Make sure the worm hangs naturally.

If you're fishing in a lake, you can cast out and let the worm settle to the bottom. You'll probably need some additional weight in the form of split-shot sinkers to both cast the worm and keep it on the bottom. A *split shot* is a small, round lead sinker with a shallow cut in it. You use it by pinching it onto the fishing line with pliers. Some split shots are designed so that they can be easily removed from the line by pinching a tiny beak on the opposite side.

Depending on the location of the lake and its water temperature, you can catch panfish, catfish, bass, trout, walleyes, carp, and suckers with this method. You can also fish the worm with a bobber, which is a float that you attach to your line. This will keep the worm off the bottom, which is an advantage when fishing very weedy lakes. (More on sinkers and bobbers in Chapter 12, "Yes, You Should Sweat the Small Stuff.")

School Notes

If you only have large worms like night crawlers on hand, but you only have small hooks, you can fish half the worm (I pinch it apart with my thumbnail). But don't keep the other half of the worm in your worm box, as it will eventually die. Sometimes this harms the other worms. It also smells horrible when you open the container a week later.

For creek, stream, or river fishing, attach the worm to a hook in the same manner and add a split shot or two on the line. Cast the worm at an angle across-stream and upstream, and let the worm drift naturally with the current. For a proper presentation, the sinker, and therefore the worm, should be making occasional contact with the stream bottom.

Make a Splash with Minnows

Many fish are predators, and small fish make up a large part of their diet. That's why minnow fishing—that is, fishing with small fish as bait—is such a successful technique. Trout, bass, walleyes, pickerel, pike, muskies, catfish, and larger panfish all eat minnows.

Shiners, chubs, dace, shad, alewifes, and sculpins are popular baitfish species used for minnow fishing. They don't grow past a certain point—from a few inches to a foot, depending on the species—and are found in all waters inhabited by gamefish. One often-repeated rule of thumb is to figure one inch of minnow for every pound of fish. As with worms, there are two ways to obtain minnows: buying them or collecting them yourself.

Many bait shops sell minnows; they are kept in large aerated tanks. You bring a bucket, and the proprietor puts as many minnows as you want (they are usually sold by the dozen) into it. The baitfish you get are typically the most prevalent species in that area's waters. If you have a choice of different sizes, use the inch-per-pound rule.

There are two ways to collect baitfish on your own: trapping and seining. You trap minnows with, logically enough, a minnow trap, which is a cylindrical mesh-wire object with small holes on either end. The holes funnel into the body of the trap, which hinders the minnows' escape once they're inside. You put bait such as bread into the trap, which comes apart at the middle via a latch, along with a rock or two for weight. Tie the trap to a rope and toss it into the shallow waters of a lake or pond. Ten minutes to an hour later, haul it in, and you should have some minnows. If not, try again in a different area.

You seine minnows with a seine net, which is a large, square, cloth net with a tight mesh, weighted at the bottom. The ends of the net are tied to sticks or poles (broomsticks work well). In a small creek, one person holds the seine net apart while another goes upstream a bit and starts walking downstream, cutting back and forth from bank to bank. The force of the current pushes the minnows into the back of the net, which balloons out in the current. The net holder lifts the net in one motion and brings it to the bank, where you pick out your minnows.

Minnows can be kept in a bucket filled with cool water. You should buy or collect your minnows just before you begin fishing (say, early that morning) so they'll stay alive. Use the water from the bait shop or from the creek, and keep the bucket in a shaded area both in your car and when fishing, so the water doesn't heat up. Never use chlorinated tap water as it will kill the minnows.

If you must buy or collect your minnows in advance, put some ice cubes in an sealed plastic bag and place the bag in the water to keep it cool. You can also buy a battery-operated aerator (similar to those used for household aquariums) to keep the water oxygenated.

Some buckets are specially designed to keep minnows. The most common type features a perforated flap on the top that swings inward via a spring mechanism when you want to fetch a minnow, but remains closed otherwise. The bucket floats, and the perforations allow fresh water to circulate inside. You keep the bucket tied to your boat or to the shore.

Cautious Casts

Most states require that persons collecting baitfish have a fishing license (which makes sense, as you are fishing). Remember to take your fishing license with you when you trap or seine baitfish.

Minnow Rigging and Fishing

If you're going to be fishing in still water, place the hook through the top of the minnow's back just behind the dorsal fin (see the figure on the next page). Don't pierce its back too low, or you will break the fish's spine and paralyze it. Add a bobber above the hook so that the minnow will swim just above the bottom or just above the tops of submerged weeds. Cast out and let the minnow swim naturally. If the minnow swims to the surface, add a split shot to keep it down. If the bobber begins moving erratically, open your bail so the predator fish won't feel line tension, and wait until the bobber disappears under the surface. When it pops back up—which may take a few seconds, and it may resurface in a different area—set the hook. (Hooksetting is detailed in Chapter 14, "Fish On! How to Keep It That Way.")

School Notes

If your minnows begin swimming to the surface in your bucket, there isn't enough oxygen in the water. Change it as soon as possible, but make sure your new water isn't too much colder, as it may "shock" the baitfish. If this happens often, you probably have too many minnows in the bucket. Split them into two containers.

If you are fishing in moving water, hook the minnow through both lips, add a split shot, and cast up- and across-stream. Let the minnow sink near the bottom and let it bump and "swim" across the bottom. Keep a fairly tight line when doing this so you can tell if a fish hits the minnow. At the end of the drift, reel the minnow slowly back to you. If you feel a fish take the minnow, stop reeling, count to three to allow the fish to take the minnow deep into its mouth, and set the hook. This technique can also be used in still water, by casting to weedbeds, rocky shoals, submerged trees, and other structures, and retrieving the minnow slowly.

Hook a minnow behind the dorsal fin (top) when fishing still waters, and through both lips (bottom) when fishing in a current.

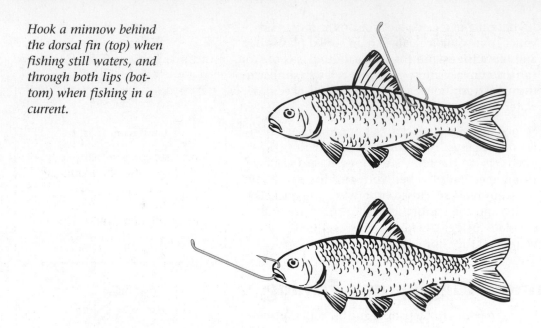

The Little Lobsters

Crayfish, or crawdads as they're sometimes called, are good bait for trout, bass, walleyes, catfish, and perch. These little crustaceans don't grow as large as lobsters, to which they are directly related, and 2 to 4 inches is the best size to use for bait. The key to crayfish is to use them where they commonly live, usually cold-water lakes, creeks, streams, and rivers.

Crayfish must molt, that is, shed their exoskeleton (shell) to grow, and they do this fairly often. Soft-shelled crayfish are especially desirable as bait, although the hard-shelled versions work well too.

Some bait dealers sell crayfish, but they are not as commonly available as worms or minnows. You can get crayfish on your own by searching small brooks and rock-strewn lake shallows. This is especially productive at night with a flashlight. Turn rocks over if you don't see crayfish. Use a net, or get an empty coffee can and remove the bottom. If you spot a crayfish, quickly drop the can around it. You can then pick up the trapped crayfish easily. You can also obtain crayfish by seining or trapping them (raw meat is the best bait) as you would minnows. Grab the crayfish around the middle of the body to avoid the pincers.

Keep crayfish in a minnow bucket. The crustaceans are somewhat hardier than minnows, but you still must keep the water cool and aerated as you would for baitfish.

Crayfish Rigging and Fishing

Rig a crayfish by passing the hook through the tail, from the bottom up. This won't kill the crayfish immediately, and it will move through the water naturally (crayfish swim tail-first) when you retrieve it. You can also strap the hook to the crayfish's body with a rubber band or pipe cleaner.

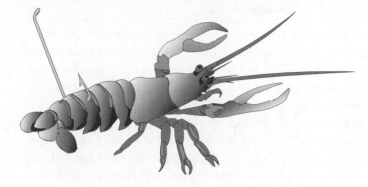

Hook crayfish through the tail.

Because crayfish dwell on the bottom of lakes and rivers, you must fish them there, which means you must put a sinker on your line. Don't use a bobber, as it will keep the crayfish above the bottom. In lakes, cast to rocky shoals and near weedbeds (but not into them, as the crayfish will hide immediately). Let the crayfish sink to the bottom and then reel in very slowly, pausing every few seconds. Occasionally lift the rod high in case the crayfish has hidden under a rock. Because of a crayfish's tendency to seek refuge, a better technique is to fish from a boat and let the wind drift you over these areas, so the crayfish slides and bumps across bottom. However, you must drift extremely slowly to keep the crayfish down where it belongs. Some anglers tie a bucket to the boat and throw it over the side to slow down the drift.

School Notes

If your crayfish is constantly using its claws to grab and hang onto underwater weeds and obstructions, break off one pincer on each claw. The crayfish will still move toward cover but can't hold onto anything, reducing your chances of getting snagged.

When fishing in a stream, cast the crayfish up- and across-stream and let it bump along the bottom with the current. At the end of the drift, reel the crayfish slowly back to you.

With either technique, if you feel a fish take the crayfish, pause for a few seconds before setting the hook, to allow the fish time to take the crayfish deep into its mouth.

Loose Lines

One spring afternoon many years ago I was fishing a trout stream in Pennsylvania right after a heavy rain and caught a few 10- to 12-inch trout. Just before dark I cast to a tree that had fallen lengthwise into the current and felt a tremendous hit. I waited a few seconds and set the hook into what turned out to be an 18-inch brown trout with a huge belly. I kept that fish to eat (to a college student, fish you catch are free food) and was astounded, while cleaning the trout that evening, when I counted 18 partially digested crayfish in its stomach. Evidently the heavy rain had quickened the stream's current, dislodging a lot of the crayfish from under rocks, and the opportunistic trout had fed gluttonously. I still wonder what I would have caught had I used crayfish for bait that day.

Grasshoppers and Crickets

These insects are prevalent during the warm-weather months. Because they fall naturally into water, many fish—especially panfish, bass, and trout—eat them readily. Crickets are an especially popular bait in the Southern states, where some bait shops keep hundreds of them in outside cages. (I heard the crickets from one such bait shop in Georgia a good half-mile before I got there.) I've never seen grasshoppers for sale, although this doesn't mean bait shops don't sell them.

You can gather grasshoppers in grassy, overgrown fields. The best time is early in the morning when they're still wet with dew or cold and less inclined to hop off. Look for them clinging onto stems and stalks and hiding under vegetation. Catching them by hand is possible (and fun), although you can cheat and use a fine-meshed net. Look for crickets in shady, bushy areas and under logs and rocks.

You can keep grasshoppers and crickets in most any non-airtight container with a lid, although one common problem is having half your bait supply jump out when you open it. This can be solved, at least when carrying only a dozen or so of the bugs, by carrying grasshoppers or crickets in an old long sock. Keep the sock closed by tying an overhand knot in it. When you need more bait, stick your hand into the sock and gently feel around for one. The sock will close around your wrist, preventing the critters from escaping.

Grasshopper and Cricket Rigging and Fishing

To bait your line with an insect, slide your hook under the collar of the insect, which is located just behind the head. A fine-wire hook is preferable, as these bugs are delicate. Don't insert the hook too deeply or you will kill it—a dead grasshopper or cricket is still good bait, but not as effective as a living, moving one. Add a split shot or two and cast out. In still water, you can add a bobber a foot or two up from the hook, to keep the bait near the surface, where they are most often found by fish. In moving water, don't use a bobber and cast at an angle up- and across-stream, letting the current carry the bug near the top of the water column. In either situation, set the hook as soon as you see the bobber move or feel a fish take the bait.

Frogs and Salamanders

These amphibians are good baits for bass, especially largemouth bass, and pickerel. Frogs can be gathered by hand, of course (ask any kid), and are easier to collect at night with a flashlight and a net. Look in shallow, weedy waters and grab them quickly. Don't bother with bullfrogs (unless you want a snack of their legs when you get home) because they're too big for bait. Instead, concentrate on the 2- to 4-inch length (without legs extended) frogs. You can keep them in a lidded container with wet vegetation.

Salamanders are found both in water and on land. You can spot the aquatic versions swimming in shallows, periodically resting on the bottom. Catch them by hand or with a net. Terrestrial salamanders frequent damp, wooded areas and often hide beneath rotted logs, which is where you should look for them. Use hand or net to catch them here as well. Keep aquatic salamanders in a minnow bucket; terrestrial salamanders in a container with some damp leaves.

Frog and Salamander Rigging and Fishing

Hook frogs through the lips, or if you're squeamish about it, strap the hook to the creature's body with a small rubber band. Always hook a salamander through the lips, from the bottom up. You won't need a sinker with a frog, though you might with a small salamander. Fish both in weedy areas.

Frogs will swim across the surface, and you should keep the frog from entering too deeply into thick vegetation, where it might foul your line. You'll know when a fish takes it from the commotion at the surface. Some fishermen are startled by the splash and try to set the hook too soon, often missing the fish. If you can, give the fish a three-count before you strike.

Let salamanders swim freely around the weeds. Because they are lip-hooked, you can retrieve them slowly and they will still look natural in the water. Reel in very slowly and pause occasionally. If you feel a fish, lower your rod tip (or put your reel in freespool) and let the fish run a bit before setting the hook.

Uncommon Baits

Some creatures are used as bait for specific species and/or in specific areas. Sometimes they are used because they are indigenous to a certain water, other times because they are the only bait in town, so to speak. These include

➤ *Hellgrammites.* These aquatic creatures could very well be named for their looks. Hellgrammites are the larval stage of the dobsonfly and are found most often in cold-water streams and lakes. A hellgrammite, which can grow to 4 inches, has three pairs of legs plus other leg-like appendages emanating from its segmented body. A pair of mandibles is quite powerful and can give you a heck of a pinch if you're not careful. They are ugly, but trout and bass in rivers love them. Some bait shops sell hellgrammites, but you can gather your own by seining in small brooks and creeks. Insert the hook under one of the segments and fish it like you would a crayfish.

➤ *Leeches.* Stuff of nightmares and B-movies, these bloodsuckers are popular forage for many gamefish species, and are especially used for walleyes. Many bait shops in walleye country (traditionally the upper Midwest) carry leeches, which you should hook through the mouth and fish as you would a night crawler.

➤ *Mealworms and grubs.* These small worm-like creatures are the larval stage of various insects, such as wasps. They are all small, typically no more than an inch long, and are good baits for panfish and trout. Another reason for their popularity is that they store easily and last a long time if kept very cold. They're also inexpensive. Rig and fish these baits as you would small worms.

➤ *Stinkbaits.* These are concoctions that you make at home and use for catfish and carp. The most simple stinkbait is a doughball, which in a pinch can be made by mixing up some flour and water. Some fishermen have elevated stinkbait-making into an art form, mixing cornmeal with substances such as anise, garlic, animal blood, and cheese (all proven carp- and catfish-attracting scents) to come up with the "perfect" bait.

To make your own, try mixing together any or all of the above ingredients, adding water slowly until it reaches a consistency that allows you to form a small, tight ball with it. When fishing, mold some of it completely around a hook, add a sinker to your line, cast out, and let it rest on the bottom. Eventually the scent will disperse in the water, and if a fish is hungry, it will follow that scent to the bait.

School Notes

Keep one rule in mind when fishing any live bait: It must appear natural to the fish. Worms don't stand still in moving water, minnows don't swim upside down, and crayfish don't splash across the surface of a lake. Your bait should look like a part of the environment.

Stinkbaits are also commercially prepared, and are one of many preserved baits you can purchase at a tackle shop, which is covered next.

Baits in a Bottle

There are two types of preserved baits: those that consist of once-living organisms, and those that don't.

➤ *Preserved minnows* can be purchased at many tackle shops. They come frozen, preserved in jars, or freeze-dried. While these are nowhere near as good as live or fresh minnows, they do catch those species that eat minnows, and they're certainly easier to handle and store, as they are already dead. You should hook preserved minnows through the lips, add some weight to your line, and retrieve them slowly after casting them out. Leeches and mealworms also come preserved, and should be fished in the same manner as fresh ones.

➤ *Salmon eggs* are popular baits for trout. They are usually sold in small jars and come plain (a pale yellow), tinted (fluorescent orange and red are two popular colors), and/or scented (cheese or anise, for example). Salmon eggs should be fished on, obviously enough, a salmon-egg hook, which is a short-shanked, gold-colored hook no larger than the egg itself. In moving water, add a split shot to your line and cast up- and across-stream, letting the egg drift with the current close to the bottom. In still water, use a bobber or let the egg sit on the bottom.

➤ *Pork rinds* are pickled strips of tough yet supple hog skin, cut in various shapes and colored in various hues and patterns. Used chiefly for largemouth bass, pickerel, and pike, pork rinds (sometimes called pork strips) undulate enticingly when slowly retrieved, and a skilled fisherman can make a pork rind look very much like a living creature. Because the rinds are so tough, they can be used over and over, even after a toothy fish has gnawed on it. Pork rinds are fun to fish in weedy areas on a weedless hook, as you can make it look like an injured minnow one moment and a distressed frog the next. Pork rinds are also used as trailers on some fishing lures (covered in the next chapter).

➤ *Stinkbaits* are also sold commercially. Some relatively new baits in this category, which previously was the sole court of carp and catfish anglers, are meant for other species. These moldable baits resemble nothing in nature but are designed to be attractive to specific species. Many of them are targeted toward trout fishermen, and are scented with ingredients that trout supposedly like. The actual ingredients are a trade secret, but they do catch fish. Fish these moldable baits as you would worms.

➤ *Fish scents* aren't baits themselves but are used in conjunction with many baits and lures. As with moldable baits, these scents—which you spray, drip, or smear onto your bait—contain certain ingredients that fish respond to. The theory is that your worm, say, is more likely to be found and eaten by a fish if you apply scent to it. Do they work? Maybe. I don't know if a trout will find a garlic-flavored worm more attractive than a plain one (to say nothing of the fact that the scent is bound to wash off sooner or later). But if there is one advantage to using scents, it's that it will hide or overcome a disagreeable odor that the angler might involuntarily get on the bait—gasoline, for instance, or even just perspiration.

Loose Lines

If you're out of bait and need some in a pinch, look in your kitchen. Salami, bologna, liverwurst, and marshmallows will catch stocked trout and some panfish as well. Catfish will eat pieces of hot dog and raw hamburger. And if you don't catch anything, you can always eat the bait.

The Least You Need to Know

➤ Worms are a good overall bait for many foraging species. They're simple to fish, inexpensive, and easy to obtain and keep yourself.

➤ Minnows, or baitfish, appeal to predatory species. They must cared for so they remain alive, which is how they should be fished.

➤ Crayfish, which are eaten by many species, must always be fished on or just above the bottom.

➤ Grasshoppers and crickets are good baits for trout, bass, and panfish. They should be fished as if they had just fallen into the water.

➤ Frogs and salamanders are eaten by bass, pickerel, and pike. Fish frogs on the surface; salamanders close to the bottom.

➤ Hellgrammites, leeches, mealworms, and grubs are good baits in certain locations for certain species.

➤ Commercially prepared baits vary widely in type and substance. They catch fish, but generally, the real thing is better.

Chapter 11

Lures: Virtual Reality to Fish

In This Chapter

➤ Feed them a spoon

➤ Lures that go round and round

➤ Plugging along

➤ Fishing with a hairpin

➤ The jig is down

➤ One word: plastics

A fishing *lure* is any inanimate object that can be used to catch a fish. Lures work by imitating the vibration, color, movement, or a combination of the three, of something a fish would eat. While a very few fishermen make their own lures, the vast majority are manufactured and sold in tackle shops, sporting-goods sections of department stores, and through mail-order warehouses. And it's a huge business: According to a 1991 survey conducted by the U.S. Fish and Wildlife Service, fishermen in the United States spent more than $621 million on fishing lures.

Such a potentially lucrative enterprise explains why there are so many lures on the market today—so many that even experienced fishermen can grow numb from poring over the selection. One recent fishing tackle catalog contains 99 pages of lures; most of them are designed to catch largemouth bass.

Obviously, you don't have to obtain one of everything. And it's difficult to suggest specific models, as there are so many out there. However, I do mention certain brand names on the following pages, only because these lures have worked well for me. So let's take a walk down the lure aisle, make a basic selection, and get you out of there before you have to apply for a second mortgage to pay for everything you think you need.

Spoons

Like the eating utensils, *spoons* are thin, rounded pieces of metal, but without the handle. Spoons are also called wobblers for their side-to-side movement in the water when retrieved.

Spoons come in two varieties: either polished on both sides, or colored on one side and polished on the other. Thus, the spoon reflects a lot of light, and flashes brightly in the water when retrieved, imitating a fleeing or distressed baitfish. The polished versions come in gold or silver; the colored versions come in a variety of hues, tones, and patterns. Spoons can feature one single hook welded solidly onto the underside (the concave side) of the spoon, or have a treble hook attached to a small ring that passes through a hole at the rear of the body, which is normally wider than the front. At the front is a hole, or another ring passing though a hole, onto which the fishing line is attached. On the single-hook versions (some of which are weedless), the line is tied to the eye of the attached hook. Some treble-hook spoons also feature a "skirt," either rubber "legs" or a length of hair (typically deer-tail hair; sometimes dyed in a bright color), tied to the treble hook for added color and attraction.

A spoon is a thin, rounded metal lure. Most feature a single treble hook.

Because of their density, spoons cast easily and accurately. They cut right through any wind present and can travel a good distance through the air. This weight also allows spoons to sink to the bottom quickly, although they can be fished at any depth.

Spoons will catch any fish that eat minnows: trout, bass, walleyes, pike, pickerel, muskellunge, and some catfish and panfish species. The particular spoon to use depends on the size of the fish you are after and the size of the prevalent baitfish in the water you are fishing. Spoons come in many different sizes, from ½-inch, ⅛-ounce bluegill sizes to 4½-inch, 1¼-ounce jobs for big pike and muskellunge. For panfish and trout in streams, go with the smaller sizes; bass, pickerel, and walleyes, the middle range; and for pike and muskellunge, the larger versions.

Spoons can be cast out and retrieved, or trolled behind a boat. Because they are heavy and sink quickly, you usually don't have to add weight to your line to keep the spoon at or near the bottom, where it belongs.

School Notes

All lures must move to catch fish because a lure exhibits "action" only when it is in motion. When fishing lures in still water, you should always keep the lure moving, whether by reeling in or by moving the boat via wind, oars, or motor.

Loose Lines

One of the oldest, and still among the most effective, spoons sold today is the red-and-white striped DarDevle (pronounced "daredevil"), manufactured by the Eppinger Company. With an elongated teardrop shape and a chrome-finished underside, and made in sizes from thumbnail to palm, this spoon has accounted for probably millions of fish for millions of anglers over the years. The DarDevle exhibits a peculiar side-to-side wobble that seems to attract fish. Although this spoon is now available in many different color combinations and patterns, the red-and-white version—for whatever reason—works well for most every species. No tackle box would be complete without one.

Spinners

A *spinner* is a lure of many parts. The base of a spinner is a thin wire shaft with a loop at the front, called the "eye" (just as one on a hook), which is where the fishing line is tied. A larger loop at the rear holds a hook, usually a treble hook. Some spinners

feature a skirt of squirrel-tail hair, either natural or dyed. The shaft features a body, which consists of colored beads, small rings, metal cylinders, or a combination of those items, to provide weight and attraction. Above the body is a clevis, which is a small C-shaped device, with the wire passing through both ends of the "C." Attached to the clevis via a hole in its top is a spinner blade: a flat, oblong-shaped piece of metal, shaped much like a spoon. The blade can be polished metal, painted, or appliquéd.

When a spinner is retrieved, the blade spins around the body of the spinner at a very fast rate of speed, emitting a great amount of vibration and flash, much like a baitfish in distress. Different shapes and thicknesses of the blades determine the rate of speed of the blade and how far away from the shaft it spins. Basically, long, thin, lightweight blades turn quickly and remain very close to the shaft, which decreases their water resistance and makes them preferable for use in moving water. Round-shaped heavy blades spin slowly and well away from the shaft, making these spinners best for stillwater use.

A spinner exhibits much flash and vibration in the water.

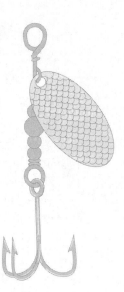

There are many variations on basic spinner design. Some don't have a clevis at all; the wire runs directly through the blade at its top. Some have two blades. Some have specially weighted bodies and/or blades. Some work in tandem with a second fish-attracting device. A good example of the latter is the Mepps Mino, which features a simulated, rubberlike silver-colored baitfish at the rear of the spinner. The combination of the flashy blade and the lifelike minnow body sometimes takes fish when other spinners won't.

Spinners come in various sizes, from $\frac{1}{12}$-ounce panfish spinners to $\frac{1}{2}$-ounce and bigger models designed for pike and muskies. Spinners catch all the predatory species, but if there is one place where spinners excel, it's in a trout stream. Because of the current, spinners start spinning as soon as they hit the water. A skilled angler can stand in one spot and fish the spinner throughout the entire water column downstream of him by casting up- and across-stream, keeping a tight line as the current moves the spinner down, and moving the rod back and forth while reeling in, sometimes pausing the retrieve when the spinner is in an area that may hold a fish, such as a deep pocket behind a rock or the "seam" between the current and still water near shore.

An unweighted spinner usually requires a sinker or two to keep it from fluttering up to the surface when retrieving, especially when fishing moving water.

Plugs

"Plug" is a term that once referred to a wooden, minnow-shaped lure. Now the term is used to refer to a whole family of lures made of hard plastic or wood that imitate all manner of baitfish, plus frogs, crayfish, salamanders, or small rodents such as mice. Most all plugs feature one, two, or three treble hooks, and vary in size from a bit more than an inch to 8 inches or so for freshwater use. How and where you fish the plug determines its specific category.

A *topwater plug* is one that floats both at rest and upon retrieval. Also called poppers or popping plugs, these imitate frogs, mice, or wounded baitfish splashing at the surface. Most topwater plugs are designed to catch largemouth bass, and are at their best when used on still, calm water near the shoreline, especially at dawn, dusk, and nighttime.

Two classic topwater lures are the Jitterbug and the Hula Popper. The Jitterbug has a round, oblong body with a wide metal lip at its front. When retrieved, the 'bug wobbles quickly from side to side, sending out small ripples and looking very much like a mouse doing a very poor job of swimming across the lake. The Hula Popper features a round, waisted body with a rubber-strand skirt and a large, slightly concave face.

School Notes

Gold and silver are the two basic choices in non-colored spoons and spinners. Which is better? Neither, although the general rule is to use silver in clear water and gold in silty or off-color water. Silver reflects better in clear, and gold matches the normal hue of baitfish in silty water.

Cautious Casts

Always use a swivel (or snap-swivel) on your line when fishing spinners. If you don't, your fishing line is sure to become twisted and kinked as the spinner rotates in the water. More on swivels in Chapter 12, "Yes, You Should Sweat the Small Stuff."

When pulled across the water, it resembles … well, I'm not sure what it resembles. But it looks like something very much alive and in trouble, as it splashes and gurgles its way back toward you.

A topwater plug, or popper. This one has a concave face, which makes a commotion when retrieved.

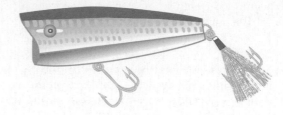

Topwater plugs are great fun to fish, because you can see the fish attack the lure, sometimes leaping out of the water to get it, other times rising directly beneath it and knocking it into the air, only to chase after it and hit it again. However, you must get the fish interested in the lure first. The most common mistake made by anglers using topwater lures is retrieving too fast. A minnow, frog, or rodent in distress acts with stops and starts, jerks and flutters. It doesn't go racing across the water like a miniature ski boat throwing up a wake. Topwater lures require patience and discipline to fish, because you must watch the lure at all times, and reel in only a little bit at a time, pausing often. One good way to fish a topwater lure is to cast it out to a likely area—say at the edge of a weedbed—and wait until all the ripples have practically disappeared. Then raise your rod and twitch the lure, once. Wait, and repeat. Then start retrieving, very slowly, taking only a couple turns of the reel handle before pausing again.

A *floater-diver plug*, as its name implies, floats at rest but dives beneath the surface when retrieved. Most floater-divers are minnow-shaped and feature a lip, which is a metal or plastic scoop-shaped device protruding forward from the bottom front of the lure. The lip allows the lure to dive and imparts action, making it vibrate, wiggle, or gyrate when retrieved. These lures work best in still water for largemouth and smallmouth bass, pickerel, pike, and larger panfish such as perch.

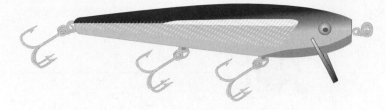

A floater-diver plug imitates a minnow. It floats at rest and dives when retrieved.

Floater-divers descend to various depths, depending on the model. The size of the lip determines how deep the lure will dive; the longer the lip, the deeper it will go. The Rapala Floater Minnow, for example, doesn't descend more than a foot or so at a normal retrieve. You can fish the Rapala like a topwater lure—cast it out and twitch it occasionally—then start retrieving, so it resembles a minnow trying to escape a predator. If you pause in mid-retrieve, it will float back up to the surface, where you can twitch it again. I've used this technique many times to catch largemouth bass in lakes and ponds.

A *crankbait* is a plug that dives relatively deep. Most float at rest like floater-divers (although some sink), and most have large lips that allow them to dive up to 20 feet (although some don't have lips). Most crankbaits exhibit a side-to-side wobbling action when retrieved, which simulates a baitfish.

A crankbait is designed to dive deep when retrieved. Some crankbaits, like this one, feature long lips.

Crankbaits are used most often for largemouth bass, though they will definitely catch smallmouth bass, walleyes, pickerel, northern pike, muskellunge, large trout in lakes, and even some catfish. As various crankbaits dive to various depths, a fisherman can outfit himself with crankbaits that will cover the entire water column, and thus be prepared to put a lure at any level. The Bomber line of crankbaits, for example, are available in models that dive to various depths in increments of 2 feet, and come in different color schemes and patterns.

A *stickbait,* or a *jerkbait,* is a plug that has no inherent action. The angler must impart action to the plug when retrieving it, by moving the rod tip side to side and/or up and down. Most stickbaits float, are large, and are designed for catching large species, such as northern pike and muskellunge.

Loose Lines

Some fishermen categorize all plugs—topwaters, floater-divers, divers, and stickbaits—as crankbaits. This has become accepted but is not really accurate, as a crankbait must be "cranked," or reeled in, for it to dive down.

Spinnerbaits and Buzzbaits

Also known as a hairpin lure because it faintly resembles a huge hairpin, a *spinnerbait* is a wire with a loop in its middle and the arms bent into a V-shape. At the end of the top arm is a spinner blade, like the kind found on spinners. It's attached to the arm via a swivel, which allows the large blade to rotate freely. At the end of the bottom arm is a hook, usually with a lead head for weight and adorned with a skirt or some other fish-attracting device. The fishing line is tied to the loop in the middle of the wire. Because the hook point rides up (in between the arms), spinnerbaits resist snagging in weeds better than many other lures.

Spinnerbaits are hairpin-shaped lures that exhibit a lot of flash and motion.

Spinnerbaits are often used by largemouth bass fishermen, although they will take northern pike and muskellunge. A popular technique is to retrieve the spinnerbait so that it rides just under the surface, creating a bulge in the surface tension. What it actually imitates is hard to pinpoint; spinnerbaits are comparatively large lures. But fish, especially bass, sometimes hit them ferociously (I once caught a largemouth bass that was only an inch larger than the spinnerbait it hit). My guess is that the combination of noise and flash created by the spinner blade, and the color and motion of the skirt on the bottom arm, resembles a large, ungainly baitfish. Maybe it seems like two minnows, and the fish is fooled into ambushing the one that seems to lag behind. Whatever, a spinnerbait certainly provokes fish, especially largemouths, into striking.

A *buzzbait* is similar to a spinnerbait except that it has a propeller-type device on the upper arm instead of a spinner blade. The upper arm, which is bent so that it's parallel to the bottom arm, passes through the center of the flashy propeller blades, which rotate very quickly when retrieved. Another popular lure for largemouth bass, the buzzbait is at its best when the angler retrieves it fast enough for the propeller to actually break the surface of the water. It makes quite a racket (hence the name) and sometimes will aggravate a bass into striking. (If it doesn't aggravate the fisherman into cutting it off first.)

Loose Lines

Spinnerbaits and buzzbaits come in many forms, with manufacturers seemingly trying to outdo each other with regard to design and components. Multiple blades and propellers, unique shapes of same, different upper- and lower-arm lengths, outlandish colors, and names that imply surefire effectiveness (should you buy the KillerKing Pro Deluxe Trophy Professional Model, or the BassBuster SecretSpin With Gyro Blades Tournament Model?) are some examples. Some of these takeoffs on original design work, and some don't. When in doubt, I suggest you choose conservatively.

Jigs

A *jig*, or a leadhead, is nothing more than a hook with a ball of lead behind the eye, yet it's probably the most versatile lure around because it can be fished in countless ways.

The jig is a relatively simple lure, but is so versatile it can catch most any species in any water.

The jig head comes in many sizes and shapes: from ⅓₂-ounce to those weighing several ounces, with heads that are round, oval, bullet-shaped, flat at the front, teardrop-shaped, cylindrical, and other forms. The shape of the head isn't very important, although a few are designed for specific purposes (the shad dart, for example, has a flat, angled face, which is supposed to make it dart in the current). The head is usually painted in white, red, black, yellow, or some other color. Many jigs sport a skirt made of bucktail or rubber legs, also available in several colors. The eye of the hook comes out of the top of the lead head.

School Notes

The most common mistake made by beginning anglers when using lures, especially jigs, is retrieving too fast. Lures must be kept in motion, but most fish won't bother to chase a lure that's speeding by.

Jigs are designed to be fished on the bottom. They have no inherent action, so the angler must impart movement to one when fishing. This is typically done by lifting the rod tip in slow, short movements while retrieving, called jigging. This makes the jig dart and hop across the bottom, resembling a minnow, a crayfish, or some other bottom-dwelling creature.

Jigs can be fished plain or with the addition of a natural or artificial bait as an enhancement. Common jig "sweeteners" include a minnow, hooked through both lips; a pork rind, hooked at the wider, thicker end; a night crawler or a leech, hooked once through the "head" (the larger end); or a plastic worm, hooked the same as a night crawler. Some plastic lures are designed specifically to adorn jigs. These are known by various names—grubs, twist-tails, flip-tails, trailers—and come in many shapes, colors, and sizes. Most of them are in the shape of a worm or a minnow but feature a flattened tail, which vibrates or twitches when moving through the water. This adds action to the jig, so all the angler has to do is reel in to attract a fish; no jigging necessary. These also allow a jig to be fished anywhere in the water column, not just on the bottom.

Jigs will catch almost every species of fish in any type of water. Tailor your jig selection to the size of the forage found in the water you're fishing—in general, $\frac{1}{32}$- to $\frac{1}{8}$-ounce for panfish and trout; $\frac{1}{8}$- to $\frac{3}{8}$-ounce for bass and walleyes; and larger sizes for larger species such as northern pike.

Plastic Lures

These are the fastest-growing segment of lure development. Soft plastic can be formed into just about any shape, can take any color, and is inexpensive when mass produced. Most important is that soft plastic feels very much like a living thing, which decreases the possibility of a fish rejecting—spitting out—a lure.

Plastic lures are made to imitate just about every forage available: worms and minnows of all sizes, crayfish, leeches, insects, frogs, salamanders, slugs, snakes, and others. These should be fished just as the real thing would be fished, except that they must be kept moving. Some imitate creatures that don't exist (thankfully, as some plastic lures are quite ghastly, with weird appendages, gigantic eyeballs, and other features). As a whole, though, they are very good at catching fish. But one of the oldest plastic lures is also one of the best lures today for catching largemouth bass: the plastic worm.

Fished properly, a plastic worm will slowly slither and gyrate along the bottom. Whether a bass actually takes it for a worm, a small snake, a slug, or a leech is anyone's guess. But if a bass is in the area and is in a feeding mood, chances are good the bass will hit it. The key, though, is if it's *fished properly*. A plastic worm must be fished *slowly*, staying on or near the bottom at all times. Sometimes a bass will grab the worm and run off, other times it will mouth the worm tentatively. The plastic-worm fisherman must keep a tight line to feel delicate takes, yet have the patience to cast out, let the worm sink completely to the bottom, and retrieve it slowly. At times one cast can take two minutes or more to complete.

Plastic worms can be purchased pre-rigged (already hooked and ready to be tied onto your fishing line) or plain. Pre-rigged versions offer the advantage of numerous hooks along the length of the worm, but those hooks inhibit the worm's natural action in the water and tend to snag on weeds easily. I prefer to rig the worm myself, which is easily done and also makes the worm extremely weed-resistant.

The most popular plastic-worm-rigging method is called the Texas rig, named for the state where it supposedly originated. Here's how to do it:

1. Put a $\frac{1}{8}$- to $\frac{3}{8}$-ounce—depending on the weight of your rod and reel—sliding sinker on your main line. (More on sliding sinkers in Chapter 12.)

2. Tie a long-shanked No. 2 to 4/0 hook to your line, depending on the size of the plastic worm you are using (a 6-inch worm works well with a 3/0 hook). Specially designed "worm hooks" feature a long shank with two 90° turns just below the eye.

117

3. Insert the hook point through the top of the head of the worm. Bring the point out of the worm about ¼-inch below the head.

4. Pull the hook through the worm until the hook eye is just protruding from the worm head.

5. Holding the worm in one hand and the hook in your other hand, turn the hook so the point faces the body of the worm. Hold the hook by the shank and lift the worm up a tiny bit. Then insert the hook point into the body of the worm, angling the point toward the front of the worm. Don't push the hook all the way through.

6. Hold your fishing line above the worm. It should hang straight and appear natural, with no bends or kinks. If the worm is bent, pull the hook point out of the worm and insert it in a different spot.

A Texas-rigged plastic worm.

Such a rig accomplishes three things: First, it keeps the worm near the bottom, where it belongs. Second, with the hook point buried in the worm, it resists snagging on weeds (the hook point passes easily through the worm when a fish grabs it and you set the hook). Third, it allows the fish to take the worm without feeling the weight of the sinker, which otherwise might cause it to drop the worm.

Some plastic worms are designed to float or remain suspended above the bottom. These worms work well when fished in and around weeds, especially when rigged Texas-style.

If you're fishing with a Texas-rigged plastic worm and you feel a fish hit it, don't set the hook right away. Wait a beat—two seconds or so—to allow the bass to take the worm, and the hook, totally into its mouth. Then lift your rod sharply.

School Notes

Plastic worms come in a rainbow of colors and color combinations, but proven colors are purple, black, blue, and a motor-oil hue. It's wise to carry some worms that have specks of glitter in them for use in muddy or tinted water.

Loose Lines

How slow should you fish a plastic worm? It's probably impossible to fish one too slowly. One summer day on a New York lake, I cast out a black plastic worm and set the rod down in the boat to take a bite of a sandwich. Hungry, I wound up eating the whole thing. When I finally picked up the rod I was shocked to feel something heavy on the end of the line. Eventually I brought a foot-long bass to boatside. While putting your rod down with line out isn't wise—a fish could grab the bait and pull your rod into the water, or your line could twist around a snag by wind or current—this does prove that fishing fast usually isn't productive.

The Least You Need to Know

➤ Spoons, or wobblers, are made of shiny metal and imitate baitfish. They can be cast far, can be fished deeply, and their various sizes take a variety of fish.

➤ Spinners feature a thin blade that revolves around a wire shaft. Spinners emit vibration as well as flash. Spinners will catch many species of fish; small sizes are especially good for trout.

➤ Plugs imitate baitfish, amphibians, or rodents. Topwater lures float, floater-divers float at rest and dive when retrieved, and crankbaits dive deeply when retrieved. They all exhibit action in the water and will take a variety of species. Anglers must impart action to stickbait plugs, which are designed for large fish.

➤ Spinnerbaits and buzzbaits emit a large amount of flash and vibration. These are popular lures for largemouth bass and members of the pike family.

➤ Jigs can be used to catch any species. They are designed to be fished on the bottom and don't have inherent action. Natural baits or plastic attractors can be put on jigs, sometimes allowing them to be fished anywhere in the water column.

➤ Plastic lures come in all kinds of shapes and sizes. Most imitate the natural forage of fish. The plastic worm is probably the best plastic lure on the market and excels at catching largemouth bass.

Chapter 12

Yes, You Should Sweat the Small Stuff

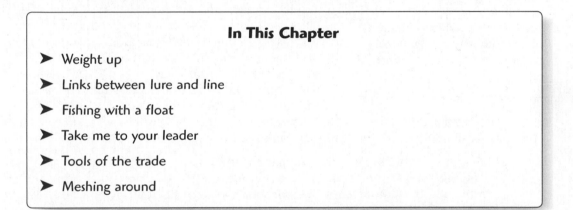

In This Chapter

➤ Weight up

➤ Links between lure and line

➤ Fishing with a float

➤ Take me to your leader

➤ Tools of the trade

➤ Meshing around

Successful fishing so often depends on paying attention to details: the proper size of the hook, the correct strength of line, the best choice of lure color. Likewise, owning and using some minor tackle accessories can make the difference between a mediocre catch and an excellent one. These "little things" such as sinkers, snap-swivels, and bobbers cost just pennies but have value far beyond their purchase price. An 89-cent bag of split shot may not look as appealing as a shiny, beautifully crafted crankbait with trophy-fish-catching promises emblazoned on its display box, but in the long run, those two-dozen little lead balls probably will help you catch more fish than the crankbait will.

Weights

Sinkers, called *weights* by some, allow a fishermen to present a bait or lure deeper in the water than if no weight were used. There are different kinds of sinkers, and all have different applications. *Split shot* are small, round lead balls with a slot cut about halfway through. Originally made from lead shotgun pellets, split shot range from BB size to pea size. You use a split shot by pinching it directly onto your fishing line with your fingers or pliers, generally about a foot or so above your hook or lure.

Cautious Casts

Never use your teeth to pinch split shot onto your fishing line. Besides the possibility of harming your tooth enamel, you don't want to risk ingesting lead particles.

Split shot are ideal sinkers because of their versatility. They are easy to put on your line, so you can add or remove them in seconds. And because they're so small and come in different sizes, you can always find the perfect combination (by adding multiple split shot to your line) to put your bait or lure exactly where you want it. For example, when fishing a trout stream with worms, you need just the right amount of weight to keep your bait bouncing naturally along the bottom. Too little weight and the worm will rush downstream close to the surface; too much weight and the worm will just sit in one spot. With split shot, you can easily find the right amount of weight to keep that worm moving around down where trout will see it. Because water depth and current speed vary tremendously throughout the length of a stream, the angler can quickly adjust the number of split shot for each situation: one or two small split shot for shallow riffles, two or three large split shot for deep pools, and so on.

Some split shot—and to me, the only kind worth buying—come with a pair of small tabs on the opposite side from the line slot. Squeezing the tabs together opens the jaws and allows you to remove the split shot from your line quickly and easily; then, you can reuse it later. You can buy split shot in small sealable plastic bags or, again my choice, in a palm-sized plastic dispenser that holds four different sizes of split shot.

Standard split shot (top) and removable split shot (bottom).

Sliding sinkers have a hole drilled completely through their middle, and are strung onto the fishing line like beads. Because the line slides through them, a fish is not as likely to feel the sinker's weight and drop the bait. There are two basic styles of sliding sinkers: *Egg sinkers* are named after their shape; they weigh ⅛ ounce and up. These are good for fishing with live bait, such as night crawlers or baitfish, on the bottom of a lake or pond. The sinker stays on the bottom, and when a fish takes the bait, the fisherman sees or feels his line move. *Bullet sinkers* are conelike, as their name implies, and are designed for use with lures, such as plastic worms. Their smooth, streamlined shape resists snagging on weeds.

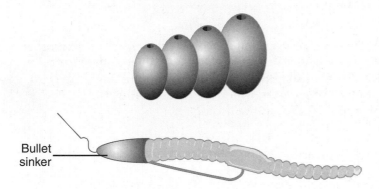

Bullet
sinker

Sliding sinkers come in two basic forms. The egg sinker (top) is ideal for fishing live bait, and the bullet sinker (bottom) works best when using lures, such as this plastic worm.

Casting or *dipsey sinkers* are used for fishing bait on the bottom, usually in deep water. These bell-shaped sinkers weigh ⅛ ounce and up. Fishing line is tied to or goes through a wire eye protruding from the top, which swivels freely to prevent line twist. A dipsey sinker is advantageous in rock-strewn bottoms, where its rounded profile is less likely to snag.

The casting or dipsey sinker has a swivel eye to prevent line twist.

Trolling sinkers are designed to be tied into the fishing line via an improved clinch knot at each end (you must cut the line to tie it in) a couple of feet above the lure or bait. These sinkers keep the offering deep in the water when slowly motoring or rowing. Most trolling sinkers are cylindrical in shape and feature bead-chain swivels on either end, to which the line is tied (see the next section for details on swivels). Some have a triangular keel to keep them straight in the water and reduce line twist.

123

Trolling sinkers are tied into the line. Some are cylindrical (top), others have a keel to reduce line twist (bottom).

Other, less common sinker styles include *walking sinkers*, which are shaped like a shallow "L" and are used to slowly move live baits directly across the bottom; *grip* or *clinch* sinkers which are cylindrical in shape with tabs at either end that clamp onto the fishing line; and *lead strips* or *strip sinkers*, which are matchlike or stringlike in shape and can be wrapped or formed around the fishing line.

Snaps, Swivels, and Snap-Swivels

Many fishing situations call for a connection between line and line or line and lure. That's where snaps and swivels come in. These tiny steel devices, which come in brass, silver, or matte-black finishes, are so inexpensive that even high-quality ones cost 25 cents or so in freshwater-fishing sizes. Yet they are integral to successful, hassle-free fishing. You can use a improved clinch knot to tie them to your line.

Snaps are tiny diaper-pin-like devices that simplify changing lures. Tie one to the end of your line and it's a simple matter to open the snap, put on a plug, close the snap, and begin casting. You can change lures in seconds, without having to cut your line and tie a new knot each time. Snaps also make it easy to change sinker weights quickly.

However, snaps should never be used to attach a baited hook to a line. The presence of a metal snap—a large object compared to the thin shaft of a fishhook—dangling off the eye of the hook and rubbing against it can look unnatural to a fish. And any lures that move slowly through the water (plastic worms and jigs, for instance) that fish might inspect closely before hitting should be tied directly to the line. Otherwise, snaps are fine—with one other exception.

School Notes

If you're fishing with bait and your sinkers are constantly getting snagged on the bottom, re-tie your hook but don't cut off the tag end of the line. Attach your split shot to that loose end. If you get snagged, the sinkers will simply slide off the line. Better to lose one or two split shot than hook, line, and sinker.

The blade on a spinner rotates so quickly around the wire shaft that inertia causes the entire spinner to turn. This effect, however, can twist a fishing line to a point where it becomes unusable unless countered. When using a spinner, therefore, it's important to always tie a *snap-swivel* to your line and attach the spinner to that. A snap-swivel is a snap that is attached to a swivel, which consists of a pair of metal line eyes that rotate freely, without kinking or torquing. The swivel absorbs the twisting motion without affecting the line, and the snap simplifies changing spinners.

Sometimes it's necessary to use just a *swivel*. For instance, when fishing for toothy species such as pike or pickerel with comparatively light line, you may have to use a leader made of heavier line that the fish can't bite through (more on leaders later in this chapter). In that situation it's wise to tie a swivel in between the line and leader, because the light line has a tendency to wrap and curl itself around the heavy leader, especially when using a live baitfish that constantly darts throughout the water. Also, when using quick-rotating spinners, a snap-swivel may not provide enough line-twist resistance. In such a case, or if you observe your line kinking near the spinner, it's a good idea to tie a swivel into the line a foot or so above the snap-swivel.

Snaps, swivels, and snap-swivels vary in design and quality. Ball-bearing swivels, for example, are stronger than barrel swivels. Because these devices don't cost much to begin with, it's wise to buy the best; that is, the most expensive.

School Notes

Snaps and swivels come in various lengths. The rule of thumb is to go with the smallest size that is still effective for the situation. A too-small snap-swivel, for example, may not completely eliminate line twist. Buy and carry several sizes.

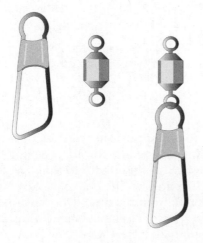

From left: snap, swivel, and snap-swivel.

Bobbers

A *bobber*, or *float*, is a device that attaches to a fishing line and floats on the water's surface, used to indicate a strike. A bobber is also used to put a bait at a particular depth. When a fish takes the bait, the bobber quivers, jerks, or goes completely underwater. And whether you are fishing for bluegills or bass, perch or pike, there are few things as exciting in fishing as seeing that bobber move around and dip beneath the surface—proof that you are a successful angler.

Bobbers are usually painted in two different colors. The portion of the bobber that floats above the water is usually white, making it easy to see and keep track of. The bottom part is typically red or some other contrasting color so the angler can easily determine when a fish is mouthing or taking the bait. Some bobbers, notably the larger versions, come weighted to ease casting.

The basic *ball bobber* is a round plastic float with recessed hooks on the top and the bottom. The angler runs the fishing line through both hooks, which are exposed by depressing the spring-loaded button on the top. Ball bobbers are good all-around bobbers. In large sizes they are especially suited for use with large baitfish, such as shiners or suckers.

A basic ball bobber. Recessed hooks, which clip onto the line, are at the top and bottom.

A *slip bobber* is a plastic or hard-foam round or pear-shaped float with a hole drilled through the middle. The angler runs the fishing line through the hole, and holds it in place with a tapered wooden or plastic stick inserted into the hole. Some slip bobbers are cut vertically through to the line hole, so the bobber can be attached and removed easily (without removing the hook from the line). One advantage of a slip bobber is the ability to fish baits in deep water with a bobber. For instance, if you want to put a minnow near the bottom in 20 feet of water, the bobber has to be about 19 feet up from your hook—and it's impossible to cast with that much line hanging down from your rod tip. With a slip bobber, though, you can simply attach a bobber stop, a little bead, 19 feet up from your hook. The bobber stop must be small enough to fit through your rod's guides, but be larger than the line hole in the bobber. Reel it directly onto your reel and place the slip bobber, minus the tapered stick, onto your line. Bait up and cast. The minnow will go 19 feet down and stay there, because the bobber stop will stop line from flowing through the bobber.

A *pencil bobber* is a long, thin float with a small hook at one end. When a fish takes the bait, the pencil stands up. Pencil bobbers are good when using small baits, such as red worms, and when fishing for small or delicately biting fish. Large pencil bobbers are also useful when fishing in windy or choppy conditions because they are more visible when a fish strikes.

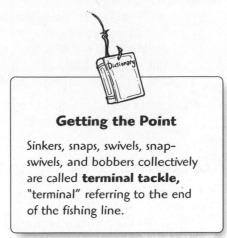

Getting the Point

Sinkers, snaps, swivels, snap-swivels, and bobbers collectively are called **terminal tackle,** "terminal" referring to the end of the fishing line.

There are many takeoffs and improvements on these three basic styles of bobbers, such as bobbers that incorporate a small light for easier visibility. Improved shapes, better bobber stops, and other features mark improvement in this area. However, no matter what kind of bobber you use, it's important to *always* be aware of the depth of the water where you are fishing. Generally you want your bait just above the bottom (or just above the top of any weeds growing on the bottom). If you set your bobber 3 feet above your hook and you wind up fishing in 20 feet of water, you probably won't get the attention of any fish in the area.

Leaders

A *leader* is a short length (1 or 2 feet in most freshwater situations) of heavy fishing line or wire tied to the end of the main line on a rod and reel. Leaders serve one of two purposes: to prevent break-offs by sharp-toothed fish; or to provide a length of clear line when using braided or heavy line that certain species in certain waters would see.

Wire leaders for use in fresh water run from 6 inches to more than a foot in length. Some leaders are nylon-coated, making them easier to handle and less subject to abrasion and kinking. Some also come with a swivel on one end and a snap-swivel on the other, which prevents line twist and simplifies lure changing. Anglers who fish for northern pike use wire leaders quite often.

In situations where a wire leader would be seen by the fish, such as in low, clear water, a length of heavy monofilament can be used instead of wire. Such "shock leaders" are used when fishing for pickerel, northern pike, muskellunge, and some large species of catfish. (Wire leaders and shock leaders are used extensively in salt water, which is covered in Chapter 21, "Tackle for the Brine.") Shock leaders also withstand abrasion from gill slits, fins, submerged rocks, and other sharp objects that the line might contact when casting or playing a fish. Shock leaders are easily tied to the main line via a surgeon's knot (see Chapter 8, "It's All on the Line").

Leaders are also used when flyfishing, although the function is entirely different in that arena. See Chapter 16, "Assembling a Flyfishing Outfit," for details.

Clippers, Pliers, and Other Important Tools

Some pocket tools are absolutely necessary to fish effectively. Primary among all the tools are clippers, which are nothing more than fingernail clippers, and are used to cut fishing line when changing hooks or lures and to trim excess fishing line after tying knots. Some clippers are made especially for fishing use and come with little accessories, such as miniature screwdrivers and bottle openers. You don't need a special fishing version, but it is wise to buy a solid model with sharp jaws, because you'll be using it quite often.

Pliers are also handy fishing tools and perform many chores, such as crimping on split shot, removing split shot, tightening loose line-tie eyes on lures, bending down barbs on hooks, and, of course, removing hooks from fish. Long-nose pliers are best for this last function, especially when removing hooks from sharp-toothed species or from any fish that have swallowed the hook. Some special fishing pliers are the long-nosed type. They typically feature non-slip handles and have a line-cutting device built into the jaws, eliminating the need to carry clippers (although I carry clippers and pliers anyway). Some are also curved at the tip, to aid in removing hooks.

De-hookers sometimes work better than pliers to remove hooks, especially deeply embedded hooks. They come in various shapes and designs. The simplest de-hooker is a long, narrow plastic rod with a slot at the end. The slot allows you to follow the fishing line down the fish's gullet to the hook. Other de-hookers are plier-like in function, but are pistol-shaped and have an extremely long, narrow "barrel" with tiny, powerful jaws at the end. It's wise to carry de-hookers when fishing for large species.

Fishing knives aren't used very often when actually fishing. Instead, these blades come into play afterward, when cleaning or filleting fish for the table (detailed in Chapter 29, "In the Pan or On the Wall?"). However, it's a good idea to take a knife with you, as

School Notes

When using clippers to trim excess line from a knot, don't clip too closely. Sometimes a knot won't pull completely tight until a lot of pressure is put on it—such as when fighting a fish—and the knot might come loose if you clipped that tag end tight. I leave $1/16$- to $1/8$-inch on the knot, depending on the line strength.

one will serve as a backup for clippers. Knives are also handy for chores that are not directly related to your tackle but are often required when fishing, such as cutting anchor line, opening a lure package, or halving a sandwich. I always pack a knife when fishing, because I often wind up using it for *some* reason.

Hook sharpeners, or hook hones, are made of a rough, rock-like material in the shape of a bar or a rod. They typically feature a shallow, narrow groove in which the point of the hook is moved back and forth in order to sharpen it. Hook sharpeners are inexpensive—five dollars will get you a good one—and they're easy to use; sharpening one hook takes 10 seconds or so.

Loose Lines

I guess it was only a matter of time before the Swiss army knife people came up with a model for fishermen. The one I have, made by Wenger, features a blade, a scissors, a hook sharpener, two screwdrivers (handy for tightening reel parts), an awl, a fish scaler (which I never use), a rudimentary hook remover, a file, a bottle opener, a can opener, tweezers, and a few other tools that I'm still figuring out. Although the knife really won't do everything, it's a handy tool that I've used plenty of times.

Landing Nets

If you don't want to risk losing a fish, you have to bring a landing let. Not only do landing nets offer a much better chance of successfully catching a fish, they also provide a safe method of removing a fish from the water and unhooking it, rather than letting the fish flop around on the ground or in the boat, where it could break the line, throw the hook, make a mess, and/or possibly hurt you (an errant fin or tooth could catch you). A net also allows you to safely capture and unhook a fish that you intend to release, for the same reasons.

Landing nets come in various sizes, with the large-hooped, long-handled version designed for large species such as northern pike and muskellunge. For smaller species such as trout, a short-handled net does the job adequately. Techniques for using a net will be covered in the next chapter.

The Least You Need to Know

➤ Sinkers, or weights, help keep your bait or lure at the desired depth in the water.

➤ Snaps are used to quickly attach and remove lures from fishing line. Swivels help reduce line twist. Snap-swivels do both.

➤ Bobbers, or floats, are used when fishing with bait. They indicate when a fish has taken the bait, and also serve to keep bait off the bottom, when necessary.

➤ Wire leaders keep toothy fish from biting off the hook or lure. Monofilament leaders do the same and are used when fish might see the wire.

➤ Clippers, pliers, de-hookers, knives, and hook sharpeners are basic and necessary hand tools.

➤ A landing net is necessary whenever you don't want to risk losing a fish.

Part 3

To Catch a Fish

It's time to get out of the classroom (or tackle shop) and put all your knowledge about fish, waters, and tackle to good use. In this section, you'll learn the best areas to cast to and how to hook a fish, play it, bring it to hand, and either keep it or put it back.

If you turned to this chapter first because you want to go out and start fishing right away, go back and read Chapter 4, "Emergency Fishing Guide." That will explain the basics of the activity. The chapters in this part go into detail of all that's covered in that chapter.

Chapter 13

On the Water

In This Chapter

➤ Lakes and ponds: fishing in still water

➤ Rivers and streams: currently speaking

➤ Do you have an attitude problem?

➤ Using lures that do it all

➤ Trolling: castless fishing

➤ Lures that need a helping hand

A good fisherman is like a master French chef: Both know that success depends largely on presentation. I happen to love *escargot*, but I doubt if I'd find the little creatures very appealing if they were served to me on white bread with ketchup for breakfast. Likewise, even an excellent bait or lure for a particular species will be ignored if it's not presented well and in the proper area. In this chapter, you'll learn how and where to make your offerings look like the makings of a five-course meal at a four-star restaurant.

Finding Fish in Lakes and Ponds

All fish relate to structure, whether it's something they (and sometimes you) can see, like rocks or weeds, or something felt, like water temperature. You have to figure out what structure the fish are partial to on a particular day, and then you have to put your lure there. It's called "reading the water," and it's not an exact science. But there are certain recognized areas that fish like, and through trial and error (and, with hope, not too much of the latter) you can eventually find fish. Here's what to look for in all still waters, from ponds to reservoirs, and how to fish them:

➤ *Weeds.* Aquatic weeds provide shelter and shade, which is why fish like them. Some weeds grow all the way to the surface, such as lily pads; others may just rise to a foot or so off the bottom. All are worth fishing, especially in waters that hold panfish, largemouth bass, pickerel, and northern pike. If you're using bait or lures, fish next to emerged weeds. Cast baits, such as minnows, right to the edge of the weedbed, and leave them there. Cast lures to the edge of the weeds and retrieve them both along the edge and back toward open water. If the weeds aren't dense, you can fish a weedless lure right in them. Spoons, topwater plugs, spinnerbaits, and plastic worms are all good lures to use in emerged weedbeds.

Baits and lures should be fished just above submerged weeds. Use a bobber to keep bait close to but not right in the vegetation. Fish floater-divers, crankbait plugs, spoons, and spinnerbaits directly over the weeds. If the weeds aren't too thick, fish plastic worms and weedless plugs right in the thick of them.

➤ *Trees.* Look for live trees with crowns that hang low over the water and fish any bait or lure beneath them. Begin casting below the outward edge of the crown and work your way in. If the tree trunk itself is submerged, cast toward it, as fish, especially largemouth bass, perch, and panfish, will seek refuge in the root system.

Fallen trees, both partially and totally submerged, also harbor fish. Cast baits and lures along the trunk. Work plastic worms and weedless plugs in the branches. Some reservoirs have submerged standing trees, long dead. These "stickups" are the remnants of a forest and are fish magnets. Work all baits and lures carefully around through them.

➤ *Points.* Ridges and other land features that angle sharply down to a lake often continue sloping down beneath the surface, usually coming to a finger-like point some way into the water. Many species, such as largemouth and small-mouth bass, northern pike, walleyes, and muskellunge, like these structures be-cause they offer quick access from deep water to bait-filled shallows. Cast lures to the edges of these points, beginning shallow and working progressively deeper. Use whatever bait is appropriate to the species, and cast topwater and shallow-running floater-divers close to shore, switching to crankbaits, plastic worms, and jigs as you fish farther out.

➤ *Dropoffs.* These are sharply angled bottoms where the depth of the water changes from shallow to deep very quickly. All fish like dropoffs because, like points (which are actually a kind of dropoff), they offer easy access to shallow water. Look for dropoffs by searching for similar land features: a sharply sloped bank, for example, or a rocky bluff. Chances are this geographic shape continues beneath the surface. As when fishing points, use all baits appropriate to the species you are after. Note that you may have to add a fair amount of weight to get your bait to the bottom. Use lures that go deep: plastic worms, crankbaits, and jigs. Jigs are especially good to use around dropoffs, as they can be "walked" down all edges of the slope.

➤ *Tributaries.* Brooks, creeks, or streams entering a lake usually bring cool, oxygenated water, and sometimes forage such as insects and baitfish. Trout, smallmouth bass, northern pike, and other gamefish will gather near tributaries, especially during warm weather. Use worms, minnows, floater-diver plugs, spinners, spoons, crankbaits, and jigs.

➤ *Boat docks and other on-water structures.* Like weeds, boat docks (and boat houses, piers, pilings, and so on) provide shade and shelter, and are used by many species, especially panfish, largemouth bass, and pickerel. Cast all appropriate baits and topwater lures, floater-divers, spoons, and plastics worms right next to the structure, even under it if possible.

➤ *Submerged humps and islands.* You can't always see these (except in ultra-clear water), but they can be found when using a boat equipped with a depthfinder, which is a sonar device that creates a map of the bottom, on either paper or an electronic screen. All fish relate to underwater humps, especially on otherwise barren bottoms, because they offer shelter and usually harbor forage. Fish these humps with weighted baits, plastic worms, crankbaits, and jigs—anything that will get down to the hump.

School Notes

If you begin catching fish around a particular structure—say, smallmouths near rocky points or walleyes near dropoffs—search out similar structures and concentrate on them. Fish prefer some structures to the exclusion of others on some days.

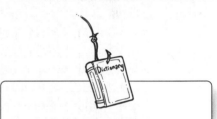

Getting the Point

Fishfinder is a general term for a sonar unit that marks fish as well as maps the bottom. These electronic units are great for pinpointing fish when on a boat, but you have to learn how to use them, they're not simple, and they don't put fish in the boat for you. They begin at $100 and go way up from there, and are worth the cost if you already own a boat.

Finding Fish in Rivers and Streams

Like still waters, moving waters have different types of structures. Some are tangible, such as rocks and shoals. Other types have to do with the current. A few types consist of both. Here's what to look for:

➤ *Holes or pools.* Any deep section in a stream or a river will hold fish. Holes offer shade, shelter (darkness), and cooler temperatures. Trout, walleyes, bass, catfish, and most other moving-water species will congregate in holes or pools where the current isn't as strong. Use weighted baits and whatever lures will get close to bottom: weighted spinners, spoons, crankbaits, jigs. Cast to the upstream side of the hole and let the current take your offering down and in.

➤ *Undercut banks.* If the water close to shore is very deep, cast your bait or lure right next to the bank. Many fish like to hide underneath a bank, which typically is overgrown with tree roots. These fish—trout, bass, catfish—stay hidden, out the current, and will dart out to take food as it passes by. Use bait, spinners, spoons, and jigs.

➤ *Current obstructions.* These can be anything from a rock the size of a toaster, to a tree that has fallen across the flow, to a piling for an interstate highway bridge. It doesn't matter exactly what it is—as long as it obstructs the current, a pocket of quiet water will exist behind it, on the downstream side—and fish will locate there, out of the current. Sometimes the pockets are so small that they're hardly noticeable, so it pays to fish small creeks carefully, casting to every rock large enough to put a dent in the flow. On large rivers, concentrate on abutments, pilings, even small islands. Cast your bait to the upstream side of the obstruction and let the current take it past, or right into, the pocket water. You can fish lures—spinners, spoons, and crankbaits—in the same manner, but be sure to retrieve them back through the pocket water.

➤ *Seams.* These are one of the most difficult structures to identify in moving waters, yet they are one of the most effective to fish. A seam is an extremely narrow section of water that exists between two currents of different speeds. Fish like seams because they can rest out of the current, but dart into it to grab forage flowing by. Seams exist downstream of large current obstructions, where the main flow is directly next to the pocket water. Seams also exist where the main current flows next to an eddy, which is a small backwards-flowing current, usually near shore. (Eddies occur when part of the main current hits a large obstruction connected to shore, follows that obstruction, and circles back to the main flow.) Fish seams by casting your bait or lure into the main flow, letting the current take it naturally into the seam. Retrieve lures back through the seam.

➤ *Bars and shoals.* Gravel bars and submerged shoals break the current. They also have wide, deep sections behind them where fish will congregate. To fish these structures, you must let your bait or lure sink naturally into the deep water and let the current take it to the fish. Cast upstream of the bar or, in the case of bars or shoals that break the surface, to its downstream edge. Sometimes you may have to cast your offering right on top of the shoal and pull it lightly into the current.

➤ *Riffles.* Many rivers and streams have riffles, which are shallow, rocky sections marked by quickly moving water (or at least faster than in other sections). Riffles draw fish, especially trout and smallmouth bass, because they offer numerous sheltered areas, and all that moving water brings a lot of forage through. Riffles are best fished with baits, spinners, and spoons. Cast to all sections; look for miniature seams, pocket waters, and shoals. Also fish sections immediately below riffles—the water has become highly oxygenated in these areas.

➤ *Dams.* The downstream side of dams is an excellent place to fish. Resembling lakes with a current, these "tailwaters" are deep, cool, well oxygenated, and provide abundant forage. Fish the area immediately below the dam and downstream from it, casting to structure as noted earlier. You will need more sinkers, or heavier lures, to fish tailwaters, as they are usually deeper and swifter than the waters above the dam.

School Notes

When fishing bait in moving waters, beware of drag, which is caused by the current pushing the line and gives the bait an unnatural appearance. Bait should ride naturally with the flow, not angle sharply across the stream or act as if it's resisting the current. Letting out a bit of line at these times will reduce drag.

Cautious Casts

Don't get too near to a dam's face, where the falling water circulates with a turbine effect. If you fall in, you may not be able to break away from the rotation, and drown. If you do fall in, wait until the rotation brings you to the bottom, then swim downstream before rising to the surface.

Rod Motion and Attitude

You must hold your fishing rod properly in order to control your bait or lure and make it appealing to fish. As well, you must always be ready for a fish to take your offering.

Bait Control

Bait should always appear natural in the water. Avoid making the bait move or behave oddly by moving the rod around sharply or keeping a very tight line. For example, if you're fishing in a lake with a minnow hooked directly behind the dorsal fin, and you're not using a bobber, any time you pull up on the rod or reel in line, the minnow will "swim" backwards. You must have a little bit of slack in the line to allow the minnow to swim freely, yet not so much that you can't reposition the minnow if it swims into thick weeds or brush. Also, if a fish takes the bait and feels tension from the line, it may spit the bait out.

When fishing bait in moving waters, you want to present the bait to as many fish as possible. This means that you should cast at an angle, up- and across-stream, and let the current carry the bait through the section of water in front of you. But you must reel in some line, called "mending," until the current brings the bait directly across from you. If you don't, too much slack will build up in the line, and if a fish takes the bait, you won't have any way of knowing it. As the baits sweeps past you, keep your rod tip at about a 45° angle, pointed above the bait, even extending your rod arm out, to keep your bait flowing naturally as you track it. Once the line straightens out, the bait will curve until it's directly downstream from you. Then you should reel in and cast again.

School Notes

If your bait or lure gets snagged on weeds and won't pull free, try this: Pull some line off your reel, then crank it back in while holding the rod differently—say, over your head or off to one side. Sometimes this pressure from a different direction is enough to release the hook.

Lure Control

Because lures should be kept in motion, you should always keep a tight line. Fish know that a lure isn't the real thing as soon as, or soon after, they take it, and they'll spit it out unless you set the hook immediately (which is covered in the next chapter). Also, lures need to be moved to attract fish; without movement, a lure is just an inert hunk of wood, metal, or plastic floating in the water or sitting on the bottom.

When retrieving a lure, keep your rod tip at approximately a 45° angle. Face the lure directly. You may find it more comfortable to cant the rod a bit to your left or right when reeling. Just be sure to maintain that 45° angle, and never point the rod tip directly at the lure. If a fish hits, you won't have the rod providing enough pressure to make a proper hookset. And never allow any slack to build into the line.

Using Lures with Built-In Action

Even though many lures—spoons, spinners, most plugs, spinnerbaits, buzzbaits, and some plastics—have inherent action, there's more to fishing some of them than just casting out and reeling in.

When fishing still water, you must allow time for the lure to sink before you begin reeling in. Spinners, spoons, crankbaits, and other heavy lures fall at differing rates of speed, and you must determine that rate, and where you want the lure to go, before you start reeling.

Let's say you're fishing a lake in 20 feet of water, and you want to retrieve a spoon 2 feet off the bottom. You can roughly determine the time it takes for the spoon to sink 18 feet by casting out and engaging the reel as soon as the lure touches water. Begin counting while the lure sinks and keep a tight line. When the lure hits bottom, the line will go slack. If that happens when you've counted to 10, you can figure that the lure falls at approximately 2 feet per second, so on the next cast, simply count to nine after the lure hits the water, and begin retrieving.

A simpler way of using this method in any water depth is to begin retrieving one second less than the time it takes for the lure to hit. This virtually guarantees that you're retrieving your lure just above the bottom.

Speed of retrieval is also critical. Although there is no one perfect speed, it's important that you crank fast enough for the lure to work—the blade on the spinner spins, the spoon wobbles, the crankbait vibrates—but not so fast that the action becomes erratic, or worse, that you take it right out of the fish zone. One easy way to determine the minimum and maximum rates of speed is to let a few feet of line hang from your rod tip and pull the lure back and forth through the water in front of you.

Using Lures Without Built-In Action

Jigs fished plain, some plastic worms, and stickbaits have no built-in action. The angler must impart action to these lures by moving the rod up and down or side to side, or by varying the rate of retrieve.

Jigs, which are often used to fish right on the bottom, are effective when moved up and down, or "jigged." The angler simply lets the jig fall to the bottom and, with a tight line, lifts the rod tip, anywhere from a few inches to more than a foot. This causes the jig to rise from the bottom and move forward. As the angler drops the rod tip back down, the jig falls back to the bottom, and he reels in a little bit to take up the slack. The jig is retrieved in this manner all the way back. Jigs can also be fished in currents of rivers and cast and retrieved accordingly.

School Notes

Sometimes a very fast retrieve works on a particular day. Other times, a very slow one takes fish. There's no set rule, though in very cold and very hot weather, slow usually works best. Experiment with retrieve rates until you find one that works.

Plastic worms can be retrieved in the same manner, though it's usually more effective to bring them in at a much slower rate, with frequent pauses and erratic lifts. This causes the worm to wiggle, waver, rise, float, and fall much like a real worm would in the depths.

Both jigs and plastic worms draw hits from fish as they fall to the bottom, and it's important to be ready for them. Whenever you cast these lures, you should always turn the reel handle to take the reel out of freespool as soon as the lure hits the water. Keep a tight line as the lure falls, whether by reeling in a bit or by moving the rod sideways.

Stickbaits should be retrieved erratically as well. The angler imparts action to a stickbait by moving the rod tip from side to side in a jerking motion and reeling in simultaneously. Some sharp lifts of the rod tip will cause the lure to rise and dip as well. Fishing a stickbait well takes practice, as well as concentration. But once mastered, you can make the stickbait look amazingly lifelike.

The Trolling Technique

One other method of fishing can be accomplished without repeated casting and re-trieving. This is *trolling*, which is pulling a lure or bait through the water from a slow-moving boat. The boat may be moved by an outboard motor, or rowed with oars. You can catch trout, largemouth and smallmouth bass, walleyes, northern pike, striped bass, and other predatory species when trolling. It's also a popular technique for many saltwater species (see Part 5, "Saltwater Fishing").

Trolling can be a productive fishing technique because it allows you to put a lure or bait in many different areas of a particular body of water. If you troll long enough, at various depths and near various types of structures, you have a good chance of catch-ing a fish. Thus, trolling is a good technique to rely on if you're unfamiliar with a particular lake or river and/or the species in it. It also helps you figure out where fish might be on a particular day, if you aren't catching them via your usual fishing meth-ods. And it's a good way to explore a body of water that you're not familiar with.

The lures or bait you use for trolling should 1) be proper for the local species; 2) ex-hibit some action or vibration when moving through the water; and 3) be able to continue that action or vibration at trolling speed, which is usually faster than typical retrieve speeds. Spoons, spinners, floater-diver plugs, crankbaits, and jigs adorned with bait or plastic trailers are all good trolling lures because they'll maintain their built-in action when trolled at varying speeds. Plastic worms and topwater plugs gen-erally don't work well as trolling lures because they're designed to be fished slowly, with frequent pauses. Spinnerbaits and buzzbaits, which exhibit a lot of flash and vibration when cast and retrieved at normal speeds, either won't operate properly or will create too much of a racket to attract fish at trolling speeds.

Minnows are good baits for trolling. They're best fished when hooked through the lips on a jig, or rigged on a "minnow harness," which consists of a double hook at the end of a short wire that has a loop on the other end. A special needle that is packaged with the minnow harness rig allows you to draw the wire through the minnow so that the double hook is situated at the minnow's vent and the loop protrudes from the minnow's mouth, which is where you tie your fishing line. This setup provides a firmer rigging than simply hooking the minnow through its mouth, because after prolonged use at trolling speeds the hook will probably tear from the minnow's lips. Minnow harnesses are available at most tackle shops.

Worms—specifically, night crawlers—can also be trolled when hooked onto a jig, or on a plain hook with an attractor device tied in to the line above it. The most common attractor is the Indiana spinner, which is a 1- to 3-inch wire with one or two spinner blades mounted onto it. Loops at either end of the wire allow it to be tied into the line: Knot the end of your fishing line to the top of the Indiana spinner with an improved clinch knot, then tie a 1- to 2-foot section of line to the bottom loop. Tie a hook to the end of that line and attach a night crawler by hooking it once through the "head," or large end. Tackle shops carry Indiana and other in-line spinners.

When using either bait or lures, you may need sinkers to keep the offering below the surface instead of skating across it. You can attach split shot a foot or two above the bait or lure; or, if you need a lot of weight to keep it down, you can use a trolling sinker (see Chapter 12, "Yes, You Should Sweat the Small Stuff"). Cut the line a foot or two above the bait or lure, and use improved clinch knots to tie the trolling sinker to both ends.

School Notes

The speed at which you troll is very important. Whether you're rowing or using an outboard, you should not go so fast that the lure or bait skips across the surface of the water, nor so slow that it occasionally lies motionless on the bottom. A speed between the two extremes is best, and you'll have to alternate speeds to find the best one for the water and for the species.

The basic trolling approach is to start in the shallows and follow the contours of the shoreline, going progressively deeper if you get no hits. Begin rowing or motoring slowly, and cast your lure or bait at least 20 or 30 feet behind the boat. Turn the reel handle to prevent excess line from coming off the spool. Now just hold onto the rod and allow the movement of the boat to pull the bait or lure. (Obviously, trolling is best done with at least two people in the boat: one to operate the oars or motor, and one to take off the rod or rods.) If you're fishing more than one rod, use a rod holder—a device that clamps onto the side of the boat, with rings into which you insert the butt of the rod to hold the entire rod upright. This allows you to troll without having to hold the rods in your hands. If the lure or bait rises to the surface, let out more line, or reel in and add more weight.

A rod holder, such as this clamp-on type, attaches to the side of the boat and allows you to troll without holding onto the rod.

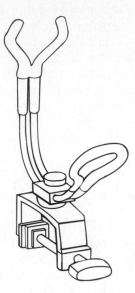

School Notes

Occasionally steer the boat in a zig-zag pattern, which will cause the lure or bait to speed up and rise in the water, then slow down and fall a bit. Such an erratic action may entice a fish into striking.

If you're fishing two lines, have one rod at the left side of the boat and one rod at the right. To prevent the lines from tangling when making a turn, make sure one lure or bait is at least 10 feet behind the other one.

It pays to fish two different types of lures or baits, which will help you figure out where the fish are that day and what they want to eat. For instance, if you're trolling for smallmouth bass in a large lake, you might fish a crankbait that dives to 10 feet on one rod, and a crankbait that dives to 15 feet on the other rod. The latter crankbait will pass through the deeper sections, while the former will remain closer to the surface. If you get a hit on, say, the deeper diver, remove the more shallow diver from the other rod and tie on a crankbait matching the one that took a fish. Also take note of where and how you caught the fish—the depth, any structures present, and your trolling speed—and duplicate your efforts in similar areas.

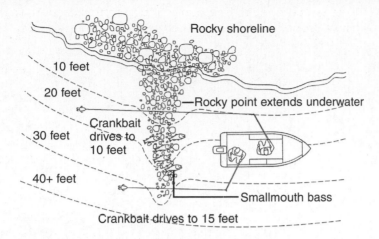

If possible, troll with two rods using different lures or baits. If you catch a fish on one of them, use that style of bait or lure and concentrate your efforts in similar areas.

Most times, fish will hook themselves when they hit a trolled bait or lure. Just be sure your drag is set properly before you begin trolling.

Again, start shallow, and troll in progressively deeper water. As you go farther away from shore, you'll probably have to switch to heavier lures and/or add more weight to your line. Alternate your speed, zig-zag the boat, and try different lures or baits. If you catch a fish, consider anchoring there and casting with the same lure or bait.

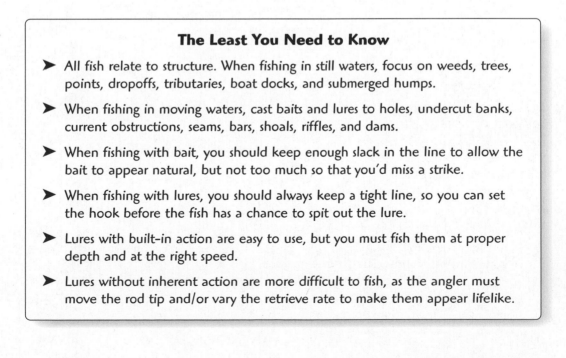

The Least You Need to Know

➤ All fish relate to structure. When fishing in still waters, focus on weeds, trees, points, dropoffs, tributaries, boat docks, and submerged humps.

➤ When fishing in moving waters, cast baits and lures to holes, undercut banks, current obstructions, seams, bars, shoals, riffles, and dams.

➤ When fishing with bait, you should keep enough slack in the line to allow the bait to appear natural, but not too much so that you'd miss a strike.

➤ When fishing with lures, you should always keep a tight line, so you can set the hook before the fish has a chance to spit out the lure.

➤ Lures with built-in action are easy to use, but you must fish them at proper depth and at the right speed.

➤ Lures without inherent action are more difficult to fish, as the angler must move the rod tip and/or vary the retrieve rate to make them appear lifelike.

Chapter 14

Fish On! How to Keep It That Way

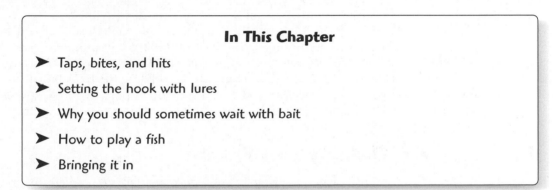

In This Chapter

➤ Taps, bites, and hits

➤ Setting the hook with lures

➤ Why you should sometimes wait with bait

➤ How to play a fish

➤ Bringing it in

Feeling the tap—or the jolt—of a fish hitting your bait or lure is thrilling for two reasons. For one, it's a signal of success. You have selected the right tackle and applied your own skills to fool—in most cases—a truly wild creature. Second, it's a highly anticipatory moment, because a lot of things may or may not happen in the next few seconds. You have to set the hook, play the fish, bring it close, and net it or at least bring the fish close enough to unhook, as described in this chapter. Besides the fact that the fish wants no part of this, some of your equipment—rod, reel, line, knots, and hook—will be tested, along with your fish-playing expertise.

Detecting a Fish

Developing a good feel for a fish taking your bait or lure requires some experience because the sensations vary greatly depending on the species, the size of the fish, the tackle you're using, the water, and the bait or the lure.

When fishing with lures, it's usually easy to tell when a fish hits, because your retrieve will suddenly be interrupted by a weight or an impediment on the line as you're turning the reel crank. Sometimes it's explosive—the rod jerks in your hands and bends way over, the drag begins screeching, and your line saws through the water. Other times it's just the weight of the fish pulling on the other end of the line, bending just the tip of your rod.

When fishing plastic worms and similar soft lures, the response can be the same, but often it's much more subtle. Because bass and other fish tend to "vacuum" plastic worms into their mouths, the angler feels a change in pressure when retrieving rather than an outright force.

If you're fishing bait and using a bobber, of course, you'll know when a fish is hitting your offering—as long as you're watching it closely, and can tell when it's just wind or waves moving the bobber. But if you're not using a bobber, or if you're fishing in a fast-moving current, you have to watch and feel your line carefully. Sometimes fish hit jarringly; other times, they'll barely peck at the bait. It's those latter times that make detection difficult, so you should constantly monitor your line for a signal.

The feel of a fish mouthing your bait won't be transmitted up your line and to the rod if you have any slack in the line. Your line should be taut enough so that you can feel any change in your bait, but not so tight that it moves the bait unnaturally or keeps it still in moving water. Watch your rod tip for a twitch or a minute vibration. With very light tackle, you'll feel the movement just by holding the rod—but it can be very slight, and you must be accustomed to it. I sometimes hold the line between the reel and the first guide in the fingers of my off hand to detect very delicate takes.

Lures: Strike Quickly and Firmly

Think about how you react when your molars first make contact with an errant sliver of aluminum foil in some potato salad. You may not spit the whole mouthful onto your paper plate (because Aunt Betsy is sitting right across from you, and it's her cookout in her backyard, and she's been eyeing you suspiciously ever since you announced to everyone present that a lot of this picnic food can double as catfish bait), but you'd at least stop chewing and try to remove the offending item.

So you can imagine how a fish reacts when it engulfs a metal or hard-plastic lure. Although the act of striking may have partially or temporarily driven at least one hook point into the fish's mouth, the point may not have penetrated past the barb. And that fish will try to dislodge the lure by opening its mouth and "shaking" its head—and unless you act quickly to set the hook (or hooks) as soon as you feel or see the fish hit the lure, there's a good chance it will succeed. That's why you should never have any slack in the line when fishing with a lure: A fish could grab the lure and spit it out without your even knowing it. Even a little slack in the line reduces your chances of setting the hook properly.

The proper hook-setting procedure when a fish hits a lure (except when flyfishing; see Part 4, "Flyfishing.") is to jerk the rod tip back over your head, or over your shoulder, as fast as possible. Most beginners make the mistake of not striking at all and simply reeling in as soon as they feel a hit. This is a good way to lose a fish. You have to whip that rod back sharply and forcefully in order to sink a hook past the barb. Many fish have tough mouths, making hook penetration difficult; many fishing lines stretch, reducing your force; and rods must bend, further decreasing that energy.

One exception to this rule is if you are fishing with large (6 inches or longer) plastic worms that are rigged with just one hook and unadorned with propellers or spinners, and you are getting hits but no hook-ups. The bass are probably grabbing just the rear of the worm and swimming off. In such cases, you should hesitate a bit—from just a couple of seconds to 10 or 15 seconds—before striking. You may be able to tell when the bass has engulfed the worm by waiting until the line stops moving. If not, you'll have to try different waiting times with each fish.

In either case, you should keep that line tight after you strike. In some cases the fish will oblige you by swimming in the opposite direction. But if it swims toward you, you'll have to reel line in quickly.

Bait: The Waiting Game

Fish usually won't drop or spit out bait, unless they feel the hook or tension from the line. Since most all bait is fished with a single hook, this doesn't happen often. But the downside to using a single hook is that it usually doesn't snag a fish by itself, as do treble hooks on many lures. Also, many species will grab a baitfish and swim off with it, turning it around inside its mouth, before swallowing it headfirst. Others will hesitantly peck at a bait, such as a worm, before finally grabbing it.

The point here is that if you strike as soon as you feel a bite, you may set the hook into nothing but water, or you'll wind up pulling the hook right out of the fish's mouth. But if you wait too long, the fish might swallow the bait, hook and all. This

Cautious Casts

If a fish hits a lure close to the end of the retrieve, use a sideways hook-setting motion. This way, if you don't hook the fish, the lure won't come flying out of the water toward your face.

School Notes

Occasionally a fish will mouth a bait and drop it. Sometimes it will take the bait again; other times it will leave it alone for good. At these times, it pays to set the hook as soon as you feel a take. You'll miss some fish, but will hook others that you wouldn't have otherwise.

School Notes

If you are constantly missing fish, on either bait or lures, check your hooks. A dull or broken point won't penetrate a fish's mouth. If the point is sharp, try using a smaller hook or a smaller lure.

Cautious Casts

Crappies are nicknamed "paper-mouths" because of the thin skin behind their lips. If you are fishing specifically for crappies, a hard hookset is not always necessary. Also keep a very tight line, as the hole created by the hook may widen as you're playing the fish.

poses no problem if you intend to keep every fish you catch, but if you don't, or if the fish is too small to keep anyway, you may be putting a fatally injured fish back in the water.

There are no set waiting times to follow for proper hook setting, because they differ for various species in various waters on various days. Even highly experienced anglers can't always set the hook at exactly the right time. This is one of those skills that you learn from experience, but there are a few guidelines.

The smaller the bait, the quicker you should strike. A trout, for example, will usually engulf a red worm or a salmon egg, while it may move a night crawler or minnow around in its mouth for a while before swallowing. Generally, strike immediately, or a few seconds after a hit, when using comparatively small bait.

When using large bait, wait. Again, the correct time varies. A largemouth bass may not take a shiner completely into its mouth for half a minute or more, but depending on the water and the day, it could swallow the whole thing in less than five seconds.

If you're using a bobber when fishing bait, wait until it goes underwater, and stays there for more than a few seconds, before striking. If you're not using bait, watch the line. Don't strike at the first twitch; instead wait until the line begins moving in a definite direction.

Set the hook in the same manner as when fishing with lures: a quick snap of the rod over your head or your shoulder. This is no time to be gentle, especially if you have a lot of line out. Remember: Your rod will bend, your line will stretch, and your hook has to penetrate past the barb into the fish's mouth, which may be bony.

Playing Your Fish

If you forget everything else when the time comes, remember this: Don't rush. Cranking in a fish as quickly as possible is an invitation to losing it, because the fish has not yet burned off its energy, and it's very difficult to control a hyperactive fish on a very short line as it runs, jumps, and digs for cover. You won't be able to respond to the fish's movements by moving your rod or turning your reel crank. Slack can build in the line, which the fish will then tangle around shoreline vegetation, the lower unit of an outboard motor, or even your feet. The fish will also surge powerfully, and if your drag isn't set properly, the line might break. Or the fish will rub the line against the bottom, wearing it thin or causing the hook to pop out. A host of other things could happen, too, none of which are in your favor, because basically you're out of control.

And that's what it all comes down to: control. Whether you're playing a pumpkinseed or a pike, you must never let the line get slack or let the fish enter cover where the line might tangle. You want to maneuver the fish into open water and let it tire by pulling against your fishing rod and taking line from the reel if necessary. Hold the rod upright and keep your hand on the reel crank. If the fish turns toward you, reel in that slack line immediately. If it turns away and begins peeling line from the drag, let it. Just keep pressure on the fish for now, pulling hard on the rod only to keep the fish away from any tangles.

Always turn your body to face the fish and keep your rod up. Don't hold it over your head; the angle lessens the effectiveness of your rod, and it's an awkward position that throws off your balance, making it difficult to adjust to the fish's movements. Hold the rod near vertical, with the reel between your waist and your shoulders.

A jump is probably the highlight of any fish fight, yet this is when many fish are able to throw the hook, because a fish can jerk its head violently from side to side. The best reaction—besides taking a moment to enjoy it—when playing most freshwater species is to keep the line tight, which lessens the chance of the hook or lure flying out.

Once the fish slows down—and this could take just a few seconds for panfish to more than five minutes for big fish—start reeling in line, just a little at first. If the fish is large, you may have to pump it in: Lift the rod up, then reel quickly as you drop it back down. As the fish approaches, be prepared for a burst of energy as it sees you, the boat, or the shoreline. Hold your rod up, take your time, and savor the experience.

Cautious Casts

If you're fishing from a boat and the fish swims beneath it, go ahead and stick the tip of your rod into the water and walk around to the other side. If you don't, the line will rub against the hull and weaken it or break it outright.

Landing Options

There are many ways to get a fish out of the water (called "landing" the fish). However, this is when most fish are lost, because, basically, fish do not *want* to come out of the water. Even tired or "played out" fish can put forth a burst of energy and try to get away from the angler. Given other factors at this time—a short line, an excited angler, possibly a rocking boat—it's not surprising that many of them succeed in escaping.

The safest and most reliable method of landing a fish is to net it. When done wrong, however, netting becomes one of the worst ways to bring a fish to hand. All large fish, such as salmon, lake trout, northern pike, and muskies, should be netted. And a large specimen of any species usually should be netted, to reduce the risk of losing it. And the easiest way to land any fish caught in moving water, particularly trout, is with a net, keeping the fish upstream and the net downstream.

Although it's a lot easier to have someone else net the fish for you, here's how to do it by yourself, whether on a boat, standing on shore, or wading:

1. Make sure the fish is played out. This is evidenced by the fish swimming in small circles or swimming on its side.

2. Reel in so that about 1½ rod lengths of line is out from the rod tip.

3. Holding the rod in your casting hand, grasp the net with your other hand and put the net gently in the water, away from the fish. The net opening should be facing the fish at about a 45° angle.

4. Keeping the net motionless, begin lifting your rod to guide the fish headfirst toward the net.

5. When the fish is just above the net opening, bring the net quickly forward and lift it up completely out of the water. If the fish shies away from the net, play it some more and try again.

Don't ever try to chase a fish with a net or drop it over a fish. Fish are fearful of overhead objects, and nets are extremely clumsy to move through the water. Besides, you may hit the line with your net and break it or pull the hook out of the fish's mouth. So if the fish recoils or jerks away as you lead it to the net, don't force it in. Play the fish some more and try again.

In other cases, you don't need to use a net to land your catch. Largemouth bass are easily brought out of the water by grasping their lower lip between your thumb and forefinger. The fish should be played out and, obviously, no hook should be protruding from that area of its mouth. Bring the bass close and lift the rod so that the bass's head is just protruding from the water. Pinch down and lift it quickly from the water; the bass will stop wiggling as this method seems to immobilize the fish. Other species without teeth on their jaws, such as smallmouth bass and crappies, can be "lipped" as well.

Average-size specimens of comparatively small species, such as panfish, can be swung out of the water and into the boat or onto the shore (although the fish should be handled delicately if they are to be released). But be very careful doing this, especially with fish that are large for the tackle you are using. Don't just derrick the thing in—all that weight puts undue pressure on the line, which is now short and offers very little stretch. And if the fish is not hooked solidly, the strain may pop the hook. Instead, hold the rod by the butt and quickly "spring" the fish out of the water and into the boat or onto land in one motion. Let the rod bear the weight of the fish instead of the line.

Never grab hold of the line above the fish to bring it in. You'll lose all advantage of the rod's elasticity, and if the fish makes a sudden move for deep water, you'll probably break the line or tear the hook out. It's much better to lip the fish if possible, try to spring it out of the water, or search for a fellow fisherman and ask to borrow his net.

Loose Lines

Occasionally I read or hear about an angler who, without a net, beaches a fish: When playing a fish from shore, he brings it close and then walks backwards, so the fish slides up out of the water and onto land, where he simply reaches down and grabs it. While this technique sounds plausible, and actually is effective when fishing the surf, where the wave action both disorients the fish and helps push it onto shore, it rarely works well with large fish in fresh water. Ideal conditions for beaching fish—a smooth (sandy or muddy) very gradual slope, with plenty of room for the angler to back up, aren't common anyway.

I found this out the hard way one summer day when I was fishing a coldwater farm pond in Pennsylvania and hooked the biggest smallmouth bass of my life. This fish ran, jumped, dived, bulldogged, and otherwise put up a tremendous fight—and one I didn't think I'd win, considering I was using ultralight spinning tackle more suitable for small-stream trout. Eventually, though, I had this fish close, swimming lazily in about 6 inches of water near my feet. That's when I realized that my net was still in the car, about a quarter of a mile away. So I tightened my line and started walking backwards. The bass came partially onto the brushy bank but wouldn't go farther because of the steep angle, so I stepped into the water and squatted down, trying to simultaneously push and scoop the fish onto shore with one hand while holding the rod with the other. It worked, but the fish started flopping as soon as it hit dry ground. I dropped the rod and squatted down, trying to trap the fish with my hands, but then the line snagged and broke on a low-lying branch, and the fish slithered into the water. It remained in the shallows, evidently stunned, and I quickly knee-walked after it. I actually got my hands around the bass's gills when its tail surged hugely and the fish rocketed out of my hands and disappeared into the depths.

A month later a friend told me that someone canoeing on the pond found a long-dead smallmouth bass floating on the surface near shore. The fish measured more than 20 inches, my friend said, and what a shame for a beautiful bass like that to die unappreciated. That's a fish you catch once in a lifetime.

Now I always bring a net.

The Least You Need to Know

➤ Fish typically hit lures forcefully, and you should set the hook immediately. Fish may not take bait or soft-plastic lures immediately into their mouths, though, in which case you should wait a bit before setting the hook.

➤ Set the hook by quickly jerking the rod tip over your head or shoulder, and begin reeling to take up any slack line.

➤ When you're playing a fish (that is, letting it tire itself out so you can land it), keep your rod pointed up, face the fish, and don't rush. Let the fish burn off energy before you begin reeling it in, but do keep it out of vegetation and other line-tangling areas.

➤ Small fish can be swung out of the water, and soft-jawed fish can be lifted out by their lower lip. But the least risky landing method is to use a net. Put the net in the water then and bring the fish to it. Don't bring the net to the fish.

Chapter 15

Keeping and Releasing Fish

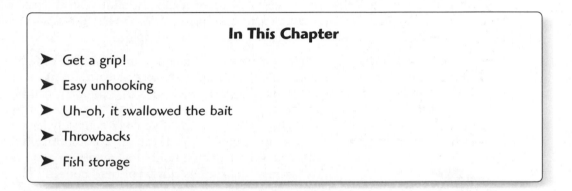

In This Chapter

➤ Get a grip!

➤ Easy unhooking

➤ Uh–oh, it swallowed the bait

➤ Throwbacks

➤ Fish storage

A fish is a wonderful thing to behold. Although the multihued trouts would win any aquatic beauty contests, even a bottom-dwelling catfish has a sort of natural elegance, with its powerful and tapered body perfectly adapted to its environment.

However, if you don't know what you're doing, a fish may not be such a wonderful thing to *hold*: cold, slimy, and wriggly, possibly with gnashing teeth and spiny fins. Such problems can be confounded when it's necessary to remove a hook, put the fish on a stringer, or handle it delicately enough to return it to the water in good condition. This chapter will tell you how to handle your fish, whether its next destination is the sparkling, placid water from whence it came, or your deep fryer.

How to Hold Your Fish

If you used a net to take your fish out of the water, the net's still the best place for it. And you may not have to touch the fish at all. You can unhook the fish while it's still in the net and return it to the water, simply by submerging net and fish and reversing the mesh. You can also put the fish on a stringer while it's still netted, or turn it upside down to deposit the fish in a cooler or creel. (Unhooking and fish-storage methods, as well as techniques to follow for returning fish to the water, are covered in the following pages of this chapter.)

It's best to put the net and fish down on the ground, or on the bottom of the boat, to unhook it. Put it down gently and press on the side of the fish with one hand so it doesn't flop around. Keep some mesh between your hand and the fish to maintain a firmer hold. Don't worry about your fishing line tangling in the mesh; you can deal with that after you've taken care of the fish (it's usually not as tangled as it seems anyway).

If you don't have a net, or if you want to remove the fish from the net to take a photo of it, store it, or release it, you have two ways to go about it. Smaller fish such as stream trout and panfish can be held by grasping the fish behind the head, with your thumb on one side and your fingers on the other, and holding the gills shut. Larger fish should be held upright with one hand on its belly and your other hand beneath its head. On fish that you intend to keep, you can also slide your thumb and forefinger partway into the fish's gill flaps to get a firmer grip. This hold tends to partially subdue fish as the internal organs put pressure on the spine.

Toothy fish such as pickerel, northern pike, and muskellunge aren't all that difficult to hold in this manner as long as you avoid putting your fingers near their mouths. When handling large specimens of these species, however, it's wise to don a pair of heavy gloves to avoid slipping, as these species are especially slimy. Another method to hold these species—and one that should be used *only* if you will definitely keep the fish—is to grasp it from the top of the head, pressing your thumb and forefinger into each eye socket. Such a hold provides a firm and positive grip, as the sockets consist of hard bone.

Soft-mouthed fish such as bass and crappies, which can be landed by grasping their lower lip, can be conveniently held that way as well while unhooking, as long as the hook isn't embedded there. This position renders the fish practically immobile.

Catfish, with sharp spines in their dorsal and pectoral fins, should be handled carefully. Grasp them from behind the head, sliding your thumb and forefinger down the fish's body to keep the pectoral fins folded flat against the body. Use the heel of your hand to fold down the dorsal fin. Very small catfish should be held from underneath, again using your thumb and forefinger to fold the pectoral fins flat.

School Notes

Fish slime is slippery stuff and makes knot tying difficult when it gets on your fingers. After handling a fish, rinse your hands in the water and dry them on a rag or handkerchief.

Out, Out Darn Hook

Hooks have barbs so they can remain in fish. That's why removing one (or more) hooks can be difficult.

Lip-hooked fish that have no teeth on their jaws are the easiest to unhook, especially those that have the shank of the hook protruding from their mouths. Simply twist the hook shank while pushing it toward the bend.

But if the fish has a lot of teeth, or if the hook is deep in the fish's mouth, long-nose pliers make the job much easier. Grasp the hook with the pliers' jaws as close to the hook point as possible. Give a sideways twist and the hook should come free. If not, try twisting in a different direction to enlarge the hole.

Removing a treble-hooked lure from a fish is more problematic. Pull out the barbs one at a time, working from the front of the fish's mouth in, until all are free.

Fish that are hooked very deeply may require a de-hooker (a long plastic rod with a slot for the line). Insert the line into the slot, follow the line down to the fish's mouth, and place the end of the rod against the bend of the hook. Push down into the fish's mouth to remove the hook.

Loose Lines

Although long-nose pliers are perfect for removing hooks, they are expensive. And since they're small and heavy, and you use them when standing in, on, or near water, you will probably lose them eventually. That's why I don't buy very expensive pliers. My cheap ones rust easily, need oiling, and don't feature plastic-coated handles, but they do the job—and when they accidentally fall overboard, I'm not heartbroken.

What to Do When the Fish Has Swallowed the Hook

It happens to every fisherman who uses bait: You bring in a fish and, when you go to unhook it, all you see is your fishing line disappearing down the fish's gullet. Maybe the fish swallowed the bait because you waited too long to set the hook, or the hook you are using is too small, or the fish took the bait without your even realizing it. What now?

Actually, you have a number of options, and the best one to use depends on whether or not you plan on keeping the fish.

First, in either event, try "tricking" the hook out. While holding the fish gently but firmly, pull—don't yank—on the line at various angles around the fish's mouth. Sometimes the hook will pop out of the fish, or at least become visible, when you do this.

Cautious Casts

If you catch a fish that you don't intend to keep, but the hook has caused the gills to bleed, consider keeping it. A fish with badly damaged gills doesn't have a good chance of survival. If the fish is smaller than the minimum size, cut the line and return it to the water quickly and with as little handling as possible.

If this doesn't work and you intend to keep the fish, you can kill the fish by bending its head back and breaking its neck, or by rapping its head with a wooden dowel or some other heavy item (some anglers carry fish "billies" for this purpose). Then you can dig deeply with your pliers and your knife if necessary to remove the hook. Or, you can simply cut the line near the fish's mouth and retrieve the hook at your leisure when cleaning the fish. Of course, this means that you'll have to retie a hook onto your line.

If the fish is too small to keep, either for legal reasons or because you don't intend to eat it, cut the line as short as possible—try to cut it inside the fish's mouth—and put it gently back in the water (more on this later). A fish that is otherwise in seemingly good condition stands a fair chance of recovery, even with a hook inside it. The hook will eventually rust and decompose. To decrease the odds of deeply hooking another fish that you don't intend to keep, tie on a larger hook, which will be more difficult for the fish to swallow.

Fishing Without Keeping

There are many reasons for anglers to put fish back: The fish is smaller than the minimum size required by state law, or the fish is legal size but too small for the angler to bother cleaning, or the angler doesn't care for the taste of that particular species, or the angler is fishing just for the enjoyment of hooking and playing fish.

Obviously it's important to do the least harm to the fish, so it can survive, grow bigger, and provide more sport another day. Certain practices help make this feasible.

The less you handle the fish, the better its chances of survival. The slime on a fish protects it from infection, and handling fish removes some of the slime. If possible, don't even net the fish or lift it out of the water. Play the fish until it's subdued, reel it close, and remove the hook with your fingers or pliers, with only the fish's head sticking out of the water.

If you must remove the fish from the water, be gentle with it. Although a net will remove some of the slime, you are better off using one instead of lifting the fish out of the water and letting it flop around on the ground or on the bottom of a boat.

If you must pick up the fish, wet your hands first. This will cause less of the slime to come off the fish.

As noted earlier, if the fish has swallowed the hook, don't try to dig it out. Cut the line as close to the gullet as possible and return the fish to the water immediately.

Sometimes a fish is so exhausted after the fight that, although it is alive, it can't move water through its gills fast enough to recuperate. If the fish you are returning to the water seems lethargic, you can revive it by moving the fish through the water, headfirst, to force water into its mouth and through its gills. Support the fish and keep it upright by placing one hand under its belly. Hold the fish's mouth open with your other hand if necessary (and if it's not full of sharp teeth) and make sure you're not keeping the gill flaps closed. Move the fish forward, gently, a few times until it swims off on its own. If you're fishing moving water, simply hold the fish with its head into the current until it revives.

Getting the Point

Some fishing waters are termed **catch and release,** which means that no fish caught there may be kept. Many of these waters offer excellent angling because of the resultant high populations of fish.

Every angler has his or her own ethic when it comes to keeping fish. Some people release every single fish they catch; they don't enjoy eating fish, or don't care to bother cleaning or filleting them. Other people—"fish hogs"—keep every single fish they catch, whether they intend to eat them or not. I've seen garbage cans at boat docks filled with fish that anglers just dumped after they brought them back. Unfortunately, a few people have some kind of wasteful, gluttonous mentality when it comes to fishing (and, probably, other things in life). Such behavior hurts not only the resource but the reputation of the sport itself.

My rule for keeping fish is this: Unless I'm absolutely positive that I and/or my family and friends will eat the fish I'm catching, I'll release them. You have to be realistic about this, too: Some fish taste better than others. You may not have the culinary skills to prepare them to your taste. Or your expectations of their taste were much higher than when you took that first bite.

You may feel like a hero bringing home enough fish to feed a high-school reunion. But you'll feel markedly different when, a year later, you come across some dried-out, freezer-burned fillets in the back of your freezer, gone to waste because you didn't feel like eating them.

Fish for the Freezer

The first step in preparing a fine fish dinner begins on the water. How you handle your fish determines how good that fish will be on the table, and for the best taste, you have to keep your fish either *alive* or *cold*.

A fish stringer is a device on which you string or clip fish. After putting a fish on a stringer, the fish end of the stringer goes in the water while the other end is tied to the shore or the boat. Some stringers are nothing more than a narrow nylon rope with a metal point on one end and a metal ring on the other. The point should be inserted through the upper and lower lips of the fish and then run through the metal circle, to ensure security before being tied off. Other stringers are chainlike devices with numerous clips hanging off of them, which operate much like safety pins: Open the pin, insert the wire through both lips, and close the pin again.

Don't run a stringer through a fish's gills. Although it seems a convenient and secure place, it will damage the fish's gills and also keep the fish from closing its mouth completely, hindering the flow of water past its gills.

Getting the Point

Some fishing boats are equipped with **livewells,** which are built-in reservoirs that can be pumped full of water and used to keep fish alive the entire day.

Stringers work well when fishing from a boat, because it's a simple matter to string a fish and toss it over the side, where it will remain alive until you're ready to clean it. Remember to bring the stringer into the boat whenever running an outboard motor. But if you are going to be taking the fish in and out of the water quite often, or if the day is hot and the water at the surface is too warm for your stringered fish to survive, you are better off keeping your catch on ice (actually, under ice) in a cooler.

Any cooler large enough to hold your fish and enough ice to last the day is fine. Kill the fish by rapping its head or breaking its neck and place it on the bottom of the cooler, with the ice on top. (If you don't kill the fish it may jump around and bruise itself, and fish that die slowly may not taste as good as quickly killed fish.) Periodically drain water from the cooler as the ice melts.

Creels are excellent for keeping your catch when walking and fishing creeks and streams. Old-style wicker creels are lightweight and fasten to your belt or your shoulder with a harness. The creel holds tackle, too. Put some wet moss or ferns above and below the fish, which will cool them as the water evaporates.

Canvas creels also cool fish by evaporation. Typically worn slung over a shoulder, these creels should be dipped in water prior to putting a fish inside. A plastic curtain on the side keeps the angler's legs dry. A plastic liner on the inside holds tackle as well.

Check on the condition of your fish throughout the day. Cool spring and fall days typically don't create problems, but in the summertime you should take whatever steps are necessary to keep your fish cool, even if it means stopping fishing temporarily.

Loose Lines

My friend John and I were fishing the Susquehanna River one spring day for "wipers," which are striped bass/white bass hybrids. I hooked, played, and finally caught one that weighed nearly 10 pounds—a tremendous fish for the river and the species, and one which I was considering getting mounted. We put the fish on a rope stringer and continued drifting down the river. Two minutes later, John fired up the outboard to head back upstream. It took awhile for either of us to realize that the stringer was still in the water. I yelled, "John, shut off the motor," and began pulling up on the rope, which was tied very close to the outboard. Thanks to a spinning propeller and some incredible absentmindedness, that fish is nothing but a memory.

The Least You Need to Know

➤ A net is the safest place to hold your fish. Otherwise, hold small fish from the top, above the head, and large fish from the bottom, using two hands. Be cautious of the spines on catfish.

➤ Pinch and twist a hook to remove it from a fish. Long-nose pliers make this job easier.

➤ If a fish swallows the hook and it won't come out with gentle tugs, cut the line as short as possible if you won't be keeping the fish, or kill the fish if it's a keeper and either dig the hook out then or cut the line and remove the hook later.

➤ Fish that you definitely won't keep should be handled as little and as delicately as possible. Tired-out fish should be manually moved headfirst through the water to help them recuperate.

➤ Keep fish on stringers, with the fish in water; in coolers, with enough ice to cover them; or in creels, which you wear and are handy when walking and fishing creeks and streams.

Part 4

Flyfishing

Flyfishing has enjoyed a tremendous resurgence in popularity lately, especially among those people who have taken up fishing late in life. The release of the motion picture A River Runs Through It, *based on the novella by Norman Maclean, promoted the elegance and challenge of the sport by showcasing the artistry of a flycaster working his rod and line in picturesque settings.*

Many of these newcomers to the sport don't realize that flyfishing is a very old sport, with one reference dating back to the Third century. And although the sport has evolved into a kind of hip, I'm-fishing-but-not-getting-dirt-under-my-fingernails trend, flyfishing is, at times, the most effective way to catch a fish. Sometimes it's the only way, as this part of the book reveals.

Chapter 16

Assembling a Flyfishing Outfit

In This Chapter

➤ Playing the numbers game

➤ Fly-rod factors

➤ The right—and wrong—reel

➤ Follow the leader

Flyfishing is different from all other forms of rod-and-reel fishing because of one basic reason: When spinning, spincasting, and baitcasting, the angler casts the lure, but when flyfishing, the angler casts the line. While this distinction may, at first, seem archaic and its practice cumbersome, it is by far the most effective way to repeatedly present an extremely lightweight lure—that is, a fly—to a fish.

This is also why flyfishing equipment differs from and is actually incompatible with other "hardware" tackle and methods. While the fly rod, fly reel, and fly line serve pretty much the same purposes as their spinning or baitcasting counterparts, their makeup and function are disparate. This chapter will show you those differences.

Fly-Line Weights, Tapers, and Sink Rates

Because a flyfisherman casts the line, not the fly, the size and type of line is the most important determination to make when putting together an outfit. The line you get will determine what type of rod and reel you should choose later.

Fly lines are categorized via a number that refers to the line's weight, not its strength, as in other fishing disciplines. Low line weights (and corresponding rod weights) are for small fish, and heavy weights are for large fish. This classification is standard throughout the industry, thanks to the American Sportfishing Association, so the weight of a particular line of one manufacturer is the same as that of another manufacturer. (The actual weight, which is determined by weighing a segment of line, is not of importance.) Fly rods and reels are also sized and classified according to this standard, which simplifies assembling a line, rod, and reel outfit. (More on fly rods and reels later in this chapter.)

The scale of weights, and the corresponding species for which each weight is generally suited, is shown in the following table.

Fly-Line Weights

Weight Range (in pounds)	Species
1–2	Panfish, small trout
3–6	Panfish, trout, small bass
7–8	Trout, bass, pickerel, small saltwater species
9–11	Large trout/bass, northern pike, saltwater species
12–15	Large saltwater species

Generally, the bigger the fish, the heavier the line necessary, because higher weights cast farther and can handle larger (heavier) flies. However, it's important to remember that these are general guidelines, not absolute rules. For instance, many anglers flyfish for large species, such as steelhead in the 8- to 10-pound range, with 6- or 7-weight outfits, because steelhead migrate up freshwater streams to spawn. Many of these streams are comparatively small, and the flies the anglers use aren't large, so the "standard" 9-, 10-, or 11-weight rods aren't always necessary.

The best "all-around" weight line and rod for the beginning flyfisherman depends on the species you fish for most often. But make sure you avoid the extremes: 1-, 2-, and 3-weight outfits are very delicate and unforgiving of casting errors, while anything above an 8-weight can be very cumbersome and difficult to cast accurately for the inexperienced (and even the experienced) fly angler. The middle of the weight ranges are the most practical; go with a 5-weight if you're going to fish for panfish, a 6-weight if stream trout will be your main quarry, and a 7-weight for bass. If you're not sure what you'll wind up fishing for, or if you might fish for all three, go with the 6-weight.

Your next decision is to pick the type of fly line, specifically its buoyancy and its taper. Buoyancy refers to the line's ability to float or sink, and there are four standardized types of line (often abbreviated as follows on the line's packaging):

➤ *Floating (F)* lines are used to fish with both floating and sinking flies. They cast easily, and their high visibility means the angler can always see the line's position on the water. They also indicate strikes very well. These all-around fly lines are the best for the beginner.

➤ *Sinking (S)* lines are used with flies that sink. They are preferred when fishing deep waters, or when the angler wants to put the fly on the bottom quickly, such as when fishing fast, deep rivers or lake bottoms. Sinking lines sink at various rates, so the deeper you want to fish, the faster sink-rate you should get.

➤ *Intermediate (I)* lines sink, but they do so very slowly. They are specialty lines, used when the angler wants to fish a fly just beneath the surface.

➤ *Floating with Sinking-Tip (F/S)* lines, commonly called *sink-tip* lines, are also specialty lines. They are used for the same reasons as intermediate lines, but in situations where the angler wants to watch that part of the line that doesn't sink to indicate strikes. They're also easier to cast than intermediate lines.

Loose Lines

Fly lines come in a variety of colors. Is there a best one? Not really. Most all sinking lines are made in dark or muted shades, so they won't spook fish. Many floating lines come in light or bright colors—white, cream, chartreuse, fluorescent orange—so that the angler can spot them easily on the water. Pick whatever color you prefer.

The taper of a fly line refers to the line's shape and diameter, and there are five basic kinds:

➤ *Level (L)* lines are the same thickness from end to end. While level lines are inexpensive, they don't cast well.

➤ *Weight-forward (WF)* lines have a single taper on one end, but directly behind it is a thick section of line, behind which the line is level. Because much of the line's weight is concentrated in the first 30 feet or so, it casts easily and can gain momentum quickly when the angler wants to make a long cast.

➤ *Double-taper (DT)* lines are tapered at both ends, with the middle section being a consistent diameter. Double-tapers cast easily and lay down on the water gently.

Cautious Casts

Beware of inexpensive fly lines: Because of manufacturing short-cuts that allow them to be sold at low prices, they won't last long and may not cast well. A $30 investment will get a fly line that won't let you down.

Although they're not good for long-distance casting, these lines are best for beginning fishermen because of their casting advantages. One advantage to a double-taper line is that it can be reversed—taken off the reel spool and cranked back on, beginning with the opposite end—when the front section becomes worn.

➤ *Shooting-taper (ST)* lines consist of two lines: one heavy section with a quick taper in front, followed by a thin, level line. These are used to make extra-long casts and are not easy to use.

➤ *Triangle-taper (TT)* lines have a short, quick taper in front, gradually increasing in diameter for about 40 feet, where it quickly tapers back down to a thin, level line. This new style is said to be a delicate line for long-distance casts.

Fly-line tapers. The line tapers have been exaggerated for clarity.

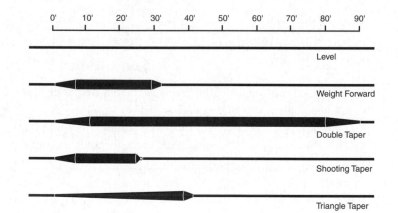

Therefore, the best line weight for the beginning flyfisherman, who will be fishing for panfish, trout, and/or bass in average-size waters under typical conditions, turns out to be a 6-weight, floating, double-taper line. Even if you wind up moving on to other weights, buoyancies, and tapers, this line will serve as a backup or a spare in many fishing situations. Consider it an investment.

When you finally purchase your fly line, be sure to pick up some backing as well. *Backing* is cordlike line that goes onto a fly reel before the actual fly line. It serves to fill the reel to capacity, which makes the fly line easier to reel in and, in case you hook a large fish, insurance in case the fish takes a long run when you already have a lot of line out.

Picking a Fly Rod

If you know what weight of fly line you need, choosing a matching fly rod becomes a process of elimination. Because the weight system of lines is standardized, all fly rods have the weight of line they are designed for—which is either one weight or two—listed right on the blank.

Fly rods are necessarily long—longer than spinning or baitcasting rods for the same fish and conditions, anyway—because of the casting angles involved (a short rod would tire you out quickly). Most fly rods designed for typical freshwater use are between 6½ and 10 feet long, with the majority measuring from 8 to 9 feet. Generally, long rods cast farther with less effort, while short rods cast quicker and are easier to maneuver in brush. Remaining with that all-around 6-weight outfit as an example, a good length would be 8½ feet: not so short that you can't get distance, but not too long so that it becomes unwieldy.

School Notes

Some manufacturers assign species names to some of their fly-line styles. These reflect line designs that supposedly will work best for the size of the flies most fly anglers use and the casting conditions they face when fishing for that species.

As a fly rod's weight rating increases, so does its actual weight. You don't need to enroll at a health club to cast, say, a 12-weight rod, but doing so can quickly tire you out if you haven't done much practicing. Most everyone, however, can easily cast a 6-weight rod.

A commonly used term in fly-rod descriptions and advertising is *modulus*. This refers to the ability of a fiber (in this case, graphite, of which most all fly rods are made today) to recover from bending. Modulus figures into casting, during which the rod bends back and forth, "loading" energy during its flex. It is measured in pounds of pressure per square inch. Basically, the higher the modulus, the stiffer the rod, and the faster it will bend back from a curve, which makes for fast casting and good distance. The lower the modulus, the smoother and more delicate the casting.

As discussed in Chapter 5, "Don't Spare the Rod," the action of a rod identifies when the rod begins to "load," or resist bending when under pressure, given the same amount of pull. Rods stop bending—that is, the rod displays a curve at a certain place under a certain amount of pressure—anywhere along the rod shaft, depending on the type of action. (See Table 5.1 for a description of rod actions.) While fast actions are quick, they aren't forgiving of casting errors. A moderate action is best for the beginner.

A fly rod is not an inexpensive investment; expect to pay a minimum of $100. Don't rely on advertising copy alone when picking the best one for you. Two otherwise identical rods from different manufacturers can feel totally different in your hands. If possible, cast with the rods outside before you decide to buy one. Most reputable sporting-goods stores should accommodate you in testing a fly rod.

Loose Lines

While it used to be true that the fewer the pieces of a fly rod, the better it would cast, advanced manufacturing techniques have made multipiece fly rods cast as smoothly as standard two-piece rods. These pack rods, which consist of four or five pieces, depending on the rod length, are very convenient to store and carry. If you'll be doing a lot of traveling with your fly rod—and especially if you'll take it backpacking or on airline flights—you'll probably be happier with a pack rod.

Reels: Single Action, Multiplier, or Automatic?

Depending on the situation and the species you are fishing for, a fly reel can range from a simple mechanism that stores line to a complex device that will determine whether you will land or lose a fish. To understand why, you must know the differences between reel types and their applications.

Single-action fly reels turn a spool one complete time for each turn of the reel handle. Resembling a squat pepper mill, a single-action reel usually has an exposed spool, which can drop out of the reel housing (on most modern reels) when you push a small release lever. Single actions are simple reels with comparatively few parts and are the most common fly reels in use today. Flyfishermen hold the line in one hand and the rod in the other, with some of the line pooled at their feet when casting. Flies are worked with that line hand, not directly off the reel. Also, when fishing for species such as panfish and stream trout, the angler does not have to play the fish directly off the reel: He simply brings in or releases line with his hand. Therefore, the reel is used mainly to keep excess line out of the way.

A typical single-action fly reel.

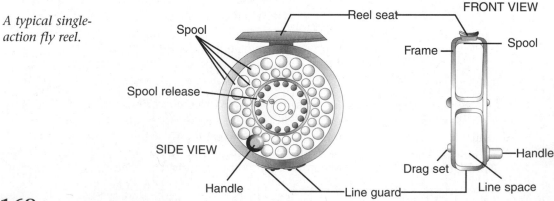

A *multiplier* reel resembles a single-action, except that it turns the spool twice or even three times for each turn of the reel handle. This makes it handy for retrieving long lengths of line in a hurry. A multiplier is advantageous when playing large fish that may pull a lot of line off the reel, then change directions, creating slack. The angler must reel in quickly to maintain a tight line, and the multiplier reel facilitates that process.

An *automatic* reel retrieves line via a spring-loaded mechanism that the angler engages by depressing a lever protruding from the front of the reel (there is no reel handle). Although they are the fastest line-retrieving reels, automatics have decreased markedly in popularity recently because they're heavy compared to single actions and multipliers, they don't offer an opportunity to play fish directly off the reel, and they have inconsistent drags.

The drag is an important component of single actions and multipliers. Although the drag on a reel may never be utilized when playing a fish, one is necessary so that the angler can strip fly line off the reel when preparing to cast (otherwise, the spool would continue to turn, resulting in a backlash). Drags on these reels are either the ratchet type or disk. The ratchet mechanism clicks as the spool rotates. The drag type has a disk that puts pressure on the spool; turning a knob adjusts the amount of drag. Because many single actions and multipliers have an exposed spool, the angler also can provide additional drag by pressing his fingers or his palm against the side of the spool as a fish takes line out. This is called "palming" the reel.

If you plan on flyfishing for panfish, stream trout, and river smallmouths, a single-action reel with a ratchet drag will serve you well. But if you're planning on fishing for largemouth bass, northern pike, steelhead, or other large species, you're better off with a multiplier reel with a disk drag.

School Notes

Some single-action and multiplier fly reels can be either left- or right-hand retrieve because the spool can be inserted in either side of the reel. I cast with my right hand, so I use reels with a left-hand retrieve. You should use whichever is more comfortable.

Cautious Casts

Fly reels start at around $20 and go up—way up—from there. While you should never buy junk, don't sink so much money into a reel that you'll short-change yourself on a rod and line. This is especially true if you'll be angling for fish that you won't need to fight off the reel.

The Logic of Leaders

The final component of a flyfishing outfit is the *leader*, which is a length of mono-filament tied to the end of the fly line. The fly is tied to the other end of the leader. Leaders are necessary because fly line is heavy and opaque. You can't tie a fly onto it, and even if you could, no fish would touch it.

School Notes

Some companies sell complete flyfishing packages—rod, reel, and line—that could get a novice started without having to fret over selecting his own balanced outfit. It may not be top-of-the-line gear, but it's not junk either, and worth looking into.

Leaders are, by necessity, tapered, so that the fly line, leader, and fly will roll out flat and straight onto the water after a cast. If the leader was the same diameter throughout, it would tangle in mid-air when casting and land in heaps of coils on the water.

Leaders average from 6 to 12 feet in length, although they can be longer or shorter. The proper length to use depends on the wariness of the fish and the clarity and condition of the water. Basically, the spookier the fish, and the lower, clearer, and quieter the water, the longer a leader you'll need. I've fished for brown trout in crystal waters where a leader less than 9 feet long would spook them, because they'd spot the heavy, thick fly line attached to it. However, long leaders are more difficult to cast well, so you should use the shortest leader you think necessary. As a rule, though, don't go any shorter than 6 feet.

The thickest part of the leader—where it is tied onto the fly line—is called the *butt*. Its purpose is to continue the taper of the end of the fly line itself. To attach the leader butt to the end of the fly line, use a nail knot. It was originally tied with a nail, but is much easier when tied with a small tube, such as an air-valve needle or the outside of a ball-point pen. (This knot can also be used to attach backing to the fly line.)

Here's how to do it, as shown in the figure on the following page:

1. Hold the tube, fly line, and leader butt as shown in the top figure.
2. Holding all three firmly, wrap the leader butt around itself, the fly line, and the tube.
3. Hold all the wraps in place and pass the end of the leader butt through the tube.
4. Continue holding the wraps and carefully slide the tube out.
5. Draw the knot tight and trim the ends.

The middle of the leader is called the *body*, and it too gradually decreases in diameter. The end of the leader, to which the fly is tied, is called the *tip* (or, when the leader is constructed of various lengths of line knotted in decreasing strengths, the *tippet*). The diameter of the tip, and its pound-test rating, are how leaders are classified.

Tippets are measured in thousandths of an inch and follow a standardized scale, called an *X-rating*. While the pound-test of the same diameter varies a bit from manufacturer to manufacturer, the approximate values are shown in the following table.

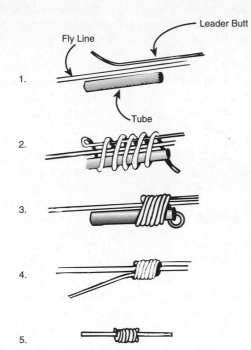

Using a nail knot to attach the leader butt to the end of the fly line.

Tippet Ratings

Tippet Size	Diameter (Inches)	Pound Test (Approximate)	Fly Size
0X	.011	12	4–6
1X	.010	10	4–8
2X	.009	8	4–10
3X	.008	6	6–12
4X	.007	5	6–14
5X	.006	4	14–20
6X	.005	2	18–26
7X	.004	1.5	20–28
8X	.003	.75	20–28

As the X-number indicating the tippet size increases, the diameter and the pound test decreases. Also note that the drop in pound test is more marked in the higher X-numbers.

Generally, the smaller the fly you use, the smaller tippet size you need, as the table shows. Going back to the previous example of that crystal-clear trout stream: I was using size-18 flies, and had to use a leader with a 6X tippet. Any size larger than that would be noticeable to the trout. Later on that day, though, I switched to larger flies—a No. 6 2X long—because I began fishing deeper, darker sections of water, and was able to use a leader with a 2X tippet. As a rule, you should use the heaviest tippet you can get away with—within reason. If the line seems too obvious, or if you're not catching fish, go to a smaller size.

Loose Lines

Dries can also be fished downstream to rises and "twitched" to entice a strike—or "skated" across the surface. Before modern manufacturing techniques made it possible to taper monofilament, all leaders were made of separate lengths of line, knotted together in order of decreasing strength: 0X, 1X, 2X, and so on. This made leader construction a bit of a time-consuming process, not to mention the matter of buying many spools of various pound-test lines. However, there is still one major advantage that knotted leaders have over knotless: They last longer. Because you lose a bit of line every time you cut off one fly and tie on another, your knotless 4X leader, say, will eventually become a 3X, then a 2X, then a 1X, and so on, not to mention the fact that it will decrease in length. With a knotted leader, it's a simple matter to tie a new length of 4X tippet material onto the end. And you can make a 5X leader out of a 4X in the same manner. While it is possible to tie tippet material onto a knotless leader, it's difficult to determine the exact diameter of the break-off point and match the right tippet material to continue a perfect taper. This is why leader manufacturers still offer knotted leaders.

The Least You Need to Know

➤ Choose your fly-line weight before you choose a rod and reel. A 6-weight, floating, double-taper line is a good all-around choice for the beginner. Don't scrimp on line quality.

➤ Pick a fly rod that matches the weight of your line. An 8½-foot, moderate-action rod is average. Try casting a number of rod sizes and styles before purchase.

➤ Use a single-action reel for panfish and trout; a multiplier reel for bass, northern pike, and other large fish.

➤ Leaders are tied onto the end of the fly line. The tip of the leader, or tippet, takes the fly. Its diameter is classified according to an "X-rating": The higher the X number, the finer the tippet.

Chapter 17

No-Fear Fly Casting

In This Chapter

➤ Get a grip!

➤ True false casting

➤ The final delivery

➤ Specialized casts

➤ Diagnosing casting ills

Casting a fly rod requires more physical coordination and practice than other casting disciplines. But it does not require brute strength, nor is it extremely difficult. Fly casting pretty much boils down to two elements: angles and timing. If you can ride a bicycle or drive a car—even one with an automatic transmission—you can fly cast.

This chapter will focus on the very basics of fly casting—not because the technique is so complex, but because most fly casting errors are rudimentary in aspect.

One other point: Fly casting is fun. Just working the rod, feeling it flex under the load of the line, hearing the hiss of the fly line as it cuts through the air above your head, and watching your line and leader straighten out and fall gently to the water—especially when on a gurgling trout stream or a mirror-surfaced lake—can be rewarding and fulfilling, whether or not you catch a fish.

Shake Hands with Your Fly Rod

That heading isn't intended to be facetious. When you hold your fly rod, you should open your hand as if you are were going to shake hands with someone (a normal handshake, not the '60s "Peace and love, brother" variety). However, don't grip the rod so hard that you put indentations into the cork handle. A fly rod should be cradled in your hand, not squeezed.

School Notes

When practicing to fly cast, don't bother to find water. You won't be fishing yet, and you need to focus on your skills, not the water. A yard or a grassy field in a park or office complex is perfect. Avoid casting on pavement, as the gritty surface will harm the fly line. And don't bother practicing on windy days.

Hold the rod with your strong hand just above the reel, which should be on the bottom of the rod. Slide your hand incrementally up and down the grip until you find a comfortable hold (grips vary in shape and width) and it feels balanced and natural. The best hold will differ from angler to angler because of varying sizes of hands and grips, and the balance point will differ because of varying weights of rods and reels.

Although there are several ways to hold a fly rod, the first-time caster should grasp it so that the thumb rests on top of the grip (the side opposite the reel). The grip should be positioned between your thumb and the first and second joints of your index finger and angle down your hand, so that it also rests against the heel of your hand, with the rest of your fingers closed on it. The exact hold will vary somewhat, again because of individual hand and grip shapes and sizes.

Always remember to keep your thumb on top of the grip. Many beginners have a tendency to "fist" the rod, or circle the grip with the thumb, when casting. Doing so will throw off your casting angles and make the whole process much more difficult. Keep that thumb on top!

Now, face your target. Pull line off your reel and, holding the rod out in front of you, waggle the rod tip so that a bit more than a rod's length of line and leader is out from the rod tip. Pull more line out from the reel so that a loop dangles between the reel and the first rod guide without touching the ground. Now you're ready to cast.

School Notes

When practicing your fly casts, always tie a fly to the end of your leader (you can snip off the end of the hook to avoid snags). This will duplicate the actual movements of the line and leader when you're fishing.

False Casting

To get enough line out and into the air to reach your target, you must "false cast," which means stroking the rod back and forth so the line loops through the air without touching down. To do this, lift your rod up sharply with your right hand (if you're right-handed) while holding the line hanging between the reel and the first rod guide with your left hand. When the line straightens out behind you, stroke the rod forward, letting some of the line in your left hand shoot through the guides, thus lengthening the amount of line in the air. When the line straightens out in front of you, stroke the rod back again. Pull more line off the reel during this back stroke if you need more line out to reach your target. You shouldn't need more than three to six strokes to get your fly where you want it. If you do, you're not letting out enough line with each stroke.

When false casting, imagine that the rod is a hand on a clock, with 12 o'clock being directly over your head. On your back cast, don't let your rod go past the 1 or 2 o'clock mark. Similarly, don't let the rod go past 10 or 11 o'clock on your forward cast. Turn your head to follow the movement of the rod behind you; what may feel like 1 o'clock may be closer to 3 o'clock. If you feel the rod "help" you on your backward and forward casts, as its flexing action works along with your strokes, you're doing it properly.

One way to help you limit your casts to those angles is to keep your wrist locked. If you bend your wrist backward, the rod will dip way past 1 o'clock on the back cast and 11 o'clock on the forward. (Some anglers even go so far as to strap the butt of their rod to their wrist to prevent bending it.) Let your forearm pivot at the elbow to move the rod backward. On the forward cast, "punch" the rod forward, moving your forearm ahead to get more power into the stroke, much like hammering a nail into a wall. You need that extra power to move that slack line in your left hand through the guides and into the air.

Now for the timing: When working the rod, you'll notice that the leader will curl above the line as you end each stroke. Let the leader uncurl and straighten out just when you begin the next cast. This happens in an instant, and requires some coordination and a bit of a "feel" for when to actually begin the stroke. If you begin the

School Notes

It helps immensely to have someone else stand to the side to point out flaws in your form. You may be doing something wrong—dropping the rod too far back, bending your wrist, or hurrying your strokes—that you may not realize, but an observer will notice it immediately. For fair play, let the observer try it when he or she starts making wisecracks.

Cautious Casts

Watch out for "wind knots," which are simple overhand knots caused by both wind blowing your tippet across your leader, and by starting a back or forward cast too early or late. These hard-to-detect knots will reduce your line strength significantly, causing it to break if you hook a powerful fish.

stroke too early, before the leader has a chance to uncurl, you'll snap the line like a whip. This reduces casting efficiency and may actually pop the fly off your tippet. If you begin the stroke too late, the line will begin to fall to the ground, requiring more power to get it back up in the air.

When working out line during your false casts, keep the line above your target, not pointed right at it. This is important because when you finally stop your forward cast, the line must float down onto it. Aiming at the target instead of above it will cause the line and leader to shoot down into the water, which will shorten your cast and possibly tangle your line.

False casting is the most difficult aspect of flyfishing for beginners to master. Don't try to cast long distances at first; it's easier to work on and correct your angles and timing with a short line. Remember: Keep the line moving, and let the rod work with you, not against you.

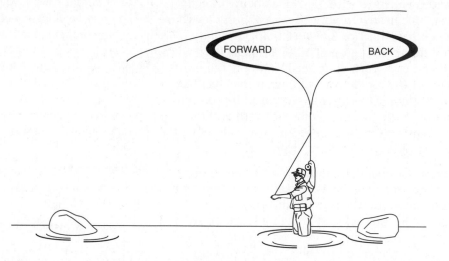

FORWARD   BACK

False cast by working the rod back and forth, putting more line into the air with each forward stroke.

Hitting Your Target

So you're working your line out in false casts, and the fly has reached that point directly above your target. What now?

Basically, let the line fall to the water. The fly should light on or in the water first, followed by the leader and then the fly line. But you must remember to stop your rod at 10 or 11 o'clock, and not drop the rod tip down too far on that final forward cast. If you do so, you'll lose the power of the forward cast by negating the flex of the rod. In other words, you'll lose distance. Also, your fly line will fall to the water first, followed by the leader and then the fly itself. This may not be a problem when fishing still waters, but in a current, it will start moving the fly line downstream before the fly has even touched the water, thus shortening the effective time of the drift. (And if you're fishing in a current, you should aim your fly upstream of your target. More on this in Chapter 19, "Real-Life Flyfishing.")

The fly should touch the water first, followed by the leader and fly line.

An easier method, which does not require so much casting, is to work out line in the air until it's close to your target. Have some extra line off of the reel hanging at your feet. Then, on the last forward cast, put a bit more power into it (remember not to drop your rod tip). The momentum of the line in the air will pull the extra line through the guides, providing enough line to reach the target.

Don't expect to hit your target perfectly the first time. You must practice the timing and the power of that last forward cast, and be able to estimate how much line it will pull through the guides. At first, chances are your cast will either fall short or go way past where you want it to go. This can only be remedied by becoming more familiar with your outfit, which translates into practice.

Now that you have all that fly line out in front of you, it's time to pick it back up and cast again. Don't try to lift it all in the air with one backward sweep of the rod; the surface tension of the water makes the line difficult to pick up smoothly. It will also cause a commotion, possibly spooking fish. Instead, strip in some line first. Hold the rod as you normally would, and use your other hand to pull in short lengths of line, grabbing hold of it between the reel and the first guide. You may find it easier to extend the forefinger and thumb of your casting hand down below the grip, to pinch the line after each pull. When you've stripped in all but 20 feet or so of line, point the rod tip down at the line in front of you. Then sweep the rod back to the 1 or 2 o'clock position and begin false casting again. With experience, you'll be able to pick up longer lengths.

179

It's not necessary to crank the line back onto the reel after you strip it back in. Simply let it gather at your feet. Fly line is slick; it won't knot up. The only time slack line may be a problem is when you're standing in a river or stream and the current takes the loops of fly line downstream. Even this won't hinder your casts, unless the loops snag on some rocks or branches in the current. If this happens, simply shorten up on your slack by reeling in some line.

Casting Ills Cured

If you're practicing your fly casting and can't seem to get over one particular problem, the cause is often easily corrected:

➤ If your line doesn't lay out straight in front of you, you're probably not putting enough power into your forward cast. Be forceful (but not overly so) with that last forward stroke.

➤ If you're not getting enough distance, you may be rushing your false casts, particularly your last back cast. Make sure the line straightens out in the air behind you before bringing it forward.

➤ If the line falls in front of you in heaps or curves, you are either rushing your back cast as noted above, or aiming your false casts too low. Cast high, above the target, and let the line fall to the water.

➤ If the line is hitting the water behind you on your back cast, you're dropping the rod back too far. Don't go past 1 or 2 o'clock on the back cast.

➤ If the line splashes into the water in front of you, you're dropping the rod too far in front of you. Don't go past 10 or 11 o'clock on the forward cast.

School Notes

When practicing in a yard or park, it helps to put out an actual target. Start with a large one—at least 3 feet in diameter—and cast from 20 feet away. You can lay out some newspaper or cardboard and hold it down with rocks. When you start hitting that consistently, increase your distance from and reduce the size of your target.

Alternative Casts

There are times when the basic overhead cast won't work, such as when you don't have enough room behind you for a back cast, or the current is running so fast that the water takes your fly line rushing downstream before the fly has a chance to go near a fish. These casts aren't difficult to make, once you can make a decent overhead cast consistently.

The simplest and probably most common alternative cast is the *roll cast*. This cast is handy when you're fishing a stream or a lake shore where your back casts would tangle in trees or brush growing at the water's edge, because fly line doesn't have to swing behind you. The roll cast is also effective when you're casting a short distance to the same area; say, to a small section of riffles in a trout stream.

The roll cast begins with line already out in front of you. Make a normal overhead cast, or if obstructions prohibit that, pull line off the reel and jiggle the rod tip. Have no more than 20 feet of line out when first practicing. Hold the line in your off (non-casting) hand, or clamp the line to the grip with your casting-hand forefinger. Now, bring the rod back behind you, to about the 2 o'clock position. Don't lift your rod hand higher than your head. Angle the rod a bit away from your body so that the line hanging from the rod tip isn't directly behind you. Without pausing, drive the rod forward and down, stopping it abruptly at about 10 o'clock (imagine you're hitting a bug on a kitchen counter with the bottom of your fist). The line should roll up from the surface in an oval and curl forward, lifting your leader and fly out of the water and dropping it as the fly line tightens.

Cautious Casts

If your fly is continually snapping off your tippet when casting, and you aren't rushing your back cast, you may be using too light a tippet for the weight of the fly. Avoid losing flies by cutting back your leader to a heavier diameter, or by using a lighter, smaller fly.

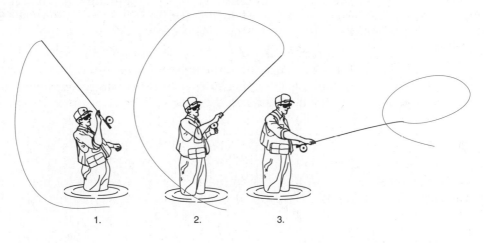

1.   2.   3.

Executing a roll cast.

The *horizontal cast* is also used when obstructions prohibit normal overhead casting. This cast becomes particularly handy when you're fishing streams that have overhanging limbs and branches from trees growing along both shorelines, or when you want to cast a fly beneath a tree hanging over a lake or pond—areas that fish frequent. To make a horizontal cast, simply hold the rod parallel to the water's surface and follow the same motions that you would for a typical overhead cast. However, you must impart much more energy into both your backward and forward casts to keep the line and leader from hitting or skipping the water. Most anglers make the mistake of not waiting for the line and leader to straighten out on backward and forward casts; snapping the leader like a whip and creating wind knots or popping the fly right off. Remember: Just put more energy into your casts without opening up your angles or changing your timing.

Although you should strive to put the line on the water in a straight, even line, there are times when you may actually want loops or wiggles to form in the line. A controlled slack-line cast lays the line down in even, consistent loops, with the leader and fly at the end of it (unlike a sloppy cast, in which the fly may fall behind or on top of the line and leader). So why would anyone want to lay down a fly line full of loops and wiggles?

The reason is drag. When fishing in a current, the heavy fly line moves downstream quicker than the comparatively lightweight leader and fly. The leader and fly eventually get pulled downstream faster than normal, and at a different angle. This causes the fly to look quite unlike natural forage, flowing along with the current. The angle of your cast to the current will delay drag to an extent, but at times you need to impart extra slack to the fly line, which increases the amount of time your fly can drift without drag.

The *S-cast* creates this kind of slack in the line. There are two ways to make one, and both are easy. The first method is to wiggle the rod tip at the end of your final forward cast, just before the line touches the water. This puts a number of curves into the line, which the current must then straighten out before dragging on the fly. The larger the angle you wiggle the rod tip, the bigger curves you get.

The second S-cast method is to shoot your final forward cast with more energy than needed, then abruptly check it. This causes the line to jerk back and fall in loops upon the water, also prolonging a drag-free drift. If you need larger loops, pull the rod back a bit just before the line lights on the water.

Make an S-cast by wiggling your rod tip at the end of your forward cast (A), or by checking your final forward cast (B).

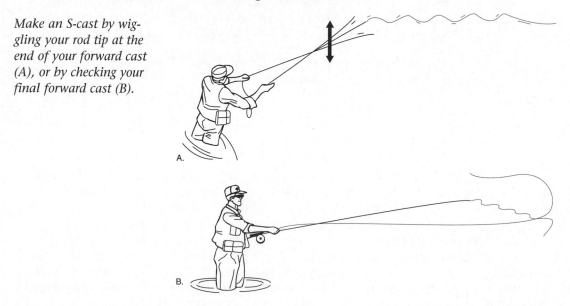

Loose Lines

Because of flyfishing's modern renaissance, a number of schools and individuals now offer professional fly casting instruction. These vary from fishing guides who advertise their services at a local marina or tackle shop (the equivalent of the country club tennis pro) to night courses at a community college, to vacation packages with meals and accommodations included at a resort destination. If you're serious about learning to flyfish, I highly recommend such instruction. Even a couple of hours of professional help can improve your form tremendously. *Black's Fly Fishing*, an annually updated guide to flyfishing equipment, instruction, and destinations, has state-by-state listings of schools and teachers. Check bookstores or call 908/224-8700.

The Least You Need to Know

➤ Hold a fly rod above the reel, with your thumb along the top of the grip. Find a position that's comfortable but gives you control of the rod.

➤ False cast the rod back and forth, pulling line from the reel to increase the amount of line in the air. Confine your back-and-forth arcs to the 10 o'clock and 2 o'clock positions, with 12 o'clock being directly overhead.

➤ Put some energy into your last cast to enable the fly to reach your target, but don't hurry the cast—particularly your back cast.

➤ After the overhead cast, the roll cast is the most practical in fishing situations.

Chapter 18

Be a Lord
of the Flies

In This Chapter

➤ Flies that float and those that don't

➤ The deadly nymph

➤ Flies that look like fish

➤ Terrestrials: the accidental flies

➤ How to bug a bass

In fishing jargon, a *fly* is a lure consisting of various materials—wool, chenille, fur, hair, feathers, tinsel, and others—tied to a hook to imitate an insect, a worm, a fish egg, a baitfish, or some other organism that fish eat. All flies fall within a certain classification and are named after the angler who created that particular pattern, or the type of forage it is supposed to simulate, or even for a certain characteristic. The creation and cataloging of flies is a study in itself, with literally thousands of patterns in existence and more being added each year. Many books have been written on flies and fly patterns; some so detailed that they focus on just one particular class of flies that imitates one particular species of insect!

While a knowledge of entomology does help the fly angler, it is not mandatory. A broad understanding of the right fly to use at the right time—and how to fish that fly—is all that's necessary to successfully catch fish on flies. For example, one friend can pick a mayfly out of the air on a trout stream, identify it by its Latin name, state its emergence date, select the pattern that it perfectly imitates, and catch a fish on it. Another friend sees "little black bugs," as he calls them, flitting over a trout stream, ties on a "little black fly," and catches a trout on it. Obviously, fishing with flies can be as simple or as complicated as you want it to be. This chapter will give you the basics.

School Notes

It's wise to buy flies from a tackle shop close to the waters you intend to fish. Insects differ regionally, and you might as well purchase flies that are known to catch fish in that area. Most tackle-shop proprietors will freely dispense advice on local hatches and the best patterns to match them.

School Notes

Although dry flies are tied with buoyant materials, they will begin to sink a bit with use. Adding some fly floatant, which typically comes in a small bottle and is sold at tackle shops, will keep your dry fly riding high.

Dry Flies: The Ones to Watch

As their name implies, *dry flies* float on the surface of the water. They imitate mayflies, stoneflies, caddisflies, craneflies, mosquitoes, and midges. Most of them are designed to imitate one of two stages of an insect's life: an adult fly, which hatches from its nymphal form on the stream bottom and rides on top of the water before it dries its wings and flies off in search of a mate; and the spent fly, which falls back to the surface of the water after mating.

Dry flies are constructed on lightweight hooks and of water-resistant materials. Directly behind the eye of most dry flies are feather fibers, called "hackles," that are wound around the hook so they are perpendicular to the shaft. The dry fly floats on the tips of these hackles, so the body of the fly, which can consist of a variety of materials, is well above the water's surface. Some dry flies have a tail, made of feather fibers, coming off the top of the bend of the hook, which also rests on the surface. Other dry flies feature hackles wound all the way from eye to bend. Wings, if any, are stiff and upright.

Many species of fish—particularly trout—will feed on one species of fly when it is hatching to the exclusion of all others. Even a perfectly presented worm, minnow, or spinner won't draw a look from a trout that is keyed into a particular hatch. Because that insect may be different in size, shape, and color from other insects, the angler must "match the hatch" with a pattern that closely resembles the emerging fly. Scores of dry-fly patterns do just that. There also are patterns that generally resemble a number of species, and patterns that match nothing in particular but are tied to stimulate a hit from a fish.

Examples of dry-fly styles, from left: divided wing, bivisible, and spent wing.

Dry flies are normally cast upstream and allowed to float downstream. Ideally, the angler spots a rise form—a dimple or pucker in the water where a fish has sipped a real fly off the surface—and casts so that his artificial fly floats over the same place. You can also fish dry flies in still waters, by casting either to likely areas or to rise forms. However, the fly must be presented upstream of the rise, so that it floats over the fish without evidence of drag. The angler tries to keep the drift drag-free by stripping in fly line (called "mending") before the current causes it to pull on the fly. (Dries can also sometimes be fished downstream to rises and "twitched" to entice a strike, or "skated" across the surface.)

Dry-fly fishermen need to carry a selection of patterns to be prepared for any situation. Although the best selection is dictated by region, as different insect species predominate in different regions, a good all-around selection is listed in the following table. These are basic patterns and sizes that will work for the majority of hatches and for general dry-fly fishing across the United States, and are recommended as a good selection for the beginning flyfisherman.

Basic Dry-Fly Patterns

Pattern	Hook Sizes
Adams	No. 12–16
Black Gnat	No. 12–16
Brown Bivisible	No. 10–14
Grey Wulff	No. 8–12
Henryville Special	No. 12–16
Irresistible	No. 8–12
Light Cahill	No. 12–16
March Brown	No. 10–14
Quill Gordon	No. 12–16
Royal Coachman	No. 10–14

Note in the table that a range of three sizes is listed for each fly (for instance, the Adams in sizes 12, 14, and 16) for a total of 30 flies. If you want to pare the list down further, simply buy the size in the middle of the range for each pattern (a No. 14 Adams, a No. 14 Black Gnat, a No. 12 Brown Bivisible, etc.). You can add to your collection as you learn about hatches in your local waters.

Loose Lines

There are two ways to obtain flies: by buying them at a tackle shop or by tying them yourself. Fly-tying is a hobby that, in the end, probably does not save the angler a fortune. But it's fun and rewarding to sit down and create flies out of thread, fur, feathers, wool, and dozens of other materials, and then go out and catch fish with them. Hundreds of books exist on fly-tying, with specifics on the tools necessary, the basic materials you need, and instructions for tying various patterns. Even more fun is to develop your very own fly pattern, based on careful study of forage in waters you fish, or simply out of your own creativity. And it's a terrific off-season pastime.

Wet Flies

Wet flies are designed to be fished beneath the surface. Depending on the pattern and how it is fished, a wet fly can imitate a variety of forage: drowned insects, drowning insects, insects hatching from their nymphal stage and rising to the surface, an egg-laying insect, or a small baitfish.

"Wets" are created from soft, absorbent materials and tied on heavy wire hooks so they sink quickly. Like dry flies, there are hundreds of patterns, with some tied to imitate a specific insect, and others tied to attract fish. The hackles on a wet fly are soft and typically angle back a bit from the hook eye, so that they undulate and appear lifelike in the water. Wings are large and also slanted back along the hook shaft. Tails, if any, are large and also are made of materials that absorb water readily.

Compared to dry flies, wet flies are typically more colorful and exhibit more flash (although some, especially those patterns that imitate specific insects, are earth-toned). They also differ from dries in the manner in which they are fished. While wets can be cast upstream and allowed to drift downstream, they can also be cast across-stream and directly downstream. The angler can allow the wet fly to drift naturally, or impart slight movement to it by jiggling the rod tip. At the end of the drift, when the fly swings directly downstream of the angler, you can move the fly into different areas by moving the rod and/or letting out line. Then you can retrieve the wet fly back to the rod in short pulls, letting the fly dart and dive erratically in the current. In this manner, the wet fly can resemble a drowned or drowning insect on the downstream drift and a hatching insect or a minnow on the upstream retrieve. Such a technique allows an angler to thoroughly fish a large section of water.

You can also fish a wet fly in still waters by casting out to a likely area, letting the fly sink—either just beneath the surface, to mid-level, or down to the bottom, depending on the water and the species—and then retrieving it, either quickly or slowly, erratically or smoothly.

It's also possible to fish with more than one wet fly at a time. You can accomplish this by tying one or two dropper lines—short lengths of monofilament—onto the leader, above the end (or point) fly. The angler can then present a number of patterns simultaneously to find out what the fish are interested in that particular day. Also, tying a large fly at the point and a small fly on a dropper gives the appearance of a large baitfish chasing an insect, or a small baitfish, which often provokes strikes.

School Notes

Generally, dry flies need to be fished on fine tippets so the fish doesn't see the line as it floats next to the fly. Because wet flies are fished under the water, where the line isn't as noticeable, it's OK to use a heavier tippet for the same-size fly.

Examples of wet-fly styles, from left: divided wing, featherwing, and hackle.

Because there are many wet-fly patterns, it's impossible to come up with a list of flies that would work for any fishing situation. However, the 10 patterns listed in the following table are a good all-around collection for the beginner.

Basic Wet-Fly Patterns

Pattern	Hook Sizes
Black Gnat	No. 12–16
Black Woolly Worm	No. 8–12

continues

Basic Wet–Fly Patterns   (continued)

Pattern	Hook Sizes
Blue Dun	No. 12–16
Dark Cahill	No. 12–16
Gold-Ribbed Hare's Ear	No. 10–14
Leadwing Coachman	No. 10–14
Light Cahill	No. 12–16
Olive Emergent Caddis Pupa	No. 12–14
Quill Gordon	No. 12–16
Royal Coachman	No. 10–14

Generally, wet flies are easier to fish than dry flies, because they're more forgiving of errors. Even if you throw your line sloppily, or your flies drag on the drift, the cast can always be salvaged at the end by retrieving the flies back to you.

Loose Lines

It's important to gain some confidence when you begin flyfishing. Don't attempt too much at first, such as trying to catch a trout in a clear-water stream. Instead, consider going for bluegills or pumpkinseeds in a pond or small lake. These panfish are voracious eaters, don't spook easily, have short memories when they do, and are scrappy fare on a fly rod. Hone your techniques on these easy-to-catch species before you graduate to bigger, warier species.

Nymphs

No, it's not a typo. *Nymphs*, without the "o," are the larval stages of insects that live on lake or stream bottoms. Most nymph patterns used by fishermen imitate mayfly, caddisfly, stonefly, dragonfly, and cranefly nymphs.

Nymphs abound in cool-water streams; check the undersides of rocks in one and you're bound to find a few of the flat, elongated creatures clinging to them.

Compared to their adult forms, nymphs are unattractive, with scaly, segmented bodies and clawed legs. But nymphs make up a large part of the diet of fish, particularly trout. It has often been repeated that "a good nymph fisherman can clean out a trout stream." I don't know if this is true, but I know some flyfishermen who use nymphs almost all the time … and they do catch a lot of trout (they put most of them back, thankfully).

The reason we don't hear of fished-out trout streams by unscrupulous nymph fishermen is because the technique is difficult—probably the most difficult flyfishing technique of all in fresh water. Fishing a nymph is very much like fishing a dry fly underwater: The nymph must be drifted through likely flows, as close to the bottom as possible, and without any drag. The angler must constantly mend line to prevent drag, turning the rod and his body to follow the nymph downstream. At the end of the drift, after it swings in the current, the nymph must be picked up and cast again, unlike wet flies, which can be retrieved all the way back to the rod. But the nymph fisherman doesn't have the sight advantage of the dry-fly fisherman; he must look for a slight twitch of the fly line or just a pause in its downstream drift. Many nymph fishermen strike every time they see the line twitch or pause during its drift; sometimes it's caused by a fish taking the nymph, but usually it's the result of the nymph bumping a rock.

Like wet flies, nymph patterns are tied on heavy wire hooks to facilitate sinking. Extra weight such as lead wire is sometimes wrapped around the hook shank before other materials are tied in to ensure that the nymph will drop to the bottom quickly. The bodies themselves consist of fur, wool, and other fibrous materials that appear lifelike underwater. Hackles, if any, are long and soft, as are the tails, also to provide motion.

School Notes

If you find tiny sticks or pebbles in a trout's belly in spring, tie on a caddis pattern quickly. Caddis nymphs construct little "houses" of those materials (which you can sometimes find sticking to the underside of a rock), and trout know it.

Examples of nymph styles: Hendrickson and stonefly (top); mayfly (bottom).

191

As with dry flies and wet flies, there is a huge number of nymph patterns. Most nymph fishermen become students of entomology to learn the range, habits, color, sizes, and other details of nymph species. However, the nymph patterns listed in the following table will work in a variety of waters during much of the year.

Basic Nymph Patterns

Pattern	Hook Sizes
Brown Stonefly	No. 12–16
Caddis Larva	No. 12–16 2X long
Gold-Ribbed Hare's Ear	No. 10–14
Large Black Stonefly	No. 6–10 2X long
March Brown	No. 10–14
Montana	No. 8–12
Zug Bug	No. 10–14

One way to figure out what size and color pattern to use on a particular day in a particular water is to pick up submerged rocks and match the most prevalent nymph you find. You can also examine the contents of a fish's stomach to find what kind of nymph the fish are eating that day. Of course, you have to catch a fish first to do that.

Loose Lines

Dry flies tend to lose their efficacy with use and age: Their stiff materials bend, break, and begin to lose water. Nymphs, on the other hand, seem to become more effective the more they're fished. Perhaps the wearing of the materials causes the nymph to undulate more provocatively underwater. Whatever the reason, a chewed-up nymph is certainly proof of its effectiveness.

Streamers and Bucktails

These "flies" imitate baitfish, and are tied on long-shanked hooks to enhance that appearance. The *streamer* has a long "wing" made of feathers, which is attached to the hook just behind the eye and extends along the top of the shank. Some streamer patterns have tails as well. *Bucktails* are streamers that have wings made of the long hair from a deer's tail, which may be dyed yellow or red, or left in its natural brown-and-white coloration. Most streamer and bucktail patterns have a body, usually a sparsely tied one consisting of a single layer of yarn or tinsel.

Some streamer patterns imitate actual baitfish species—such as the Black Nose Dace—while others resemble nothing at all, with improbable color combinations and oversized eyes. These attractor patterns are meant to induce strikes through their flash and vibrancy.

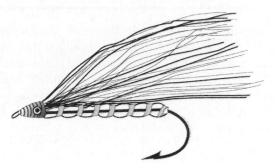

A bucktail streamer (top) and a feather streamer (bottom).

As with the other flies, there are hundreds of streamer and bucktail patterns to choose from. The following table lists some popular and proven patterns.

Basic Streamer Patterns

Pattern	Hook Sizes
Black Nose Dace	No. 6–10 3X long
Gray Ghost	No. 8–12 3X long

continues

Basic Streamer Patterns (continued)

Pattern	Hook Sizes
Marabou (White, Black)	No. 6–10 2X long
Matuka (Olive, Black)	No. 6–10 2X long
Mickey Finn	No. 6–10 3X long
Muddler Minnow	No. 4–8 2X long
Woolly Bugger (Tan, White)	No. 4–8 2X long
Zonker (White, Olive)	No. 4–8 3X long

Unlike dry flies, wet flies, and nymphs, you should keep streamers in motion almost all of the time they are in the water. In a current, the angler should cast directly across-stream, twitching the streamer as it drifts. You can also put the streamer into pockets and seams by mending the line and manipulating the rod tip. When the streamer is all the way downstream, retrieve it back to the rod by stripping in line, again working the rod to place the streamer into likely areas. In still waters, the angler should cast to all likely areas and retrieve the streamer at various speeds, working it through all levels of the water column.

Loose Lines

If I had to fish with just one streamer, it would be the Muddler Minnow. It's probably the most versatile streamer pattern in existence, because it can imitate a variety of forage depending on how it's fished. Made of deer hair and turkey feathers with a gold tinsel body, the Muddler floats if unweighted, making it look remarkably like a grasshopper struggling in the current. When retrieved at the end of the drift, the Muddler can resemble a minnow breaking the surface of the water or a mouse swimming across the flow. If weighted, the Muddler can look like a large nymph bumping along the bottom, or a sculpin minnow seeking shelter among the rocks. Muddler Minnows are tied in a variety of sizes and colors, but I'm partial to the lifelike original brown/white/gold pattern.

Terrestrials

So named because they mimic creatures normally found on land ("terra"), *terrestrials* imitate a wide variety of insects that get blown, washed, or otherwise deposited into the water accidentally. These insects—ants, beetles, blackflies, crickets, grasshoppers, and others—are basically helpless, and fish feed upon them constantly, because they're available every day throughout much of the open-water season.

Examples of terrestrial flies, from left: ant, beetle, grasshopper.

Terrestrials are fished much like dry flies—they should be cast upstream and allowed to float down—but some patterns, such those that imitate grasshoppers and crickets, can be twitched and even retrieved to simulate a struggling insect. Although terrestrials don't hatch as do mayflies and other aquatic insects, some species are widespread at certain times of year, and fish will key on them. Look for an abundance of ants, grasshoppers, inchworms, or some other creatures, and match them with one of the flies listed in the following table.

Basic Terrestrial Patterns

Pattern	Hook Sizes
Ant (Black, Brown, Red)	No. 16–20
Beetle	No. 12–16
Cricket	No. 8–12
Hopper	No. 8–12
Inchworm	No. 16–20 2X long
Jassid	No. 18–22

Many patterns for the same terrestrial exist; this table shows generic patterns. You should pick styles that seem to match forage in your region.

Bass Bugs

Although they're called bugs, these fly-rod lures actually imitate larger forage: frogs, mice and other rodents, and large insects such as bees and dragonflies. They are used most often for largemouth and smallmouth bass, and all of them float.

Bass bugs fall into two categories: deer-hair bugs and solid-body bugs. Deer-hair bugs have bodies made of that material, which is laid across the shank of the hook and tied tightly, which causes the hairs to stand perpendicular. When a number of lengths of deer hair are tied on in this manner, they can be clipped into various shapes and forms. (And because deer-hair folli-cles are hollow, the bug floats extremely well.)

Solid-body bugs are constructed of cork, balsa wood, or hollow plastic, and painted to resemble forage. Some are streamlined in shape; others have a cupped face that will gurgle and spit when retrieved. These are called "popping bugs."

These "flies" are best fished near weeds for large-mouths, or in rocky, gravelly shallows for small-mouths. The deer-hair and streamlined solid-body bugs should be retrieved slowly, and the poppers per-form best when twitched erratically so they actually make a popping sound.

Solid-body bass bugs (top) and deer-hair bugs (bottom).

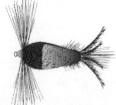

Bass bugs will take more than bass, however. The small deer-hair versions work well on trout and panfish, particularly during twilight hours in summer. Large poppers and deer-hair bugs that resemble mice will take pike and pickerel as well as bass.

Bass bug patterns are mostly proprietary; manufacturers are constantly introducing new styles and shapes. They also don't have to exactly match the forage they are imitating (to a bass, a 2-inch frog is a 2-inch frog). Carry a few of each style to be prepared.

The Least You Need to Know

➤ Dry flies float on the surface of the water. Most dry flies match specific aquatic insects that hatch into winged adults, and are presented to fish feeding on the prevalent insect.

➤ Wet flies sink beneath the surface. They resemble drowned or drowning insects when drifted, and hatching insects or small baitfish when retrieved.

➤ Nymphs mimic the larval stage of aquatic insects. They should be drifted close to or on the bottom.

➤ Bucktails and streamers imitate baitfish. They should always be kept in motion when in the water.

➤ Terrestrials resemble land-based organisms that have fallen accidentally into the water. They float, and are usually fished like dry flies.

➤ Bass bugs simulate frogs, rodents, or large insects such as bees. They are designed to be retrieved across the surface. Bass bugs also take panfish, trout, pickerel, and pike.

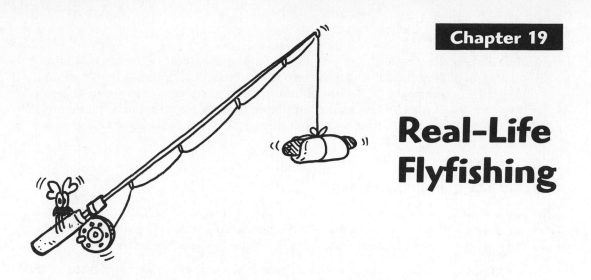

Chapter 19

Real-Life Flyfishing

In This Chapter

➤ Think before you cast

➤ The dreaded D-word

➤ Strike time

➤ Don't touch that reel—yet

One of the best all-around fly fishermen I know isn't a world-class fly caster. He keeps his casts very short, preferring to walk or wade close to his target rather than make long reaches. He isn't an expert in entomology, either, although he can identify the basic insect species that fish feed upon. And he doesn't own the finest tackle; some of his stuff is actually pretty beat up.

But this flyfisherman is a master at putting his fly in front of fish. He spends just as much time looking at the water, studying its condition, and moving into place as he does casting his line. He's always in complete control of the fly rod and fly line, and he rarely blows a cast or spooks a fish.

That's what this chapter is all about: using your flyfishing tackle to catch fish, rather than to exercise your arms on a Saturday afternoon.

Where to Cast

Here's where you *shouldn't* cast first: directly at the fish. Most beginners make the mistake of aiming their first cast so the fly falls directly on or over a fish or where they think a fish might be. Think about it from the fish's perspective: Out of nowhere drops an object directly into its field of vision, possibly with a bit of a splash, or with the line slapping the water as well. That fish won't stay there long—much less take the fly.

Stillwater Fly Casting

An absolutely perfect cast directly over a fish might work well in still water if you are using a dry fly. But you stand the risk of overcasting, which will put the leader and possibly the fly line over the fish, and will definitely spook the fish.

If you see a fish, or the rise form of a fish, in a lake or pond, make your first cast deliberately short. Lay the fly down gently. If you're using a dry fly, let it sit. If you're using a nymph, let it sink, then bring it back with minute strips of the line. Allow wet flies and streamers to sink, then retrieve. Let a bass bug sit on the surface until the water disturbance dissipates before retrieving.

Extend the length of your next cast a bit and follow through similarly. Continue to lengthen your casts until you're putting the fly right over the fish. Remember that fish have large fields of vision, and a feeding fish will see a fly some distance away from it. If the fish doesn't take your fly, or if it moves off, look for other rises and work your casts gradually toward the fish. This method guarantees that you won't spook a fish or put it down by overcasting.

If you're not casting toward a specific fish or rise form—such as when casting bass bugs in a lake or pond—again, don't try to hit the mark with your first cast. If you want to work the edge of a weedbed with your popper, aim your first cast so that the bug falls a few feet out from the edge. Retrieve, then cast again, dropping it closer. Continue this until you put the bug right next to the weeds. By following this routine you won't overshoot the target and tangle your line in weeds or spook fish with your heavy fly line.

Casting in a Current

Fish usually face upstream in rivers and streams, and your fly line, leader, and fly all start moving downstream as soon as they hit the water. Therefore, you must always cast above your target, whether it's a fish, a rise form, or a general area.

When fishing with dry flies or terrestrials, you should usually stand downstream of your target and cast up- and across-stream, so the fly lands above the target, with your line angling to the side and downstream of it. This way, the fly will float over the target without the fly line following it. As the fly progresses downstream, you can mend line (strip it in) and lift your rod to ensure that the faster-floating fly line doesn't drag on the fly. (See "How to Avoid Drag" below.) After the fly floats past the target, or begins exhibiting drag, lift the line and cast again.

Wet flies are generally best cast directly across stream or at an angle downstream. The fly sinks in the water as the current pulls it downstream, and line tension at the end of the drift will pull the flies around in an arc in front of your target. Then the fly can be worked around the target and into different areas by lifting and swinging your rod. Finally the fly is slowly retrieved.

Nymph fishing is similar to dry-fly fishing, except that the angler works a general area rather than a specific fish. Cast nymphs up- and across-stream and mend line to keep the nymph drifting naturally underwater as close to the bottom as possible. As the nymph passes in front of you, mend more line and lift the rod. Wait until the nymph swings around in an arc as the line straightens downstream, then pick up the line and cast again.

The best way to fish a streamer or bucktail in a current is to cast it directly across-stream, or a bit upstream if the water is fast and/or deep. Allow the streamer to sink a bit, then retrieve with quick strips of the line. By continually recasting to a point just a bit downstream of the previous cast, you can cover an entire section of water below you. On your downstream-angle casts, be sure to let the streamer arc completely across the current before you begin the retrieve.

School Notes

If you're trout fishing but no hatch is on, try casting a big, heavy hackled fly like a Bivisible to pools, runs, and seams. Make several casts to each area. Sometimes trout can't resist what appear to be big juicy flies floating past them.

School Notes

Sometimes fish appear to be rising but they won't take a dry fly that matches the insects you see flying about. Often, these fish are taking hatching flies before they reach the surface. Switching to a wet fly of the same pattern and casting it upstream, like a dry fly, may take these fish.

How to Avoid Drag

Drag occurs whenever your fly, dry or wet, travels on or through the water faster than the current in which it is drifting. It occurs most often when your heavy fly line, which is extending across the river or stream, is subject to currents of various speeds and travels downstream faster than the fly is traveling, thus pulling the fly along with it.

Drag can be the ruin of the dry-fly fisherman casting to a rising fish. A trout, for example, might be stationed in a current seam during a hatch, rising up to take an insect about once a minute. All these insects drift past the fish at the same rate of speed. So the angler wades down- and across-stream from the trout and casts so that his dry fly, which exactly matches the hatching insects in size and color, will float directly into that trout's lie. He casts perfectly, but just when his dry fly is about the enter the feeding area above the trout, his fly line—which is already downstream of the fly—gets caught in a fast flow and causes the dry fly to skate across the surface, putting a little V-wake above the lie. The trout takes off for deeper water and skulks there, thinking spooked-trout thoughts, and the frustrated angler moves on.

Drag can also affect nymph fishermen, especially in fast, deep currents. These anglers must cast far enough above their target to let their flies sink to the proper level; often, the current takes the heavy fly line quickly downstream before the flies even enter the strike zone.

Loose Lines

Although it happens rarely, sometimes drag can actually help you catch a fish. When fishing the Albany River in the northern Ontario wilderness one spring, our group of five anglers fished for almost two days without catching one of the native brook trout for which this flowage is famous. On the afternoon of the second day, I spotted a rise on a 10-foot-wide offshoot of the main river, which was surrounded with brush and practically covered with a canopy of branches. My only approach was from downstream from the opposite bank, and I took it. My first cast fell short. On my second cast, the fly floated perfectly over the area where I thought the fish was—but no take. My third cast was too long, and I hastened to pull in fly line before it floated over the fish, spooking it. I was a little late reacting, though, and the fly skittered across the surface as I stripped in line. To my surprise, the trout smashed the fly.

We discovered later during the trip that lemmings were part of these trouts' diet. The little rodents occasionally swam across the river, and the trout slurped them up. One of my fishing partners had brought a hat adorned with bass bugs, including some deer-hair mice, on that trip—only because it was his favorite fishing hat, not because he was planning on using the big flies on a trout stream. But after I caught that fish, and we figured out why, that stained and ugly little crusher became more an object of desire than a flush toilet.

A few methods to defeat drag have been mentioned in the previous chapters. Here they are in summary:

1. *Cast up- and across-stream.* Your fly will float longer without drag than if you had cast down- and across-stream.

2. *Mend line.* As the fly and fly line cross in front of you, strip in line with your free hand. Simultaneously jerk your rod tip every few seconds to flip the fly line a bit upstream, which will prolong the fly's natural drift.

3. *Cast from another angle.* Sometimes moving a few feet upstream or downstream will reduce the current's effect on the fly line.

4. *Make S-casts.* These put more slack into your fly line, which will delay the current's effect on it.

5. *Try a different approach.* Unless you must use dry flies, such as during a hatch, try fishing a troublesome area with wet flies or nymphs, letting the fly arc across your target on the line's downstream swing.

Setting the Hook

No matter what kind of fly you're using, never wait to set the hook. Artificial flies don't feel at all like the real ones, and fish are quick to spit them out.

When fishing with dry flies, you'll know when to strike. As soon as the fish sips that fly off the water, lift the rod tip sharply while holding the line between reel and first guide firmly in your off-hand. Just make sure the fish actually has the fly first. It's possible to pull the fly away from the fish if you don't have much line out and you see the fish rise up to inspect the artificial fly. Don't react to the sight of the fish. Wait until the fly disappears before you lift the rod.

It's important that you don't have too much slack line on the water. Although you often need slack to prevent drag, don't have so much line out that you won't even move the fly when you lift the rod. To prevent this, always mend line as your fly drifts toward you.

School Notes

If you're fishing with a fine leader, don't forget about its low breaking strength when you're setting the hook. Lift the rod when a fish hits your fly, but don't put too much energy into it.

It's difficult to detect a strike when drifting a nymph or a wet fly before it arcs downstream and the line straightens out. Because the nymph is beneath the surface, and the line isn't under tension, a strike isn't obvious, and you certainly can't feel one. Closely watch the end of your fly line and strike sharply when you see a slight dip or a momentary pause in its drift. Often, that's the only clue you'll have that a fish has taken the fly. That's why many nymph fishermen strike at any seemingly unnatural movement of the line.

One aid to detecting a strike is a strike indicator, which is nothing more than a brightly colored bit of yarn, cloth, or wood that attaches to the leader butt via a knot or glue. It's a rudimentary bobber, and when it dips or disappears, you set the hook. Strike indicators are sold at tackle shops and through mail-order outlets.

It's relatively easy to detect a strike when fishing wet flies and nymphs downstream of you, or when retrieving a streamer. You'll feel the tension at the same time you see some of the line disappear underwater. Set the hook immediately—a fish has definitely taken your fly!

How to Play Your Fly-Caught Fish

For the majority of freshwater flyfishing situations, and excepting big species like northern pike, and when hooked into a larger-than-average fish that will make long runs and deep surges, the fish should be played by hand. That is, the rod hand holds the rod while the other hand strips in line.

The reason: In most circumstances, you will have a certain amount of slack line hanging at your feet between the reel and the first guide. But the fish is hooked, and it's jumping and surging, and your off-hand is holding the line. Although fly rods are comparatively long and will absorb a lot of the energy of the fish by bending and flexing, you may have to let some line slip gradually through your fingers at first, so you don't break off the fish when it's first hooked and at its strongest. Now is not the time to drop the line and crank in all that slack line; releasing pressure might allow the fish to throw the hook or tangle the leader and break you off. Just let the fly line puddle at your feet as you start bringing in the fish.

School Notes

When moving from one stretch of water to another, you can save time by looping the line around your reel handle, hooking your fly to a middle guide, and reeling up the slack. The line will stay tight against the rod when you're walking, but is easily unlooped, with 10 to 12 feet of line already out from the rod tip.

Obviously, you'll have to release the line after you strip some in so you can grab the line farther up to continue bringing in the fish. To maintain pressure on the fish, extend the forefinger of your rod hand and clamp the line against the rod grip, or against your thumb, after you draw in line with your off-hand. Then reach up and grab the line below your finger and repeat.

If the line hanging off the reel becomes an impediment—say, if it starts tangling around your legs, or if it's floating in front of you, barring you from reaching for or netting the fish—clamp the line against the grip and crank it in. But don't do this early in the fight, when the fish is still strong and may surge unpredictably. Take your time and play the fish until it's tired out and swimming in circles in front of you.

In the event you hook a truly large fish, you may have no choice but to play it off the reel. Any slack line you have hanging off the reel will disappear anyway as the fish zooms off. Your spool will be spinning against the drag, letting out more line. You can try to slow the fish down further by palming the spool (making sure you don't put too much pressure on it, and possibly breaking the line), and begin cranking in line whenever you can. Hold the rod up, but not over your head, and let the fish burn off its energy while you maintain control. Chase the fish if it runs too far or enters a section of water where it might break the line. Most of all, make sure you enjoy it. Go ahead and whoop if you feel like it, because this is what flyfishing is all about.

The Least You Need to Know

➤ Make gradually longer casts toward your target when fishing still water instead of trying to hit it with your first cast, so you don't risk overcasting and spooking fish.

➤ In a current, work gradually toward your target, and always cast upstream of it, so the fly enters the fish's vision naturally.

➤ Drag is caused by the fly line drifting faster than the fly. Avoid this by casting upstream, mending line, casting from another angle, or allowing more slack in your line.

➤ Set the hook as soon as a fish hits. Make sure the fish has taken the fly when dry-fly fishing, and strike at any movement of the line when drifting a nymph.

➤ Play fish by holding the line in your off-hand and drawing it in, using your rod-hand forefinger to clamp the line against the grip when necessary. Large fish should be played directly off the reel.

Part 5

Saltwater Fishing

Life supposedly originated in the ocean, and maybe that's why so many of us are drawn to it. Swimmers and sunbathers swarm the beaches every summer, as ski boats, yachts, and other pleasure craft ply the inshore waters. Northern-state residents flock to the warm-weather beaches of Florida, Texas, and the Caribbean every winter. Saltwaterfront property—not just oceanfront but bayfront, estuary front, tidal riverfront, and even muddy backwaterfront property—is among the most expensive real estate in the nation, reflecting this innate attraction to the sea.

The fishing can be great, too. With hundreds of species of different sizes, shapes, and attributes, and dozens of ways to fish for them, salt waters offer a lifetime of fishing opportunities. Whether you want to put together the makings of a delicious fish dinner, or attempt to hook one of the gamest fish in the world, or battle a fish that's two, three, even four times bigger than you, salt waters should be your destination.

The following chapters will run down the basics of saltwater fishing and strategies. The species and the best techniques vary tremendously across the country; consult a regional guide or magazine when you're ready to hit the salt.

Chapter 20

Finding Saltwater Fish

In This Chapter

➤ Hold the salt

➤ Fit to be tide

➤ Hitting the beach

➤ Inland ocean water

➤ Deep thinking

There are many different environments in salt waters, each with individual conditions that suit particular species. Yet these marine habitats and their residents are all connected, forming a perfect symbiotic balance. The empty snail shell you find on the beach becomes a home for the hermit crab, which is eaten by the blackfish, which is preyed upon by the shark, which dies and decomposes and eventually becomes food for the snail.

Luckily, you don't need a degree in marine ecology to figure out where to cast your sandworm to catch a flounder. However, you do need knowledge of preferred habitats of the species you're after, how they are influenced by the tide, how they feed, and how to increase your chances of catching them.

Why Saltwater Fish Are Different

Although freshwater species and saltwater species appear identical in form, freshwater fish would die if placed in salt water, and vice versa. The reason: Although both types need salt to survive, they get it in different ways.

Salt has a tendency to diffuse from areas of high concentrations to those of low concentrations. Therefore, freshwater fish lose the salts in their body via osmosis. To counteract this loss, the kidneys of freshwater fish rid the fish of water while retaining salts. Freshwater fish have glands that retain salts as the fish moves through the water.

Saltwater fish don't need these glands. However, because saltwater fish have less salt in their bodies than is in the water around them, they tend to gain salt—and lose water. To compensate for this loss, saltwater fish actually swallow water, and eliminate excess salts via their respiratory and digestive systems. (That's why a mouthful of ocean water tastes terribly salty, but you still shake some salt on your codfish fillet.)

Otherwise, saltwater fish are biologically and physiologically much the same as freshwater fish. However, their behavioral patterns differ markedly, due to the influence of the tide.

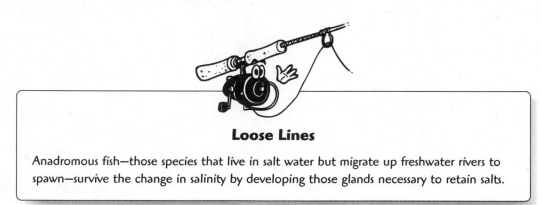

Loose Lines

Anadromous fish—those species that live in salt water but migrate up freshwater rivers to spawn—survive the change in salinity by developing those glands necessary to retain salts.

The Tidal Influence

Most saltwater species are affected either directly or indirectly by the tide, which raises and decreases shoreline water levels. Tide is caused by the gravitational pull of the moon and the sun. Basically, the water that rushes in and out of bays and estuaries creates strong currents and flushes forage out of cover, which usually triggers fish into feeding.

The tide changes four times every 24 hours: two high tides and two low tides. In most U.S. waters, low tide occurs about six hours after a high tide. And each day, the time of a tide occurs 50 minutes to one hour later than that tide on the previous day. At the culmination of each tide is a slack period, where no water moves.

In chronological order, an incoming tide is called a flood tide. Its peak, about six hours later, is called high-water slack. As the water starts draining out, it is called an ebb tide. About six hours after that is low-water slack, also called dead low tide.

The amount of the change in water level is dictated by the phase of the moon. Each month, the moon goes through four distinct changes: new (meaning the moon is not visible from earth), first quarter, full, and last quarter. A new moon and a full moon, which occur when the sun, earth, and moon are in a direct line, cause higher-than-normal tides. These are called spring tides. When the moon is at the first-quarter and third-quarter phases, the sun and moon form a right angle, with the earth at the center. Because the gravitational pull is decreased, tides are lower than normal. These are called neap tides.

The wind can also affect the height of a tide. If a strong wind is blowing toward the shore simultaneous with a flood tide, the water level will be higher than normal.

Saltwater fishermen should become familiar with tide times (which are published in area newspapers, shown on some television weather reports, and listed on "tide charts" that are available at many tackle shops) and patterns because they greatly influence fish behavior. During slack periods, forage fish can seek refuge in cover. When the tide starts moving, these fish are pulled along with the flow, where predatory fish feed on them.

Whether the flood tide or ebb tide makes for better fishing depends on the locale. Generally, an ebb tide draws forage fish out of shallow-water cover, because the dropping levels force the fish into deeper water. This usually means good fishing in areas where the currents are forced into narrow areas, such as tidal rivers and creeks— especially during a neap tide, when less water will remain near shore. In other areas, though, an incoming tide will allow gamefish access to areas they couldn't reach during low-tide periods, such as the shallow, weedy waters of a bay, where forage fish will hide. This is especially true during a spring tide, when the high-tide waters reach a higher-than-normal level.

Getting the Point

Brackish waters are those areas of rivers and creeks that contain salt, but that are not as salty as ocean water. Frequently, both freshwater and saltwater species inhabit brackish waters, which also usually exhibit some tidal influence.

Still, there are exceptions. For instance, in one tidal creek I frequent, the summer flounder fishing is much better on the flood than on the ebb. Why? I'm not sure. I have noticed, however, that a lot of vegetation and other debris gets sucked into the flow of the outgoing tide. My line gets fouled with weeds quite a bit during this period, but not often enough to keep a fish from finding my bait. But the actual reason isn't as important as my recognizing that pattern, which is what all saltwater fishermen should strive for: reading the tide and recognizing how it influences the fish in your waters.

Surf and Jetty Fishing

Just standing on a beach with the wind and salt spray blowing in your face while huge breakers crash at your feet can prove exciting and invigorating. Perhaps that's why so many people love to fish the surf, even though it is among the most difficult and challenging fishing venues.

There are actually three places to fish the surf: *beaches*, which are open stretches of sand and/or gravel; *groins*, which are man-made fingers of rock, wood, metal, or concrete that jut from the beach into the water; and *jetties*, which are groins that extend into the ocean from both sides of a tributary. (Groins are frequently referred to as jetties as well.) We'll look at each type individually.

Although a beach may look flat and featureless, the bottom beneath the surface usually isn't. If you walk along a beach at dead low tide, you'll see sandbars, holes, humps, and channels, often in a seemingly random pattern. Gamefish such as striped bass, bluefish, and redfish (red drum) use these bottom structures (when they're covered with water) to prey on forage. As the waves wash up on shore, and as the tidal currents—which always move up or down the beach—contribute to the turbulence, baitfish and other forage such as mollusks and crustaceans get caught in the flows. Gamefish will use the deeper sections, such as a *cut* (a channel perpendicular to the beach between two sandbars) or a *slough* (a channel that runs parallel to the beach, close to shore) to get to the forage without being tossed around by the turbulent waters. A surf fisherman should always check a beach at low tide to find these structures.

Fish often frequent a cut between two sandbars, which you can recognize by its lack of waves; and a slough, which is a deep section just off the beach behind the breakers.

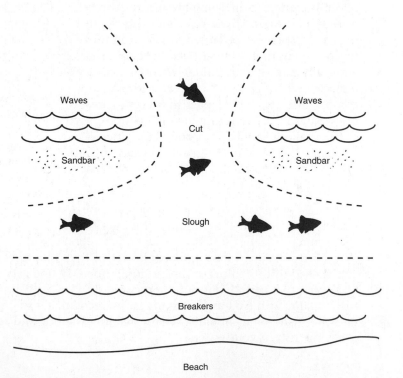

But sometimes the tide doesn't recede far enough to expose such structures. Then the angler must read the water to find suitable places to cast. The most common area lies beyond the point where ocean waves begin breaking. Waves fall when the circular motion of the water within the wave reaches shallow water, which causes the wave to grow higher, until it eventually falls on itself. Obviously, the water is deeper just beyond the wave-break point—sometimes it's a substantial dropoff—and gamefish will also congregate there. You'll often have to make a long cast, which requires a long rod, to reach this area. (Saltwater tackle is covered in the next chapter.)

A cut can also be recognized by certain wave patterns. Look for a break, or a relatively calm, flat area along a waveline. This indicates a deeper section in between two shallow areas. Gamefish will use the cut as a "highway" of sorts to access forage close to the beach.

School Notes

Many surf fishermen bring two rods, casting their baits far out with one and in close with the other, to narrow down their search for fish. This also allows an angler to fish bait on one rod and cast a lure with the other. Seasoned surf fishermen may bring three, four, or five rods, if legal, to cover all likely areas and try different baits.

Groins, which are typically constructed to prevent beach erosion, also draw gamefish. A lot of small marine life grows on groins, which attracts baitfish and other forage, and hence gamefish. Because tidal currents move parallel to a beach, one side of the groin is always deeper than the other. Frequently, bluefish and striped bass prey on forage on the deep side, or ambush bait at the tip of the groin as it washes past in the current curling up and around the groin. Other gamefish, such as blackfish and sea bass, stay tight to the groin, foraging for crustaceans. Don't cast too far out from a groin; you're liable to put your bait or lure too far from a fish.

Groin fishing can be difficult, and even dangerous, for the uninitiated. The rocks are typically slippery, sometimes requiring metal cleats or grips on boots or waders (always available in area tackle shops). On some groins, a high tide will leave the tip exposed while inundating the rest of it, thus leaving a fisherman stranded in the middle of a roaring, crashing surf. Never venture all the way out on a groin in bad weather, or if you're not familiar with tide heights in that area; and don't venture out on one at all if you're not wearing firm-gripping soles or cleats.

Jetty fishing (also called inlet fishing) is similar to groin fishing, and you can use the same techniques (and heed the same warnings) just described. But jetties offer the added feature of water moving in and out of the mouth. Inlets are often sites of conflicting currents, such as when a tributary is still emptying out from ebb tide as a flood tide begins. These conflicting currents are called "rips," often characterized by what look like standing waves. Rips attract gamefish because a lot of forage is rendered helpless in the turbulence.

Search for fish on the deep side of a groin and at its tip.

Fish will congregate at rips, or areas of conflicting currents marked by standing waves, outside of inlets on outgoing tides and inside of inlets on incoming tides.

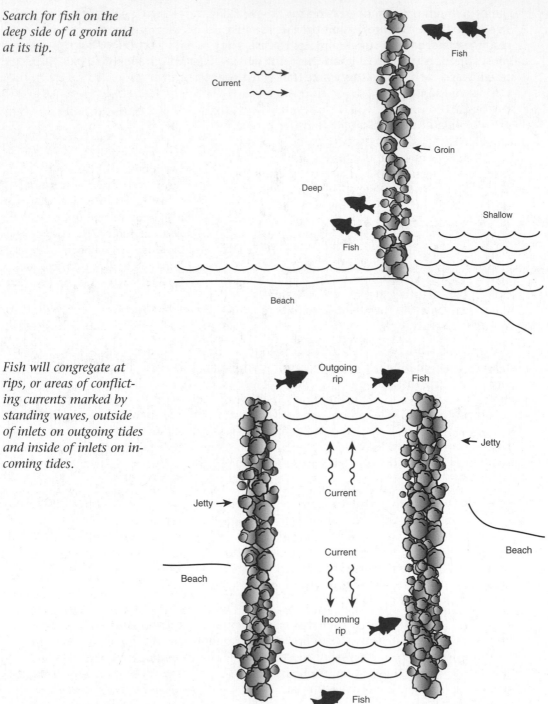

Gamefish, sometimes whole schools of them, often move into a tributary on a flood tide to feed. They all must pass through the inlet, concentrating their numbers. Once in a while, a school of fish—notably bluefish—will "herd" a school of baitfish into an inlet, where they can feed upon them easily. An angler who happens to be standing on a jetty at such a time can experience outstanding fishing.

Tidal Rivers and Bays

Much saltwater fishing takes place on inland waters, where many saltwater species can be caught. Inland waters are better protected from wind and high waves, provide easier access, and often produce good fishing. For the boatless fisherman, tidal rivers, creeks, bays, and backwaters offer thousands of miles of shoreline from which to cast. Also, many businesses offer small boats that can be rented by the hour or by the day.

Although these inland waters aren't frequented by oceanic species such as tuna, many other popular fish, such as flounder, bluefish, striped bass, redfish, sea trout, weakfish, kingfish, and a variety of saltwater panfish, can be found there. As in the surf, these fish are influenced by the tide, but are found in specific places.

Many inland waters are crisscrossed by navigation *channels*, which are deeper sections or stretches of water and are marked by buoys. Boats must travel in channels so they don't run aground in the shallower water surrounding the channel. During low tide, some boats—even relatively small ones—can't stray from the channel in some sections, or they'll hit bottom. Some channels are natural, but many are man-made. All are good spots to fish, because gamefish remain in the deeper water and feed upon forage that flows into it during a tide. The edges of a channel are usually more productive than the middle of one, as gamefish often lie just below the edge to ambush bait.

Bridges also attract fish, as the tidal currents rip around the bridge abutments and pilings, funneling forage. Also, navigation channels, another obvious target, must run under bridges. Fish usually congregate on the down-tide side of bridges.

Piers and *dock pilings* attract fish for the same reason. Occasionally holes or depressions form to the sides or in front of these structures, the result of tidal currents hitting the obstructions and scooping out the bottom.

Drop-offs are found in many inland waters. Again, these may be natural (one side of a sand or gravel bar) or man-made (a retaining wall). Concentrate your efforts on the side of the drop-off, where gamefish typically congregate.

Cautious Casts

If you're fishing from a boat, don't drift or anchor in the middle of a navigation channel. Not only is it inconsiderate, it also puts you in danger of boaters who might not see you or are running too fast to avoid you. Drift the channel edge, where you can leave it quickly, or anchor outside of it and cast in.

In tidal rivers and bays, look for fish near piers, bridge pilings, on the sides of navigation channels, and near dropoffs by sandbars and gravel bars.

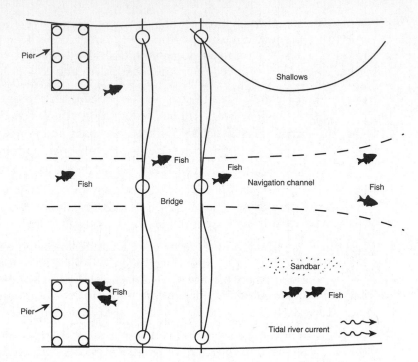

Other good inland areas are regional, such as a warm-water discharge from a power plant. The only way you'll find these areas is to consult a regional publication, ask at a local tackle shop, or—and I'm not above this—fishing where others seem to be having luck.

Ocean Fishing

This style of saltwater fishing is done necessarily from a boat. The species involved range from 1-pound flounder and sea bass to 1,000-pound-plus sharks and marlin. Although it would be impossible to detail the specific fishing methods for each species in this space, all these methods are based on five approaches:

➤ *Trolling* is pulling a bait or a lure behind a moving boat, and is used to catch a variety of species. While any seaworthy boat can troll, some are specially set up for this technique. Rod holders, which are pipe-like devices built into or attached to the stern (back) and/or the gunwales (sides) of the boat, hold the rod at an angle toward water, allowing a fisherman to operate the boat while trolling one or more lines. Outriggers are long poles that jut out perpendicularly from both sides of the boat. A line-clip device holds the fishing line, which gets moved to the end of the outrigger via a pulley. Outriggers, which are commonly used on boats that troll for billfish (marlin, swordfish, and sailfish), put baits or lures well to the side of the boat, where they won't tangle with those baits or lures being trolled from rods on the stern or transom (which are called flat lines when outriggers are used).

➤ *Bottom fishing* is just that: fishing baits or lures directly on the ocean floor. The boat is anchored, so that it remains directly over a particular area that should hold fish. Many ocean fishermen use a sonar unit to find a structure, which may be a reef, a boat wreck, rubble, or any object or objects that attract fish. You'll find many species such as blackfish, sea bass, and porgies around a structure. A boat may also anchor over comparatively open bottom—a mussel bed or a raised portion of the ocean floor—to fish for other species, such as cod, mackerel, and whiting.

➤ *Drifting* involves a couple of types of fishing. With this method, the unanchored, unpowered boat floats over a likely area, driven by the wind, the tide, or a current. In some situations, the boat operator may have the motor running at very light throttle to keep the craft on a particular course. You can fish with bait or lures directly on the bottom, as when flounder fishing, or at mid-levels, for species such as bluefish. Sometimes drifting is used to find a concentration of fish, in which case the boat is anchored or drifted repeatedly over that spot.

➤ *Chumming* is the use of ground-up bait to attract fish close to the boat, where they are then fished for with lures or bait. Depending on the species and the situation, the boat may be anchored or drifting. You can make chum on the boat by grinding up baitfish into a souplike consistency and ladling it over the side of the boat, so that a "chum slick" spreads out across the water. Gamefish will scent the slick and follow it to the boat, where anglers will have lures or baited lines out. You can also disperse chum in the water by freezing it solid and letting it melt in a crate tied to the hull. The rocking of the boat lifts the chum block in and out of the water, creating a steady slick. Chumming is used extensively by bluefish anglers.

➤ *Chunking* is very similar to chumming, except that small pieces of bait are tossed out into the chum slick. The difference is that chum is basically liquid in form, with specks of flesh in the suspension that are too small to satisfy the appetite of a large fish. The chum's purpose is simply to attract the fish. When chunking, however, you are actually feeding the fish to keep them around. This is necessary when fishing for fast-swimming, wide-ranging species such as tuna, which may leave a chum slick if they can't find forage.

Getting the Point

Inshore fishing generally refers to angling that takes place in the ocean close to or within sight of land. **Offshore fishing** means fishing out of sight of land, often hundreds of miles out.

217

Some specialized equipment is often necessary on ocean fishing trips. When large species are the quarry, a gaff, which is a pole with a large, sharp hook at the end, is usually employed to bring the fish over the side. If you're fishing for extremely large fish—sharks and some species of tuna—a flying gaff may be put into the fish. This device resembles a basic gaff except that the hook can be released from the pole. A rope is tied to the hook, so that the fish can then be pulled or winched in. Other big-gamefish boats have fighting chairs, which are bolted to the deck, facing the stern. The angler is strapped into the chair and the rod butt is placed into a gimbal, located at the front of the seat of the chair in front of the angler's groin. The gimbal pivots from front to back, allowing the angler to pump the fish in. This fish-fighting technique and other specialized methods are detailed in Chapter 24, "The Big-Game Fishing Trip."

The Least You Need to Know

➤ Saltwater fish are biologically and physiologically the same as freshwater fish, except for the way their bodies retain and eliminate salt.

➤ Saltwater fish are affected either directly or indirectly by the tide, in which the moon's and sun's gravitational pull on the ocean causes the water level to rise and then fall about twice every 24 hours.

➤ Surf fishing refers to fishing the ocean from the shore; jetty fishing means fishing from a structure that protrudes from the shore. It's necessary to read the beach and the water for fish-holding locations.

➤ Tidal rivers and bays host numerous saltwater species, hold a lot of fish-attracting structure, and are generally easily accessible.

➤ Five approaches are used for ocean fishing: trolling, bottom fishing, drifting, chumming (adding a ground-up fish mixture to the water to attract fish), and chunking (chumming with large pieces of fish, to keep fish in the vicinity).

Chapter 21

Tackle for the Brine

In This Chapter

➤ A rod for the sand

➤ The (almost) all-around pair

➤ Outfits for the ocean

➤ Tackling the heavyweights

While freshwater fishermen generally choose their type and size of rod and reel according to the size of the fish that's targeted, saltwater anglers must take other factors into account: the length of the cast that's necessary to reach fish, the weight of the sinker needed to keep bait on the bottom in turbulent waters, and the amount of line a fish might peel off the reel when first hooked. Even the presence of other anglers next to you on a boat will dictate a rod-and-reel style.

As you'll learn in this chapter, these requisites sometimes lead to using outfits that may seem too heavy for the fish you catch. Last summer, for example, I walked out onto a jetty early one morning to fish for striped bass. A few minutes after I had cast my clam bait out a bit from the rocks, I felt a slight *tap-tap* on the 17-pound-test line and reeled in, on the 9-foot rod, a sea robin—a generally undesirable bottom fish common to the East Coast—that weighed perhaps 12 ounces. Feeling a little silly about the obvious overkill, I unhooked and released the fish, rebaited, and cast out again to a different spot. That's when a fish—probably a striper—hit that clam bait so hard that I actually lost my grip on the rod, and I fell to my knees trying to regain control of it. I didn't get to set the hook on that fish, but neither did I continue to feel as if I was using too much rod.

Needs for the Surf

Rods used to fish the surf are long, ranging from 8 to 12 feet, because the angler must often cast long distances to put a bait or lure in the right spot, which is often behind the breakers. At high tide, this could be 75 yards out or more. And because heavy sinkers are often required to keep bait on the bottom in all that turbulence, the rod must be strong enough to handle weights upwards of 3 ounces. This translates into a reel that can hold at least a couple hundred yards of fishing line that tests in the 15- to 20-pound range.

There is a law of diminishing returns (actually diminishing casts) regarding length. A friend told me how he custom-built a 14-foot surf rod in order to reach way out in the surf. It didn't work, because the rod was so long that it became unwieldy, even for his 6½-foot, 200-pound-plus frame. The rod overpowered him, and his casting distance actually fell off.

Most surf rods are two-piece, so that you can transport them easily. Some die-hard surf anglers still believe that a one-piece rod has better casting ability, and will go through the bother of storing and transporting one or more 10-foot, one-piece rods. But rods are made so well these days that a two-piece rod has no shortcomings. These rods also feature large butt sections with long grip areas so that you can use two hands to cast out.

Surf rods and reels are available in both spinning and baitcasting styles. Many seasoned anglers use baitcasting outfits because they'll cast longer than a comparable spinning rig: Line peels directly off the revolving spool and through the guides on a baitcasting outfit. On a spinning reel, however, the line comes off the stationary spool in loops, slapping against the first guide on the rod as it travels out. Surf spinning rods are made with extra-large guides to decrease this friction, but a certain amount still occurs.

School Notes

Always keep surf-reel spools filled to capacity, especially spinning models. Line will rub against the lip of a partially empty spool, creating friction and shortening the potential distance of the cast.

A baitcasting rig also offers the advantage of freespool mode, which is handy when "livelining," or fishing a live baitfish or eel, which is usually done off of a jetty. This allows you to stand on a jetty with the reel in freespool, keeping your thumb lightly on the spool. If a fish grabs the bait and runs—which is usually the case—it won't feel pressure from the rod and drop the bait. Also, you can let the fish take line out, but use your thumb to keep the reel from overrunning and creating a tangle. (Most baitcasting reels have a "clicker" device that makes a ratcheting sound when the line is pulled off the reel; it serves as a warning and also provides some protection against overruns.) Finally, baitcasting reels are inherently stronger than spinning reels, which is a consideration for those anglers who target fish that can weigh more than 50 pounds.

However, baitcasters aren't easy to master, especially when trying to make extremely long casts. Also, modern spinning reels are stronger than ever, and new materials have eliminated much of the weight, which was a problem in the past. And some manufacturers have eliminated the bail on some versions of their surf spinning reels, because the bail spring on these reels often broke under the tough conditions where you use surf tackle. They are called "manual pickup reels," because you must use your finger to pull the line away from the line roller before casting (instead of flipping the bail) and to put it back under the roller in order to reel in.

The best all-around surf-fishing outfit for the first-timer is a 9½- or 10-foot, medium-action spinning model rated for up to 5- or 6-ounce lures. The matching reel should be capable of holding at least 200 yards of 15- or 17-pound-test line. This outfit can be used successfully to catch fish practically anywhere on both coasts. You may also want a sand spike, which is used to hold your rod for you when you need a break from holding it.

Getting the Point

A **sand spike** is a long hollow tube used to hold a surf rod after a bait is cast out. You just push the spike into the sand and slide the rod butt inside. A pin inside the spike supports the butt and keeps the reel from rubbing against the edge.

This is a surf-style spinning reel. Note the large, deep spool to hold a large amount of line.

Light Saltwater Rods and Reels

Probably the majority of saltwater fishing is done in inland waters—bays, tidal rivers, and estuaries—and just off the beach, where the depth averages from 5 to 20 feet. Although the size ranges of the fish caught in these places vary, the weight of the lures used here are an ounce or less, and the sinkers necessary to put bait on the bottom weigh 1 to 3 ounces. Therefore it's possible to pursue most all of the fish encountered here with one or two outfits. Spinning rods that fall into this "light saltwater" category are from 6 to 7 feet long with a moderate or fast action, and are capable of handling monofilament that tests from 8 to 12 pounds and lures that weigh up to an ounce or so. Light saltwater baitcasting outfits have rods that average about 6 feet long, are designed for 10- to 17-pound-test line, and lures that weigh up to 3 ounces. The reels for both outfits fit the same criteria, and feature large line capacities—at least 150 yards—and heavy-duty drag systems. These size ranges are average; the species, water conditions, and lures or bait used in your waters will govern the exact sizes and specifications. Generally, the deeper the water you'll be fishing, the heavier the tackle you'll need, because you'll need a heavy sinker or lure to reach bottom without being pushed off course by the currents.

If you read the chapters in Part 2, "Tackle and How to Use It," you'll note that these specifications are similar to those for some freshwater fishing applications, specifically those for larger species such as northern pike. Thus, it's possible to own one or two rod-and-reel pairs that can double as heavy freshwater/light saltwater outfits.

Cautious Casts

Always wash off your rods and reels with fresh water after using them in saltwater to avoid corrosion of metal parts. Rinse or wipe down all portions of rods, and hold reels under a gentle stream of water. Remove spinning reel spools and rinse separately. Let dry and spray the reels with a protective aerosol lubricant.

But don't let the tail wag the dog (or, more appropriately, the rod cast the fisherman). You don't want to fish in salt water with tackle that isn't up to the demands. While in some places (typically shallow waters) and at some times it's possible to fish for saltwater species with medium or even light freshwater tackle—small bluefish (called "snapper blues") in protected inland waters in the Northeast, say; or grunts and snappers along the Florida coast—the weight of the sinker or lure, and/or the tidal currents combined with the strength of some fish, make doing so impractical or impossible. Casting a 2-ounce sinker with a slow-action, medium-weight rod with 8-pound-test line resembles David hurling a rock at Goliath with a sling more than it does fishing.

I use two light saltwater outfits for most of my inland and inshore fishing. The first is a 6½-foot, medium-power, fast-action spinning rod rated for ⅜- to 1-ounce lures and 8- to 14-pound-test line, mated with a reel that holds about 200 yards of 12-pound-test line. The second is a 6½-foot baitcasting rod, heavy power and fast action, rated for 1- to 2-ounce lures and 10- to 25-pound-test line, with a reel that holds about 200 yards of 15-pound-test line. The rods have long butt sections, enabling me to use both hands when casting a heavy lure or bait, and the reels feature smooth-running drag systems. I often bring both outfits with me when fishing. Generally, I use the spinning rig when I'll be doing a lot of distance casting with lures, and choose the heavier baitcasting outfit when fishing on the bottom with bait or when needing to cast lures that might be too much for the spinning rod. With these two outfits I'm ready for practically any fishing situation in those waters.

Ocean Outfits

School Notes

You can use one spinning rod-and-reel outfit for different applications by buying an extra reel spool (or two) and putting different line on it. One of my outfits is good for river bass with the 6-pound spool, but becomes a light saltwater rig with the 10-pound spool.

As a rule, big saltwater species are caught in big water. Although this includes offshore fishing, it's not necessarily confined to it. Many species that grow to large sizes, such as striped bass and bluefish, are caught close to the beach by boat anglers fishing in inlets, in areas of conflicting currents, or in deep waters. Other species, such as blackfish, live on the bottom among rocks and other structures.

Fishing for these and other species requires stout tackle. A 5-pound blackfish, 15-pound bluefish, 30-pound striper, or 60-pound cod would overpower most light saltwater outfits. Also, the conditions in these waters—which range from 20 to 80 feet deep, produce strong currents, and may feature snag-filled, line-breaking structures—demand that you use an outfit with which you can control the fish once it's hooked. Finally, the baits, sinkers, and lures used to catch these fish are bigger and heavier than those used in inland waters.

As when fishing with light saltwater tackle, the species and the situation will dictate whether you'll be casting to the fish with lures or drifting or bottom-fishing with bait. Sometimes you'll have the opportunity to do both on one fishing trip: A school of fish may move within casting distance when you're bottom-fishing, for example. Although one spinning outfit will suffice for both bait fishing and lure fishing in some situations, it won't have enough backbone and winching potential to effectively fish with large sinkers or lift heavy fish up from the bottom. The well-equipped angler will have both a spinning and a conventional (not a baitcasting) outfit. Conventional reels, often called boat reels, are heavier than baitcasters of their size. They feature narrower, deeper spools that can hold more and heavier line. The inherent strength of the conventional setup makes it easier to manage heavy sinkers, lift large fish away from the bottom, and maintain control of them throughout the fight.

Keeping in mind that the best outfit to select depends upon your regional conditions and the size of the species you'll be fishing for, a good all-around ocean spinning outfit would consist of a 7-foot, heavy-weight, medium- or fast-action rod rated for up to 1½-ounce lures and 12- to 20-pound-test line, and a reel spooled with about 200 yards of 15- or 17-pound-test line. (You may have noticed that the spinning reel recommended for surf fishing earlier in this section has the same specifications.) The conventional rod should be about 6 feet long (but no longer than 6½ feet), heavy weight, with a medium- or fast-action and a long butt section, which you can put under one arm when cranking in a big fish. It should be rated for 15- to 30-pound-test line and handle lures weighing from 2 to 6 ounces. The reel should be able to hold approximately 300 yards of 20-pound-test line, and feature a quality star-type drag.

You don't want a conventional rod longer than 6½ feet because anything bigger than that becomes extremely cumbersome when fishing on a boat, especially on a party boat (a large commercial craft that makes half-day to full-day trips to fishing grounds, with customers boarding on a first-come basis) where the rail may be lined shoulder-to-shoulder with anglers. Not only will a long rod get in the way of other anglers, it also makes it more difficult to put leverage on a fish and get it up to the surface.

I own two outfits that fit these specifications, and have used them successfully on a number of ocean-fishing trips, catching a variety of species in various sizes. Both are about ten years old, but I have no reason to change—they're perfect.

Trolling Tackle

Now we enter the realm of truly big fish: billfish, tuna, and some sharks. The fishing takes place offshore on boats large enough to navigate the potentially rough seas, designed with a large, open stern that provides room for anglers to move about when battling fish. Some of these offshore boats can be as small as 20 feet or as long as 70 or 80 feet. These larger boats have one or two fighting chairs for use when an extremely large fish is hooked on one of the baits and/or lures being trolled behind the moving boat. And the tackle, besides being heavy, has some specific and necessary adaptations.

School Notes

It's perfectly fine to use spinning rods with sinkers that are heavier than the rod's lure-weight rating. In most cases you'll simply be dropping the bait-and-sinker rig over the side of the boat—no casting necessary. Once the sinker reaches bottom it'll relax the bend in the rod, returning sensitivity and control.

School Notes

It's a good idea to label all your reels (or the spools on spinning reels) with the pound test of the line on it and the date it was put on. You'll know at a glance whether the line is strong enough for your intended use, and if it needs replacing.

Unless you already own a boat large enough to make such offshore trips, you'll probably never need to purchase trolling tackle. Charter boats (which take small parties of anglers fishing for a half- or full-day trip, by reservation only) that make offshore trips already supply the rods and reels. But it's important to understand the type of tackle used for trolling and how it operates.

First, let's distinguish trolling tackle from tackle used for trolling. While the former is large and specifically designed for fish that can weigh from 50 to more than 1,000 pounds, the conventional outfits described in the previous section—for fishing in water from 20 to 80 feet deep, for fish weighing from the single digits up to 60 pounds—can also be used to troll for those size fish in those depths. Sometimes you can use wire line, which sinks rapidly, to reach the fish. Other times you can employ a downrigger. This is a device that lowers a heavy weight, called a "cannonball," on a cable into the water to a specific depth. The fishing line runs from the rod down through a release clip on the cable or the cannonball. A bait or lure is trolled behind the cannonball, and when a fish hits, the line pops free of the release, so you can fight the fish on a direct line. (Downriggers are also used for freshwater fishing and are common on boats in the Great Lakes.) But both wire lining and downrigging are specialized, advanced fishing methods; besides, you have to buy a boat before you buy a downrigger. Let's at least become familiar with the tackle before you decide to sell the house, buy the *Miss Take* and become a charter-boat captain in Aruba.

Saltwater trolling reels weigh from 1 to 10 pounds or more, depending on their size. They're not designed for casting, and thus have no antibacklash devices, thumb-operated freespool releases, or other such features. Trolling reels are rugged, corrosion-resistant, and very expensive, starting at more than $100 and entering the $1,000 realm. Because they are often used to subdue tremendous fish, they have relatively low gear ratios; the fastest is only about 3.5 to 1. Many trolling reels feature clamps that securely bolt the reel to the rod. Some have lugs on the top of the housing that permit the reel to be harnessed to the angler.

Most trolling reels have a simple lever on the side plate that takes the reel in and out of freespool. The reel handle, or crank, is usually oversized, permitting you to put more muscle into the fight. Finally, trolling reels have, or should have, superb drag systems, as some fish can tear a couple hundred yards of line off the spool in a matter of seconds. It's usually a star-type drag, although some reels feature a two-stage drag system operated via a knob and a lever.

The size rating system of trolling reels is based on the reel's line capacity and designated by a number followed by a slash and a zero. The higher the number, the larger the reel and the more line it will hold. Reels range from 1/0, which holds approximately 350 yards of 20-pound-test monofilament, up to 16/0, which has a capacity of 1,000 yards of 130-pound-test Dacron line. Most reels in use fall into the 2/0 to 12/0 range.

*A saltwater trolling reel,
with a harness to hold it
firmly to the rod.*

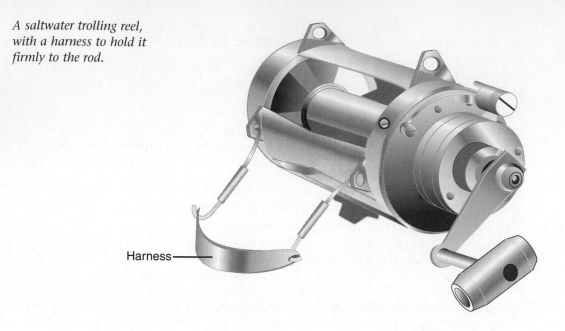

Harness──

Trolling rods are classified by the International Game Fish Association (IGFA), a record-keeping organization (see Appendix B for details). The categories range from ultra-light (used with 6- to 20-pound-test line) to unlimited (130- to 180-pound-test line). The rods themselves consist of an upper section with guides (called a "tip section") and a butt section. The IGFA sets certain standards for rods, such as minimum tip lengths and maximum butt lengths, and will not consider for a record any fish caught on a rod that falls outside their specifications. This prevents someone from "catching" a record fish on a rod and reel that are more suited to pulling tree stumps out of the ground than for sport fishing.

Most trolling rods have roller guides nearest the butt and at the tip, or along the entire length of the tip section. Resembling miniature steel rolling pins, these help to reduce friction caused by line shooting through the guides as a big fish runs. The butt section may be straight or bent into a shallow U shape, which gives you more fish-fighting leverage. It also has a powerful locking reel seat and a butt fitting that allows it to fit into the gimbal—a swiveling cuplike device—on the fighting chair.

Getting the Point

Stand-up fishing refers to battling a fish while standing instead of strapped into a fighting chair. The angler wears a belt harness with a gimbal that holds the rod butt. Some anglers feel that stand-up is more sporting; others believe it's a more effective technique to wear a fish down because you can move about the boat to apply leverage on the fish.

The Least You Need to Know

➤ Surf rods must be long—8 to 12 feet—in order to make long casts with sinkers up to 6 ounces in weight. Large reels should hold enough line for the cast and for a fish to take out.

➤ Light saltwater outfits are similar to heavy freshwater rods and reels. Spinning outfits should be able to handle up to 1-ounce lures; baitcasters should accommodate a 3-ounce sinker without strain.

➤ Spinning outfits for ocean use should be rated for 1½ ounces of weight, with conventional outfits handling up to 6 ounces or more.

➤ Trolling tackle is specialized equipment used to take fish that weigh anywhere from 2 pounds to hundreds of pounds. It consists of very large conventional reels and rods classified according to the strength of the line they are designed to handle.

Chapter 22

Au Naturel or Artificial?

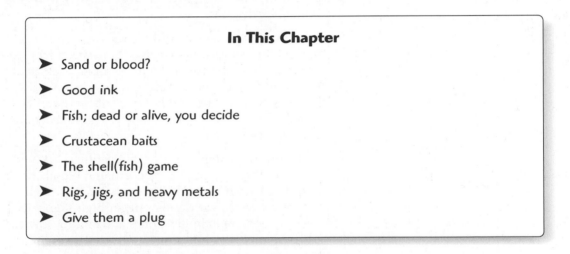

In This Chapter

➤ Sand or blood?

➤ Good ink

➤ Fish; dead or alive, you decide

➤ Crustacean baits

➤ The shell(fish) game

➤ Rigs, jigs, and heavy metals

➤ Give them a plug

A cornucopia of life exists in and around salt waters, and humans have taken advantage of this bounty for thousands of years. That's even before the first Red Lobster restaurant opened its doors.

Part of that bounty is the tremendous variety of baits that we can collect and use to catch fish. To me, one of the most fascinating aspects of saltwater fishing is figuring out which of the dozens of possible baits would be best for a certain species that day. Sometimes it doesn't matter—the fish will hit just about anything—but other times they'll refuse everything except one particular type of forage. In this chapter I'll examine all those baits commonly available to saltwater fishermen and the basics of using them.

Sandworms and Bloodworms and Pincers, Oh My

A number of marine worms are eaten readily by many saltwater species. Some fish feed extensively on worms; others don't normally frequent areas where worms are found but will grab them without hesitation. Sea bass, striped bass, flounder, halibut, blackfish, weakfish, sea trout, and a host of saltwater panfish species will eat worms.

Cautious Casts

Never store sandworms and bloodworms in the same container. The two species are natural enemies, and the bloods may kill the sands.

Cautious Casts

Cull dead bloodworms or sandworms immediately, as they tend to sicken the others (meaning the worms, but possibly your friends, too). Also, don't keep pieces of worms with whole live ones for the same reason.

Bloodworms and sandworms are the two most common types of marine worms used by fishermen. Bloodworms average about 6 or 7 inches long and have a smooth, pinkish or reddish skin with short appendages along the sides. Its suckerlike mouth, which can extend and retract, holds two pairs of small, yet sharp, curved pincers. They will latch on to your finger painfully if you're not careful—always hold a bloodworm firmly just behind the mouth. And make sure you know at which end the mouth is. Cut a bloodworm in half and you'll discover why they're called bloodworms.

Most sandworms are 9 to 10 inches long. They're a reddish-tan color with a green or blue sheen and have numerous tentacle-like appendages along their flanks, and have a slightly flattened body. Sandworms also have retractable pincers (only one pair) and can also inflict a nasty bite; these should be held just behind the head as well.

Both worms are found along the Atlantic coast, with sandworms from Long Island north and bloodworms from the Carolinas north. They inhabit flats, which are areas covered with water only at high tide, and burrow in the mud under stones and among seaweeds, with the sandworms burrowing deeper than the bloodworms. Both can be obtained by digging, raking, or by searching at night with a flashlight when they leave their burrows; the process is much like looking for night crawlers.

While some fishermen obtain their own worms, the majority purchase them at local bait shops, where the price varies widely according to availability and season (most are collected in Maine and shipped south). They are usually packed in seaweed, must be kept cold, and out of direct sunlight. Bloodworms have tougher skins than sandworms, and stay on the hook longer. They're also a bit hardier and tend to cost more. But both work well.

These worms can be fished whole when you're going for large (and large-mouthed) species such as striped bass and weakfish. Be sure to insert the hook through the worm's mouth first. Continue drawing the hook through the worm's body until just the hook shank (from eye to beginning of bend) is covered. For smaller species, a half, third, or even quarter of the worm, threaded on the hook from the eye to the point, is enough.

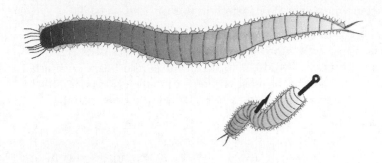

A sandworm (shown) or a bloodworm makes a good bait for many saltwater fish. Use part of the worm when fishing for smaller species.

Squid Marks

The squid is one of the most common saltwater baits. Its strong odor, bright-white flesh, and sturdy composition make it a favorite of both fish and fishermen.

Squid are typically sold frozen at bait shops, or refrigerated at grocery stores under the name "calamari." While offshore fishermen sometimes troll large, whole squid for tuna and billfish, most squid is fished in strips by anglers fishing inshore and inland waters.

To cut a squid into strips, defrost it in a bucket of seawater. Pull the head and tentacles off; save the latter if you'll fish for small species such as croaker. Peel the skin from the remaining tube, slice from bottom to top with a knife or scissors, rinse out the ink and remove any remaining carti-

School Notes

Try to prepare a supply of squid strips before you begin fishing. They'll be fine if you keep them cold, and you won't have to put your rod down and prepare more strips if the fishing gets good suddenly—which often happens in salt water.

lage, leaving you with a flat white sheet of squid meat. Use knife or scissors to cut long, tapered strips of meat that come to a point on one end. These pennants wave enticingly in the current or when retrieved. Keep your squid strips cold, preferably in a container with a bit of seawater. Don't let the squid strips sit in fresh water, as they'll turn mushy.

Fish such squid strips plain on a hook, as a "sweetener" on a jig or other lure, or in tandem with a baitfish. Always put the point of the hook into the base of the wide end, so the rest of it will wiggle and flutter. The additional color and scent of a squid strip will often trigger fish into striking a bait or lure that they'd otherwise leave alone.

A Cut Above: Cut Bait

This category encompasses a variety of baitfish species that are sold dead, either fresh or frozen. The term is a bit misleading as sometimes the fish are small enough to be used whole. Bunker, herring, mackerel, and mullet are common species. They're all oily and emit a lot of scent when drifted or fished on bottom.

Small whole fish can be hooked through the head, or through the head and body with a double hook, and fished on bottom or retrieved. Larger specimens can be chunked (cut to resemble miniature swordfish steaks) for use on bottom, or filleted (cut lengthwise) and fished on bottom or retrieved, also on single hooks or double-hook rigs. The head and tail sections are especially good, and durable, baits.

The type of bait to buy and the fish to use it for are largely determined by region. As most bait shops rely on local suppliers for their bait, what you see in the freezer there is probably going to be the best choice. As always, ask the proprietor for details on what species are taking what baits.

Loose Lines

Cut bait is frequently used when chumming. The idea is to begin a chum slick made with the same type of bait you'll be using: Fish will follow the scent of a particular baitfish to the boat, where they'll find the real thing drifting in the slick.

A Live One

Minnows are a popular and effective bait for a variety of saltwater species. Actually, some of the baitfish used for some species are too large to be called minnows; some striped-bass anglers fish live bunkers weighing almost a pound. However, many of them—herring, killifish (or killies), mullet, anchovies—are smaller.

Here again, the prevalent baitfish found in particular waters, and sold in those areas, varies from region to region. Local bait shops will carry the predominant species.

Small baitfish such as killies, which average two to four inches, can be caught in a minnow trap. Weight the trap, bait it with bunker or some other oily fish, and place it in shallow, weedy areas.

Larger baitfish, such as mullet, are best obtained by throwing a cast net, a large-diameter (from 6 to 14 feet and higher), round net that is weighted at the edges. To use a cast net, softly wade the shallows or drift in a boat. When you sight a school of minnows, throw the net out so that it opens up in midair and falls upon the school. A rope, attached to your wrist, draws the bottom of the net closed when you pull it in. Throwing a cast net is a lot of fun but challenging to do properly; although they are sold with directions, the technique is best learned by having a proficient thrower teach you.

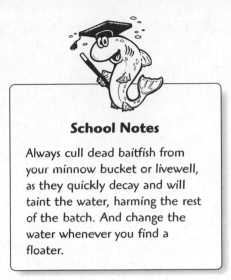

School Notes

Always cull dead baitfish from your minnow bucket or livewell, as they quickly decay and will taint the water, harming the rest of the batch. And change the water whenever you find a floater.

Typically, you can collect bunker and other large baitfish with a rod and reel, usually by sighting a school of them and snagging them with weighted treble hooks. Because large baitfish are difficult to keep for an extended period of time, and doing so involves extremely large livewells with aeration systems, most anglers obtain these baits just prior to fishing with them.

Eels are a popular bait for striped bass in many areas. Eels can be caught or trapped, but again are difficult to keep, so many anglers simply purchase them at bait shops. Hooked through the lips and allowed to drift and swim off jetties and in other noted striper haunts, the slimy creatures account for a lot of big bass every year.

As with the live freshwater versions, saltwater baitfish should be hooked through the lips when being cast and retrieved or drifted, and through the back behind the dorsal fin when fishing on the bottom. Baitfish also work well when attached to a jig. Hook the fish through the lips, from the bottom up.

Crabs and Shrimp: Fish Like Them, Too

Crabs are used primarily but not solely for bottom-feeding fish, where these crustaceans are found. The type of crab to use and how it is fished depends on the region, but they are always fished on or near the bottom.

You can use blueclaw, green, fiddler, and other crabs to catch redfish, sea bass, cod, grouper, haddock, hake, halibut, ling, snapper, and many other species. Small crabs, which, depending on the species, can be 1 to 4 inches long, are usually fished whole. Larger crabs are broken in half before being hooked. In either case, insert the hook through the body at the base of a leg or a claw. Be aware that there may be regulations regarding the size and possession of blueclaw crabs; check with the fish and game department of your state if you're not certain of them.

When using small crabs such as fiddlers for bait, break off one claw and insert the hook at the base.

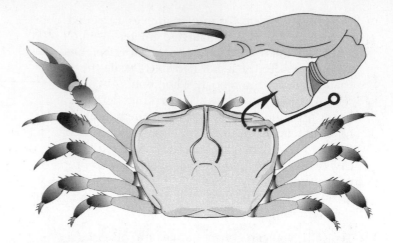

Crabs can be trapped (and are often accidentally caught when bottom fishing with worms, squid, or cut bait, which is often annoying but can be viewed as free bait) but you can buy them at bait shops. One exception is the mole crab, commonly called the sand flea. This little crustacean can be dug up on beaches at low tide with a shovel, a sturdy rake, or your hands and feet. These inch-long creatures are popular fish forage wherever they are found.

Hook sand fleas through the underside of the body.

Shrimp are used as bait on both coasts but most notably in the South. Grouper, redfish, ladyfish, snapper, snook, bonefish, sea trout, weakfish, and many other species feed on shrimp. There are many different species of shrimp; all work equally well in their home waters. They can be cast-netted, but can also be purchased at bait shops.

Live shrimp are much preferred as bait over dead ones, though the latter can still be used effectively. They are typically hooked from the rear of the tail, with the hook shank running up under the carapace and back out the bottom. They can be fished on the bottom, drifted with the current, or used to sweeten a jig. Always keep shrimp in a minnow bucket out of direct sunlight, and change the water often.

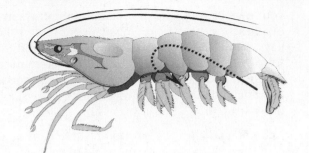

When fishing a live or dead shrimp, run the hook from the base of the tail up through the body and back out again.

Loose Lines

Many saltwater species are opportunistic feeders, sometimes taking advantage of high numbers of a certain forage that they don't normally eat. A few years ago, for instance, I was fishing for summer flounder, or fluke, off the New Jersey beaches with a friend in his boat. We caught a fair number of fish drifting squid-and-killie combos, but not enough to call it an outstanding day. Later, while filleting the fluke, we discovered that all their bellies were absolutely stuffed with blueclaw crab parts. For whatever reason—a storm that kicked the bottom up, or maybe a local migration—a lot of blueclaws were on that bottom, and the fluke filled up. This occasion also marked the very first time that I caught flounder stuffed with crabmeat.

Baits on the Half Shell

The meat from both clams and mussels is fished on the bottom for a number of species. Clam is a good bait for striped bass, black drum, redfish, and ling. Mussels, which are smaller than clams and don't contain a lot of meat, take winter flounder, blackfish, and a number of panfish.

Both clams and mussels have a "foot," which is a wide, flat protuberance. It's the toughest part of the bait, and the bigger the clam or mussel, the bigger the foot. Always hook your shellfish baits through this foot, because the rest of the meat is too soft to stay on the hook for a long time.

Both clams and mussels are sold at bait shops. The clam meat is usually shucked and sold frozen in a plastic bag; mussels come whole. You can gather these shellfish on

School Notes

Clam and mussel shells make effective chum. Break up the shells with a hammer and occasionally toss a handful overboard. The scent of the shellfish, as well as the sparkle and flash of the shell bits falling to bottom, will attract fish. This technique works best when used in combination with other chum.

your own as well. Look for clams along the surf line of a beach, or feel for them with your feet in shallow bays. (Note: You may need a special clamming license to collect clams. Inquire at bait shops or contact your state fish and game department.) Look for mussels at low tide attached to jetty rocks, dock pilings, and other structures.

And you can always stock up on these baits at a grocery store. Sometimes it's possible to get a good deal on older or broken clams and mussels from the seafood department at a supermarket.

In both cases, remember that the bigger the shellfish, the bigger the foot, and the better it will stay on the hook. When fishing for large species such as striped bass, impale the clam meat on the hook as many times as possible until you have a glob of it. If small fish are your quarry, you need only a piece of mussel or clam large enough to cover the hook.

Basic Bait Rigs and Components

Although there are as many ways to rig baits as there are baits themselves, they all share the basic components of hook, leader, and sinker. The type and size of the hook, the strength and length of the leader, and the weight and shape of the sinker determine the type of rig it is and what it is designed for. Some rigs have other features that further distinguish their applications.

The most common setup is the basic *bottom rig*. At the heart of this and many other rigs is a three-way swivel. The running line (the line from the end of your fishing rod) is tied to one eye. On the second eye is a sinker snap, which is a snap with arms that open on both ends. The small end is attached to the swivel, and the large end opens up to accept a sinker. On the third eye is a leader, which, as a rule of thumb, should be monofilament that's double the pound test of the running line. When fishing for bluefish, sharks, or some other sharp-toothed species, a wire leader is necessary.

The sinker you choose should be heavy enough to hold on bottom and resist movement by the current. If you're casting to a sand bottom when surf fishing, you should use a pyramid sinker (see Chapter 12, "Yes, You Should Sweat the Small Stuff"). This three-sided sinker plunges point-first into the sand and tends to hold well there. If you're fishing on a rocky bottom, you should use a bank sinker, which is teardrop-shaped. It will slide over the obstructions, while the angular pyramid will get stuck on them.

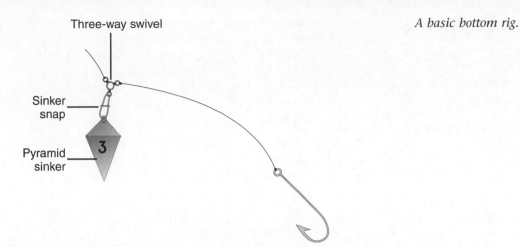

Three-way swivel

Sinker snap

Pyramid sinker

3

A basic bottom rig.

Generally the leaders on bottom rigs are kept short—they run from 6 inches to a foot—because there's no need for a long leader when the bait will simply be resting on the bottom. Also, a long leader will tend to throw very soft baits off the hook when you cast; even if you reel the sinker up very close to the rod tip, a long leader will hang down, and the inertia of your cast may sling the bait away.

Some bottom rigs, particularly those designed for surf use, feature a moveable float strung onto the leader, to lift the bait off of the bottom and away from pesky bait-stealing crabs. Of course, crabs often swim off the bottom to grab the bait anyway, but the float does seem to deter them a bit.

Other rigs resemble bottom rigs but are designed to be fished from a moving boat, either drifting or under power, or cast and retrieved. These *drift rigs* are marked by a long leader, anywhere from two to four feet. The long leader is necessary to prevent both tangling on the running line and to allow the bait to dart and wave close to bottom, moving with pauses and jerks, much like bait flowing naturally with the current. Many of these rigs are assembled with a three-way swivel, as described previously. Others feature a length of line, usually between 1 and 3 feet long, between the sinker and the swivel. This allows the bait to be presented at a level off the bottom when fishing for non-bottom species such as striped bass. Many anglers use very weak monofilament for this line when fishing in obstruction-filled waters, so that if the sinker becomes irretrievably snagged, that line will break before the running line will, requiring only replacement of the sinker rather than the whole rig.

A *multi-hook rig* features two or more hooks on separate leaders, which attach to loops tied into the main leader. A sinker is tied to the bottom of the main leader, and two or more loops, spaced 10 to 12 inches apart, hold leaders with hooks above it. The leaders are shorter than the space in between the loops to help prevent tangling. Multi-hook rigs offer fish a lot of baits at once, immediately improving your odds of catching fish. They also provide an opportunity to experiment with different baits. However, multi-hook rigs are generally not used to fish for large and fast species such as bluefish because bringing in two of these fish at once would prove extremely difficult.

237

A drift rig.

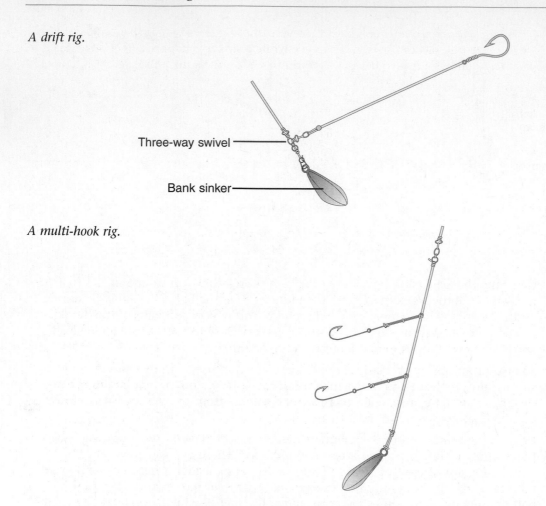

Three-way swivel

Bank sinker

A multi-hook rig.

Another type of rig is called the *sliding rig*. The running line passes through a sliding sinker (oval in shape with a longways hole through it; also called an egg sinker) and is tied to a swivel; a leader with a hook on the end is tied to the other end of the swivel. Such a setup allows a fish to take a bait without feeling the weight of the sinker.

A sliding rig.

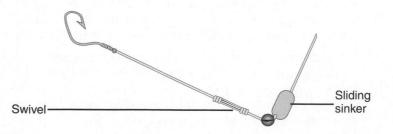

Swivel

Sliding sinker

A *fish-finder rig* relies on a small plastic sleeve with a sinker snap coming off its middle. The running line passes through the sleeve while a sinker is clipped to the snap. Such a setup also allows a fish to take a bait and run with it without feeling the sinker.

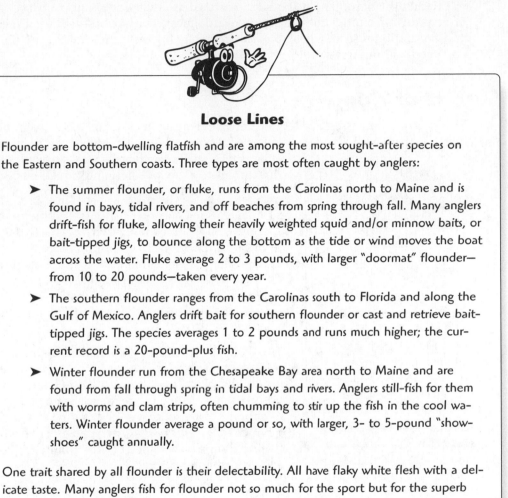

Loose Lines

Flounder are bottom-dwelling flatfish and are among the most sought-after species on the Eastern and Southern coasts. Three types are most often caught by anglers:

➤ The summer flounder, or fluke, runs from the Carolinas north to Maine and is found in bays, tidal rivers, and off beaches from spring through fall. Many anglers drift-fish for fluke, allowing their heavily weighted squid and/or minnow baits, or bait-tipped jigs, to bounce along the bottom as the tide or wind moves the boat across the water. Fluke average 2 to 3 pounds, with larger "doormat" flounder—from 10 to 20 pounds—taken every year.

➤ The southern flounder ranges from the Carolinas south to Florida and along the Gulf of Mexico. Anglers drift bait for southern flounder or cast and retrieve bait-tipped jigs. The species averages 1 to 2 pounds and runs much higher; the current record is a 20-pound-plus fish.

➤ Winter flounder run from the Chesapeake Bay area north to Maine and are found from fall through spring in tidal bays and rivers. Anglers still-fish for them with worms and clam strips, often chumming to stir up the fish in the cool waters. Winter flounder average a pound or so, with larger, 3- to 5-pound "showshoes" caught annually.

One trait shared by all flounder is their delectability. All have flaky white flesh with a delicate taste. Many anglers fish for flounder not so much for the sport but for the superb meals a good catch will yield.

Lures for the Salt

Effective as baits may be for catching saltwater species, there are times when a lure will do just as good a job—or better. Various lures can be retrieved rapidly, cast forcefully, and otherwise stand up to hard, repeated use that would cause a bait to fall off or be thrown from the hook. Also, there are times when the best bait for a species and/or location just isn't available, leaving a lure the only choice. Here are the lures you should know about.

Metals of Honor

This term encompasses a variety of saltwater fishing lures, all of which are solid metal, usually with a buffed, hammered, or chromed finish. Metals are popular and effective lures because they cast far, sink quickly, resist the current to a great degree, and can be retrieved, jigged, or trolled.

School Notes

Metal lures with large single hooks are usually preferable to those with treble hooks. The wider gap of the single hook holds fish better, and they're much easier to remove from fish—a consideration when casting to a school of fish that may move on at any moment.

Some metals for saltwater fishing resemble freshwater spoons, with a curved body that wiggles or darts when retrieved. Others look like nothing more than a rectangular slab of metal, but also exhibit action upon retrieval. They feature either single hooks or treble hooks, often with a hank of deer hair or a colored-plastic tube attached to the hook shank for added attraction.

The diamond jig is a long, four-sided metal lure. Its solid-metal body is tapered at both ends. While diamond jigs aren't true jigs, with a lead head and an upturned hook, they can be jigged readily. Because diamond jigs are so heavy—they range in size from 1 ounce to 2 *pounds*—they are very effective when fishing from a boat in deep water. Diamond jigs can also be cast and retrieved.

Heads of Lead

The leadhead jig is probably the best all-around saltwater lure because it can be fished in a variety of ways to imitate a lot of different forage. Dragged along the bottom it can look like a crab. Jigged it can simulate a squid. Retrieved just off the bottom, it appears to be a shrimp. When quickly reeled in, it looks like a baitfish.

Many saltwater jigs have a length of deer hair, usually white or dyed, tied to the hook-shank. These bucktail jigs can be fished plain or with a squid strip, shrimp, worm, or baitfish attached to the hook. These and plain jigs also can be adorned with a plastic worm, eel, shrimp body, or twist-type tail to further attract fish.

The jig you use should match the size of the predominant forage. You can buy jigs in just about every color. But if I had to pick one color of jig to use in salt water for the rest of my life, it would be white with a hint of red, as that combination seems to catch the most fish for me.

Pop, Pop, Fish, Fish

As with the freshwater versions, saltwater plugs come in assorted colors, sizes, and shapes, though not in as wide a selection. Most all saltwater plugs are swimming plugs, which sink or dive upon retrieval. Many of these plugs are designed to be cast from shore or boat; others are for trolling use. Generally, plugs with lips are for casting; lures without lips are for trolling.

Many plugs are designed to imitate specific forage fish, such as mackerel or bunker. As always, ask in a local bait shop if you're not sure about the best color and size of bait in the waters you'll be fishing. When in doubt, choose yellow, silver, and black plugs, and experiment to find which one produces.

Poppers, or topwater plugs, are excellent lures to use when fish are busting bait on the surface, and often attract fish when no such activity is occurring. Some poppers have concave faces, just like the freshwater versions, and gurgle and splash upon retrieval. Other poppers (notably "pencil" poppers, which are long, thin and don't have concave faces) require manipulation. By lifting and moving the rod from side to side, you can make such a popper swim, dart, and cause a commotion that looks incredibly like a distressed baitfish.

The Old Softies

Most saltwater plastic lures are used in conjunction with a metal lure or a jig, as mentioned previously. An array of jig bodies that imitate all sorts of forage—baitfish, shrimp, squid, crab, worms, eels, even creatures that exist only in some lure designer's mind—are sold. Again, match the forage in the waters you'll be fishing.

Rigged eels are actual-size, soft-plastic eels mounted on spoons that have a second hook placed midway down the eel's body. These lures look very much like the real thing, especially when retrieved and manipulated so that it slithers and darts in the water. Rigged eels will take striped bass, bluefish, cobia, and other predatory species.

Some very large plastic lures are used to troll for billfish and tuna offshore. These generally imitate squid and are trolled on the surface at a high rate of speed so the lure actually leaves a wake in the water.

The Least You Need to Know

➤ Sandworms and bloodworms take a variety of saltwater species. Use a whole worm for large fish, and just enough to cover the hook for smaller fish. Squid, crabs, shrimp, clams, and mussels also make good bait.

➤ Live baitfish are effective for most species. Large baitfish are snagged or cast-netted; smaller ones can be trapped. Cut bait refers to whole or sectioned baitfish. These can be fished on bottom or drifted, usually in conjunction with chum.

➤ Bottom rigs are for bottom fishing. Multi-hook rigs are for smaller fish. Drift rigs have long leaders. Sliding and fish-finder rigs prevent the fish from feeling the weight of the sinker.

➤ Metal lures imitate baitfish and work well in deep water. Leadhead jigs are the best all-around saltwater lures because they can imitate a variety of forage.

➤ Swimming plugs sink or dive and imitate baitfish. Poppers float and simulate a baitfish in distress.

➤ Most plastic lures are used in combination with jigs or spoons. They are made in just about every forage configuration.

Paying for It

Sometimes the easiest and most practical way to fish in salt water is to pay someone else to bring you to the fish. It can be difficult for someone who lives some distance from the ocean to figure out what species are hitting, where, on what tide, and what to use to catch them. While all these challenges are part of the fun of fishing, surmounting them is sometimes difficult, frustrating, and extremely time-consuming. In many cases, you'd need a boat just to *begin* your search.

Party boats and charter boats take much of the potential hassle out of fishing, leaving you to concentrate on the catching. This benefit comes at a price, of course, which varies according to what you want to fish for and how much comfort you desire when doing it. But most everyone who has taken such a trip regards it as money well spent. Some fishermen even consider the boat trip itself rewarding enough for the cost of the fare.

The heck with that. Let's catch some fish.

Party Boats

Party boats, also called head boats or open boats, are large sea-going craft that are designed to allow a large number of anglers to fish simultaneously. Averaging from 60 feet to more than 125 feet in length, and capable of holding from 60 to 140 anglers, all sides of party boats have open decks where anglers stand and drop their lures or baits in the water. Most all party boats dock at large marinas in protected bays or rivers. They specialize in fishing for prevalent species in nearby waters.

Party boats sail on a regular basis—sometimes every day during the fishing season. They leave port and return at predetermined times. Some party boats fish all day; others make two half-day trips, say from 8:00 A.M. to 12:30 P.M. and again from 2:00 P.M. to 6:00 P.M. Yet others will sail at night, departing in the evening and not returning until after midnight.

Typically you don't need to reserve a spot on a party boat. All you have to do is show up at the dock before the departure time and get on board. On a weekend morning during the height of the fishing season, however, you may have to arrive an hour or two early to ensure getting a spot. The fare averages $25 to $30 but may be more or less depending on the location, the length of the trip, and the species involved.

And it's almost always a bargain. Party boat captains are highly experienced fishermen, and you're paying for that knowledge. It's their job to know where the fish might be on any given day during the season. They also have to know the best baits, lures, and techniques to take the fish. They must be able to calculate the influences of the tides, the weather, fishing pressure, and many other variables to find fish, day after day. And they have to position the boat just so to give all anglers the best possible shot at the fish. Your job is simply to show up on time.

Party boats provide bait for their passengers and will chum if necessary for some species. Both are included in the cost of boarding. If you don't own the proper rod and reel, you can rent an outfit for a small fee; usually $5 plus a deposit. Party boats also have toilets and a roofed cabin with cushioned benches. Most also have a galley (kitchen), where snacks, soft drinks, and sometimes warm food can be purchased.

Party boats advertise in newspapers (usually in the sports section) and in state and local outdoor magazines and circulars. These ads usually give the name and size of the boat, where it docks, what species the boat is currently fishing for, and the times it leaves port. It's always wise to call the phone number listed and verify that information.

Also be sure to ask questions when you call: the boarding cost, how the fishing has been recently, what kind of tackle you need, how much it costs to rent tackle if you don't own the right kind, how early you should arrive at the dock, and so on.

And ask about the weather. Ocean weather is usually different—sometimes markedly so—from inland weather, and the forecast for your area probably won't be the same for the coast and offshore. (Party boats sail in all kinds of conditions, and rain usually doesn't affect the fishing anyway; though the wind might make for a choppier ride, depending on the region and the waters fished.)

Don't wear clothes that you can't wash or don't want to risk getting stained by fish blood. Wear shoes with non-skid soles—sneakers or boat shoes are fine in warm weather, rubber boots are best in cool or cold months. And dress in layers, no matter what the weather. You will be subject to wind, sun, possibly rain, and salt spray, and temperatures that may go much higher or lower than those inland. You'll be more comfortable adding or removing a sweatshirt and a jacket as conditions dictate, rather than bring one heavy parka along and alternating between freezing and sweating.

School Notes

Generally, the preferred spot to fish from on a party boat is the stern (back), as it is closer to the water than the starboard (right) and port (left) sides and doesn't rise and fall as much as the rest of the boat. Stern spots are the first to go, so get there early and claim it by tying your rod to the handrail.

Every party boat I know of has a fishing pool on each trip. Any angler who wishes to can enter the pool, which averages about $5 per angler (though it can cost more, and sometimes there are two different pools for different amounts). The fish are weighed on the trip back to port and whoever caught the biggest fish wins the pool, which can be a couple hundred dollars. But if the boat is large, and a lot of fishermen are on board, and a lot of them enter the pool, the biggest fish can mean some serious money. One acquaintance tells of a codfishing trip out of Long Island a few years ago on which his father won more than $1,600. While some seasoned party boat anglers fish specifically for large fish (they'll bring different baits or use large lures), many pools are won by first-timers, kids, or someone's indulgent date.

The best advice for winning the pool: Make sure your tackle is in good shape, your hooks are sharp, and you play all fish carefully but firmly. Finally—and this advice comes from Captain Tony Bogan, who pilots the 125-foot party boat *Jamaica*, has taken tens of thousands of fishermen out off the New Jersey coast, and has witnessed all kinds of errors made when a potential pool-winning fish was on someone's line— don't screw the drag down tightly in the mistaken idea that you'll bring a fish in easier. And don't touch the drag when you're fighting a fish; let it take the line out. That's what the drag is supposed to do.

Even though party boats offer a lot of services, you should bring a few things along. The following list covers the basics:

➤ Cash for fare and pool

➤ Rod, reel, and tackle (if you don't choose to rent it)

➤ Cooler with ice (in warm weather) or burlap bag for fish

➤ Food and drinks (if not sold on board)

➤ Rain gear or poncho

➤ Hat (with visor in sunny weather) and sunglasses

➤ Extra top (shirt, windbreaker, or coat, depending on season)

➤ Rag or towel

➤ Seasickness remedy (administer before leaving port)

➤ Optional items include: rubber boots, sunglasses, sunscreen, and gloves, depending on the season. You might also want to bring a camera to take a picture of you and your pool-winning fish.

Loose Lines

Many party boats that fish in cold weather have heated handrails. Experienced party-boat fishermen swear by these as they allow you to remain a bit more comfortable in raw conditions, thus affording more fishing time.

Charter Boats

A charter boat is a craft that can be rented by one or more anglers to fish for one day to one month or more. While party boats take customers on a first-come basis, a charter boat is for the exclusive use of the anglers—like a hired limousine compared to a city bus.

The size of a charter boat depends on the region, the species of fish involved, and the method of fishing. Charters on inland rivers and bays that fish for striped bass, redfish, snook, and tarpon with light saltwater outfits may be 20 feet or less and take just one to three anglers. Ocean charter boats that fish the same near-shore and offshore waters for those and other mid-size species such as grouper, bluefish, and cod generally run 20 to 30 feet in length and usually can take three to five anglers. Offshore charter boats that go for dolphin, king mackerel, tuna, and billfish run to 45 feet and longer, and can accommodate four to six or more paying customers.

Smaller charter boats may be owned by captains who make their boats "available for charter" on a part-time basis and use the boat for their personal fishing at other times. The larger offshore boats, however, are floating businesses, which are worth hundreds of thousands of dollars and may or may not be owned by the captain.

Charter boats are in evidence at practically all saltwater ports, docks, and marinas. Great numbers of them exist in popular fishing sites, such as Islamorada and Key West in the Florida Keys, the Caribbean islands, Long Island, and many California coastal towns and cities. A lot of resort hotels and inns have agreements with charter boats and will arrange in advance for guests to fish on a particular day.

School Notes

On some charter boats there may be more lines out than there are anglers on board. Figure out beforehand who gets to play the first fish (flip a coin if you can't decide) and the rotation after that.

The cost of a charter is much more than the fare on a party boat. Depending on the size of the boat, the duration of the trip, and the location, the price could range from as little as $100 for a half-day trip on a small boat that fishes inland waters, to more than $1,000 for a party of four or six to fish offshore for marlin and tuna. Generally, the farther the boat has to travel and the more gasoline or fuel it has to consume, the more expensive the trip will be. The timing of the trip is another cost factor. Weekend trips are usually more expensive than weekday ventures, as are trips scheduled during a time when a particular species is most likely to be in the area.

What you get for this cost, in addition to the captain's expertise, is the use of the boat's rods, reels, and tackle (you don't need to bring any); a whole boat to yourself and your friends; and personalized instruction and tips about anything from casting to and playing fish. The day is yours; the boat, to a certain extent, is yours as well. You can indicate preferences regarding species and fishing techniques, and the captain will do his or her best to accommodate you. There's an excellent chance that you will catch fish, and the possibility that you'll get a lot of them and maybe a trophy. In addition, the captain is usually a tremendous source of knowledge about the fish, wildlife, and vegetation found in and around those waters, and just talking and asking questions will often prove fascinating. In short, it's an experience that will probably create a lot of lasting memories.

Check newspaper ads and regional fishing magazines for names of charter boats. When calling, ask what species the boat will target. Tell the captain your level of experience and ask him or her if that will be a factor. Get the cost straight, and ask what it includes. (You'll probably have to bring your own lunch and drinks, though the captain may provide those for an additional fee.) Ask what time you should show up at the dock and what time the boat will return to the dock.

Even though you're paying for the charter, there are a few rules you should follow when on board to ensure a good trip for everyone involved. Captain John Wilson, who charters in and around the Indian River in Stuart, Florida, for redfish, sea trout, snook, tarpon, and other species, offers the following recommendations:

➤ *Show up on time.* Why keep the boat waiting when you're paying for it?

➤ *Don't drink.* Alcohol will dull your senses as well as your reaction time, and will dehydrate you quickly on a warm day. (My advice: Save it for your big-fish celebration when you return. You'll enjoy the drinks more then anyway.)

➤ *Wear old clothes.* Just like on a party boat, you may come into contact with bait and fish blood.

Cautious Casts

A boat is no place for horseplay, with hooks, gaffs, and expensive equipment lying about, not to mention the possibility of falling overboard when the boat is underway. Keep any children, and yourself and your friends, under control.

➤ *Ask questions.* The captain wants you to have a good time—he also wants your return business. On a charter boat, no question is a stupid question.

➤ *Bring PFDs (Personal Flotation Devices, or life vests) for your children.* The adult sizes, which every charter boat carries, may not fit the kids properly.

➤ *Don't hook the captain.* (John insisted this has happened to him.) In other words, don't be careless with the tackle.

A few more factors are involved when chartering a big boat for an offshore big-gamefish trip, which is detailed in the next chapter.

The Mate

All party boats and large charter boats have at least one mate, who is in charge of all those duties other than piloting the boat. A party boat mate (there may be more than one) collects the fares, organizes the pool, rents out tackle, prepares and distributes bait, helps set the anchor, prepares and disperses chum, nets or gaffs fish, sometimes helps unhook fish, clears tangled line, settles disagreements among passengers, weighs fish for the pool, swabs the deck, and assists docking the boat.

The mate on a charter boat performs many of the same duties and also readies the rods, reels, hooks, bait, lures, line, and leaders; sets out lines; operates outriggers and/or downriggers; coordinates multiple hook-ups; straps anglers into fighting chairs when necessary; offers advice on fish playing; and, in the event of a very large fish coming to boatside, unhooks and releases it or gaffs the fish and subdues it.

Always listen to the mate; he or she probably knows more about the boat and the fishing than anyone else on board except the captain. If you have what seems an unresolvable problem with the mate, ask to bring it to the captain's attention.

Party boat mates will clean fish for a fee. It is usually inexpensive—for $5 or $10 they'll clean a burlap bag of fish. This saves you a chore later on, possibly late at night, and is worth the money just to watch a mate produce perfect boneless fillets in minutes. On charter boats, the fish-cleaning cost is part of the fare.

Mates work hard and deserve a tip at the end of a trip. Like waiters and waitresses, mates have a low hourly or daily wage and make most of their money (which isn't a lot) on tips. On boats with more than one mate, they will pool their tips and take equal shares. A minimum amount for both party-boat and charter-boat mates is 10 percent of the fare. If you feel the mate doesn't deserve a tip, for whatever reason, you should inform the captain.

School Notes

When fishing on small charter boats that do not have a mate, it is customary to tip the captain. Ten percent of the fare is a reasonable minimum.

Seasickness

Some people never get seasick (I'm extremely lucky in that regard). Others get the dry heaves just thinking about boats. Many anglers fall somewhere in the middle—they can handle a typical boat ride, but when the swells get high and the boat rocks up, and down, and up, and down; and the thick, greasy diesel fumes hang in your face; and the mate starts ladling out bunker chum in front of you, and you hear it slopping into the water; well, lunch is often revisited.

While you can't permanently rid yourself of motion sickness, there are some steps and preventatives you can take to minimize it. Dramamine is a common over-the-counter drug that helps prevent, or at least minimize, nausea and wooziness. However, it does tend to make you sleepy. (Go on a full party boat and I guarantee you'll find someone inside the cabin taking a Dramamine nap.) But you must take the Dramamine a half-hour to one hour before you step onto the boat.

Scopolamine is another anti-motion-sickness drug. It is administered transdermally—a patch that you stick behind your jaw line, just below your ear. Scopolamine users claim the stuff is great, with dry mouth being the only side effect. However, my wife used it on an offshore fishing trip and took a one-hour nap on board and another one when we returned home. Still, she didn't get seasick, and she's very prone to it. Scopolamine is still a prescription drug in the U.S.

Don't eat a big, greasy, hard-to-digest meal just before going on board; this will worsen any nausea you experience. On the other hand, don't go on the boat with an empty stomach, either. Eat light foods and snack occasionally rather than wolfing a huge sandwich. If you're on board and feeling queasy, don't go in the cabin. Get outside, preferably on the upwind side of the boat (usually the bow). Look out at the shore, or the horizon line, instead of focusing on near objects. And don't fight the urge to vomit: Lean over the rail and let it go. You'll probably feel better, and you can always tell your friends that you did it because you thought the mate wasn't putting out enough chum.

Loose Lines

Some anti-seasickness aids consist of elastic bracelets with little bumps that put pressure on nerve endings on your wrist. I've read that they work well if placed properly, but I don't know anyone who has used them. But I do know people who are willing to try *anything* to combat sickness, and if nothing else these bands might be psychosomatically effective.

The Least You Need to Know

➤ Party boats are large crafts that take people fishing on a first-come basis. They sail almost every day during the fishing season and the fares are low.

➤ Be sure to bring cash, tackle, a cooler, food and drinks, rain gear, a hat, extra clothing, a rag, a seasickness remedy, and sun protection when fishing from a party boat.

➤ Charter boats vary in size and are hired for the exclusive use of the customers, generally one to six in number. The cost is much more than that of a party boat.

➤ Mates perform all duties on the boat other than piloting the craft. Their advice should be followed, and tipping 10 percent of the fare is customary.

➤ Take seasickness medication before you go on board. Eat lightly. Remain outside the boat in an upwind spot if you feel queasy.

The Big-Game Fishing Trip

When I was 14 years old, I was invited by a friend and his family to spend a week fishing off the Florida Keys. Although I'd fished a lot with my father up until then, both fresh water and salt water, it was the first time I'd fished so far from home. Every morning we'd get up, have a quick breakfast, and jump on the big sportfishing boat, which the captain would take far offshore for the day. We caught dolphin and barracuda, and on the afternoon of the fourth day, when it was my turn to take the next fish, a sailfish hit one of the trolled baits. I'll never forget being strapped into the fighting chair by the mate and putting my hands around a rod that was bent tautly over as the reel spool whirred into a blur, giving up line to 7 feet and 4 inches of pure wild muscle. That fish leaped completely out of the water numerous times, tore line off the reel time and time again, and dived beneath the boat when I finally got it close. But the mate was able to gaff the sailfish and bring it aboard. The mount of that fish still graces my parents' rec-room wall, and I'm reminded of how much that experience meant to me every time I see it.

Although killing and mounting big-game fish isn't as widely practiced now as it was then, fishing for them has grown in popularity. Being far from shore, trolling baits that are big enough for your dinner, waiting for the sight of or a strike from a huge, beautiful, predatory game fish—which could happen at any moment—is unequaled in anticipation. Actually hooking one and fighting it is exciting beyond belief. And although a lot of the work involved in getting you into that position is done by other people, the experience is fulfilling on its own. Here's how to put together such a trip and enjoy it to its fullest.

Planning the Trip

As discussed in the previous chapter, an offshore charter trip isn't cheap, costing hundreds of dollars per person. Many people can't afford such a trip; for others, it's a once-in-a-lifetime luxury. This is not a time for spontaneity; you want to make sure you're picking the right boat, the right place, and the right time to fish.

Obviously, the more people that charter a boat with you, the less the cost per person. Charter-boat captains will, of course, put together a trip of individual anglers, and everyone might get along fine. But you'll probably enjoy it more if you fish with friends or family members. Planning the trip is part of the fun, as is reminiscing about it later. This also gives you the opportunity for advance discussions on who gets the first fish, whether you'll want a fish mounted, who will take pictures, and other aspects of the trip.

If you live in an area of the country close to ports or marinas where offshore sport-fishing boats dock, your job is much easier. You can visit the marina one day to look over the boats, find out what species of fish the boats target, and get an idea of prices. Most marinas have a headquarters or dockmaster's building where a lot of that information is available. Pick up pamphlets and brochures and ask the proprietor for some recommendations.

Loose Lines

Offshore boats frequently fly a pennant that indicates an angler on board caught a fish. The pennant can indicate what species was caught and whether it was kept or released.

You'll also learn more about the fishing by being at the dock when the boats come back in, which is usually late afternoon. Note what kind of and how many fish they bring back. Ask the departing anglers on a couple of boats how they did, and if they would recommend that boat and crew.

If you don't live within a few hours' driving distance of the coast, you'll probably want to combine your big-game fishing trip with a vacation, as you'll have to be away from home for at least two or three nights to go on a one-day fishing trip. Fortunately, big-game fishing boats proliferate at most ocean-oriented vacation destinations in the U.S. However, the best fishing period may not coincide with your vacation time, so start making phone calls now. Up to a year in advance isn't too early. Call the chambers of commerce or the tourism boards—these can be state, county or local in scope—of a few different destinations and ask for all the information they have on big-game fishing: docks, boats, costs, accommodations, species available, and *the best time of year* to fish for those species. This last point is of extreme importance, because many big-game species—tarpon, tuna, and some billfish—are migratory and may not be in area waters when you get there. Some popular fishing destinations such as the Florida Keys have some type of big-game species available almost all year round, making the choice easier.

Call some charter-boat captains from the list you acquired from the tourism board (if you haven't done so by now) for specifics. Tell him or her your tentative plans—the time of year you'd like to go, the number of people with you, the species you'd like to fish for—and ask for the captain's thoughts. It's very possible that the boat's totally booked up for the time of year you want to go. In that case, ask the captain to recommend other boats and captains and make more calls. If *they're* booked, take it as a sign that you've called some good charter captains and have narrowed down the best time of year. Either make a reservation for the following year, or find a new destination and start over again. This sounds like a lot of advance work, but you'll be assured of getting a good boat at a good time of year.

School Notes

Most charter captains will require a deposit when you book a trip. Be sure you won't change your mind, as you may have to forfeit part or all of the deposit if you cancel within a certain period of time before your trip. Make sure you understand the terms under which the deposit is refundable.

Cautious Casts

Avoid being talked into spontaneous trips by charter captains or mates when walking on a dock. Although they may offer you a discount off the usual rate, they're probably trying to piggyback you onto a small fishing party and thus make a larger profit on the trip. The boat *might* be a good one, but you have no way of knowing for sure.

The Species

In the following sections, you'll read about the most common and sought-after big-game fish found off North American waters.

Atlantic Sailfish

This billfish is easily identified by its huge cobalt-blue, black-spotted dorsal fin, which is higher than the depth of its body. Its slab-shaped body has a steel-blue back with white or silver sides and thin light-blue bars. This coloration, combined with a long, slender bill, makes for an especially handsome and streamlined fish. Most sailfish caught by anglers are in the 7-foot, 40-pound range, although longer and heavier fish are occasionally taken.

The Atlantic sail is a showy and spectacular fighter. It often jumps clear of the water half a dozen times or more when hooked up, waving its head and falling back sideways into the water.

This species ranges in the Atlantic Ocean from Venezuela to Cape Hatteras, although it has been caught as far north as Massachusetts. Along the U.S. coast, sailfish seem to migrate northward from Florida in spring (though a concentration of them remains off that state's east coast) and move back down as the weather cools in the fall.

Most Atlantic sailfish are caught by trolling strip (filleted) baits, whole baits such as mullet, and lures. Under certain conditions they also can be caught on a fly rod (covered in the next chapter).

Pacific Sailfish

This fish is pretty much a western version of the Atlantic sailfish, with similar shape and coloring. Actually, some taxonomists doubt if it is really a separate species. It does grow larger, however, averaging from 60 to 100 pounds.

The Pac sail ranges from southern California south to Ecuador and is found in waters off of Hawaii and throughout the South Pacific. Fishing methods are the same as those for Atlantic sails.

Blue Marlin

This species is probably the most famous and sought-after billfish because of its outstanding fight—it jumps and dives and "greyhounds," or runs in one direction, quickly jumping in and out of the water—and the fact that it grows to immense proportions. Its cylindrical body is dark blue along the back, turning silvery along the sides that are marked with horizontal hash-mark-like bars. Its dorsal fin comes to a well-defined point above its gills and quickly slopes down to continue along its back.

The average blue marlin caught by anglers weighs 200 to 500 pounds, though female marlin (males don't get much larger than 300 pounds) can grow to a ton or more.

Blue marlin are found in warm and temperate waters worldwide, ranging as far north as Massachusetts in the Atlantic and southern California in the Pacific. There are particularly large populations of them off the North Carolina coast in summertime and farther south in winter.

These fish are principally caught on trolled whole baits, flying fish, mullet, strip baits, and lures.

White Marlin

Although this species doesn't grow nearly as large as the blue marlin—it averages 50 pounds but can reach a bit more than 150 pounds—it is very popular with offshore anglers because of its willingness to hit baits and lures and its propensity to jump often and go on long runs when hooked. The white marlin's back is a bright blue while its flanks are silvery-white, both of which are marked with light-blue vertical bars. Its dorsal fin is rounded, rather than sharply pointed like the blue's.

White marlin are found only in the Atlantic Ocean, from Brazil north to Nova Scotia. The species migrates north as the weather warms, and concentrations of white marlin show up off Maryland and the east end of Long Island. They hit a variety of trolled baits and lures, and often are targeted by anglers specializing in light offshore tackle.

Black Marlin

This fish shares the distinction with the blue as being the largest of marlins, reaching a ton in weight. The color of the black marlin varies, although its back is often a deep slate blue with whitish sides. It is distinguished from all other marlins by the fact that its pectoral fins protrude rigidly at a right angle from its body and can't be folded flat.

The black marlin is mainly a fish of the Pacific and Indian oceans. It is primarily found from Peru north to Mexico, with some fish entering waters off southern California. Trolled baits and lures take most of these fish, though drifting with live bait is a common method in some areas.

Striped Marlin

This marlin runs much smaller than the blue and black marlins. It averages around 200 pounds, but can reach more than twice that weight. It has a high, sharply pointed dorsal fin with a steel-blue back that gradually fades to white along the sides, which are marked with wide white or blue vertical bars.

Like the black marlin, the striped marlin inhabits the Indian and Pacific oceans, and is caught as far north as southern California. It will take trolled baits, lures, and drifted live baits.

Loose Lines

Although sailfish and marlins are edible, they're uncommon enough to warrant your re-leasing them after the fight instead of keeping them for food.

Swordfish

Also called broadbill, the swordfish is found worldwide in temperate and tropical waters. It is readily identified by its dark brown or black back, fading to lighter shades along the sides. The dorsal fin is high and sickle-shaped, and the sword is quite long and flat compared to those of other billfish. Swordfish average 100 to 200 pounds, but some have been known to reach more than 1,000 pounds.

This species is much sought-after by commercial fishermen, who sell the meat. Anglers catch them by trolling baits and drifting live baits. Shy and selective feeders, swords are often spotted basking on the surface, and the boat must slowly and delicately present the bait to the fish without noise or surface disturbance. They're also caught at night on deep-fished baits.

Bluefin Tuna

The bluefin is the largest of all the tuna species, with "giants" reaching 1,000 pounds and more. ("School" bluefins average from 5 to about 70 pounds.) Its thick, double-tapered body resembles a giant football, explaining why school tuna are sometimes referred to as "footballs." They are found worldwide in temperate and subtropical waters, ranging from the coast of Canada south to The Bahamas in the Atlantic. They're less common in the Pacific, seeming most abundant in waters around Catalina Island. They generally migrate northward as the water warms, reaching Nova Scotia waters in September.

Bluefins are among the most powerful and tenacious of big-game fish, putting up heated battles that may last for several hours. They are caught by chumming (both while drifting and anchored), baiting with cut or whole baits, and by trolling with whole fish and squid. Bluefin are popular food fish and now are subject to quotas for both commercial and sport fishermen.

Sharks

Ever since Peter Benchley's *Jaws* debuted in book and movie form in the mid-1970s, sharks have been popular targets of fishermen in the U.S. Although the great white shark gets most of the press—the "man-eater" can weigh up to a ton—many other species grow to large sizes, hit readily, and offer superb sport, including blue, tiger, thresher, and hammerhead sharks. (And they're dangerous, too.) Sharks are found in all temperate, tropical, and subtropical waters around the world.

When going specifically for sharks, nearly all offshore anglers will chum from a drifting (though sometimes anchored) boat and set out two or three lines, baited with strip or whole baits, at different depths throughout the chum slick. Sharks will also hit trolled baits usually intended for other species.

Of all the sharks, the mako is probably the most prized, for both its fighting ability and its flesh. Makos, which range as far north as Massachusetts, make spectacular leaps when hooked, and rival swordfish as table fare. Unfortunately, the fishing pressure on the mako and some other shark species has resulted in a noticeable decline of large specimens, and many anglers now release all the sharks they catch.

Other Species

While the previous fish are most frequently sought-after by big-game fishing boats, other, smaller species are often caught. Though these fish are sometimes considered secondary or incidental, many times they are equally prized.

Dolphin (the fish, not the mammal) inhabit tropical and subtropical waters worldwide and often hit trolled baits and lures intended for billfish. They average from 5 to 15 pounds but can reach weights in excess of 60 pounds. Their flesh is delicious; they fight long, hard, and acrobatically; and they have a striking blue, green, and yellow body; so most experienced anglers look forward to hooking some dolphin. These fish usually forage in small schools and will stay together even when one is hooked. Many fishermen stop the boat when one dolphin hits a trolled bait and have other anglers on board cast smaller baits or lures to the remaining school members. Dolphin frequently relate to floating debris or seaweed, making it possible to watch one or more dolphin speed out from under such flotsam to strike a trolled bait.

King mackerel are found in the Atlantic from Florida to the Carolinas and occasionally further north, and in the Gulf of Mexico. They average 5 to 15 pounds but can reach weights of 100 pounds. They are long, streamlined fish that are silvery-blue on top, fading to a gold color. They often hit fast-trolled lures and baits and go on long, sizzling runs when first hooked. The flesh is good.

Loose Lines

Don't confuse the dolphin fish with the bottlenose dolphin, which is a mammal. Dolphin fish are called mahi–mahi in Hawaii and in restaurants across the U.S., where patrons might otherwise think they're about to be served a Flipper steak.

Great barracuda are frequently caught when trolling for big-game fish. Although they can reach weights of 100 pounds, most of those caught offshore weigh much less than half that. Although the barracuda is a great sporting fish, its fight is often diminished by the heavy trolling tackle. Cudas are common off Florida and in the Caribbean, ranging as far north as the Carolinas. This long, slim, silvery-blue fish has a mouthful of large, pointed teeth, which matches its aggressive disposition. Many great barracuda carry a poison in their flesh and thus are not safe to eat.

Fighting a Big Fish

You're sitting in a chair on the stern deck, watching the baits surf and skip on the water behind the boat. You've been trolling for an hour or two with no action. But that's okay; you're enjoying the sun and the solitude of the ocean as the drone of the boat's engines lull you into a kind of trance.

Suddenly, tumult. The captain on the bridge above you roars out something you didn't quite understand, and the mate literally leaps to one of the rods, yanking it out of the rod holder. At the same time the line from that rod pops loose from the outrigger, and the mate puts the reel in freespool, paying out line. The captain roars again—it's your name he's shouting!—and your friends pull and push you toward the fighting chair as the mate closes the reel and starts whamming the rod back over his head to set the hook. You find yourself being strapped into the chair by the captain (where did he come from?) as the mate sets the rod into the gimbal in front of you. Now everyone is shouting at each other, and as you go to grab the rod you look out and see a fish—a huge fish; it's much bigger than you—leap magnificently out of the water, completely airborne, and fall back in with a tremendous splash. Everyone whoops. "Don't lose him!" one of your friends yells in your ear.

Now what?

Follow directions. Not from your friend, your brother-in-law, or the guy from accounts payable, but from the mate. He's been in this situation hundreds of times before, and he and the captain will work together, often in an unspoken manner, to help you bring that fish in. That expertise is part of what you're paying for.

School Notes

Make sure that you and all your fellow fishermen bring a camera. Everyone should take plenty of photos during a fish fight to ensure some quality shots of what may be a once-in-a-lifetime experience. If you're fighting the fish, remind the others to take pictures. Those with cameras shouldn't stand in the middle of the action.

A lot of the tricky work will already have been done for you. When having a party of inexperienced anglers aboard (we're assuming you're one, of course), the mate will already have set the hook. This can be a difficult maneuver because oftentimes fish will not hook themselves when they strike the bait. Sometimes they just rise up to inspect it or mouth it; other times they'll grab it and swim away but not swallow it. The captain and mate know what to do in each case. Oftentimes it involves speeding up or slowing down the boat, and/or "dropping back," which means putting the reel in freespool so that the bait stops and sinks in the water, allowing the fish to grab it or run with it. Sometimes the fish won't take the bait at all.

But let's assume that it does, and you're up. Although the mate and captain will be guiding you the whole way, the first rule is: Don't touch the drag setting on the reel. Big-game reels have fine-tuned drag mechanisms, sometimes two of them, and it'll be set properly. The fish is *supposed* to peel line off the reel; that's part of what tires it out. If, for some reason, you have any doubt about the drag setting, tell the mate. Keep your hands off of it.

The mate or captain will strap you into the fighting chair and place the rod in the gimbal in front of you. At first, don't reel. You won't have much of a choice anyway; the fish will be taking out line at an incredible rate and you'll have enough of a time holding onto the rod with both hands. The mate may adjust the drag a bit at this time.

Eventually, the fish will stop taking line off the reel. Now it's time to gain some of it back. Place your feet on the chair's footrest. With your hands around the rod grip above the reel, lean back, using your legs and back to bring the rod to a near-vertical position. Then drop the rod and simultaneously reel in slack line. Then repeat; for as long as it takes to bring the fish in.

The fish may go on another long run after a while, taking out all that line that you gained back. When this happens just hold the rod and let the fish run. Don't reel against the drag; it'll twist the line and will just serve to tire you out.

Cautious Casts

Don't feel pressured to get a fish mounted. There's nothing wrong with keeping a true trophy fish, but don't let others—including the captain or mate, who may be getting a percentage of the taxidermist's fee—talk you into it. When in doubt, have extra pictures taken and let the fish go. (See Chapter 29, "In the Pan or On the Wall?" for details.)

Throughout the fight, the fish will probably move to the sides of the boat. It's important to always face the fish when fighting it, so the mate will swivel the chair to keep you pointed in the right direction.

If and when you get the fish close to the boat, it may sound, or dive deeply. This is when the job can get very tough, as you have to winch the fish—which may be hundreds of feet down—to the surface by pumping and reeling repeatedly.

Most fish are lost close to the boat just before landing. It's very important to do exactly what the mate says—specifically "reel" or "don't reel," because the fish may jump, sound again, or even take off on another run. Any slack line could allow the fish to throw the hook or roll on the line, breaking it or tearing out the hook.

When the fish is ready to be boated, the mate will grab the leader with a gloved hand and either gaff the fish and hoist it over the side or bring it in through a gate in the stern. Very large fish may need to be roped around the tail to be brought in. Be ready to vacate the chair as soon as the mate tells you to, as a large fish can jump and writhe powerfully and may cause injury. If the fish is to be released, the mate will cut the leader as close to the hook as possible.

Now you can relax, have something to drink, and start telling your story.

The Least You Need to Know

➤ Book a charter trip well in advance, and first research the area, the best time of year to fish, and the charter boats available.

➤ Sailfish, various marlin species, swordfish, bluefin tuna, and sharks are the most popular quarry of offshore anglers. Dolphin, king mackerel, and barracuda are common secondary catches.

➤ Follow the mate's instructions exactly when fighting a fish. Use your legs and back as well as your arms to bring the rod up, and reel in slack as you drop it down.

Chapter 25

Ultimate Sport: Flyfishing the Salt

In This Chapter

➤ The big eight species

➤ Leave your trout rod at home

➤ Flies in the brine

It may seem unrealistic or even inconceivable to use a tool as wispy and as delicate as a fly rod to catch fish that normally are fished for with huge baits, thick monofilament line, and rods that have barely more action than a broomstick. But new technology has enabled manufacturers to produce lightweight, manageable fly rods that can cast heavy fly line and help tame fish that weigh more than 100 pounds. Reels have been developed that can hold hundreds of yards of line, with superb drag systems that can withstand long, scorching runs—also of a weight that won't tire you out after a few casts.

Not that saltwater flyfishing is easy. Actually, forms of it, including those for species that don't grow much larger than 10 or 15 pounds, are among the most challenging fishing to be found anywhere; some anglers consider it the pinnacle of the entire sport of fishing. And it is increasing in popularity every year. Here's why.

The Species

Most of the species that are targeted by saltwater flyfishermen are those that feed on the surface or within reasonable reach of a sinking line—in other words, no fishing for groupers a couple hundred feet down. You cast to the fish while wading, when standing in a small boat, or from the deck of an offshore boat. Such wide parameters make it possible to flyfish for dozens and dozens of saltwater species (and it's done), but there are eight species that seem to get most of the attention:

➤ *Bonefish* are probably the saltwater species most sought after by fly rodders. These streamlined silvery-blue fish are found worldwide in tropical waters and typically roam flats (large expanses of shallow water) singly or in small schools during high tides, searching for crabs, shrimp, and other forage along the bottom. You can search for these fish while wading or from "flats boats," which are open-decked, fast-running craft that can get around in very shallow water, looking for fish or signs of them. Because bonefish are bottom feeders, it's possible to see their tails sticking up out of very shallow flats. But they're incredibly flighty and will spook from the scrape of your foot along the bottom or even the shadow of your fly line.

Although bonefish reach 20 pounds, most fish caught by anglers weigh 3 to 5 pounds. They are incredibly powerful for their size; a hooked bonefish will generally peel 50 to 100 yards of line off your reel in its first run.

➤ *Permit*, another tropical-water species, are silver and green, narrow, deep-bodied fish (somewhat resembling a sunfish) that average 10 to 40 pounds. Like bonefish, they come up on flats to feed on crabs and other crustaceans on a high tide, but are even more sensitive to sight and sound. Just hooking one on a fly is considered an accomplishment. Bringing one in, after it takes more than 100 yards of line off your reel, is a feat.

➤ *Redfish*, also called red drum or channel bass, are more accessible than bonefish and permit to U.S. fishermen—they occur along the Atlantic coast from Massachusetts to Texas. Although they don't put up as spectacular a fight as those two species, they often feed in shallow water along the bottom and can be sighted and cast to. Copper or bronze in coloration, reds grow to 80 pounds, but most of those fish caught in shallow water by fly anglers run from 5 to 20 pounds.

➤ *Snook* range throughout tropical U.S. waters and are found in great numbers in Florida and Texas. These long, thick, silvery-brown fish are famous for their outstanding fighting ability, running, jumping, and diving powerfully. They generally relate to somewhat deep waters—channels and estuaries—but often are found near structure such as dock pilings and will enter shallow waters to feed. Most snook caught by flyfishermen weigh less than 10 pounds, but they can grow to 40 pounds and more.

➤ *Spotted Sea Trout* occur along the southern U.S. Atlantic coast and in the Gulf of Mexico. These bluish-gray speckled fish are extremely popular with Southern anglers for both sport and food, especially in Florida. Flyfishermen go after sea trout because of this species' propensity to feed on shrimp in grassy areas of relatively shallow waters. Sea trout average 2 to 3 pounds but will reach 15 pounds.

➤ *Striped Bass*, which were the mainstay of saltwater surf, bay, and river fishermen along the north and mid-Atlantic coast for years, suffered from extensive commercial harvest in the 1960s and 70s and only now are making an amazing comeback thanks to season closures and stringent minimum-size laws. Fly-fishermen have found a new quarry in stripers, given their tendency to prowl jetties, rock pilings, and other near-shore structures. Silvery white with black horizontal lines, stripers are strong fish and fight well, ranging from 5 to 10 pounds when young and more than 50 pounds when mature.

➤ *Sailfish* (detailed in the previous chapter) have become popular with more experienced saltwater fly anglers. Hooking them on a fly rod requires teamwork on an offshore boat, as a fish must be trolled up on a teaser, which is a hookless lure usually in the shape of a squid. The teaser is brought close to the boat, with the sailfish following it. The teaser is quickly pulled out of the water at the same time that the fly angler drops a big popping fly in that area, which the sailfish—with luck—will strike.

➤ *Tarpon* may be last alphabetically but rank first in the minds of many saltwater flyfishermen. This is because tarpon are among the strongest of all saltwater species. They can grow to great sizes, with 200-plus-pound fish caught every year. And they often feed in relatively shallow waters, allowing you to search for and stalk fish from a flats boat. Just seeing a school of these huge creatures cruise and feed in shallow water is exciting. Approaching and casting to them without spooking the school, and then witnessing one of them come close to your fly and prepare to eat it can give you the shakes. If you manage to do everything right and actually hook it, that fish will probably jump completely out of the water and take off on a sizzling run, often emptying your spool of line and most of the backing, requiring you to chase the fish with the boat just so you can gain line back.

Tarpon, sometimes referred to as "silver kings" for their coloration and their esteem by anglers, live in tropical and subtropical waters of the Atlantic Ocean, with many fish caught in Florida. Wherever you fish for them, it's not a sport for the faint-hearted.

Many other species are sought by fly rodders but don't have as much appeal, perhaps because they are comparatively plentiful. But many are easier to catch and provide a lot of opportunity for practice experience. Two of them, bluefish in northern waters and dolphin in southern, offer the additional advantage of being good to eat.

Bluefish inhabit inshore and offshore waters from spring through fall along much of the Atlantic coast. They are a staple of the party boat and charter boat industry, being

ravenous feeders and great brawlers. Many fly anglers will go for bluefish from small craft in bays and tidal rivers and offshore when seas are calm. A popular technique is to look for sea gulls and other birds circling and diving into the water, feeding on baitfish driven up to the surface by a school of blues, and casting their streamer fly into the boil. Broiled or grilled on the day they are caught, bluefish are excellent eating (although they don't keep well in the freezer).

Dolphin, trolled up by offshore boats as explained in the previous chapter, can be teased to the boat in the same manner as sailfish. (Not all offshore charter captains are familiar with the technique, however.) When I fished on the *Ocean Fancy* out of Marathon, Florida, a couple of years ago, Captain Eric Johansen had his mate tease in a couple of big dolphin that were seeking cover under a small mat of weed well offshore. The mate cast out a bait close to the weeds and began reeling it in immediately. One of the dolphin followed, and I cast a big popper to the fish as the mate pulled the bait out of the water. It took a few tries (which is one of the advantages of flyfishing for bluefish and dolphin—you can make a mistake but still catch a fish), but I finally hooked into a 14-pound fish that tasted superb at dinner that evening.

> ### School Notes
>
> Even if you've become an accomplished freshwater flyfisherman, you should always retain a fishing guide for your first saltwater foray. Guides know their home waters and the species that inhabit them intimately, and what you'll learn from a guide in one day would take months to learn on your own.

> ### Loose Lines
>
> If you need another excuse to take up saltwater flyfishing, consider that many of the fun-to-catch species are found in waters near popular vacation destinations. The coasts of North and South Carolina, Florida, and Texas, and many Caribbean islands such as The Bahamas, offer excellent saltwater flyfishing opportunities. Many anglers who can afford it will take a family vacation to one of these areas and reserve a day or two (or more if possible) to flyfish, while the non-fishing family members can enjoy a laid-back beach or resort vacation. Sure, it's an expensive and somewhat transparent ploy, but definitely an efficacious one.

Rods, Reels, and Line

Most saltwater flyfishing can be divided into two categories: that for "small" fish, or those that weigh less than 30 or 40 pounds, and that for larger fish. The popular smaller species frequent inland and inshore waters, while many of the larger fish are fished for in deep waters or offshore.

The smaller species can be fished for with a variety of fly rod weights; the 8/9-weight outfit is probably the best all-around size for most of them in most situations. A 12-weight rod will handle most of the bigger fish. However, all of the species encountered when saltwater flyfishing are extremely powerful for their size. Long casts are frequently necessary to reach them, and they can burn a lot of line off your reel once hooked. When also considering the corrosive nature of the saltwater environment, it's obvious that specialized equipment is necessary: long, beefy fly rods that can get fly line way out there and stand up to the surges of powerful fish; fly lines that match these rods but can still be used to make a delicate presentation; reels with great line capacities, excellent drag systems, and corrosion-resistant parts. Most freshwater tackle just isn't sturdy enough for the task.

Manufacturers have quickly responded to the increased interest in saltwater flyfishing with rods, line, and reels specifically designed for salt water use. Rods are generally fast action and have particularly heavy butt sections. Many also feature a ball-like "fighting butt," allowing the angler to comfortably place the bottom of the rod against his or her body to apply more leverage to a fish when fighting it. Saltwater fly lines are sturdier as well, with hard finishes and longer tapers to facilitate long casts. Many lines are customized for fishing for a certain species—bonefish, tarpon—and are labeled as such, as well as with its weight, taper, and buoyancy.

School Notes

Some saltwater fly reels are available with an anti-reverse drive. This means that as line is taken off the reel, the spool turns but the reel handles don't. This is a nice feature to have when playing fast-running fish. You'll save a bloody knuckle or two and will regain control of the reel handle much faster.

Fly reels are perhaps the most specialized (or different from freshwater versions) part of the saltwater outfit. Besides the necessity of corrosion-resistant parts, saltwater reels must be sturdy and have a large line capacity. Most important is the drag system. Ratchet-type drags have no place in saltwater fishing. A disk drag reel is mandatory because many popular species are incredibly fast swimmers; a standard ratchet-drag reel wouldn't even start to tire a fish out. Disk-drag reels have a knob that adjusts the amount of drag; palming of the spool is still possible but not absolutely necessary as it is with ratchet-drag reels.

Of course, all of this equipment doesn't come cheap. Serviceable saltwater fly rods start at about $100; decent ones at about twice that. And that's the low end. Reels have a similar but somewhat higher pricing structure, with about $125 price tags on the acceptable models. A good line will cost about $40. When adding incidentals—backing, leaders, some flies—figure on spending at least $300 just to get into the game.

Right now it may not seem worth that cost, plus more down the road, just to catch a fish that you're probably going to release anyway. But the incredibly fast growth of this sport does suggest that many people, upon discovering its unmatched challenge and excitement, think it's a bargain in comparison.

Flies and Other Tackle

The forage consumed by saltwater species is represented by flies that, with few exceptions, look much different from those you'd use for trout, bass, or pike in fresh water.

Shrimp flies, for instance, are tied in various patterns that closely or somewhat resemble that crustacean. These flies, which are popular for bonefish, permit, sea trout, and redfish, are weighted so they will sink to the bottom quickly with the hook point up, where they're retrieved in short hops. Popular patterns include the Crazy Charlie and the MOE (Mother of Epoxy, which has an epoxy head).

Streamers are tied in various sizes in a rainbow of colors and patterns. Some imitate specific forage species; others are considered attractor patterns. They're used for most all species, with the Lefty's Deceiver, Clouser Minnow, and SeaDucer being good all-around patterns (in the proper sizes) for bonefish, redfish, snook, and striped bass. Specific-forage patterns resemble bunker, squid, mackerel, anchovies, and sand eels.

Crab flies are usually intended for permit but will take bonefish, redfish, and other bottom-oriented feeders. Del's Merkin Crab is a good pattern.

Flies for tarpon are smaller than you'd suspect for such a huge fish. They're tied on wide-gap hooks to better penetrate a tarpon's bony mouth. A variety of patterns work, with some patterns being favored on a local basis. The Huff Tarpon Fly and the Ruoff Tarpon Fly are popular.

Poppers effectively take redfish, snook, and sailfish, as well as bluefish and dolphin. They're also exciting to use, as fish will sometimes blast the popper hard enough to knock it out of the water. Ruoff's Backcountry Popper will take a variety of species.

Big-game flies are used for sailfish. These are extra long (generally longer than 6 inches), flashy, and often have a second trailing hook to ensure a hookup. Curcione's Big Game Fly is used successfully.

Most saltwater species have teeth as well as sharp dorsal fins and gill covers, and many will take your line into abrasion-filled cover. Therefore, it's necessary to tie a shock leader—usually about a foot in length—onto the end of your leader. The strength of the shock leader varies from 20- to 100-pound test, with the lightest used for redfish and the heaviest for sailfish. (Shock leaders are covered in more detail in Chapter 12, "Yes, You Should Sweat the Small Stuff.") Shock leaders can be attached to the end of the leader with a surgeon's knot (see Chapter 8, "It's All on the Line").

As many species will make long runs, sometimes emptying your spool of fly line, it's essential to have enough backing on your reel. Two hundred yards of 20-pound-test backing on an 8/9-weight outfit for bonefish and permit is cheap insurance.

As long casts are often necessary to reach salt-water species, it's necessary to have as much as 50 feet of line laying loosely at your feet so it can shoot easily through the rod guides on your final cast. This is rarely a problem when fishing from a flats boat. But if you're wading after bonefish, permit, or redfish, all that line may tangle in your legs as the tidal current pulls at it. The line must lift from the water before it shoots through the guides, decreasing its energy. And striped bass fly-fishermen often cast from rock jetties and groins, where the line easily gets tangled and even damaged on the rubble. The solution is a stripping basket, which is nothing more than an open plastic box that straps to the caster's waist. Cones inside the box distribute the line evenly as the angler deposits it into the box when preparing for a cast or retrieving a fly, and it lifts out of the box smoothly when casting for distance. The basket sounds too simple an idea to work, but it does.

School Notes

Although you can get by with basic flycasts, some saltwater situations require special casting methods and techniques. If you're going to invest in an expensive trip, you should strongly consider taking casting instructions from a professional (see Chapter 17, "No-Fear Fly Casting"). Some fishing guides will provide lessons for an additional fee.

Loose Lines

Some charter boat captains, especially those in the Chesapeake Bay area, specialize in fly-fishing trips for bluefish and striped bass. To get the fish close to the boat, they begin a standard chum slick. But they've found that the best fly pattern to use in such a situation is one that was developed in that region: a chum fly, which is tied to resemble a bit of fish flesh. Blues and stripers in the slick will often pick up such morsels, and are fooled by the fly.

The Least You Need to Know

➤ Bonefish, permit, redfish, sailfish, snook, spotted sea trout, striped bass, and tarpon are the most popular species targeted by saltwater anglers. Bluefish and dolphin, in their regions, are secondary flyfishing species.

➤ Putting together a decent saltwater flyfishing outfit—rod, reel, line—costs about $300. Prices can go much higher, as the equipment must be top-notch to withstand the saltwater elements and the strength of the fish.

➤ Saltwater flies—shrimp and crab patterns, plus streamers, poppers, and huge big-game flies—are much different from freshwater versions. Shock leaders and a lot of backing are also necessary.

Part 6

The Complete Angler

The evolution of an average person into a fisherman is marked by two devel an increasing wealth of practical outdoor know-how and a burgeoning collec stuff.

The former entails a lot of methods, tricks, and other knowledge that make efficient, safe, and comfortable—things like knowing the basics about boats as the best hat to wear on a particular day, how to remove a fishhook from (or your own) finger, the proper procedure for measuring a fish, and filleting so that not one bone is found by your dinner companions. Some of this con perience; some must be learned. But all of it is important. The second devel an accumulation of rods, reels, lures, hooks, line, and flies—presents a mo immediate need, so we'll look at some solutions for that, too.

Fishing Boat Basics

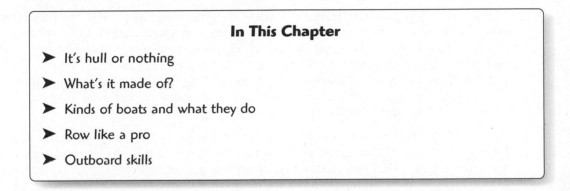

In This Chapter

➤ It's hull or nothing

➤ What's it made of?

➤ Kinds of boats and what they do

➤ Row like a pro

➤ Outboard skills

Pass by any river, lake, reservoir, or bay during the non-winter months and chances are good that you'll see people fishing from boats. If you're there and planning to fish from the bank or the beach, you'll probably feel some envy when you watch those boaters rowing or motoring around, fishing in all those places you can't get to, and possibly catching more fish and fish bigger than you are. That's why so many people every year go out and buy their first boat. (Of course, many of the same people wind up hating their boat, but that's another story.)

Still, so much fishing is done from boats that it's helpful to recognize boat types, and the advantages and disadvantages of each. (Two good resources for learning all about boats are *The Complete Idiot's Guide to Boating and Sailing* and *Guide to Freshwater Fishing Boats*; see Appendix D, "Species and Resource Guide," for details.) Also, because thousands of boat liveries on waters across the country rent boats by the hour, day, or week, the beginning angler should be familiar with the rudimentary aspects of boat handling and safety. You may never own a boat (a sign I've seen hanging in more than one den reads "Boat: A hole in the water into which one throws money"), but knowing boat basics will make you a better fisherman when you're in one.

Getting the Hull Story

The outside bottom of every boat is called a *hull*, and the shape and design of the hull dictate the boat's performance and use.

The simplest hull configuration is the *flat bottom*. Boats with flat bottoms maneuver easily and are very stable in calm waters. (The johnboat, a very common small fishing boat, has a flat bottom. More on johnboats later.) Flat-bottomed boats make a good choice of boat for a fisherman who is going to use his craft on small, protected inland waters such as ponds or small lakes, and in cases where speed is not a factor. In even moderately choppy water, though, the flat bottom provides a very rough ride.

The *semi-V* hull resembles a flat-bottom, except for a shallow V shape in its front portion. This shape provides a bit more stability than does the flat bottom, as the V helps cut through the water instead of riding with it.

The *deep-V* hull has a sharply angled V shape running from the front of the boat (the bow) all the way to the rear of the boat (the stern). Boats with deep-V hulls are intended for use in rough water, as the hull slices through waves instead of being tossed around by them. Because of the sharp angle of the V, however, boats with deep-V hulls sit lower in the water than do others, and aren't suitable for fishing in shallow water. Also, although deep-V boats are generally very seaworthy, they tend to rock from side to side when not under power.

The *modified-V* hull resembles a deep V, except the angle of the V isn't as sharp. A boat with a "mod-V" hull represents a good compromise in hull shape and makes a good all-around craft: It's maneuverable enough to get around easily, offers a fairly smooth ride in rough water, doesn't rock from side to side as easily as a deep V, and can enter shallow (though not too shallow) water.

The four most common hull types on fishing boats are the flat bottom, semi-V, deep-V, and modified-V. The perspective here is from the front of the boats.

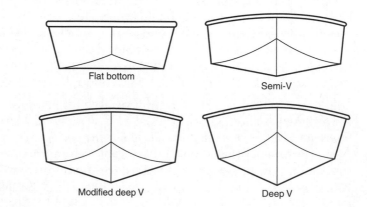

Flat bottom

Semi-V

Modified deep V

Deep V

for redfish and the heaviest for sailfish. (Shock leaders are covered in more detail in Chapter 12, "Yes, You Should Sweat the Small Stuff.") Shock leaders can be attached to the end of the leader with a surgeon's knot (see Chapter 8, "It's All on the Line").

As many species will make long runs, sometimes emptying your spool of fly line, it's essential to have enough backing on your reel. Two hundred yards of 20-pound-test backing on an 8/9-weight outfit for bonefish and permit is cheap insurance.

As long casts are often necessary to reach saltwater species, it's necessary to have as much as 50 feet of line laying loosely at your feet so it can shoot easily through the rod guides on your final cast. This is rarely a problem when fishing from a flats boat. But if you're wading after bonefish, permit, or redfish, all that line may tangle in your legs as the tidal current pulls at it. The line must lift from the water before it shoots through the guides, decreasing its energy. And striped bass fly-fishermen often cast from rock jetties and groins, where the line easily gets tangled and even damaged on the rubble. The solution is a stripping basket, which is nothing more than an open plastic box that straps to the caster's waist. Cones inside the box distribute the line evenly as the angler deposits it into the box when preparing for a cast or retrieving a fly, and it lifts out of the box smoothly when casting for distance. The basket sounds too simple an idea to work, but it does.

School Notes

Although you can get by with basic flycasts, some saltwater situations require special casting methods and techniques. If you're going to invest in an expensive trip, you should strongly consider taking casting instructions from a professional (see Chapter 17, "No-Fear Fly Casting"). Some fishing guides will provide lessons for an additional fee.

Loose Lines

Some charter boat captains, especially those in the Chesapeake Bay area, specialize in fly-fishing trips for bluefish and striped bass. To get the fish close to the boat, they begin a standard chum slick. But they've found that the best fly pattern to use in such a situation is one that was developed in that region: a chum fly, which is tied to resemble a bit of fish flesh. Blues and stripers in the slick will often pick up such morsels, and are fooled by the fly.

The Least You Need to Know

➤ Bonefish, permit, redfish, sailfish, snook, spotted sea trout, striped bass, and tarpon are the most popular species targeted by saltwater anglers. Bluefish and dolphin, in their regions, are secondary flyfishing species.

➤ Putting together a decent saltwater flyfishing outfit—rod, reel, line—costs about $300. Prices can go much higher, as the equipment must be top-notch to withstand the saltwater elements and the strength of the fish.

➤ Saltwater flies—shrimp and crab patterns, plus streamers, poppers, and huge big-game flies—are much different from freshwater versions. Shock leaders and a lot of backing are also necessary.

Part 6

The Complete Angler

The evolution of an average person into a fisherman is marked by two developments: an increasing wealth of practical outdoor know-how and a burgeoning collection of stuff.

The former entails a lot of methods, tricks, and other knowledge that make you more efficient, safe, and comfortable—things like knowing the basics about boats, as well as the best hat to wear on a particular day, how to remove a fishhook from someone's (or your own) finger, the proper procedure for measuring a fish, and filleting that fish so that not one bone is found by your dinner companions. Some of this comes from experience; some must be learned. But all of it is important. The second development— an accumulation of rods, reels, lures, hooks, line, and flies—presents a more immediate need, so we'll look at some solutions for that, too.

Fishing Boat Basics

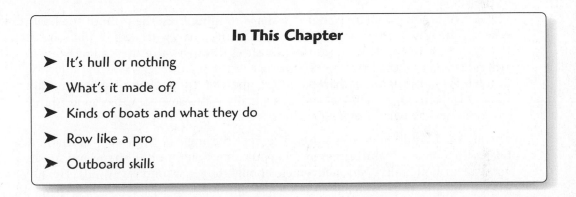

In This Chapter

➤ It's hull or nothing

➤ What's it made of?

➤ Kinds of boats and what they do

➤ Row like a pro

➤ Outboard skills

Pass by any river, lake, reservoir, or bay during the non-winter months and chances are good that you'll see people fishing from boats. If you're there and planning to fish from the bank or the beach, you'll probably feel some envy when you watch those boaters rowing or motoring around, fishing in all those places you can't get to, and possibly catching more fish and fish bigger than you are. That's why so many people every year go out and buy their first boat. (Of course, many of the same people wind up hating their boat, but that's another story.)

Still, so much fishing is done from boats that it's helpful to recognize boat types, and the advantages and disadvantages of each. (Two good resources for learning all about boats are *The Complete Idiot's Guide to Boating and Sailing* and *Guide to Freshwater Fishing Boats*; see Appendix D, "Species and Resource Guide," for details.) Also, because thousands of boat liveries on waters across the country rent boats by the hour, day, or week, the beginning angler should be familiar with the rudimentary aspects of boat handling and safety. You may never own a boat (a sign I've seen hanging in more than one den reads "Boat: A hole in the water into which one throws money"), but knowing boat basics will make you a better fisherman when you're in one.

Getting the Hull Story

The outside bottom of every boat is called a *hull*, and the shape and design of the hull dictate the boat's performance and use.

The simplest hull configuration is the *flat bottom*. Boats with flat bottoms maneuver easily and are very stable in calm waters. (The johnboat, a very common small fishing boat, has a flat bottom. More on johnboats later.) Flat-bottomed boats make a good choice of boat for a fisherman who is going to use his craft on small, protected inland waters such as ponds or small lakes, and in cases where speed is not a factor. In even moderately choppy water, though, the flat bottom provides a very rough ride.

The *semi-V* hull resembles a flat-bottom, except for a shallow V shape in its front portion. This shape provides a bit more stability than does the flat bottom, as the V helps cut through the water instead of riding with it.

The *deep-V* hull has a sharply angled V shape running from the front of the boat (the bow) all the way to the rear of the boat (the stern). Boats with deep-V hulls are intended for use in rough water, as the hull slices through waves instead of being tossed around by them. Because of the sharp angle of the V, however, boats with deep-V hulls sit lower in the water than do others, and aren't suitable for fishing in shallow water. Also, although deep-V boats are generally very seaworthy, they tend to rock from side to side when not under power.

The *modified-V* hull resembles a deep V, except the angle of the V isn't as sharp. A boat with a "mod-V" hull represents a good compromise in hull shape and makes a good all-around craft: It's maneuverable enough to get around easily, offers a fairly smooth ride in rough water, doesn't rock from side to side as easily as a deep V, and can enter shallow (though not too shallow) water.

The four most common hull types on fishing boats are the flat bottom, semi-V, deep-V, and modified-V. The perspective here is from the front of the boats.

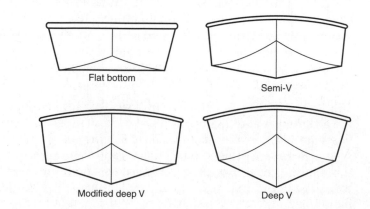

Flat bottom

Semi-V

Modified deep V

Deep V

There are many other hull shapes, some of which are proprietary to specific manufacturers. But those listed here are the most common, and are the basis for most other hull shapes you may see.

Boat Materials

The first boats were made of wood, and some boats still are. Many rental boats at marinas are wooden, because they stand up to near-daily use and, sometimes, abuse. They also tend to leak a lot. But most fishing boats sold to the public these days are made of either aluminum or fiberglass, and each substance has its pros and cons.

Aluminum boats are made of narrow sheets of the metal, welded together at the joints. Most aluminum boats are less than 18 feet long. Aluminum is rigid yet lightweight, so aluminum boats can be transported easily; small ones can be hand-carried by two people. Aluminum is also inexpensive, making boat ownership affordable for many people. Other than needing paint every few years, aluminum boats are virtually maintenance-free.

But aluminum isn't perfect. Its light weight makes it prone to bouncing around, making for an uncomfortable ride. It's also noisy; clanking an anchor or a tackle box on the bottom of an aluminum boat will send sound waves through the water, scaring nearby fish. (Carpeting does help deaden such vibrations, though.) Still, aluminum boats are choice for most small-boat fishing.

Fiberglass, which refers to layers of various types of polyester resins laid onto a wood and/or plastic frame, is very strong, compared to aluminum, and can withstand pounding waves better than aluminum. It's also heavy, which translates into stability. Also, fiberglass can be formed into a very streamlined, hydrodynamic shape, with delicate curves.

But the very weight of fiberglass is its biggest detraction. You need proportionately larger motors to power fiberglass boats, compared to aluminum boats of the same size.

School Notes

Although there are hundreds of boat manufacturers, most boat dealers will carry less than a dozen lines—and sometimes only two or three. Additionally, dealers usually stock those types of boats that are desirable for use on nearby waters. So the hull designs you see at one dealer aren't representative of the entire family of hulls.

Getting the Point

A **cartopper** boat is any boat that can be carried on top of a vehicle or in the bed of a pickup truck. The term "cartopper" is generally applied to aluminum rowboats 12 feet long or less, as they are lightweight and easily carried from car to water and back.

Kevlar, the stuff from which bullet-proof vests are made, makes for an incredibly strong yet lightweight craft. Basically, it has the best features of aluminum and fiberglass, with none of the detractions—except for price. Kevlar is so expensive that few boat manufacturers make Kevlar boats.

Fishing Boat Types

Although boats come in many different flavors, all fishing boats generally fall into the following classifications:

➤ *Rowboats* are typically 14 feet or less in length. Although they can be powered by a motor attached to the rear (called an outboard motor), rowboats can also be maneuvered by a pair of oars (not paddles—those are for canoes). They have benches running from side to side, and no other features. Most are made of aluminum (though many rental rowboats are wooden) and have semi-V or modified-V hulls.

➤ *Canoes*, because of their streamlined shape and easy maneuverability, are good for navigating on moving waters. Most are made of aluminum, and are very portable compared to other fishing craft. Canoes are paddled (though some can be fitted with an outboard motor), and require a certain amount of skill to use properly. They can also overturn if you're not careful, no small accident in rough water and/or cold weather. I like to canoe, and I like to fish, but often the two don't mix—I know of two very experienced fishermen who spilled a canoe before they traveled 100 yards in a slow-moving creek. Beginning fishermen should stick with boats.

➤ *Johnboats* are basically flat-bottomed rowboats, ranging from 10 to 18 feet long. These also can be rowed or powered by an outboard. Nearly all johnboats these days are made of aluminum. Johnboats were developed in the Ozark Mountains, and were designed to easily slide over the many shoals of that region. A johnboat can carry a lot of weight for its size because of its generous width (or "beam," nautically) in proportion to its length. Johnboats are lightweight, inexpensive, and very stable in calm waters, making them perfect for fishing small, protected water. However, johnboats don't handle rough water very well, and their square bow can shovel water right at you if taking a wave head-on. And in strong winds, a johnboat can easily be blown from side to side when rowing. But on ponds and small lakes, a johnboat is hard to beat for stability and maneuverability.

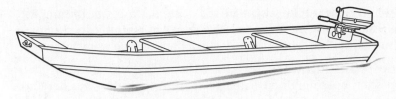

A johnboat, with its flat bottom and wide beam, is a good choice for fishing small, protected waters.

➤ *Utility boats*, as the name implies, refer to craft that were designed for all-around use. Utilities feature semi-V or modified-V hulls, and run from 12 to about 18 feet in length. Many have special fishing features such as seats instead of benches, storage for rods and other tackle, compartments (called livewells) for keeping baitfish, and other niceties. Most utilities are made of aluminum to keep their overall weight down, and are fitted with outboard motors. Basically they're souped-up rowboats, and are the most common fishing craft on large lakes and reservoirs. You may also hear them referred to as "multispecies" boats or "super utilities," as they can be used to fish a variety of waters, for a variety of species.

Loose Lines

Bass boats were introduced in the 1960s as the perfect craft for getting around the large lakes and impoundments throughout the southern states, where largemouth bass flourish.

Made of fiberglass, bass boats run from 16 to more than 20 feet long. They're low to the water and carry high-horsepower outboards to allow quick access to all areas of the lake. Most have comfortable seats and a platform in the front for stand-up casting. The hull is usually a sharp V, which begins at the front of the boat and tapers down to a flat "pad" at the stern. This design allows the boat to get up "on plane," or lift partially out of the water when under power, allowing the boat to speed along the surface.

Bass boats feature steering consoles, allowing the operator to steer the boat like a car (though doing so is actually quite different). These boats are not for the inexperienced angler or the faint of heart. Nor are they the choice craft for fishing anywhere other than large, calm bodies of water.

Other, larger fishing boat types exist, but these are the ones that most beginning fishermen are likely to be fishing from, as they're relatively easy to use and don't require special training or advanced skills.

Although the remainder of this chapter explains the basics of boat handling, beginners should take a course on boating, or have an expert show them how it's done. For more information, contact your state fish and game department (see Appendix A).

Row, Row, Row Your Boat

You've probably been a passenger on a boat while someone else rowed, or you've at least seen it done while you watched from shore. It's not hard at all, but a few pointers will help.

First, sit on the middle bench of the boat. Face the rear of the boat. You can tell on most boats because the pointed end is the front. On a johnboat, where both ends are square, the front will curve up, and the sides won't be as long. Unlike driving a car or riding a bike, you won't be facing the direction you'll be going.

To your left and your right, you'll see a little vertical metal tube a few inches long mounted just below the edge of the boat. Those are the oarlocks. Now, pick up an oar (you have your oars, don't you?) and you'll notice a metal Y-shaped device mounted along the middle of the oar. Put the bottom part of the Y into one of the oarlocks. Then do the same with the other oar on the other side.

Now you're ready to go. If the boat is roped to something, untie the knot, and push away from the dock or shore. You can use one of the oars to push yourself off. Better yet, have your companion do it. After all, you're doing all the work here. If you're on shore, someone—not you, of course—may have to walk the boat out until it's floating.

Cautious Casts

Just like cars, all boats must be registered. Make sure the one you are using has a current sticker. If you are considering buying a boat, contact your fish and game department for registration information.

At this point you should have a destination in mind, say a weedbed on the other side of the lake. But since you're not facing front, you won't know if you're going in the right direction, right? You can solve this by taking a bearing:

➤ Look over your shoulder, and use the oars to align the front of the boat with the weedbed (details on oar use are coming up).

➤ When the boat is pointing directly at the weedbed, face rear again, and find something directly behind the boat. It could be a dock, a house, a certain tree, or the space midway between a house and a tree.

➤ Keep that spot directly behind you as you're rowing.

As long as you're rowing straight *away* from that spot, you'll be rowing straight *toward* the weedbed.

Now, stay seated, and grasp each oar at the end with each hand. Extend your arms away from your body so that the other ends of the oars—called the blades—are behind you and out of the water. Then, all at once but not too quickly, bring your hands up, toward you, and down again. Basically your hands should be tracing the top half of a circle. If you look at the oar blades while you're doing this, the blades should have entered the water behind and to either side of you, swept past, and lifted partially out of the water. And the boat should have moved forward.

Now, push your hands down and away from you, as if you were tracing the bottom half of a circle. This movement lifts the oars completely out of the water and brings them back through the air, where you're ready for another stroke.

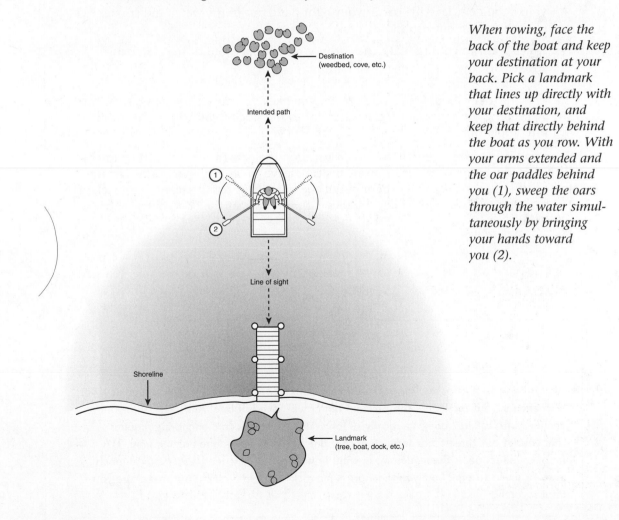

When rowing, face the back of the boat and keep your destination at your back. Pick a landmark that lines up directly with your destination, and keep that directly behind the boat as you row. With your arms extended and the oar paddles behind you (1), sweep the oars through the water simultaneously by bringing your hands toward you (2).

You'll soon see that your hands are tracing a complete (though flattened) circle through the air. If you keep your hands synchronized while describing this circle pattern, the oar blades will enter, push through, and leave the water at exactly the same time, allowing you to go in a straight line.

If you look over your shoulder occasionally to make sure that you're staying on course to the weedbed, you'll probably notice that you're *not* going in a straight line. This could happen for a number of reasons: A slight wind is pushing you off-course; you aren't rowing in a synchronized movement (since most of us favor one arm, you're probably going to row a little bit harder on one side); or the weight in the boat is unevenly distributed, causing it to veer to one side. In that case, you'll have to make a course correction once in a while:

➤ Look over your shoulder. If you want the boat to go left (as you're looking over your shoulder), take the oar in your right hand out of the water and stroke with the oar in your left hand.

➤ If you want to go right, take the oar in your left hand out of the water and stroke with the oar in your right hand.

One or two strokes should be enough to get you back on course. You can hasten the turn by keeping the other oar in the water out to the side of you while you stroke with the proper one.

When you get to your destination, don't just drop the oars in the water; they might pop out of the oarlocks and float away. Instead, leave them in the oarlocks. Lift the blades out of the water and let them rest at the outer edges of the seat in the back of the boat. This way the oars will be parallel with the sides of the boat, out of the way but secure.

Loose Lines

Always bring an anchor and rope when fishing from a boat. Rental boats should come with anchors, but sometimes the previous renter will have lost one. And make sure your anchor rope (called "rode," nautically) is long enough, too. Secure anchoring requires that you let out three times as much anchor line as the depth you're anchoring in. This ratio, called scope, is the minimum. In wind or waves, you may need a scope of as much as six or seven to one. Lose your anchor? A big rock works in a pinch. Just make sure you tie it securely.

Running an Outboard

Row a boat enough and you'll start wishing for an outboard motor. These gas-powered engines mount on the back of a boat and use a submerged propeller to move the boat forward.

Outboards on most small fishing boats have a tiller—a horizontal arm that allows you to turn the boat left and right. Most outboards today also have the throttle located on the tiller. It's a twist-type throttle, much like on a motorcycle. If you're going to rent a boat with a motor, this is probably what you'll wind up with.

To operate the outboard, sit in the rearmost seat or bench. Although the motor is centered on the stern, you have to sit on the right side of the bench in order to operate the tiller with your left hand.

To start the outboard, first make sure it's in neutral. Typically there is a small lever mounted on the motor itself above the tiller, with R–N–F designating reverse, neutral, and forward. Next, clip the kill-switch cord to a belt loop or somewhere else on your person. (If pulled out of its clip on the outboard, this cord will automatically shut off the engine. If, for some reason, the operator of the boat should get thrown overboard, the boat will stop running.) Make sure the kill switch itself is in the "on" position. If the outboard is cold, adjust the choke (usually a pull-out lever). Adjust the throttle so it is in the "idle" position; if this is not marked on the throttle, just move it down a tiny bit. Then, grab the pull cord and, in one mighty movement, pull it straight out. The outboard will not start.

At least, it probably won't. Only once have I ever had a cold outboard start on the first try. Maybe I just use cheap outboards, but I've found that it usually takes a good half-dozen pulls to get one going.

If you've pulled at least a dozen times and the motor won't start, take a break and re-assess. Gas tank full? Engine in neutral? Kill switch on? Choke adjusted? If you smell gas, shut off the choke, wait a few minutes, and try again. If you don't smell gas, open the choke and/or adjust the throttle to allow more fuel to reach the carburetor, and give it another try. If you still can't get it started, get some help from the marina operator, or get a different boat.

But let's say you've got the motor running, and you're itching to get away from the dock. Hold on! Getting the hang of steering with the tiller and adjusting speed with the throttle at the same time takes some practice.

First, make sure the boat is pointed in a safe direction, away from the dock and from other boats. Then, with the motor idling, move the gearshift into the forward position. You'll hear and feel a slight clunk. The boat may start moving forward a tiny bit at that point. Your left hand should now be on the throttle. Twist the throttle just a bit to give it some gas as you simultaneously get the boat pointed in the direction you want to go. To make the boat go to the left, pull the tiller to the right (toward you). To make the boat go to the right, push the tiller to the left. Proceed slowly at first until you get a feel for adjusting the throttle and moving the tiller.

279

Loose Lines

Many outboard motors are two-cycle, which means that you have to mix oil with the gas. If you're renting a boat, the fuel should already be mixed. Some newer models are four-cycle, so there's no mixing involved. Outboard motors fall under stringent environmental regulations now, so the noisy, smoke-belching outboard is becoming more and more a rarity.

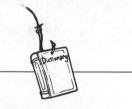

Cautious Casts

Never leave the dock without some sort of life preserver for each person on board. Not only is it common sense, it's the law. Many boat cushions double as life preservers. Small children, though, need wearable pre-servers that fit properly, and the kids should keep them on at all times.

Don't go fast. There's no need. You're already going faster than anyone who's rowing. Pay attention not only to what's in front of you, but also what *will be* in front of you, especially other boaters who may not see you. Don't get too close to the bank or you'll hit bottom.

Sooner or later you'll encounter a wave (or, more properly, a swell) probably made by another boat. The best way to take on a wave is at an angle. (Take one head-on or broadside and you may lose control of the boat for a while, or worse, upend the boat.) With an upcoming wave, slow down and turn the front of the boat into the wave at about a 45° angle. Once you're over the wave, throttle back up again.

The Least You Need to Know

➤ The shape of a boat's hull dictates the type of water it's best used in. Basically, flat hulls are for calm waters, V-shaped hulls are for rough or choppy waters.

➤ Most boats today are made from either aluminum or fiberglass. Aluminum boats are lightweight and inexpensive but bouncy and noisy. Fiberglass is strong and suitable for hydrodynamic designs, but heavy.

➤ Rowboats, johnboats, and utility boats are the best craft for the beginning fisherman to consider. Canoes are good for fishing moving water but require experience before they're used for fishing.

➤ Row a boat by facing the back of the boat and pulling forward with the oars. Keep your strokes synchronized for most efficient movement.

➤ Outboard motors are steered by a tiller, which has a throttle located on the end, allowing you to adjust direction and speed simultaneously.

Chapter 27

A Place for Everything

In This Chapter

➤ The best box

➤ Tackle garments

➤ Over the shoulder and around the waist

➤ Close your flies

Fishing tackle doesn't store well. This given has proved to be the downfall of many anglers, some of whom have been known to wake up every member of a household at a pre-dawn hour because they couldn't find some strategic piece of equipment, such as a rusty bait-cutting knife.

Tackle organizers—boxes, vests, creels, and other devices—enable anglers to store, compartmentalize, and carry their gear with a minimum of hassle. This chapter will explain the various types of organizers and guide you to the best one for your style of fishing.

Tackle Boxes

Modern tackle boxes are like toolboxes on steroids. Made of impact-resistant, light-weight plastic, they feature individual compartments in various sizes to hold lures, hooks, sinkers, spools of line, and other equipment. They're much improved over older models, which were made of metal and squeaked, rusted easily (especially when used around salt water), and clanged on the bottom of a boat, scaring fish.

An older, but still popular, plastic design opens via a latch in the front, like a standard toolbox; or separates in half from the top (envision a huge rectangular oyster). Trays in the box, which can be slid out like dresser drawers or cantilevered open, hold the compartments. The size of the compartments can be adjusted on newer tackle boxes because the sides of each compartment are removable and can be fitted into various slots situated along the inside edges of each tray.

Other tackle boxes are simply plastic shells that hold stacks of utility boxes, which are flat and have a hinged lid on the top (somewhat like a jewelry box). These clear or translucent utility boxes also feature adjustable compartments. A benefit to this style is that the boxes can be used to store different types of tackle and can be labeled as such on their sides—"hooks," "trout spinners," "spoons," and so on. You'll know what's in each box just by glancing at it and won't have to pull all of them out or open each one to get what you want. This style also allows you to bring just one or two boxes on a short trip if you want to and leave the rest at home, thus lightening your load.

Plastic tackle boxes can have compartments for individual lures and/or storage for utility boxes.

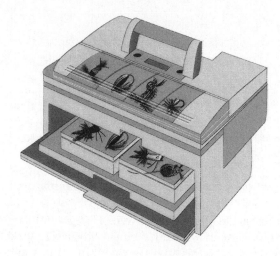

The most recent tackle-box design consists of a padded nylon case that holds an array of utility boxes. The outer shell repels water, opens via a zipper or a set of clasps, and is fitted with a strap, allowing you to carry it over your shoulder. Many of them have separate smaller compartments designed to hold reels, spools of line, or food and beverages. These soft-sided tackle boxes, or tackle bags, were originally designed for anglers traveling by air to distant destinations, as they could be checked as baggage and would survive the rough handling en route—which would destroy most standard hard-sided boxes. But their durability, light weight, ease of handling, and inherent quietness on a boat has made them popular with all fishermen.

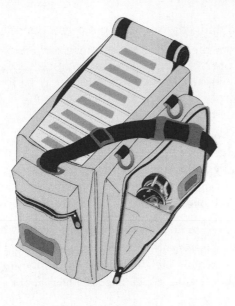

Soft-sided tackle boxes hold stacks of utility boxes and can stand up to rough handling.

All of these tackle box styles are manufactured in a variety of sizes. But you don't necessarily need a huge box because you own lot of lures. Why carry a dozen pike-size spoons when you're fishing for bass and bluegills at a farm pond? The key to good tackle organization begins not only with separating your equipment according to species, but being able to quickly add or remove tackle as the situation dictates (although you won't need those pike spoons at the farm pond, you will need hooks and sinkers). Therefore, if you often fish for two or more separate species that require different-sized lures, you're better off buying two or more smaller tackle boxes and separating your tackle according to your needs instead of lugging along one giant tackle box on each trip.

School Notes

If you have a choice, always choose white or light-colored tackle boxes. Dark colors absorb light and can become warm enough inside to partially melt soft-plastic lures, ruining them.

The soft-sided bags offer a different alternative. You can keep all your tackle in separate utility boxes in one bag, and bring with you just what you need, leaving the rest of your tackle at home or in your car. Although the bag may be large, it is very lightweight, and the space created by those utility boxes you pulled out can be filled with other items, such as extra clothing or rain gear, sunscreen, a thermos, or a radio.

Tackle boxes, which cost from $20 to almost $100, depending on size and quality, are excellent for anglers who will be fishing from a boat or from one spot along a shoreline, as you can put the box in front of you and reach into it to get what you need whenever you want it. But fishermen who will be wading a stream or lake shallows, or otherwise moving from place to place, are better off using a tackle organization system that doesn't require them to find a dry spot and put down their tackle box and fishing rod to change a lure or find an extra split shot. There are a few options for such mobile anglers, and they're covered next.

Loose Lines

Some miniature tackle boxes are designed to fit into a shirt or jacket pocket. These "pocket packs" usually have lids and compartments on both sides and can hold a fair amount of tackle. Filled with an assortment of lures, hooks, and sinkers, they're ideal for stowing in a car trunk along with a travel rod for a spontaneous fishing trip or as backup gear.

Fishing Vests

Fishing vests are garments that feature numerous pockets and attachment devices specifically for storing tackle. Fishing vests are most commonly worn by anglers who wade creeks, rivers, streams, and lake shores, and often by anglers who fish from a canoe, which normally does not have enough deck room for a large tackle box.

Most fishing vests are short, ending above the waist so that anglers can reach into their pants pockets. Some are cut very high, ending above the hips, so that the vest won't get wet when you wade into deep water. (The bottom section can be zipped off on some models.) Most are made of a cotton/polyester blend and dyed in an earth tone—tan, gray, olive—so that it won't stand out to wary fish. Some vests are made of nylon mesh, which allows air to circulate and keeps its wearer cooler in hot weather.

The pockets on most vests—and some have as many as 30 of them—have Velcro, snap-button, and/or zippered flaps. They're sewn and shaped to hold various sizes of small utility boxes, bait jars, prepackaged snelled hooks, spools of line or tippet material, sunglasses, and other items. (A pocket on one vest I own seems perfectly tailored for a 12-ounce beverage can.) Many have large zippered pockets sewn onto the back, where you can carry large items, such as a couple of sandwiches and an apple. The idea is to fill the boxes with all your necessary tackle for stream fishing and keep them in the pockets of your vest. When you want to fish, simply put on the vest and go. Keep the small utility boxes replenished with hooks, lures, and sinkers as needed.

Fishing vests are ideal for flyfishermen, who often wade streams for trout and usually carry an assortment of gear: a huge selection of flies, extra leaders, extra tippet material (sometimes an extra reel with a different type of fly line on it), fly floatant, and other things. Some flyfishing vests have a patch of sheepskin sewn or buttoned onto the front. The wool makes a good temporary and readily accessible place to keep flies, allowing an angler to change patterns without having to repeatedly search for and open boxes to put flies back while fishing.

Most vests have at least a few D-rings attached to the front, onto which the angler can fasten tools such as line clippers and pliers. An elastic or retractable cord holds the cord to the D-ring so it won't accidentally fall into the water. And there's usually a large D-ring or a cloth loop sewn onto the back of the vest below the collar, which will hold a landing net out of the way but within easy reach. Another elastic or retractable cord allows the angler to stretch the net in front of him.

School Notes

Instead of keeping snaps, swivels, and snap-swivels in a utility box, where they often creep into different compartments and tangle on hooks, string them onto a safety pin and attach it to the front of your vest. They're much more accessible there, too.

Another useful device, which isn't featured on all vests but is one I look for, is a rod keeper. This consists of a small loop of cloth or cord at the bottom front of the vest and a loop that closes via a snap button midway up the vest. To use it, drop the rod butt through the bottom loop. The reel will keep it from falling through. Then snap the rod to your body with the other loop. This device is invaluable when you're standing in the middle of a stream and need both hands to do something—search through a large utility box, apply sunscreen, or open that beverage can. It's a lot easier than tucking the rod under one arm, and makes for better balance when standing in fast waters.

Like most garments, vests are priced according to quality. They range from $30 to more than $100, but $40 to $50 will get you a very good one that will last for years. Before buying, make sure the vest is large enough (you might be wearing a lot of extra clothing beneath it on cold days), is easily washable (vests tend to get rank, especially if you use bait), has enough pockets for your needs, and has flaps that close securely but aren't difficult to open with one hand.

Fishing vests feature an array of pockets for tackle storage.

Creels, Tackle Belts, and Buckets

The wicker creel is the tackle box of yesteryear. These "fish baskets," which are worn via an adjustable harness that goes over the shoulder and around the waist, were much more popular in the days when a trout caught was a trout kept, because wicker creels are designed to hold tackle as well as fish.

Wicker creels are made of thin woven sections of split willow, shaped like a rounded rectangular box, with one side concave to fit against the angler's body at hip level. A hinged lid held shut with a snap, buckle, or wooden pin allows access. They allow you to carry all of your tackle with you, leaving both hands free to fish. A vest, of course, allows this as well, but it's not wise to put a fish in your pocket. With a creel, you can keep fish cool and moist by keeping them between layers of wet ferns or moss. The spaces between the wicker sections allow air to circulate and water to drip out, keeping fish cool by evaporation.

Canvas creels, which are purse-like bags with shoulder straps, are similar to wicker creels in that they hold fish. An internal plastic liner allows you to carry tackle in it as well. These also keep fish cool via evaporation; just dunk the creel into water after you place a fish inside, and rewet as necessary. A plastic sheet on the outside of the creel keeps the angler dry. These creels work well, but aren't exactly sweet-smelling after a few years of use.

Canvas creels (left) and wicker creels (right) allow anglers to carry both tackle and fish.

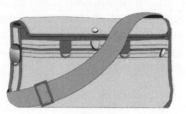 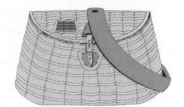

School Notes

If you want to use a wicker creel, be sure to apply a couple of coats of spar varnish, both inside and out. If you don't, the un-protected wicker will absorb fish, bait, and other odors that will become unpleasant with time.

A tackle belt has various pockets that hold utility boxes and other gear. It's basically a soft-sided tackle box that you wear cinched around the waist. While a vest actually affords easier access to tackle, these belts are practical when you must walk or hike long distances in warm weather, when wearing a vest would make you sweat after a while.

Some saltwater surf and jetty fishermen use tackle belts as well, as they allow easy maneuverability. But you must carry your bait separately, which is why many beach fishermen carry all their gear in a plastic 5-gallon bucket. It keeps sand and water from getting on your tackle, and you can use the bucket to bring your fish home, too.

Loose Lines

Wicker creels are back in vogue in sort of a Martha Stewart fashion, being used as decorations in country-style homes. Because I trout-fished in my adolescent and teen years while wearing a wicker creel—keeping many worms, salmon eggs, and dead trout in it over that time—I can't help but laugh when I see one perched on a mantelpiece like an *objet d'art*.

Fly Boxes

While most flyfishermen will find a vest most practical, they still have to store the flies themselves. Small utility boxes will work to a degree, but you'd have to carry a lot of boxes with a lot of sections to keep a good variety of flies on hand. It's common to carry a couple dozen (or more) different patterns, each in two or three different sizes, of dry flies, wet flies, streamers, and nymphs when fishing a trout stream. The problem is one of organization.

School Notes

With a lot of use, the hinges or the snap closures of utility and fly boxes may break. They can be fixed temporarily with a rubber band or some duct tape, but invest in a new one as soon as possible. I learned the hard way that broken boxes have a way of coming apart again and dumping their contents into the stream.

Numerous designs of fly boxes solve that problem. These are flat (some are no more than an inch deep) metal or plastic boxes that hold flies magnetically, on tiny clips, or by holding the point of the fly in a sheet of plastic foam. Others have clips on one side of the box and tiny compartments on the other. Many other styles of boxes exist; almost all of them work very well and can hold scores of flies.

Make sure you buy the right type of box. Dry flies, with their stiff hackles, wings, and tails, must be stored loosely in a sealed compartment or held upright on a clip. They can't be folded together, or the fly materials will mat together or bend and not float properly. Wet flies and most streamers and nymphs, however, can be stored tightly. For these types of flies, some anglers use fly wallets, which are zippered leather or cloth cases with sheep-skin interiors; or fly books, which are similar to wallets but have foam "pages" onto which flies are attached.

Fly boxes vary in design, with some having foam or sheepskin interiors and others having small plastic compartments.

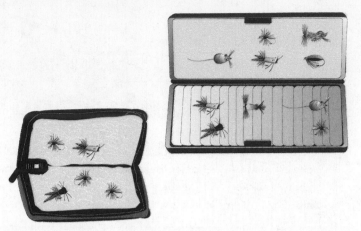

The basic rule of fly storage is to keep dries, wets, streamers, and nymphs in separate boxes, and to organize them into different sections or compartments according to pattern and size, labeling the sections as such when your collection gets large. Otherwise, the choice of fly-box style and design is a personal one.

The Least You Need to Know

➤ Tackle boxes are like plastic toolboxes with many small compartments to hold lures, hooks, and other tackle.

➤ Modern tackle boxes are made of cloth and hold a number of individual boxes, each with separate compartments. Tackle boxes are the best choice for stationary—that is, boat or bank—fishermen.

➤ Fishing vests have numerous pockets sized to hold small boxes of tackle and other fishing gear. They're best for anglers who wade streams and lake shallows.

➤ Creels, both wicker and canvas, are designed to hold both fish and tackle.

➤ Fly boxes hold numerous flies in a practical manner, with some designed to carry dry flies without bending the hackles, wings, and tails.

Chapter 28

Sense and Safety on the Water

In This Chapter

➤ Hip or chest?

➤ Heads up

➤ Staying dry

➤ Bug out!

➤ Screens and shades

➤ Getting off the hook

It was my first saltwater fishing trip of the year, and I couldn't wait to get out on the water. The tide would be coming in about 10:00 A.M. and the summer flounder, I thought, would be biting well. But we arrived late at the beach house where we'd be staying for the weekend, and I quickly drove to the dock, applied sunscreen, and jumped into the boat.

The fluke *were* hungry that day, a day that became so hot that I removed my shirt. It wasn't until late in the afternoon, when I sat in the car to drive back to the beach house, that I felt that tight tingly sensation signaling the onset of a bad sunburn. Then it dawned on me that in my haste I had forgotten to put sunblock on my back.

That turned out to be the worst case of sunburn I ever had, forcing me to miss work and take medication for the pain. My back peeled for weeks, and I still cringe when I think about the damage to my skin.

Such oversights aren't rare among fishermen, who often let the anticipation of the trip overshadow their need to take care of themselves. Similarly, we sometimes don't properly prepare for being outdoors for an extended period of time. You might not think you'll need that extra sweater if you're planning your trip while sitting in a comfortable, climate-controlled living room with a full belly. (Heck, it's springtime!) But get out there on the streambank, with a damp, cold wind working its way down your spine, and you'll wish you had brought two sweaters.

Here, then, are some rules, tips, and recommended gear to make your fishing trip a comfortable and safe one.

Shoes and Boots

No matter where you'll be fishing, don't ever assume that your footwear will remain dry. Banks and shorelines get muddy; boats get sprayed; it rains. And there's always that rock just offshore, that great-looking spot to cast from, that you can probably reach if you take a running jump ...

Forget it. Plan on having to walk in water, or at least on getting your shoes wet, when fishing. This narrows your choice considerably.

Calf-high, lace-up rubber boots are the all-around (if clichéd) preferred footwear for bank and shoreline anglers. Even if you're not planning on wading (covered next), you can step into water past your ankle and not worry about wet feet. You can buy a very good pair of boots for less than $50, and they'll probably last you a decade.

In hot weather, where wet feet won't be a problem, an old pair of shoes or sneakers will work just fine (and will be more comfortable than rubber boots anyway). I save my worn-out running shoes for this purpose, changing into them when I get to the water. I've tried the popular "water shoes," which are made of stretchy lightweight nylon with a thin sole, and found them to be fine for strolling on the beach but lacking in support and protection when fishing.

Don't wear lace-up rubber boots when fishing from a boat. In the unlikely event you fall in, their weight may make swimming difficult. Still, you should be wearing a life vest—PFD, for Personal Flotation Device—if you can't swim, and when fishing in very rough water even if you can.

Laceless slip-on rubber boots are best in very cold and wet conditions. In spring and fall, ankle-high shoes with rubber bottoms and leather uppers work well. Sneakers or Topsider-type "deck shoes" are fine in warm weather.

Cautious Casts

Boating laws require that every craft carry one PFD per occupant. Often the boat's seat cushions double as PFDs. In any case, be sure you're carrying enough PFDs for everyone in the boat, and become familiar with their use.

Wear wool socks with all-rubber boots; your feet will perspire in them but wool will keep you warm even when wet. Cotton will keep your feet cool in warm weather. In hot weather, I go sockless.

Hip Boots and Chest Waders

These are used by anglers to walk in the water. Hip boots are boots that extend to crotch level and are held up via straps that loop around your belt. Some have a lace-up arrangement inside the boot around the shin. Chest waders come up to a point just below the armpits and are held in place with suspenders.

Cautious Casts

Don't wear sandals or "flip-flops" when fishing; they're not stable on uneven ground and leave the top of your feet and your toes exposed to rocks, thorns, insects, errant fishhooks, and other potential dangers.

Almost all hip boots are boot-footed; that is, the bottoms have a heel and sole and a reinforced ankle area. Waders come in either boot-foot or stocking-foot (which end in a sock shape) versions. You must wear special wading boots over stocking-foot waders.

Hip boots cost less than waders and aren't as heavy and cumbersome to wear. They're also much cooler in warm weather. If you only fish small streams and brooks where you won't enter water much past your knees, hip boots are all you need.

But if you fish in deeper water, waders are the better choice: You'll have more access to more water, will stay warmer in cold weather (and you can get very cold standing in a stream for three or four hours), and they will keep you drier in the rain.

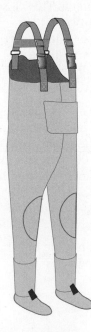

Most waders come to mid-chest level and are available in stocking-foot (shown) or boot-foot versions.

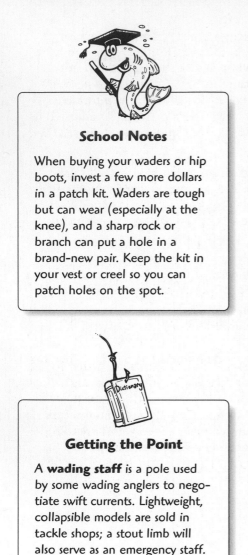

Boot-foot waders are cheaper than stocking-foot waders, as you won't have to buy wading shoes. They're also quicker and easier to put on and take off. But stocking-foot waders afford better traction only because they, and the wading shoes, fit your feet much better. Boot-foot waders are somewhat buoyant, as air is trapped in and around your foot. This and the somewhat loose fit of the built-in boot combine to give you a somewhat unsteady feeling. Stocking-foot waders and wading shoes feel practically like wearing normal boots.

Various sole types are available on hip boots, waders, and wading shoes. The standard rubber-lugged sole may feel firm-footed in the store, but slip easily on algae-covered rocks. Much better are felt soles, which provide more stability. Felt-soled hip boots and waders are more expensive, and the soles wear out with use and must be replaced (kits are available), but are worth the money if you fish in slippery streams. Some boot-foot waders and wading boots come with studded soles, which greatly enhance traction. Slip-on studded sandals, which fit over boot-foot waders, are another option.

Hip boots and waders are made of various materials. Rubber, coated nylon, and coated canvas types have been around for years, but have been largely supplanted by neoprene. This closed-cell, foam-like material is warm, lightweight, strong, and flexible. Its only downside may be its insulative qualities when fishing on a warm day; you'll sweat in them. Manufacturers still make uninsulated coated-nylon waders, typically called "flyweight" waders, for use in hot weather.

You can buy a pair of coated-nylon hip boots for less than $50. Neoprene waders range from $70 to $250, depending on the quality and the thickness of the neoprene. Wading shoes add another $50 to $100. This sounds like a lot of money until you accidentally step into a 50° trout stream while wearing your tennis shoes.

The Perfect Fishing Hat

The above line notwithstanding, I have yet to find one hat that works in all fishing situations. But I have settled on four for the time being.

The first one is a white cotton baseball cap with a long visor. The hat is perfect for fishing on warm, sunny days because the visor blocks the sun from my eyes, and its underside is dark green, which prevents glare. Its white outside doesn't absorb sunlight so it keeps my head cool, and the cloth hat band on the inside absorbs perspiration. Most hats of this nature have a plastic hat band, which is very uncomfortable in warm weather and leaves a red indentation across your forehead. The hat is adjusted with those cheap snap-together plastic tabs on the back, so it's not perfect. But it's the best I've found so far.

For fishing in cold weather I wear a wool watch cap (often called a ski hat). It's gray, to match the color of the sky in such weather. (On cold *and* sunny days, sometimes I'll wear it over a visored cap.) I can pull it down over my ears when the wind blows hard, and it keeps my head warm. Because you lose a lot of body heat through your head, a warm hat is essential on cold days.

The third hat is a standard visor-size, heavy cotton ball cap with a leather hat band. Its brown visor prevents glare, and the hat is adjustable via a small leather belt with buckle. I wear this hat for late spring and early fall fishing, as it keeps my head warm early and late in the day but isn't uncomfortable on mild afternoons. I'll also wear this hat when fishing small, clear streams, as its color (drab green) won't stand out and spook wary trout.

Last is my billfisherman's cap, named for those offshore trollers who popularized it. The cotton hat's super-long visor and pull-down flaps protect your face, ears, and neck from the sun, both direct and reflected from the water. Small ventilation holes let some air circulate around my head. I wear this hat whenever I'm fishing in tropical waters, where the sun is intense. I suppose I could wear this in lieu of the white ball cap—and it would do a better job of protecting me from the sun—but I feel a little self-conscious wearing a billfisherman's cap when, say, drifting for fluke off Asbury Park. Sporting-goods stores that are near salt water and mail-order fishing-supply houses (see Appendix D, "Species and Resource Guide") sell billfisherman's caps.

Hat choice is personal, so I can't recommend the best one for you. Just make sure you're adequately protected from the sun and the cold.

Loose Lines

I've worn a wide-brimmed Western (or cowboy) hat when fishing Rocky Mountain trout streams. While that hat felt appropriate in that wide-open country, I found that it tended to get knocked off my head when wading smaller, brushy eastern waters.

Garments Throughout the Seasons

Wearing improper clothing can ruin a fishing trip. One common mistake is not wearing enough clothing; another is wearing the wrong kind.

Moderate temperatures in late spring and early fall call for long pants, a long-sleeved shirt, and a jacket or windbreaker. It's always colder near the water, so bring an extra layer—a sweatshirt or another jacket.

In summertime, shorts and a T-shirt may be all you need by mid-day. But again, cooler temperatures near water might necessitate long pants and a light jacket early and late. On sunny days, and when fishing in tropical waters, it's wise to wear light-weight pants and a long-sleeved shirt to protect your skin from damaging ultraviolet rays. And use sunblock (covered later in this chapter).

When fishing in early spring and late fall, dress as you would for winter on land: long underwear, heavy pants, and shirt, coat or sweater, and jacket. You'll probably need gloves (cut the fingertips off an old pair for improved dexterity).

When choosing clothing for your trip, keep these tips in mind:

➤ Wear cotton garments in warm and hot weather because cotton breathes and absorbs perspiration.

➤ For the same reason, avoid cotton in cold weather. And if you perspire while getting to the water or somehow become wet, all that moisture held by the cotton will rob your body of heat. You'll chill quickly with no way to get warm.

➤ Wear wool or synthetic fleece outer garments in cold weather. Wool is a great insulator and will keep you warm even when wet; fleece can be wrung out and dries quickly.

➤ Dress in layers no matter what the weather. Air trapped between the clothing acts as an insulative barrier, and you can add or remove clothing as the temperature dictates.

And always be ready for rain, because it will.

School Notes

When fishing farther than a short drive from home, bring extra clothing—just in case you fall in. It's happened to me and to almost every fisherman I know.

School Notes

Wear extra clothing when fishing from a boat. It's usually colder and windier out on the water than on shore, and the movement of the boat produces a wind–chill effect.

Rain Gear

Yes, fish do bite in the rain (one of the best days of largemouth bass fishing I ever had was on a rainy day in late spring), but you must be prepared for it.

A poncho with a hood works well as rain gear for fishing because you can slide it over whatever you're wearing, including a fishing vest. If you wear a poncho in combination with waders, you'll stay dry in even the heaviest downpours.

But if you're not wearing waders, your legs will get wet. That's when you need a rain suit: a combination of plastic or coated-nylon pants (that fit over your regular pants) and a jacket with hood. Rain suits work well when fishing from a boat (as long as you have rubberized or otherwise waterproof footwear), and a decent set costs about $40.

But while plastic or coated-nylon suits keep rain out, they also keep moisture (from perspiration) in. A few times I've fished all day while wearing rain gear and wound up almost as wet inside as I would have been had I not worn it. Better suits have flaps and vents to allow air to circulate and pull moisture away. A better (but more costly) alternative, especially if you plan on fishing a lot, is a rain suit made with Gore-Tex. This fabric contains microscopic pores—nine billion per square inch, according to the manufacturer—that prevent water from penetrating but allow water vapor to escape, keeping you dry on the inside. I spent $150 on a complete set of Gore-Tex rain gear five years ago and consider it one of my wisest investments.

Keeping Bugs at Bay

Mosquitoes, blackflies, deer flies, horseflies, and other winged pests can become so irritating at times that they can drive you off the water. A number of insect repellents are on the market today, but the most effective ones have DEET as the active ingredient.

Repellents in waxy stick form adhere to your skin better than the liquid or aerosol versions. They're also easy to carry, and you can reapply the stuff with one hand. Put it on all exposed areas of your

School Notes

If you're stuck without rain gear, you can fashion an emergency poncho out of a large plastic garbage bag by cutting holes for head and arms.

Cautious Casts

Heavy applications of DEET have been associated with seizures (the Environmental Protection Agency has recorded 13 cases since 1960, four of them fatal), particularly among children. Apply DEET-based repellents to clothing instead of skin, and avoid using on children. DEET also disintegrates some materials, including monofilament fishing line, so wash your hands after applying it.

skin (but don't get the stuff in your eyes), paying particular attention to your ears and the backs of your hands. Use a spray to apply repellent to your clothing.

In areas where the bugs are numerous, you may have to wear long pants and a long-sleeved shirt just to keep them away. A headnet, which covers your head, face, and neck with a mesh screen, is also necessary in some areas. Such measures are mandatory in regions where deer flies proliferate, as these insects seem impervious to repellent.

Cautious Casts

Always bring plenty of liquids when fishing on hot days, and drink often to prevent dehydration. Avoid caffeine and alcohol, as these are diuretics and you'll lose any benefit of hydration.

School Notes

Take with you fishing (or have nearby, such as in your car) a first-aid kit (containing bandages, antiseptic, antibiotic cream, topical painkiller, aspirin or acetaminophen, and the like). Include any special medication, extra eyeglasses, and other personal items.

Sun Protection

A lot of sun can lead to a painful but temporary sunburn. Too much sun over the years, however, can lead to melanoma (skin cancer), and anglers are at risk if they don't take precautions. Always apply a water-resistant sunblock with an SPF (sun protection factor) rating of at least 15 before fishing, and reapply it often during the day.

In regions of extreme sun, you should cover your skin with light-colored, lightweight pants and a long-sleeved shirt. Apply sunscreen before donning these garments, as ultraviolet light can partially penetrate clothing. Be sure to wear a long-billed hat as well. Although I don't have a pale complexion, one fishing guide in the Florida Keys refused to take me out until I had put on long pants and a long-sleeved shirt.

Sunglasses are a must as well. Polarized sunglasses, which reduce glare, will actually help you see into the water, which is a great aid when sight-casting to trout, bonefish, and other shallow-water species. A good pair of polarized fishing glasses costs about $20. Make sure they offer UV protection, to protect your eyes from these harmful rays.

Removing a Hook

When a fishhook penetrates your skin, most times it's a simple matter to pull it out and continue fishing. But if the hook penetrates past the barb, removal isn't so simple.

There are two ways to remove such hooks without the assistance of professional medical help. The first is to push the hook so the hook point and barb break through the skin in a different area. This sounds painful, but it's necessary. Then cut the hook below the barb with wire-cutting pliers, then back the hook out of the flesh. Clean the wound, then apply antiseptic and a bandage.

The second method sounds too easy to work, but it does: Make a foot-long loop of strong fishing line (double the line if it's 10 pound test or less) by tying together the ends of a 2-foot section. Put the knotted end around your wrist and bring the rest of the loop up against your palm and hold it between your thumb and forefinger. Slide the end of the loop over the hook shank so it's lying against the bend. Then push down and backward on the hook shank (this is important) with one hand while jerking the line sharply back with your other hand. The hook will pop free. Clean, disinfect, and bind the wound.

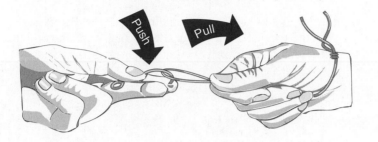

Remove an embedded fishhook by passing a loop of fishing line around the hook and pulling sharply while pressing down and back on the hook shank.

The Least You Need to Know

➤ Wear waterproof shoes or boots in cool and moderate weather and lightweight shoes or sneakers in hot weather.

➤ Hip boots come to crotch level and are fine for walking in shallow waters. For large rivers and streams, wear waders, which come up to mid-chest.

➤ Wear a light-colored cotton hat with a visor in warm, sunny weather and a wool cap in cold temperatures.

➤ Cotton clothing will keep you cool in hot weather. Choose wool outer layers in cold temperatures. Layer your clothes, and bring an extra garment or two.

➤ A poncho provides good and inexpensive protection from the rain. Better yet is a full rain suit made with Gore-Tex.

➤ Prepare for biting bugs by applying repellent to your clothes and skin. Wear long pants, long-sleeved shirts, and a headnet in bug-infested areas.

➤ Use a sunblock with a high SPF rating on sunny days, and cover your skin in intense sun. Wear polarized glasses to cut glare on the water.

➤ Remove a fishhook from your flesh by pushing it through the skin and cutting it off at the barb, or by pulling it out at the bend with fishing line while pushing down on the shank.

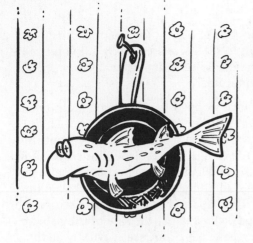

Chapter 29

In the Pan or On the Wall?

In This Chapter

➤ How to gut a fish

➤ Filleting: no bones about it

➤ Freezing in a flash

➤ What's for dinner?

➤ Mounting considerations

➤ Say it in pictures

In college I shared an apartment with two other guys who loved to fish, as I did. This was fortunate for us personally but unfortunate for our collective grade-point averages, as we spent a little too much time matching the hatch instead of cracking the books. Nevertheless, by the time we (eventually) graduated we were quite adept at catching, cleaning, and preparing a variety of fish species in a number of ways. While this chapter won't cover some of those creative specialties (crappies and eggs with beer was a favorite), it will go over the basics of gutting, filleting, preparation, and cookery; as well as what to do if the fish you catch is just too big to eat.

Gutting Fish

Any fish can be gutted in preparation for pan frying, baking, or broiling. This method is best for small fish, which would be difficult to fillet (covered next). All you need is a sharp knife of any kind and some water, preferably running water. With practice, you can completely gut a fish in less than a minute.

Clean your catch as soon as possible after you've stopped fishing to maintain freshness. If the fish is still alive, rap it on the head with a heavy blunt object, such as the dull side of your knife blade. Fish that are to be cooked whole (except for trout) need to be scaled first. Use a scaling knife, which is a dull, serrated blade that costs a dollar or two and is available at tackle shops and many grocery stores. (A dull kitchen knife, such as an old butter knife, will also work.) Lay the fish flat and stroke the knife edge repeatedly against the side of the fish, at about a 45-degree angle. Some scales will fly about, so this chore is best done outdoors. If you're inside, hold the fish underwater in a sink or a basin when scaling.

You might want to leave the head on the fish for aesthetic reasons, especially if you're planning to bake the fish. But if you'll be grilling or pan-frying it, removing the head will leave you more room in the pan. Remove the fish's head by cutting from the top down so the knife passes just behind the pectoral fins. Some organs will come out of the fish when you pull the head away.

Gut the fish by holding it on its back, with its tail toward you. Large fish can be laid on their side. Hold the knife with the edge face-up and insert the point of the knife into the vent, or anus. Then draw the knife up through the belly skin, all the way to the gills. Cut through any small bones near the gills to complete the cut. Remove all organs. Pull or cut out all the gills from the fish.

You will see a dark line lying against the backbone of the fish. This is the kidney. It's easily removed by running your thumbnail or a narrow spoon up the spine.

That's it. You can cut off the fins now if you wish, but they're much easier to remove after cooking; each fin and its interior bones will slide right out of the fish.

If you won't be preparing the fish immediately, wrap it tightly in plastic wrap followed by heavy-duty aluminum foil. Seal the package with tape and freeze it quickly.

School Notes

When freezing fish, label each package with the kind and number of fish inside and the date that you caught it. This way you won't have to unseal the package to find out what it is, and you'll know when you have enough to make a meal.

School Notes

How long will fish last in the freezer? A lot depends on the type of fish and how well the package is sealed, but I don't like to keep any species longer than two months, when freezer burn and an ensuing loss of quality become evident.

Filleting Fish

Many species can be filleted, which is cleaning a fish so that no bones remain in the flesh. Except for very small fish (and for trout and members of the pike family, which don't fillet well because of their bone structure), I prefer this method to gutting because it makes for more uniform cooking and more confident eating.

Species such as bass, walleyes, perch, bluegills, and many saltwater fish fillet up easily and well. You'll need a fillet knife, which has a long, narrow, and flexible blade; and a cutting board (it's best to dedicate an old one for this chore). A table covered with newspapers will work but can be slippery.

To begin, lay the fish flat on the cutting board with its head to your left. Pick up the pectoral fin and place the edge of the fillet knife on the rear side of its base. Cock the blade so that its tip angles to the left but is not over the gill plate. Now cut straight down to, but not through, the backbone (you'll feel it with your knife).

Now spin the fish so its back is toward you. Hold the knife parallel with the cutting board and, starting at the top of the fish's head at your first cut, begin slicing down the fish along the backbone. Don't cut through the rib cage; just slide your knife point past it. Keep your knife edge just above the dorsal fin. Once past the rib cage, and keeping the knife flat, push it through the fish so the point protrudes through the belly. Now slice all the way down to the tail, keeping your knife flat against the spine.

Next, grasp the top part of the slab you've created and use your knife to slice it free of the ribs, following the curve of the rib cage, until the slab comes free of the fish.

Repeat on the other side of the fish so you're left with two slabs of fish with the skin on.

Lay one slab on the board with the skin side down. Hold an edge of the skin with your fingertips at the small (tail) end and slide the knife edge between skin and flesh. Keeping the blade pressed flat, use a sawing motion to slice down to the wide end, freeing the skin from the flesh. If your fillet knife isn't flexible enough for this work, move the fillet to the edge of the board or the table to provide room for your hand. Now feel the wide edge of the fillet with your fingertips for small bones. If they're present, cut a little triangle out of the wide end to remove them. Repeat with other slab.

School Notes

You can defrost frozen fish quickly by placing it in a sealed plastic bag (if not already frozen that way) and putting the bag in a sink or bowl of lukewarm water. Replace the water a few times if necessary, and cook the fish immediately.

1. Cut down to the spine without severing it.

2. Slice down the back-bone to the tail without cutting into the rib cage.

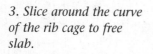

3. Slice around the curve of the rib cage to free slab.

4. Hold skin and slice flesh free of skin with sawing motion.

You're now left with a pair of fillets—no skin, no bones—and you're ready to start cooking. If you won't be consuming them that day, freeze them immediately. Fillets freeze best when covered in water. I put fillets in a sealable plastic bag and fill it with just enough water to cover them. Hold over a sink and press out all the air. Lay the bag on its side in a freezer.

Cooking Your Fish

The secret to a delicious fish dinner has little to do with detailed recipes, special sauces, or hard-to-find species. The best fish is fresh fish, period. If you handled your catch properly—killed it quickly, kept it cool, cleaned or filleted it as soon as possible, and froze it immediately or put it in the refrigerator for preparation in a few hours—that fish is guaranteed to taste better than anything you could possibly buy in the seafood department of a grocery store.

I don't like to hide the taste of fish beneath a lot of pungent spices or creamy sauces. If it's fresh, there's no need. Besides, the budding fish chef should concentrate on cooking the fish properly rather than messing with time-consuming preparations. So the following recipes—all of my favorites—and recommendations may seem simple, but all are guaranteed to please. As you progress, you may wish to check some of the hundreds of cookbooks now on the market that list thousands of different fish recipes.

Fried Fish Fillets

You can follow this recipe with any fillets that are less than half an inch thick (bass, walleyes, panfish, flounder, etc.). Because the size and number of fillets will vary, you'll have to judge exact amounts of ingredients for yourself:

> Flour
>
> 1–2 eggs
>
> Milk
>
> Bread crumbs (Italian-flavored) or cornmeal
>
> Vegetable shortening or peanut oil

1. Pat the fillets with a paper towel and coat them in flour. You can put the flour and fillets in a bag and shake them, or pour flour on a plate and roll them.

2. Break one egg into a medium-size bowl and beat with a fork until consistent in color. Add about ½ cup milk and beat again.

3. Pour bread crumbs onto a large plate and spread from edge to edge.

4. Dip one fillet at a time into the egg-and-milk mixture until completely wet. Transfer immediately to the bread crumb plate and roll and press the fillet until completely coated. Stack fillets on a separate plate.

5. In a large skillet on medium-high heat, melt enough vegetable shortening until the level is just beneath that of the thickness of your fillets. Continue heating until shimmery (it's ready when a tiny drop of water "dances" on the surface).

6. Place the fillets gently into the pan. Turn when golden brown and fry the other side. Place on rack or brown-bag paper to drain.

School Notes

To avoid getting giant, bread-crumb-covered fingertips when coating fish, use one hand to dip and remove the fillets from the egg-and-milk mixture and your other hand to press and roll them in the bread crumbs.

Fish prepared in this manner aren't as greasy as you'd imagine because the double coating seals the fish. You'll probably see some of the fillets "popcorn" up a bit as the fish steams inside. Serve with salad or cole slaw and fried potatoes. If the fish is done right, you won't need tartar sauce.

Batter-Dipped Fillets

This recipe comes straight from the Banana Bay Resort & Marina in Marathon, Florida, where the chef prepared the finest dolphin I have ever tasted (friends and I had caught the dolphin that day). It works well for that species and for other large fish such as grouper, and is deceptively simple:

> Flour
>
> Ice water
>
> Peanut oil

Cautious Casts

Don't use standard vegetable oil or corn oil when frying fish—it smokes when you bring it to a high temperature, and won't get hot enough to properly seal the fish in the coating or batter.

1. Prepare a deep fryer for cooking with enough peanut oil to cover the fish. Cut the fillets into 3- to 5-inch sections.

2. Quickly mix equal parts flour and ice water (yes, it must be icy cold) and a pinch of salt, in a bowl you have kept in the refrigerator. Don't mix until smooth; the lumpier the batter, the better. Dip the fillets in the batter until completely coated and drop immediately into the hot oil.

3. Remove when golden brown and place on rack to drain. Serve immediately.

Grilled Fillets

This recipe works best with fillets from dolphin, grouper, walleyes, redfish, and other large species.

> Olive oil
>
> Tarragon vinegar
>
> Lime juice (lemon juice may be substituted)

1. Marinate whole fillets in a bowl or large sealed plastic bag in the refrigerator with three parts olive oil, one part tarragon vinegar, and one part lime juice for at least two hours.

2. Place directly on medium-hot grill. (You may have to line your grill with aluminum foil—and poke numerous holes in it—to prevent the fish from falling through.)

3. Cook until white on bottom and turn once. Remove from grill when fish separates easily.

Foiled Fish Fillets

Strong-flavored fish such as bluefish and striped bass are delicious when prepared in this manner.

Olive oil

Red wine vinegar (Italian salad dressing may be substituted for the oil and vinegar)

Tomatoes

Onions

Lemons

Old Bay seasoning

Salt and pepper

Cut the tomatoes, onions, and lemons into slices and layer haphazardly on a large sheet of aluminum foil. Place whole fillets on top and sprinkle with salt, pepper and Old Bay. Layer more tomato, onion, and lemon slices on top and drizzle with oil and vinegar. Seal the foil tightly by bringing the edges together and folding over numerous times. Place on medium-hot grill and close cover. Turn the package when you hear loud sizzling and cook for only a few more minutes. Leave the foil sealed until ready to eat.

Whole Fried Fish

This is the simplest way to prepare a fish you haven't filleted, such as panfish, trout, snappers, and comparatively small fish.

Vegetable shortening or peanut oil

Flour

Cornmeal

One egg

Milk

Butter or margarine

Salt and pepper

1. Combine equal parts flour and cornmeal and spread evenly on a large plate.
2. Beat egg in medium bowl and add ½ cup milk.
3. Dip fish in egg-and-milk mixture and press in bread crumbs.
4. Melt shortening or add oil to large frying pan until bottom is covered with about ¼ inch. Heat until shimmery.
5. Salt and pepper the body cavity of the fish and add a few small pats of butter. Fry until coating is golden brown; turn once and repeat.
6. Drain on rack. Serve with lemon wedges.

To eat a whole fish, pull out the fins and attached bones (an extra plate in the center of the table can hold scraps). Cut the skin down the center of the fish to expose a horizontal line on the flesh. Use your knife to separate and push the fish away from the bones along this line. Repeat on other side.

Campfire Trout

You can use a grill instead of a campfire for this simplest of all recipes (and you can substitute other species as well), but there's something about eating a freshly caught trout that you've cooked on an open wood fire that just can't be duplicated.

Butter or margarine

Salt and pepper

Clean the trout, salt and pepper the cavity, and place a few pats of butter inside. Wrap tightly in foil and drop right into the hot coals of a campfire that has burned for at least an hour. Turn occasionally with a stick, and remove when sizzling steadily. For a side "dish," you can throw a few potatoes (plain or wrapped in foil) onto the coals about a half-hour before the fish.

Getting Your Fish Mounted

A mounted (often incorrectly referred to as "stuffed") fish can make a unique and attractive addition to many rooms. Most anglers decide to mount a large fish, or one that they have never caught before, to commemorate the event.

A *taxidermist* is one who prepares fish and game for mounting. They are artists as well as craftsmen, for their goal is to render the specimen into a lifelike position that very closely resembles the size, shape, and coloration of the fish when it was alive. Taxidermists usually advertise in the Yellow Pages, and sporting-goods stores can recommend some local ones.

When preparing a fish to be mounted, the taxidermist will very carefully remove the entire skin from the fish and preserve it. He will then mount the skin on a styrofoam "form" that he customizes to that fish's particular shape. He then paints the skin, matching the fish's tones and patterns. The work is delicate, time-consuming, and requires specialized knowledge, training, and techniques.

The cost of mounting a fish ranges from $8 to $12 per inch, depending on the species to be mounted, the region of the country, demand, and other factors. The wait runs from three months to a year. Most taxidermists require a 50 percent deposit.

The decision to mount a fish is a personal one. Some anglers set goals, such as a 10-pound walleye or a 20-inch trout, and won't mount a fish under that predetermined weight or length. Others will decide to mount a fish because it is the biggest or the best-looking of that species they have ever caught. Still others will mount a fish that they caught on a fishing trip at a faraway destination—one they may never be fortunate enough to visit again.

If you catch a fish and decide to get it mounted, a few steps will help you get the best mount possible:

1. Take pictures of the fish right away, of both sides and from different angles, as soon as possible after you catch it. Colors on fish fade soon after death, and the photos will aid the taxidermist in making it look exactly as it was when it was alive.

2. Take notes about the fish—"vivid pink stripe, distended belly, prominent black dime-sized spots on flanks"—to back up your photos, especially if you don't have access to a camera soon after you caught it.

3. Keep the fish in cold water as long as possible while fishing. When returning home, wrap the fish completely in wet rags (never in newspaper, which can dry out the skin) and place in a plastic bag. If you won't be going immediately to a taxidermist, freeze the fish.

4. Be careful not to penetrate or bruise the fish's skin. Taxidermists can fix some damage, but not all.

Cautious Casts

You can't have your mount and eat it, too. As the taxidermist must use preservatives when preparing a fish for mounting, the flesh must be disposed of.

309

The Replica Alternative

Catch-and-release fishing is widely practiced these days, even on waters where such a rule is not enforced. The idea is to put back any fish that you won't eat. But what if you catch a fish that you don't want to kill but would like to get mounted?

One solution is to get a replica mount. These fiberglass forms, which cost about $10 per inch, can be created to look exactly like the fish you caught, without your needing to provide the actual fish.

What you *do* provide is a detailed description. Take photos and notes as described previously, and measure the fish. Length (from tail to tip of snout) and girth (the circumference around the widest part of the fish) are most important. But since the whole idea behind replicas is to release the fish alive, the photos and measurements must be taken quickly so the fish can be put back without harm.

School Notes

Many large marinas have cold storehouses on the premises where large fish to be mounted are kept. The fish are picked up from time to time by the commercial taxidermist service.

Large Fish Mounts

Commercial taxidermist operations—those that mount large saltwater species such as billfish, tarpon, and sharks—often combine the features of a standard mount and a replica mount. The whole fish is delivered to the taxidermy plant and measurements are taken. Then, a fiberglass replica of the fish is made. Often, some actual fins are preserved and used on the mount, as well as the bill on billfish and the jaws on sharks.

It would be very difficult or impossible to create a standard mount of such huge fish. Besides all the work that would be involved in skinning and preserving, the fish themselves are often not in good enough shape—with holes from gaffs and abrasions from being moved about—to make the job worthwhile.

Prices for large fish mounts vary; ask the captain of your charter boat what the going rates are before you decide to kill and mount a fish.

Fish Pictures

A good photograph of you and your catch is almost as gratifying as a mount. In some cases it's better, as you can release the fish if you want, and you can record the water, the day, your expression, and your fellow anglers as well. Photos taken immediately after the catch are much better than those taken at home in a driveway or kitchen with a misshapen, washed-out fish and/or angler.

But a good fish picture isn't easy to take. The following tips will help you get one worth framing:

➤ *Don't just take a snapshot.* Compose the photo first: Make sure that the angler and his fish will be prominent in the picture. No objects such as bait buckets, coolers, or someone's foot should be in the foreground.

➤ *Prepare the angler.* No cigars or cigarettes in the mouth. Remove sunglasses to better capture expression. If wearing a visored hat, remove it or tilt it up so no shadow will fall on his or her face.

➤ *Use the sun.* Make sure sunlight shines directly on the angler and fish, but be careful not to let shadows from the photographer or nearby objects show in the picture. If it's a cloudy day, use the flash.

➤ *Keep the fish wet until you're ready to shoot.* The fish will shine and look natural, and its colors will be vibrant.

➤ *Hold the fish properly.* The angler should hold the fish so its side is presented to the camera. Large fish should be held with two hands to better display their size. In most cases, the fish should be held high and a bit to the side of the angler, without blocking his face. Try some shots with the angler looking at the fish instead of at the camera.

➤ *Don't skimp on film.* Bracket your shots if possible (shoot a number of photos at different exposure times and apertures) and have the angler stand in different poses in different areas. Try using your flash for a couple of shots, even if your camera meter says you don't need it. Such "fill flash," especially on sunny days, can eliminate all shadows and make the difference between a good shot and a great one.

Loose Lines

The "disposable" cameras on the market take very good pictures and are convenient to carry, as they're lightweight and can be carried in a tackle box or fishing vest with no noticeable difference in weight.

The Least You Need to Know

➤ Fish are easily gutted. This cleaning technique is best for small fish.

➤ Filleting takes some time and skill, but results in pieces of boneless fish.

➤ Fresh fish don't need heavy sauces or pungent spices to taste good. Always cook on medium-high heat to seal the fish, and don't overcook.

➤ Taxidermists prepare a life-like rendition of a fish you caught. This "mount" may consist of the actual skin of the fish, or may be a fiberglass replica.

➤ Photos of fish are best taken on the water as soon as possible after the fish is caught. Compose the photograph carefully and shoot a number of frames to assure a good shot.

Chapter 30

Hello, Warden

In This Chapter

➤ License, please

➤ Is it legal?

➤ The tale of the tape

Effective management of freshwater and saltwater fisheries would be impossible without a system of rules and regulations governing when people may fish, how many of each species they may catch, and how big the fish must be in order to keep them. States must sell fishing licenses to derive the funds necessary for such management and law enforcement.

Each state necessarily has different fishing regulations, and it is the angler's responsibility to know about them, as well as to abide by them. This chapter will explore some of those regulations, the reasons behind them, and some tips on how to stay within the law.

Fishing Licenses

Most states require that anglers possess a license when fishing in fresh waters. Some coastal states also require separate saltwater fishing licenses. A resident fishing license is sold to residents of the state, who generally must prove that they have lived in the state—a *bona fide domicile*—for six months. Normally a current driver's license is valid proof. Nonresident licenses are sold to out-of-staters.

Resident fishing licenses average in the $15 to $25 range, and are valid for the calendar year. Nonresident annual fishing licenses are more expensive, usually costing from $25 to $35. (License fees often increase incrementally every couple of years.) Many states sell nonresident licenses that are valid for a limited time, generally from three to ten days, and are cheaper than an annual nonresident license. These short-term licenses are typically bought by anglers visiting a distant state for a short period.

School Notes

You can fashion an emergency or temporary license holder if needed by putting it into a plastic sandwich bag (eat the sandwich first) and affixing it to your shirt or coat with a pin or even a fishhook.

Cautious Casts

Many fishermen affix their license to their fishing hats, on the assumption that they won't forget their license because they'll never forget their hat. But I've lost too many hats due to wind gusts and fast boats. A better idea: Pin it to your fishing vest or keep it in your tackle box.

Fishing licenses are generally not required for children or seniors. Kids younger than 14 or 16, depending on the state, don't need a license. However, some states do require junior licenses for teens, which are cheaper than adult licenses; and senior fishing licenses for those over a certain age, usually 65 or so.

A number of states require special tags or stamps for those who will be fishing in a particular water, or for a particular species, usually one that is stocked, such as trout, or one that is suffering from either overfishing or loss of habitat due to pollution or human encroachment. This provides the state with an extra source of revenue for hatchery operations or for research programs. These stamps generally cost from $5 to $15, depending on the state, the species, and the classification (resident or nonresident), and must be purchased *in addition to* the regular fishing license. The regular license usually has a space where the species stamp is to be affixed.

Sometimes the species stamp is necessary just for fishing in waters that hold that species. In New Jersey, for example, a trout stamp (along with a regular fishing license) must be purchased by anyone who will be fishing in waters that hold trout. Even if you're fishing specifically for another species—catfish, say—in a designated trout water, you must have the trout stamp affixed to your license.

Pennsylvania serves as a good example of various licenses and their costs. A resident annual fishing license costs $17; no license is required by anglers younger than 16. Residents 65 and over can purchase a senior fishing license for $4. Nonresidents of Pennsylvania pay $35 for an annual fishing license, $30 for a seven-day tourist license, and $15 for a three-day license. Both resident and nonresident anglers who fish for trout must also purchase a $5.50 trout stamp.

Most fishing licenses are made of paper, with spaces for your name, address, physical description (hair and eye color, height, and weight), and date and place of birth. In all states, you must have the fishing license on your person when actually fishing. The license must be produced when requested by a law enforcement officer or a by a landowner when fishing on his property. A few states require that the license be displayed— pinned onto your shirt, coat, or hat—when fishing, in order to simplify license checking by state fish department officers. Special transparent license holders with a built-in safety pin cost about a dollar and make license display easy.

School Notes

Some states give you a carbon copy of your license along with the actual document. Keep the carbon in a safe place, your wallet or at home, so you can use it or get a replacement license if you lose the original. Contact your state fish department for details on replacements.

Licenses and stamps are typically available at bait and tackle shops, sporting goods stores, and the main and branch offices (if any) of the state fish department. The license is usually filled out in triplicate, with one copy kept by the angler, another copy retained by the issuing agent, and the third sent to the state fish department for their records.

Also available at these outlets are state fishing compendiums, which are summaries of fishing laws and regulations. These small booklets are pocket-sized so they can be carried by anglers and easily referenced when on the water.

It's always the angler's responsibility to be aware of license requirements. If you're not sure, obtain a compendium at a license outlet or contact the fish and game department of your state. Addresses and phone numbers of all departments are listed in Appendix A, "State Fish and Game Departments."

Sizes, Limits, and Seasons

States regulate the size and number of fish taken by anglers, and when they can take them. While some abundant species such as carp and some panfish have little or no regulations pertaining to their capture, most others do.

Most states enforce minimum-size regulations for bass, trout, walleyes, pike, pickerel, muskies, and other gamefish so that anglers don't keep young fish—those that have not reached spawning age. Generally, young fish are easier to catch than old fish, and are certainly more abundant in a given body of water. If anglers removed many young fish from a particular lake or stream, that water would wind up missing both that age-class of fish and its progeny. Such a change in the makeup of the lake environment would skew its whole balance, effectively ruining the fishing. Although nature seems to have its own system of checks and balances, with another species

Getting the Point

A **possession limit** is the number of fish that an angler may own at one time. This rule allows prosecution of unlawful anglers who may have gotten away with catching more than the daily limit, and are found to have too many fish in their car or at their residence. Possession limits may be one or more times the creel limit.

Getting the Point

A **slot limit** refers to a law that puts both a minimum and a maximum size on a species. This allows the buildup of a trophy fishery and allows mature fish to spawn repeatedly.

possibly moving into the "space" created by the missing fish, it might not be a desirable one from an angling standpoint.

To protect these young fish, state fish departments set minimum sizes on many species. It may be 8 inches for trout, 12 inches for bass, 16 inches for walleyes; whatever the state determines. Anglers cannot keep fish under the set minimum size. Any fish caught under the minimum must be returned to the water immediately. It is the angler's responsibility to carry a ruler or some other measuring device to check their fish.

Another protective law is a "creel limit" or "daily limit," which is the maximum number of fish of a particular species that an angler can keep in one day. Such limits keep anglers from removing too many fish from a body of water. Though it may seem difficult to catch more than, say, six walleyes over 16 inches on one day, it is possible to do so when conditions are right.

States also set fishing seasons to both protect fish stocks overall from too much fishing, and to keep anglers from fishing during a particular species' spawning season. This obviously gives the fish a chance to reproduce and provide more fish for the future. Also, fish are very protective of their nests, and will attack anything that, to them, poses a threat to their eggs or young—including fishing lures. For example, a number of states don't open their largemouth bass season until some time in May or June, because the fish spawn in spring and those on the nests are comparatively easy to catch.

In almost all states, when the season for a particular species is closed, you can't fish for them. However, in some states it is legal to continue fishing for a particular species even after you have taken your creel limit.

All fish caught thereafter must be immediately returned to the water unharmed. But note that not all states allow this.

Again, it is up to the angler to know and abide by the state fishing laws and seasons.

316

Weighing and Measuring Fish

You can hold a ruler against the fish, or the fish against a ruler, and measure it. What's so hard about that?

Not much, except that you may be measuring it the wrong way. There are a couple of ways to measure fish, and you should know the method required by the laws of the state you're fishing in to make sure you're not keeping undersized fish.

For instance, some fish species have forked tails. Your state fish department may have a "fork length" minimum, meaning that the fish must be measured from the tip of its jaw to the fork—not either tip—of its tail. This could mean the difference of a couple of inches or more, so you might wind up keeping an illegal fish if you measure improperly.

Some states require that the mouth of the fish be closed when measuring. Others make no such distinction, meaning that the fish can be measured from any point. The overall length of some fish is increased when the mouth is open, as the lower jaw may protrude incrementally farther, and it also allows a fisherman to angle the ruler (which gives a whole new meaning to the term "angler"). Some fishermen—certainly not I!—have been known to squeeze the ends of a fish's tail together to gain a few sixteenths of an inch.

> **School Notes**
>
> A better alternative to carrying a ruler (or a yardstick) when fishing is buying a plastic adhesive ruler and sticking it on the side of your tackle box. Even simpler is to mark off 1-inch increments on your fishing rod with an indelible marker or nail polish, so you'll always have a measuring device handy.

States do not use the weight of a fish to determine its legality. However, knowing a fish's exact weight as well as its length is interesting and fun, if not disappointing at times. Numerous models of fishing scales are sold at tackle shops and through mail-order houses. Most are small and relatively accurate. You simply hang the fish from the scale and read the weight on the face of the scale. A few models have built-in retractable measuring tapes, so you can carry one device instead of two.

The Undersized-Fish Dilemma

It happens to every angler, and sooner or later, it will happen to you, too: You catch a fish that is below the minimum size, but by the time you unhook it, the fish is so badly injured that you know it will never survive. So do you do the proper thing from a legal standpoint and put it back in the water, watching it sink into the depths or float away in the current to become a meal a few days later for crows, crayfish, or crabs; or do you keep the fish and eat it for dinner and hope you don't get caught with it?

According to the law, of course, there is no argument here: There are no exceptions for undersized fish. Ethically, however, there is at least room for discussion.

I've caught undersized fish that were injured due to my own negligence. I mishandled the fish, dropping it on the shore or on the deck of a boat; I used too small a hook or waited too long before setting the hook, allowing the fish to swallow it; I used too much force in removing the hook or lure from the fish's mouth. In all those cases the fault was mine, and I took steps to decrease the chances of it happening again by handling fish carefully, using a larger hook, striking quickly, and taking my time unhooking.

But quite a few times I've brought in undersized fish that were bleeding profusely from the gills because it struck a bait too hard, or because a trailing hook became caught beneath the gill plate. These fish had no chances of surviving, through no error or miscalculation on my part.

It boils down to this: Is it worth the risk of a fine—generally $50 to $100—to keep a small fish? Conversely, is it ethical to put a basically dead fish back in the water, although it's the lawful thing to do?

I hope that state fish departments one day recognize that imperfection in fishing laws and institute some type of regulation that would allow the possession of, say, one undersized fish. It would be considered part of the daily creel limit, so that the angler won't kill yet another fish to fill his limit.

In the meantime, the decision is up to the individual angler. And I've already made mine.

The Least You Need to Know

➤ You must buy a state fishing license to fish for freshwater and some saltwater species. There are resident, nonresident, junior, and senior licenses available.

➤ Minimum size refers to how long a fish must be in order to be kept. Creel limit or daily limit means how many of a certain species you may keep per day. The season refers to when during the year you may fish for a particular species.

➤ Fish are measured in different ways according to the rules the state sets: from either the open or closed mouth to either the fork or the tip of the tail.

State Fish and Game Departments

Contact these government agencies for rules, regulations, license costs, and other information pertaining to fishing in each state. Web sites for the departments, which are listed here, can provide a good idea of the fishing opportunities in that state—popular species, stocking programs, special regulations waters, etc.—and often include up-to-date information regarding seasons and license fees.

Alabama Department of Conservation and Natural Resources
64 N. Union Street
Montgomery, AL 36130
334-242-3471
www.dcnr.state.al.us

Alaska Department of Fish and Game
P.O. Box 25526
Juneau, AK 99802-5526
907-465-4100
www.state.ak.us/local/akpages/FISH.GAME/adfghome.htm

Arizona Game and Fish Department
2221 W. Greenway Road
Phoenix, AZ 85023-4312
602-942-3000
www.gf.state.az.us/welcome.html

Arkansas Game and Fish Commission
#2 Natural Resources Drive
Little Rock, AR 72205
501-223-6300
www.agfc.state.ar.us

California Department of Fish and Game
1416 9th Street
Sacramento, CA 95814
916-653-7664
www.dfg.ca.gov/dfghome.html

Colorado Division of Wildlife
6060 Broadway
Denver, CO 80216
303-297-1192
www.dnr.state.co.us/wildlife

Connecticut Bureau of Natural Resources
79 Elm Street
Hartford, CT 06106-5127
860-424-3010
http://dep.state.ct.us/rec-nat.htm

Delaware Division of Fish & Wildlife
89 Kings Highway
Dover, DE 19901
302-739-5295
www.dnrec.state.de.us/fw/fwwel.htm

Florida Fish and Wildlife Conservation Commission
620 South Meridian Street
Tallahassee, FL 32399-1600
850-488-4676
www.state.fl.us/fwc/index.html

Georgia Department of Natural Resources
2189 Northlake Parkway
Building 10, Suite 108
Tucker, GA 30084
770-414-3333
www.ganet.org/dnr

Hawaii Department of Land and Natural Resources
P.O. Box 621
Honolulu, HI 96809
808-587-0400
www.hawaii.gov/dlnr/Welcome.html

Idaho Department of Fish and Game
P.O. Box 25
Boise, ID 83707
208-334-3700
www.state.id.us/fishgame/fishgame.html

Illinois Department of Natural Resources
600 N. Grand Avenue W.
Springfield, IL 62701-1787
217-782-6431
http://dnr.state.il.us

Indiana Department of Natural Resources
402 W. Washington Street, Room W255B
Indianapolis, IN 46204-2748
317-232-4020
www.state.in.us/dnr/index.html

Iowa Department of Natural Resources
Wallace Building
502 E. 9th Street
Des Moines, IA 50319-0034
515-281-FISH
www.state.ia.us/government/dnr/fwdiv.htm

Kansas Department of Wildlife and Parks
900 SW Jackson Street
Suite 502, Topeka, KS 66612-1233
785-296-2281
www.kdwp.state.ks.us/fishing/fishing.html

Kentucky Department of Fish and Wildlife Resources
#1 Game Farm Road
Frankfort, KY 40601
1-800-858-1549
www.state.ky.us/agencies/fw/kdfwr.htm

Louisiana Department of Wildlife and Fisheries
P.O. Box 98000
Baton Rouge, LA 70898-9000
225-765-2800
www.wlf.state.la.us

Maine Department of Inland Fisheries and Wildlife
284 State Street
41 State House Station
Augusta, ME 04333-0041
207-287-8000

Maine Department of Marine Resources
21 State House Station
Augusta, ME 04333
207-624-6550 (for saltwater fishing information only)
http://janus.state.me.us/dmr

Maryland Department of Natural Resources
580 Taylor Avenue
Tawes State Office Building
Annapolis, MD 21401
410-260-8021
www.dnr.state.md.us

Massachusetts Department of Fisheries
Wildlife and Environmental Law Enforcement
100 Cambridge Street, Room 1901
Boston, MA 02202
617-727-1614
www.magnet.state.ma.us/dfwele

Michigan Department of Natural Resources
P.O. Box 30028
Lansing, MI 48909-7528
517-373-1280
www.dnr.state.mi.us

Minnesota Department of Natural Resources
500 Lafayette Road
St. Paul, MN 55155-4040
651-296-6157
www.dnr.state.mn.us

Mississippi Department of Wildlife, Fisheries and Parks
P.O. Box 451
Jackson, MS 39205
601-362-9212
www.mdwfp.com

Missouri Department of Conservation
P.O. Box 180
Jefferson City, MO 65102-0180
573-751-4115
www.conservation.state.mo.us

Montana Department of Fish, Wildlife and Parks
1420 E. Sixth Avenue
P.O. Box 200701
Helena, MT 59620
406-444-2535
http://fwp.mt.gov

Nebraska Game and Parks Commission
2200 N. 33rd Street
Lincoln, NE 68503-0370
402-471-0641
http://ngp.ngpc.state.ne.us/gp.html

Nevada Division of Wildlife
P.O. Box 10678
1100 Valley Road
Reno, NV 89520
775-688-1500
www.state.nv.us/cnr/nvwildlife

New Hampshire Fish and Game Department
2 Hazen Drive
Concord, NH 03301
603-271-3211
www.wildlife.state.nh.us

New Jersey Department of Environmental Protection
Division of Fish, Game, and Wildlife
P.O. Box 400
Trenton, NJ 08625-0400
609-292-2965
www.state.nj.us/dep/fgw

New Mexico Game and Fish
P.O. Box 25112
Santa Fe, NM 87504
505-827-7911
www.gmfsh.state.nm.us

New York State Department of Environmental Conservation
50 Wolf Road
Albany, NY 12233
518-457-5420
www.dec.state.ny.us

North Carolina Department of Environment and Natural Resources
1601 MSC
Raleigh, NC 27699-1601
919-733-4984
www.enr.state.nc.us/ENR

North Dakota Game and Fish Department
100 N. Bismarck Expy.
Bismarck, ND 58501-5095
701-328-6300
www.state.nd.us/gnf

Ohio Department of Natural Resources
1952 Belcher Drive, Building C-1
Columbus, OH 43224
614-265-6565
www.dnr.state.oh.us

Oklahoma Department of Wildlife Conservation
1801 N. Lincoln
Oklahoma City, OK 73105
405-521-3851
www.state.ok.us/~odwc

Oregon Department of Fish and Wildlife
2501 SW First Avenue
Portland, OR 97207
503-872-5268
www.dfw.state.or.us

Pennsylvania Fish and Boat Commission
P.O. Box 67000
Harrisburg, PA 17106-7000
717-657-4518
www.state.pa.us/PA_Exec/Fish_Boat

Rhode Island Department of Environmental Management
9 Hayes Street
Providence, RI 02908
401-222-3075
www.state.ri.us/dem

South Carolina Department of Natural Resources
Rembert C. Dennis Building
1000 Assembly Street
Columbia, SC 29201
803-734-3888
water.dnr.state.sc.us

South Dakota Game, Fish and Parks Department
523 East Capitol Avenue
Pierre, SD 57501-3182
605-773-3485
www.state.sd.us/gfp/gfp.html

Tennessee Wildlife Resources Agency
Ellington Agricultural Center
P.O. Box 40747
Nashville, TN 37204
615-781-6575
www.state.tn.us/twra

Texas Parks and Wildlife Department
4200 Smith School Road
Austin, TX 78744
512-389-4800
www.tpwd.state.tx.us

Utah State Department of Natural Resources
1594 W. N. Temple
Suite 316
Salt Lake City, UT 84116-3193
801-538-7200
www.nr.state.ut.us

Vermont Agency of Natural Resources
Department of Fish and Wildlife
103 S. Main Street
Waterbury, VT 05671-0501
802-241-3701
www.anr.state.vt.us/fw/fwhome/index.htm

Virginia Department of Game and Inland Fisheries
4010 W. Broad Street
P.O. Box 11104
Richmond, VA 23230
804-367-1000
www.dgif.state.va.us

Virginia Marine Resources Commission
P.O. Box 756
Newport News, VA 23607
757-247-2200 (for saltwater fishing information only)
www.state.va.us/mrc/homepage.htm

Washington Department of Fish and Wildlife
600 Capitol Way N.
Olympia, WA 98501-1091
360-902-2230
www.wa.gov/wdfw

West Virginia Division of Natural Resources
1900 Kanawha Boulevard East
Charleston, WV 25305
304-558-2771
www.wvweb.com/www/travel_recreation/fishing/fishing.html

Wisconsin Department of Natural Resources
P.O. Box 7921
Madison, WI 53707
608-266-2621
www.dnr.state.wi.us

Wyoming Game and Fish Department
5400 Bishop Boulevard
Cheyenne, WY 82006
307-777-4600
http://gf.state.wy.us

Freshwater and Saltwater Record Fish

The following is a partial listing of the largest fish ever caught with a rod and reel—known as "all-tackle" records—as listed by the International Game Fish Association (IGFA). The IGFA also keeps separate "line class" records—the largest fish caught on various strengths of fishing line—and maintains junior categories for children. Contact the IGFA (300 Gulf Stream Way, Dania Beach, FL 33004; 954-927-2628; www.igfa.org) for comprehensive listings, updates of records, and details on how to submit a fish for record entry.

Barracuda, great, 85 lb., Christmas Island, Rep. of Kiribati, April 11, 1992, John W. Helfrich

Bass, black sea, 9 lb. 8 oz., Rudee Inlet, Virginia Beach, Virginia, USA, Jan. 9, 1987, Joe Mizelle, Jr.

Bass, black sea, 9 lb. 8 oz., Virginia Beach, Virginia, USA, Dec. 22, 1990, Jack G. Stallings, Jr.

Bass, giant sea, 563 lb. 8 oz., Anacapa Island, California, USA, Aug. 20, 1968, James D. McAdam, Jr.

Bass, largemouth, 22 lb. 4 oz., Montgomery Lake, Georgia, USA, June 2, 1932, George W. Perry

Bass, rock, 3 lb., York River, Ontario, Canada, Aug. 1, 1974, Peter Gulgin

Bass, smallmouth, 10 lb. 14 oz., Dale Hollow Lake, Tennessee, USA, April 24, 1969, John T. Gorman

Bass, spotted, 9 lb. 9 oz., Pine Flat Lake, California, USA, Oct. 12, 1996, Kirk M. Sakamoto

Bass, striped, 78 lb. 8 oz., Atlantic City, New Jersey, USA, Sept. 21, 1982, Albert R. McReynolds

Bass, striped (landlocked), 67 lb. 8 oz., O'Neill Forebay, San Luis, California, USA, May 7, 1992, Hank Ferguson

Bass, white, 6 lb. 13 oz., Lake Orange, Virginia, USA, July 31, 1989, Ronald L. Sprouse

Bluefish, 31 lb. 12 oz., Hatteras, North Carolina, USA, Jan. 30, 1972, James M. Hussey

Bluegill, 4 lb. 12 oz., Ketona Lake, Alabama, USA, April 9, 1950, T.S. Hudson

Bonefish, 19 lb., Zululand, South Africa, May 26, 1962, Brian Batchelor

Bullhead, black, 7 lb. 7 oz., Mill Pond, Wantagh, Long Island, New York, USA, Aug. 25, 1993, Kevin Kelly

Bullhead, brown, 6 lb. 1 oz., Waterford, New York, USA, April 26, 1998, Bobby Triplett

Bullhead, yellow, 4 lb. 4 oz., Mormon Lake, Arizona, USA, May 11, 1984, Emily Williams

Carp, common, 82 lb. 3 oz., Lake Roduta, Romania, May 26, 1998, Christian Baldemair

Catfish, blue, 111 lb., Wheeler Reservoir, Tennessee River, Alabama, USA, July 5, 1996, William P. McKinley

Catfish, channel, 58 lb., Santee-Cooper Reservoir, South Carolina, USA, July 7, 1964, W.B. Whaley

Catfish, flathead, 123 lb. 9 oz., Elk City Reservoir, Kansas, USA, May 14, 1998, Ken Paulie

Catfish, gafftopsail, 8 lb. 14 oz., Indian River, Florida, USA, Sept. 21, 1996, Larry C. Jones

Catfish, white, 18 lb. 14 oz., Withlacoochee River, Inverness, Florida, USA, Sept. 21, 1991, Jim Miller

Cobia, 135 lb. 9 oz., Shark Bay, W.A. Australia, July 9, 1985, Peter William Goulding

Cod, Atlantic, 98 lb. 12 oz., Isle of Shoals, New Hampshire, USA, June 8, 1969, Alphonse J. Bielevich

Cod, Pacific, 35 lb., Unalaska Bay, Alaska, USA, June 16, 1999, Jim Johnson

Crappie, black, 4 lb. 8 oz., Kerr Lake, Virginia, USA, March 1, 1981, L. Carl Herring, Jr.

Crappie, white, 5 lb. 3 oz., Enid Dam, Mississippi, USA, July 31, 1957, Fred L. Bright

Croaker, Atlantic, 3 lb. 12 oz., Escambia River, Pensacola, Florida, USA, Sept. 29, 1992, Tina Marie Jeffers

Dogfish, smooth, 26 lb. 12 oz., Galveston, Texas, USA, March 2, 1998, George A. Flores

Dogfish, spiny, 15 lb. 12 oz., Kenmare Bay, Co. Kerry, Ireland, May 26, 1989, Horst Willi Miller

Dolly Varden, 19 lb. 4 oz., Unnamed River, Alaska, USA, Sept. 4, 1998, Gary D. Ordway

Dolphinfish, 88 lb., Highbourne Cay, Exuma, Bahamas, May 5, 1998, Richard D. Evans

Drum, black, 113 lb. 1 oz., Lewes, Delaware, USA, Sept. 15, 1975, Gerald M. Townsend

Drum, red, 94 lb. 2 oz., Avon, North Carolina, USA, Nov. 7, 1984, David G. Deuel

Eel, American, 9 lb. 4 oz., Cape May, New Jersey, USA, Nov. 9, 1995, Jeff Pennick

Flounder, gulf, 6 lb. 4 oz., Dauphin Island, Alabama, USA, Nov. 2, 1996, Don Davis

Flounder, southern, 20 lb. 9 oz., Nassau Sound, Florida, USA, Dec. 23, 1983, Larenza W. Mungin

Flounder, summer, 22 lb. 7 oz., Montauk, New York, USA, Sept. 15, 1975, Charles Nappi

Flounder, winter, 7 lb., Fire Island, New York, USA, May 8, 1986, Einar F. Grell

Grouper, black, 114 lb., Galveston, Texas, USA, Jan. 2, 1997, Stanely W. Sweet

Grouper, gag, 80 lb. 6 oz., Gulf of Mexico, Destin, Florida, USA, Oct. 14, 1993, Bill Smith

Grouper, giant, 263 lb. 7 oz., Anguruki Ck., Groote Eylandt, Australia, Sept. 9, 1988, Peter C. Norris

Grouper, Nassau, 38 lb. 8 oz., Bimini, Bahamas, Feb. 14, 1994, Lewis Goodman

Grouper, Warsaw, 436 lb. 12 oz., Gulf of Mexico, Destin, Florida, USA, Dec. 22, 1985, Steve Haeusler

Halibut, Atlantic, 355 lb. 6 oz., Valevag, Norway, Oct. 20, 1997, Odd Arve Gunderstad

Halibut, Pacific, 459 lb., Dutch Harbor, Alaska, USA, June 11, 1996, Jack Tragis

Jack, crevalle, 57 lb. 14 oz., Southwest Pass, Louisiana, USA, Aug. 15, 1997, Leon D. Richard

Kingfish, northern, 1 lb., 10 oz., West End, Long Branch, New Jersey, USA, Aug. 5, 1998, Joseph R. Anelli

Kingfish, southern, 1 lb. 14 oz., Dauphin Island, Alabama, USA, Sept. 9, 1997, Marcus R. Kennedy

Kokanee, 9 lb. 6 oz., Okanagan Lake, British Columbia, Canada, June 18, 1988, Norm Kuhn

Ladyfish, 6 lb., Loxahatchee River, Jupiter, Florida, USA, Dec. 20, 1997, Michael Baz

Ladyfish, 6 lb., Sepetiba Bay, Rio de Janeiro, Brazil, Jan. 24, 1999, Ian Arthur de Sulocki

Mackerel, Atlantic, 2 lb. 10 oz., Kraakvaag Fjord, Norway, June 29, 1992, Jorge Marquard

Mackerel, king, 93 lb., San Juan, Puerto Rico, April 18, 1999, Steve Perez Graulau

Mackerel, Spanish, 13 lb., Ocracoke Inlet, North Carolina, USA, Nov. 4, 1987, Robert Cranton

Marlin, black, 1,560 lb., Cabo Blanco, Peru, Aug. 4, 1953, Alfred C. Glassell, Jr.

Marlin, blue (Atlantic), 1,402 lb. 2 oz., Victoria, Brazil, Feb. 29, 1992, Paulo Roberto A. Amorim

Marlin, blue (Pacific), 1,376 lb., Kaaiwi Point, Kona, Hawaii, USA, May 31, 1982, Jay Wm. De Beaubien

Marlin, striped, 494 lb., Tutukaka, New Zealand, Jan. 16, 1986, Bill Boniface

Marlin, white, 181 lb. 14 oz., Victoria, Brazil, Dec. 8, 1979, Evandro Luiz Coser

Muskellunge, 67 lb. 8 oz., Lake Court Oreilles, Hayward, Wisconsin, USA, July 24, 1949, Cal Johnson

Muskellunge, tiger, 51 lb. 3 oz., Lac Vieux-Desert, Michigan, USA, July 16, 1919, John A. Knobla

Perch, white, 4 lb. 12 oz., Messalonskee Lake, Maine, USA, June 4, 1949, Mrs. Earl Small

Perch, yellow, 4 lb. 3 oz., Bordentown, New Jersey, USA, May 1865, Dr. C.C. Abbot

Permit, 56 lb. 2 oz., Ft. Lauderdale, Florida, USA, June 30, 1997, Thomas Sebestyen

Pickerel, chain, 9 lb. 6 oz., Homerville, Georgia, USA, Feb. 17, 1961, Baxley McQuaig, Jr.

Pike, northern, 55 lb. 1 oz., Lake of Grefeern, West Germany, Oct. 16, 1986, Lothar Louis

Pollack, 50 lb., Salstraumen, Norway, Nov. 30, 1995, Thor-Magnus Lekang

Pumpkinseed, 1 lb. 6 oz., Mexico, New York, USA, April 27, 1985, Heather Ann Finch

Sailfish, Atlantic, 141 lb. 1 oz., Luanda, Angola, Feb. 19, 1994, Alfredo de Sousa Neves

Sailfish, Pacific, 221 lb., Santa Cruz Island, Ecuador, Feb. 12, 1947, C.W. Stewart

Salmon, Atlantic, 79 lb. 2 oz., Tana River, Norway, 1928, Henrik Henriksen

Salmon, chinook, 97 lb. 4oz., Kenai River, Alaska, USA, May 17, 1985, Les Andersen

Salmon, chum, 35 lb., Edye Pass, British Columbia, Canada, July 11, 1995, Todd A. Johansson

Salmon, coho, 33 lb. 4 oz., Salmon River, Pulaski, New York, USA, Sept. 27, 1989, Jerry Lifton

Salmon, pink, 13 lb. 1 oz., St. Mary's River, Ontario, Canada, Sept. 23, 1992, Ray Higaki

Salmon, sockeye, 15 lb. 3 oz., Kenai River, Alaska, USA, Aug. 9, 1987, Stan Roach

Sauger, 8 lb. 12 oz., Lake Sakakawea, North Dakota, USA, Oct. 6, 1971, Mike Fischer

Sea robin, striped, 3 lb. 6 oz., Mt. Sinai, Long Island, New York, USA, June 22, 1988, Michael B. Greene, Jr.

Sea trout, spotted, 17 lb. 7 oz., Ft. Pierce, Florida, USA, May 11, 1995, Craig F. Carson

Shad, American, 11 lb. 4 oz., Connecticut River, S. Hadley, Massachusetts, USA, May 19, 1986, Bob Thibodo

Shark, blue, 454 lb., Martha's Vineyard, Massachusetts, USA, July 19, 1996, Pete Bergin

Shark, bull, 490 lb., Dauphin Island, Alabama, USA, Aug. 30, 1986, Philip Wilson

Shark, dusky, 764 lb., Longboat Key, Florida, USA, May 28, 1982, Warren Girle

Shark, great hammerhead, 991 lb., Sarasota, Florida, USA, May 30, 1982, Allen Ogle

Shark, lemon, 405 lb., Buxton, North Carolina, USA, Nov. 23, 1988, Colleen D. Harlow

Shark, sand tiger, 350 lb. 2 oz., Charleston Jetty, South Carolina, USA, April 29, 1993, Mark Thawley

Shark, shortfin mako, 1,115 lb., Black River, Mauritius, Nov. 16, 1988, Patrick Guillanton

Shark, tiger, 1,780 lb., Cherry Grove, South Carolina, USA, June 14, 1964, Walter Maxwell

Shark, white, 2,664 lb., Ceduna, South Australia, April 21, 1959, Alfred Dean

Sheepshead, 21 lb. 4 oz., Bayou St. John, New Orleans, Louisiana, USA, April 16, 1982, Wayne Desselle

Snapper, gray, 17 lb., Port Canaveral, Florida, USA, June 14, 1992, Steve Maddox

Snapper, mutton, 30 lb. 4 oz., Dry Tortugas, Florida, USA, Nov. 29, 1998, Richard Casey

Snapper, red, 50 lb. 4 oz., Gulf of Mexico, Louisiana, USA, June 23, 1996, Doc Kennedy

Snapper, yellowtail, 8 lb. 9 oz., Gulf of Mexico, Ft. Meyers, Florida, USA, Sept. 13, 1996, William M. Howard

Snook, common, 53 lb. 10 oz., Parismina Ranch, Costa Rica, Oct. 18, 1978, Gilbert Ponzi

Sturgeon, white, 468 lb., Benicia, California, USA, July 9, 1983, Joey Pallotta III

Sunfish, longear, 1 lb. 12 oz., Elephant Butte Lake, New Mexico, USA, May 9, 1985, Patricia Stout

Sunfish, redbreast, 1 lb. 12 oz., Suwannee River, Florida, USA, May 29, 1984, Alvin Buchanan

Sunfish, redear, 5 lb. 7 oz., Diversion Canal, Georgia, USA, Nov. 6, 1998, Amos M. Gay

Swordfish, 1,182 lb., Iquique, Chile, May 7, 1953, Louis B. Marron

Tarpon, 283 lb. 4 oz., Sherbro Island, Sierra Leone, April 16, 1991, Yvon Victor Sebag

Tautog, 25 lb., Ocean City, New Jersey, USA, Jan. 20, 1998, Anthony R. Monica

Trout, brook, 14 lb. 8 oz., Nipigon River, Ontario, Canada, July, 1916, Dr. W.J. Cook

Trout, brown, 40 lb. 4 oz., Little Red River, Heber Springs, Arkansas, USA, May 9, 1992, Howard L. (Rip) Collins

Trout, cutthroat, 41 lb., Pyramid Lake, Nevada, USA, Dec. 1925, John Skimmerhorn

Trout, golden, 11 lb., Cooks Lake, Wyoming, USA, Aug. 5, 1948, Chas. S. Reed

Trout, lake, 72 lb., Great Bear Lake, N.W.T., Canada, Aug. 19. 1995, Lloyd E. Bull

Trout, rainbow, 42 lb. 2 oz., Bell Island, Alaska, USA, June 22, 1970, David Robert White

Trout, tiger, 20 lb. 13 oz., Lake Michigan, Wisconsin, USA, Aug. 12, 1978, Pete M. Friedland

Tuna, bigeye (Atlantic), 392 lb. 6 oz, Puerto Rico, Gran Canaria, Spain, July 25, 1996, Dieter Vogel

Tuna, bigeye (Pacific), 435 lb., Cabo Blanco, Peru, April 17, 1957, Dr. Russell V.A. Lee

Tuna, blackfin, 45 lb. 8 oz., Key West, Florida, USA, May 4, 1996, Sam J. Burnett

Tuna, bluefin, 1,496 lb., Aulds Cove, Nova Scotia, Canada, Oct. 26, 1979, Ken Fraser

Tuna, yellowfin, 388 lb. 12 oz., Isla San Benedicto, Revillagigedo Islands, Mexico, April 1, 1977, Curt Wiesenhutter

Walleye, 25 lb., Old Hickory Lake, Tennessee, USA, Aug. 2, 1960, Mabry Harper

Weakfish, 19 lb. 2 oz., Jones Beach Inlet, Long Island, New York, USA, Oct. 11, 1984, Dennis Roger Rooney

Weakfish, 19 lb. 2 oz., Delaware Bay, Delaware, USA, May 20, 1989, William E. Thomas

Terms and Definitions

anadromous fish   Fish that migrate from the ocean to freshwater rivers to spawn. Various species of salmon that have been transplanted to the Great Lakes still exhibit this behavior, moving from the lake to a tributary to spawn.

angler   One who fishes (derived from the Sanskrit word "anka," meaning bend, referring to a curved fishhook).

backing   Cord-like line that goes onto a fly reel before the actual fly line. It serves to fill the reel to capacity, which makes the fly line easier to reel in, and, in case you hook a large fish, acts as insurance in case the fish takes a long run when you already have a lot of line out.

barb   A small, sharp protrusion below the point of a fishhook that keeps the hook embedded in a fish.

barbless hook   A hook without a barb. Although barbless hooks don't hold as well as barbed versions, some fishermen—such as those who intend to release all the fish they catch—prefer them because they are easier to remove from a fish. These are required on some regulated catch-and-release waters.

bass bugs   Fly-rod lures that imitate frogs, mice, and other rodents, and large insects such as bees and dragonflies.

blank-through handles   A feature on modern fishing rods on which the rod blank, or shaft, extends all the way down through the handle. This provides for more sensitivity when holding the rod, because vibrations caused by a fish hitting a bait are more easily felt by the angler.

brackish waters   Those areas of rivers and creeks that contain salt, but are not as salty as ocean water. Frequently, both freshwater and saltwater species inhabit brackish waters, which also usually exhibit some tidal influence.

buzzbait A lure similar to a spinnerbait except for a propeller-type device on the upper arm instead of a spinner blade. The upper arm, which is bent so that it is parallel to the bottom arm, passes through the center of the flashy propeller blades, which rotate very quickly when retrieved.

cartopper Any boat that can be carried on top of a vehicle or in the bed of a pickup truck. The term is generally applied to aluminum rowboats 12 feet long or less.

catadromous fish Fish that migrate from freshwater rivers to oceans in order to spawn.

catch and release A term for a body of water where no fish caught there may be kept; or the practice of releasing all fish caught.

charter boat A craft that can be rented by one or more anglers to fish for one day to one month or more.

crankbait A plug that dives relatively deeply.

creel A wicker or canvas container for storing and carrying tackle and fish that is worn by an angler via a harness.

drag (1) The action of a fly drifting on or through the water faster than the current in which it is drifting.

drag (2) A device on a fishing reel that slows the outward flow of line when the reel is in gear.

dry fly A fly that floats on the surface of the water. Dry flies imitate mayflies, stoneflies, caddisflies, craneflies, mosquitoes, and midges.

fishfinder A general term for a sonar unit that displays fish as well as bottom contours on paper or a video screen. Also called a depth finder or chart recorder.

fishing lure Any inanimate object that imitates something that fish eat and has hooks in order to catch a fish.

fly A lure consisting of various materials—wool, chenille, fur, hair, feathers, tinsel, and others—tied to a hook that imitates an insect, worm, fish egg, baitfish, or some other organism that fish eat; typically fished on a fly rod.

foul-hooked fish A fish that is hooked anywhere besides the mouth—the body, gill, or tail. Sometimes fish hit a lure or bait so explosively that they don't get it in their mouth, but manage to hook themselves anyway.

gaff A pole with a large, sharp hook at one end, used to bring large fish over the side of a boat.

hook keeper A small wire loop attached to the rod directly above the reel seat (where the reel is attached). This is a convenient place to store a hook or lure that's tied to your line when you're moving from place to place.

inflatable boat One that can be carried in the trunk of a car and filled with air at the fishing area. Most have hard floors and can even be fitted with an outboard.

inshore fishing Angling that takes place in the ocean close to or within sight of land.

jig A lure consisting of a hook with a ball of lead behind the eye. It's usually painted, and hair or feathers is sometimes tied to the hook shank for added attraction to fish.

leader Tapered line tied to the end of a fly line.

levelwind A device on certain baitcasting reels that distributes the line evenly along the length of the spool when the handle is turned. Sometimes a reel with such a device is referred to as a levelwind.

livewell A built-in reservoir on a fishing boat that can be pumped full of water and is used to keep fish or bait alive.

long-cast reels Spinning reels with extra-tall spools that allow line to spiral off easily and with little friction, increasing the casting distance. This has proven to be such a successful design that some manufacturers are incorporating long-cast spools into all their spinning reel models.

nymphs The larval stages of insects that live on lake or stream bottoms, or the flies that imitate them. Most nymph flies used by fishermen imitate mayfly, caddisfly, stonefly, dragonfly, and cranefly nymphs.

offshore fishing Fishing out of sight of land.

party boat A large sea-going craft that is designed to allow a large number of anglers to fish simultaneously. Also called a head boat or open boat.

plug One of any of a whole family of lures made of hard plastic or wood that imitate all manner of baitfish, plus frogs, crayfish, salamanders, or small rodents such as mice.

possession limit The number of fish that an angler may keep at one time.

practice plug A lure-sized, hookless, soft-plastic, or rubber object designed to be used for practice casting. These are obviously safer to use than the real thing and won't hook interested bystanders or inquisitive pets. Tackle shops carry them.

reel A device attached to a fishing rod that dispenses and retrieves fishing line via a crank.

rod A long, slender, and extremely lightweight tube made of fiberglass, graphite, or a composite of the two. Don't call your rod a pole (unless you want to pretend you're Huckleberry Finn), which is made of cane (and thus heavy and thick) and which doesn't take a reel.

sand spike   A long hollow tube used to hold a surf rod after a bait is cast out. The spike is pushed into the sand and the rod butt slid inside. A pin inside the spike supports the butt and keeps the reel from rubbing against the edge.

shock leader   A short, strong section of line tied to the end of a fishing line, used when large and/or toothy fish are the quarry.

sinker   A weight that attaches to a fishing line.

slot limit   A law that puts both a minimum and a maximum size on a species.

spinner   A fishing lure with a thin metal blade that revolves around a wire shaft.

spinnerbait   A lure consisting of a wire with a loop in its middle and the arms bent into a V-shape. At the end of the top arm is a spinner blade, like the kind found on spinners, attached to the arm via a swivel, which allows the blade to rotate freely. At the end of the bottom arm is a hook, usually with a lead head for weight and adorned with a skirt or some other fish-attracting device. Fishing line is tied to the loop. It is also called a hairpin lure.

split shot   Small, round lead sinkers with a slot cut about halfway through them which allows them to be pinched onto fishing line.

spoon   A thin, rounded metal fishing lure. Spoons are also called wobblers for their side-to-side movement in the water when retrieved.

stand-up fishing   Playing a large gamefish while standing instead of strapped into a fighting chair. The angler wears a belt harness with a gimbal that holds the rod butt. Some anglers feel that stand-up is more sporting; others believe it's a more effective technique to wear a fish down because you can move about the boat to apply leverage on the fish.

streamer   A fly that imitates a baitfish.

stringer   Either a rope with a large needle on one end and a metal ring on the other, or a chain with large locking snaps. A stringer is a convenient place to keep fish while fishing.

terminal tackle   Fishing-line accessories, such as sinkers, snaps, swivels, snap-swivels, and bobbers.

terrestrial   A life form that lives on or in the ground ("terra firma") instead of in the water; and a fly that imitates such a life form.

tippet   The end or last section of a flyfishing leader, to which the fly is tied.

wading staff   A pole used by some wading anglers to negotiate swift currents.

wet fly   A fly designed to be fished beneath the surface. Wet flies imitate drowned or drowning insects, insects hatching from their nymphal stage and rising to the surface, egg-laying insects, or small baitfish.

Species and Resource Guide

This final appendix in *The Complete Idiot's Guide to Fishing Basics, Second Edition* provides basic reference information that can help you learn more about key fish species, as well as lists of resources that you can consult to learn more about a fishing topic. Additionally, this appendix lists some mail-order sources for fishing tackle and related gear.

Selected Freshwater Fish Species Profiles

Although there's not enough room in this book to provide you with detailed descriptions of all fish, I've profiled the 14 freshwater species that are most sought after by anglers. See Chapter 25, "Ultimate Sport: Flyfishing the Salt" for notes on common inshore saltwater species. For details on offshore saltwater species, see Chapter 24, "The Big-Game Fishing Trip."

The next section of this appendix, "Books," notes several resources that can provide more detail about some of the species covered here.

Largemouth Bass

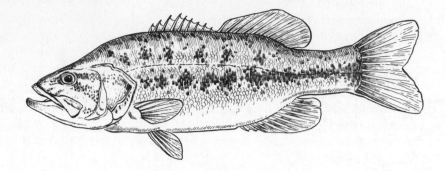

Among anglers, the largemouth bass *(Micropterus salmoides)* is the number-one fresh-water species in the U.S. Indigenous to warm-water lakes and rivers in the eastern and southern regions of the country, the largemouth's range now extends to waters throughout the lower 48 states, from half-acre farm ponds to miles-long reservoirs. Largemouths—which actually belong to the sunfish family, *Centrarchidae*—average 1 to 3 pounds, depending on the range, although larger fish are common in southern and western waters.

Largemouths are not known for having a selective diet. Smaller fish, crustaceans, worms, insects, frogs, snakes, mice, and even small birds are all part of this gamefish's menu. However, many anglers have come home after a day of fishing with nothing to show for their efforts. Largemouths can "turn off" their feed, and nothing you throw at them will provoke a strike. Also, these fish change locations constantly. They will inhabit water from shallow to deep, depending on time of year, water type, and water temperature.

A largemouth angler's arsenal includes bait such as minnows, crayfish, frogs, and insects; and lures such as crankbaits, spoons, spinners, flies, and plastic worms. This last offering is arguably the most effective largemouth bass lure throughout its range, and is usually fished on bottom with a slow retrieve.

Smallmouth Bass

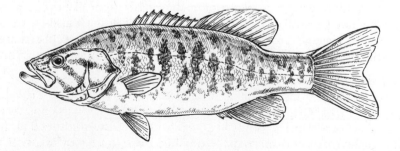

The smallmouth bass *(Micropterus dolomieui)* is native only to the Lake Ontario and Ohio River drainages, although widespread stocking has introduced the "smallie" to waters from the Canadian border south to Alabama and Texas and west to California. The smallmouth prefers clean and cold water such as fast-moving rivers and spring-fed lakes with rocky bottoms. A member of the sunfish family (as is the largemouth), the smallmouth gets its name from comparison to the largemouth: The "hinge" on the upper jaw extends past the eye on the largemouth, and falls even with the eye on the smallmouth.

But that's the only small aspect of the smallmouth. One of the scrappiest fighters in fresh water, this bass will give a spirited battle all the way to the boat. A half-pound smallmouth—which is the average in many streams; about twice that in lakes—will give the fight of a largemouth two or three times its size.

Smallmouths prefer minnows, crayfish, worms, and assorted insects, with crayfish being the preferred forage where these crustaceans exist and when they are available. These baits, and lures resembling them such as jigs, spinners, and small crankbaits, all will take smallmouths.

Walleye

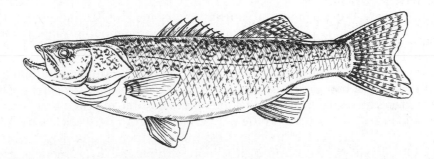

The walleye *(Stizostedion vitreum)* is the favorite gamefish of anglers in the northern Midwest states, although it is pursued in many other regions. Originally inhabiting the cool lakes and large rivers of the northern U.S., the walleye has been introduced throughout the East and South and parts of the West.

Often erroneously called the walleyed pike—it's actually a member of the perch family—the walleye gets its name from its oversized, moonlike eye. The species is favored table fare because of its mild and tasty white flesh. It also grows to decent sizes; these fish average 2 to 3 pounds in most areas. Larger specimens are frequently taken, although the 10-pound walleye is a benchmark trophy for most anglers.

Walleye are usually bottom-oriented, feeding on minnows, worms, leeches, and the aquatic stages of insects. As such, the angler would do well to use these baits, fished close to the bottom. One of the most effective walleye offerings consists of a small jig "sweetened" with a minnow, night crawler, or leech, slowly bumped along the bottom. Small crankbaits and spinners, also fished close to the bottom, will also take walleyes. A slow presentation is best.

341

Chain Pickerel

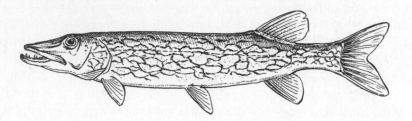

The chain pickerel *(Esox niger)* is found throughout the eastern and southern states and is easily distinguished from its cousins in the pike family by the distinct chain-like markings on its flanks. With a long, wide mouth filled with long, sharp teeth, the pickerel averages around 2 pounds, with larger specimens reaching weights two and three times that. Pickerel like to ambush their prey and thus are denizens of the weedbeds, typically ponds, backwaters, and coves with depths ranging from 2 to 15 feet or so.

Surprisingly, few fishermen specifically pursue chain pickerel. These fish often are by-catches of anglers after largemouth bass, as the habitats of the two species overlap. One reason, perhaps, for the pickerel's relative unpopularity is that its flesh, while mild and tasty, is quite bony and difficult to prepare. Still, the pickerel provides plenty of sport and is a favorite of young anglers throughout its range because of its feeding habits, which are quick, ferocious, and frequent.

A favorite fishing method is also quite simple: hooking a shiner or other minnow a few feet below a bobber and casting it near or into a weedbed. In clear waters, and if the angler is attentive and quiet, it's sometimes possible to watch a pickerel "stalk" its prey and eventually pounce on the minnow with lightning speed. Many other baits and lures will take pickerel, too. Diving crankbaits, spoons, and plastic worms are the most effective. Flyfishermen find great sport with pickerel by using large streamers fished slowly in and around the weeds.

Northern Pike

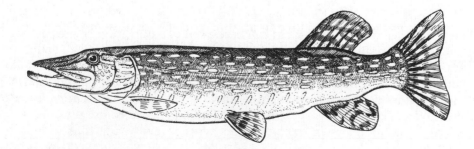

Originally found in the larger waters of the northeast and northern midwest states, stocking has broadened the range of the northern pike *(Esox lucius)* as far south as Pennsylvania and as far west as Montana. Like the chain pickerel, the northern pike has a long and thin body with a large, toothy mouth, but reaches much greater lengths and weights. It also shares the pickerel's voraciousness; pike have tremendous appetites and an attack-style of feeding.

The average size of northern pike depends on the locale—2 to 4 pounds in some waters, 5 to 7 in others—although some lakes routinely give up pike in the 10- to 20-pound class. Northerns range throughout the water column but seem to frequent weedbeds in lakes with close access to deep water, as well as humps or bars in deep river pools.

These opportunistic predators don't have a finicky diet, except that they seem to prefer large forage (they have been known to eat ducklings). Yellow perch, suckers, and panfish are well known as favorite forage for northern pike. These fish, as well as large shiners and chubs, will take pike when fished with a bobber in the weeds or close to the bottom in pools and holes. Many fishermen prefer to use artificial lures for pike, with the red-and-white spoon being a time-honored favorite. Large spinners and crankbaits, especially those that resemble a yellow perch where that species is found, also take northern pike.

Yellow Perch

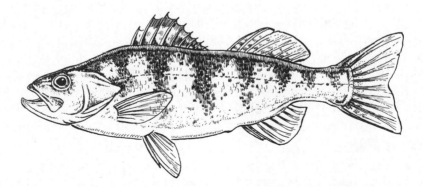

The yellow perch *(Perca flavescens)* can be viewed as a transition species between gamefish and panfish in that it is pursued both for sport and for food. Found throughout the East, Midwest, and in some western states, the yellow perch can be found in all manner of lakes, ponds, and some rivers in its range. Schools of perch generally roam in search of food, often remaining in one area where forage is abundant, and the angler who lucks onto such a school can literally fill a bucket with them.

Average weight for the species runs less than 1 pound, although a school of "jumbo" yellow perch may contain fish twice that weight. Yellow perch aren't very finicky feeders, but their forage is limited because of their comparatively small size. Small fish, insects, small crayfish, and snails make up a perch's diet. Probably the best bait for yellow perch is a small minnow fished live on a small hook, either suspended below a bobber or fished with weight close to bottom. Small spinners, jigs plain or tipped with a minnow, and worms also take yellow perch.

Yellow perch are delicious, which is why many anglers strive to fill that bucket. Their firm white flesh is considered one of the tastiest of all freshwater species. A commercial perch fishery exists in some northern waters, but is limited because of this species' comparatively diminutive size.

Striped Bass

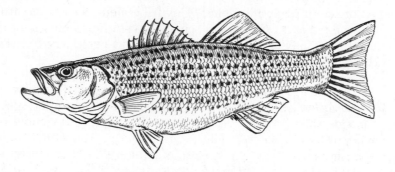

The striped bass *(Morone saxatilis)* is an anadromous species, meaning that it dwells in salt water but ascends freshwater tributaries to spawn. Its original range is along the eastern seaboard and the southeast Gulf Coast, but the striped bass has been introduced to coastal waters on the West Coast and, most notably, in large freshwater lakes and reservoirs in the East and South. These "landlocked" stripers have thrived well beyond the expectation of fishery managers and have created a large and popular fishery.

Striped bass in fresh water don't get as large as those in salt water, but they do grow to tremendous sizes. Stripers range in weight from a couple of pounds to the 20-, 30-, and 40-pound class and beyond.

This fish can be difficult to find as they can be anywhere in the water column depending on temperature, time of year, and forage present. This last can include any manner of fish, but is usually a specific species of baitfish such as gizzard shad that has been stocked along with the stripers to provide a large enough source of forage. Sometimes deep trolling with crankbaits and jigs is necessary to catch stripers; other times still-fishing with live or cut bait—large shiners, gizzard shad, even small trout where legal—can take them. At times a school of stripers will herd a school of baitfish to the surface, at which time anglers can catch them by casting surface or shallow-running lures at the commotion.

Bluegill

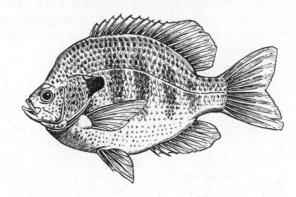

Practically every state in the lower 48 has waters that support a population of blue-gills *(Lepomis macrochirus)*. This scrappy panfish is the most common species in farm ponds and smaller waters everywhere. Hardy (they tolerate a wide range of water quality), abundant (one female bluegill may deposit as many as 38,000 eggs in her nest), sporting for its size (it typically swims at right angles to the angler when hooked, and pulls extremely hard when doing so), and usually not finicky about feeding (insects, snails, small baitfish, worms, and, as many a kid has discovered, bread balls), the bluegill provides about as much guaranteed sport as any species can. They also are superb table fare, ranking with the yellow perch and walleye in that category.

The downside, if any, is the bluegill's size. A 1-pound bluegill is a whopper; unfortunately, bluegills are so prolific that a population of them can quickly become stunted if fish are not removed regularly.

Best baits include garden worms and red worms, grasshoppers, crickets, grubs, and small minnows. Lure fishermen can use small jigs and spinners, miniature crankbaits, and small soft-plastic baits. Flyfishermen can enjoy quick, tremendous sport by casting small dry flies, wet flies, and nymphs.

Black Crappie

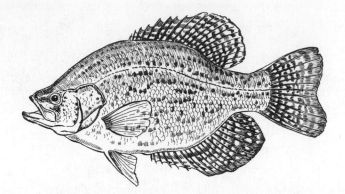

Also called the calico bass, the black crappie *(Pomoxis nigromaculatus)* is a close cousin to the white crappie and the two have been known to hybridize. Together, the two panfish species provide millions of hours of early-spring fishing (which is immediately prior to their spawning period), and in some waters constitute the primary target of fishermen. The reasons: Crappies are not difficult to catch, once they are located; they are fun to fish for, as one school can provide hours of non-stop catching; and their flesh, while a bit on the soft side, is excellent.

As with most panfish, crappies don't grow to large sizes. A foot-long crappie, which is of admirable size anywhere, will weigh only a pound or so.

Crappies range throughout the East, South, and Midwest states, and have been transplanted into a number of western waters. In spring these fish are found near cover prior to spawning: downed trees, weedbeds, and undercut banks.

Crappies forage on all manner of things—small fish, snails, small crayfish, and insects—but it's hard to beat a small live minnow, fished a few feet below a bobber, as crappie bait. Some anglers troll very slowly with weighted minnows until catching a crappie, then they anchor and bobber-fish live minnows near the closest cover or bank. The best artificial lure for crappies is a small jig or a pair of them, fished with or without a bobber and slowly retrieved in the vicinity of shoreline or submerged cover.

Brown Trout

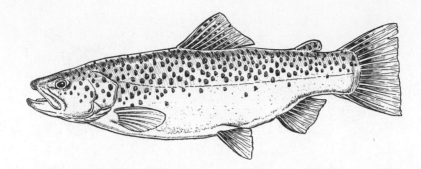

The brown trout *(Salmo trutta)* is actually a European immigrant, transplanted to the United States late in the last century. Its present range includes the Northeast and down through the Appalachians, the upper Midwest, and the mountainous regions of the West. The hardiest of all trout species, browns can withstand comparatively impure and warm water. In fact, brown trout have taken over many rivers and lakes in the U.S. that, because of pollution, tree cutting, and other human impacts, can no longer support native brook trout.

Brown trout can be difficult to catch and so can grow to spectacular sizes, especially in large waters such as some Great Lakes. Average size depends on the habitat: from ½ to 2 pounds in rivers, and double that in still waters. Larger specimens are very often taken in both water types.

For all the difficulty in getting them to hit your bait or lure, brown trout eat a wide variety of organisms: aquatic and terrestrial insects, crustaceans, small fish (even their own young), frogs, and mice. The challenge in catching brown trout is twofold: They are highly nocturnal creatures, and they can be very selective when a particular food source presents itself in abundance, such as mayflies or stoneflies during a hatch.

The best lure and bait choices for brown trout depend entirely on the habitat and the time of year. Generally, live bait, such as garden worms and small minnows, and artificials, such as spinners and small spoons, work well, especially early and late in the year in rivers and smaller lakes. Flyfishermen do well with nymphs and streamers in early spring and move to wet and dry flies when insect hatches occur. In large lakes and reservoirs, fishing live bait—especially the prominent forage type, such as smelt—will take browns, as will trolling crankbaits and spoons imitating the forage.

Rainbow Trout

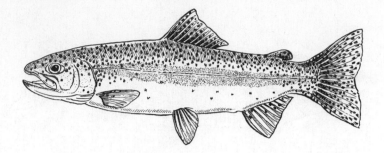

If you hook a trout and it jumps out of the water frequently and spectacularly, chances are good it's a rainbow trout *(Oncorhynchus mykiss)*. This trout species is native to the Pacific drainage of the United States, but transplanting has increased the rainbow's range throughout the West and parts of the East and Midwest. Some rainbow trout are migratory, spending part of their life in the ocean or one of the Great Lakes, and ascending freshwater streams to spawn. These types are called steelhead.

Rainbow trout require clean, cold, well-oxygenated water, and in rivers, show a preference for fast-moving riffles and runs. Rainbows in lakes have similar needs and they will ascend tributaries if present to spawn. They average from ½ pound to a couple of pounds in rivers, and about twice that in lakes. Steelhead run much larger.

Rainbow trout are usually not as difficult to catch as brown trout, but they certainly aren't pushovers. The majority of a rainbow trout's diet consists of aquatic insects (which, along with their acrobatics, makes them a favorite of flyfishermen), but will readily feed on terrestrial insects, worms, and small fish. Fly-rodders should try to "match the hatch" if one is present; if not, brightly colored wet flies or streamers are a good bet. Spinfishermen do well with the baits previously mentioned, as well as brightly colored spinners and small spoons. Rainbows and steelhead also display a liking for fish roe, so baits such as salmon eggs and egg sacs are worth trying. In large lakes, rainbows and steelhead are usually caught by anglers fishing with live bait and/or lures that resemble the particular forage base in that water, such as alewife.

Lake Trout

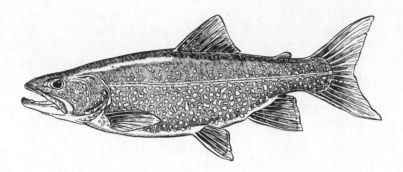

Actually a member of the char family, the lake trout *(Salvelinus namaycush)* is a denizen of deep, clear, cold lakes of the northern states and in some Great Lakes, and has been introduced into some waters of the western states. Typically bottom-oriented fish, lake trout can be caught in 20 feet of water early in the year but later move to the depths—up to 100 feet, with some subspecies moving as deep as 500 feet.

Because of the short "growing season" in their region, lake trout don't get big very quickly. However, they do reach impressive sizes. Average size depends largely on the locale; from 2 to 5 pounds or so is typical. Commercial fishermen have caught lake trout weighing more than 100 pounds.

Lake trout can be caught by flyfishermen and light-spin-tackle anglers in spring when the fish move to shallow water. Best offerings to use at this time are minnow simulations: streamers, spinners, spoons, and diving crankbaits. But the majority of lake-trout fishing is done at depth by trolling with large spoons and live bait, such as smelt. In the past, heavy, unwieldy conventional rods and reels outfitted with wire line were necessary to reach the depths required. However, the advent of downriggers has allowed comparatively light-tackle anglers to fish for lake trout successfully.

Brook Trout

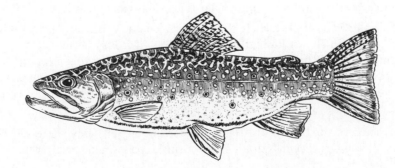

Also a member of the char family (although not referred to as one), the brook trout *(Salvelinus fontinalis)* is native to the Northeast and parts of the north-central U.S. A stunningly beautiful fish, the brook trout is also the most demanding—perhaps "delicate" is a better term—regarding water quality. Although its name suggests a running-water habitat (and most brookies these days are found in small, usually mountainous streams), brookies dwell in ponds and lakes that usually have an incoming source of cold water, such as a tributary or a spring. Unfortunately, the encroachment of civilization has severely cut back the brook trout's range, although stocking efforts by state fisheries departments allow a put-and-take brook trout fishery in many areas.

Native brook trout in streams may average only 6 inches or so (but these streams may be only 6 feet wide). In lakes, brook trout grow to larger sizes, although still not as big as other trout species. Brookies eat a variety of forage, although in most places it's limited to aquatic and terrestrial insects, baitfish, and crustaceans. Brookies are not difficult to catch, but at times these fish will "turn off" and frustrate even the most dedicated fishermen. In streams, flyfishermen should use bright wet flies, small streamers, and nymphs; spin-fishermen do well with live bait such as garden worms and small minnows and with miniature spinners and spoons. Baits and lures for lakes are similar and can be somewhat larger.

Brown Bullhead

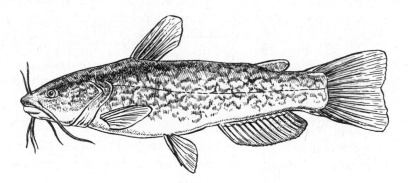

This popular and common catfish shares many characteristics with its cousins, the black bullhead and the yellow bullhead. Distributed from Maine south to Florida and throughout much of the Midwest, the brown bullhead *(Ictalurus nebulosis)* is found in lakes, ponds, and slow-moving streams and canals. The species seems to prefer muddy, weedy bottoms, although it does quite well in waters with sandy, gravelly bottoms.

Like other catfish, the brown bullhead is a bottom feeder. They forage there for insect larvae, mollusks, crustaceans, small fish, worms, leeches, and even aquatic plants.

Bullheads are relatively easy to catch using worms, live or dead minnows, shrimp, or stinkbait fished directly on the bottom. Given this species' wide distribution and propensity to eat a variety of baits, thousands of bullheads are caught each year by anglers fishing worms from the shores of lakes and ponds.

Brown bullheads average about a foot long, weighing nearly a pound at that length, sometimes reaching 19 to 20 inches and 4 to 5 pounds. Like all catfish, bullheads have sharp spines in their dorsal and pectoral fins, which become erect when caught. A toxin in the spines can be quite painful if you get jabbed by a spine. Avoid these spines as you handle the fish, which is worth the risk for its delicious flesh.

Books

Stores and libraries are filled with dozens of fishing books. Most of them focus on one particular species, aspect, or approach, such as flyfishing, bass fishing, or surf fishing. But the following ten volumes will form an excellent base for your own fishing book collection:

Advanced Tactics for Bass & Trout by Jerry Gibbs; Stackpole Books/Outdoor Life Books; 1987. Professional advice on the best tackle and fishing techniques for the two most popular freshwater species in the U.S.

Black's Fly Fishing; Black's Sporting Directories; JFB Inc. An annually updated guide to flyfishing tackle manufacturers, instructors, guides, and destinations.

Coastal Angling Guide by Tom Schlichter; Stackpole Books/Northeast Sportsman's Press; 1989. Species, tactics, and tackle for popular Northeast saltwater species, with a special section on party-boat fishing.

The Complete Idiot's Guide to Boating and Sailing by Frank Sargeant; Alpha Books, 1998. An excellent source of information on operating a motorboat, written by an expert in the field (and water).

The Complete Idiot's Guide to Fly Fishing by Michael D. Shook; Alpha Books, 1999. All the details on flyfishing equipment, casting, fly patterns, and more.

Guide to Freshwater Fishing Boats by Mike Toth; Hearst Marine Books; 1995. Yes, this is a shameless plug. Covers the basic design and uses of all freshwater craft, with a special section on freshwater species.

Ken Schultz's Fishing Encyclopedia by Ken Schultz; IDG Books Worldwide; 1999. At 1,936 pages (the book weighs 9¼ pounds!), and with details on more than 800 species of fish, this is the latest and most authoritative reference on fishing available today.

The New American Trout Fishing by John Merwin; Macmillan Publishing Co.; 1994. A modern treatise (see *Trout* following) on the sport today.

Practical Fishing Knots by Mark Sosin and Lefty Kreh; Crown Publishers, Inc.; 1972. A thorough instructional guide on tying all types of knots for all types of fishing.

Smallmouth Strategies for the Fly Rod by Will Ryan; Lyons & Burford; 1996. A well-written, complete guide to flyfishing for smallmouth bass in all types of habitat throughout the year.

Surf Fishing the Atlantic Coast by Eric B. Burnley; Stackpole Books; 1989. An easy-to-read and well-illustrated guide to fishing beaches and jetties from Maine to Florida.

Trout by Ray Bergman; Alfred A. Knopf, Inc. First published in 1938, this second, revised edition has become a classic treatise on trout fishing in the United States. Its age is advantageous in that it allows the beginner to learn about the modern-day infancy of the sport.

Magazines

Check newsstands for these and other periodicals pertaining to fishing:

Bassmaster, published 10 times a year by the Bass Anglers Sportsman Society, Montgomery, AL. This magazine, which is mailed to members of B.A.S.S., focuses on tactics, tackle, and waters of the most popular gamefish in the U.S.

Field & Stream, published 12 times a year by Times Mirror Magazines, Inc., New York, NY. The largest-circulation general-interest fishing and hunting magazine in existence, with editions covering specific fishing destinations in the East, South, Midwest, and West.

The Fisherman, published weekly by The Fisherman, Shirley, NY. With four editions—New Jersey/Delaware Bay, Long Island, New England, and Florida—this magazine offers where-to and how-to advice and timely reports on local waters, with a focus on saltwater fishing.

Fly Fisherman, published six times a year by Cowles Magazines, Harrisburg, PA. A very informative publication on flyfishing tackle, methods, and destinations, with an emphasis on trout fishing.

Outdoor Life, published 10 times a year by Times Mirror Magazines, Inc., New York, NY. Many articles on fishing tactics and technique, with an emphasis on the adventure of the outdoors.

Saltwater Sportsman, published monthly by Times Mirror Magazines, Boston, MA. Covers saltwater fishing tactics and tackle, with regional articles about local waters and species.

Fishing Tackle Makers and Suppliers

The following are some of the larger sporting-goods mail-order companies and fishing tackle manufacturers. Check Web sites or call for a catalog.

Bass Pro Shops; 2500 E. Kearney, Springfield, MO 65898; 1-800-227-7776; www.basspro.com. Rods, reels, lures, hooks, line, and other gear, for both largemouth bass and other species.

Cabela's; One Cabela Drive, Sydney, NE 69160; 1-800-237-4444; www.cabelas.com. "The World's Foremost Outfitter" of fishing, hunting, and outdoor gear offers good prices on a wide variety of fishing tackle; some catalogs are more than 400 pages long.

Daiwa Corp.; 12851 Midway Place, Cerritos, CA 90703; 562-802-9589; www.daiwa.com. Makers of freshwater and saltwater rods and reels.

Eagle Claw Fishing Tackle; 4245 East 46th Avenue, Denver, CO 80216; 303-321-1481; http://righttrak.net/eagle. Makers of fishing hooks, plus rods, reels, and other fishing tackle.

Flambeau Products Corp.; 15981 Valplast Road, Middlefield, OH 44062; 440-632-1631; www.flamprod.com. Makers of tackle boxes and bags, bait containers, storage boxes, and other fishing accessories.

L.L. Bean; Freeport, ME 04033; 1-800-221-4221; www.llbean.com. Famed suppliers of clothing, boots, and flyfishing tackle.

Normark Corporation; 10395 Yellow Circle Drive, Minnetonka, MN 55343; 612-933-7060; www.normark.com. Makers of Rapala, Storm, and Blue Fox lures.

Offshore Angler; 2500 E. Kearney, Springfield, MO 65898; 1-800-463-3746; www.offshoreangler.com. Part of the Bass Pro Shops' corporate family, this division offers saltwater-fishing–related tackle and other equipment.

Orvis; Historic Route 7A, Manchester, VT 05254; 1-800-548-9548; www.orvis.com. Manufacturers and distributors of quality fishing tackle, with an emphasis on flyfishing gear.

Penn Fishing Tackle Mfg. Co.; 3028 West Hunting Park Avenue, Philadelphia, PA 19132; 215-229-9415; www.pennreels.com. Makers of rods and reels, with an emphasis on saltwater use.

Plano Molding Co.; 431 East South Street, Plano, IL 60545; 630-552-3111; www.planomolding.com. Makers of tackle boxes and bags, bait containers, and other fishing accessories.

PRADCO Outdoor Brands; P.O. Box 1587, Fort Smith, AR 72902; 501-782-8971; www.lurenet.com. Parent company of numerous lure makers—Bomber, Cotton Cordell, Creek Chub, Heddon, Lazy Ike, and others—plus other fishing product manufacturers.

Pure Fishing; 1900 18th Street, Spirit Lake, IA 51360, 877-777-3850; www.purefishing.com. Parent company of Berkley, Fenwick, Abu Garcia, and Coleman Fishing products.

Shakespeare Fishing Tackle; 3801 Westmore Drive, Columbia, SC 29223; www.shakespeare-fishing.com. Makers of rods, reels, line, and other fishing products.

Shimano American Corp.; One Holland, Irvine, CA 92618; 949-951-5003; www.shimano.com. Makers of rods and reels for both freshwater and saltwater use.

Stren Fishing Lines; 870 Remington Drive, Madison, NC 27025; 1-800-243-9700; www.Stren.com. Makers of fishing line and other fishing accessories.

Water Gremlin Co.; 1610 Whitaker Avenue, White Bear Lake, MN 55110; 651-429-7761; www.watergremlin.com. Makers of all types of fishing sinkers.

Zebco; 6101 East Apache, Tulsa, OK 74115; 918-836-5581; www.zebco.com. Manufacturers of affordable rods and reels.

Index

S